Criminal Justice M:

M000315732

Criminal justice students and practitioners in criminal justice agencies know first-hand the value of effective management; they understand the vital need to develop organizations that meet the expectations of their community members as well as those of their workers. Employing an innovative, student-friendly approach this fully updated second edition of *Criminal Justice Management: Theory and Practice in Justice-Centered Organizations* examines the complex subjects associated with operating justice-centered agencies.

Authors Mary K. Stohr and Peter A. Collins interweave their comprehensive research with humor and personal anecdotes to make the study of criminal justice management accessible—and interesting—to students. Chapter exercises and study questions provide a springboard for lively class discussion, encouraging students to discover relevant applications for these provocative topics. Through its dedicated pedagogy, this text challenges readers to:

- Initiate human relations management practices
- Develop and maintain strong ethical practices
- Provide support for the professional development of staff
- Use proactive, collaborative and shared responsibility forms of leadership
- Implement evidence-based best practices in agency programming
- Build strong bridges within an engaged and informed community

With an emphasis on putting theory into practice, *Criminal Justice Management* is an invaluable resource for the development of efficient, dynamic, and resourceful justice-centered agencies. It is perfect reading for criminal justice students, particularly those looking to enter a career in the criminal justice sector.

Mary K. Stohr is a professor in the Department of Criminal Justice at Washington State University. She earned her PhD (1990) in political science, with specializations in criminal justice and public administration, from Washington State University. Previously she worked at Missouri State, Boise State, and New Mexico State Universities for a total of 23 years. Before academe Stohr worked in an adult male prison in Washington state as a correctional officer (for less than a year) and as a correctional counselor (for about two years). Stohr has published over 80 academic works of one sort or another in the areas of correctional organizations and operation, correctional personnel, inmate needs and assessment, program evaluation, gender, and victimization.

Peter A. Collins is an Assistant Professor in the Criminal Justice Department at Seattle University. He received his PhD in criminal justice from Washington State University in 2011 with specializations in corrections, cost-benefit and evaluation research, and criminal justice organizations. His research interests include criminal rehabilitation, substance abuse issues, community corrections and criminal reentry, the intersection of criminological theory and public policy analysis, criminal justice management and organizations, and criminology within the context of popular culture.

Criminal Justice Management

Theory and practice in justice-centered organizations

Second edition

Mary K. Stohr and Peter A. Collins

Routledge
Taylor & Francis Group

LONDON AND NEW YORK

First edition published 2009
by Oxford University Press, Inc.

Second edition 2014
by Routledge
2 Park Square, Milton Park, Abingdon, Oxon, OX14 4RN

and by Routledge
711 Third Avenue, New York, NY 10017

Routledge is an imprint of the Taylor & Francis Group, an informa business

© 2014 Mary K. Stohr and Peter A. Collins

British Library Cataloguing in Publication Data
A catalogue record for this book is available from the British Library

Library of Congress Cataloging-in-Publication Data
Stohr, Mary K.
Criminal justice management : theory and practice in justice
centered organizations / Mary K Stohr, Peter A Collins.
    pages cm
    Includes bibliographical references.
    1. Criminal justice, Administration of. I. Collins, P. A. (Peter A.)
    II. Title.
    HV7419.S746 2014
    364–dc23
    2013022986

ISBN13: 978-0-415-54050-6 (hbk)
ISBN13: 978-0-415-54051-3 (pbk)
ISBN13: 978-0-203-10725-6 (ebk)

Typeset in Baskerville
by Sunrise Setting Ltd, Paignton, UK

Printed and bound in Great Britain by
TJ International Ltd, Padstow, Cornwall

Mary Stohr: To my husband Craig Hemmens and daughter Emily Rose Stohr-Gillmore for all you do and are to me.

Peter Collins: To my wife Sancheen, daughter Kaiya, and son Lucas.

Contents

Figures and Tables

Boxes

Preface

As with the first edition, this book was inspired by the students of, and practitioners in, criminal justice agencies. These people, as well as those interested enough to pick up this book, know the value of effective management and they understand (or soon will in the case of students) the need for organizations to fit the desires of community members and the needs of workers to what is possible. We wrote and, in the case of the second edition, revised this book as a means of addressing the truths—as we understand them—about justice-centered agencies, their management, and their operation. One such truth is that we believe that workers deserve to be included in the management process, both for their own sake and sanity and to advance the accomplishment of the publicly determined goals of the agency.

Another truth, which unfortunately falls under the heading of "sad but true," is that students often see management and organizational topics as dry and irrelevant. In recognition of this, we did our best to provide a student-oriented text that gives serious attention to the relevancy of all topics for people who hope to understand and effectively negotiate their work lives within criminal justice organizations.

We also wrote this book as a means of addressing some critical organizational issues that are not always given sufficient attention in texts, namely, understanding ethics in the organizational environment, the ins and outs of personnel processes, the twenty-first-century workforce, and budgeting. As we indicate in these chapters, such topics are terribly important to the operation of any criminal justice agency and therefore to the education of our students.

As a reader of this text, you should also know that it was pure pleasure for us to write and revise! Sure, there was the tedium of looking up references and making sure the headings were correct. But in general writing this book, much like teaching this topic, provided us with the opportunity to explore the seminal management issues of our time as they are distilled through the prism of everyday criminal justice agencies—how much more fun could two people have?

As with any project of this size and scope, there are many, many people to thank for their assistance and inspiration, and we would be remiss if we did not at least attempt to acknowledge some of their efforts. We apologize in advance if anyone is left out of these acknowledgements.

First of all, we want to thank Routledge's commissioning editor, Thomas Sutton, for encouraging us to proceed with a second edition. Second, we are also thankful for the diligence and patience of Nicola Hartley, editorial assistant with Routledge. We remain thankful for the work of Jennifer Ashley and Sancheen Collins for their editing and research assistance on the first edition and for the similar labors of Brittney McClure and most especially Jamie Kim, Heather Burns, and Mary Jordan on the second edition. In addition, our writing was informed by several students and entire classes of criminal justice management students (in particular Seattle University Fall Quarter 2011, Spring and Fall Quarters 2012, and Spring Quarter 2013 CJ organizations students!), fellow scholars in the criminal justice and public administration fields, and justice-centered practitioners in the field. We are indebted to them all for shaping this work.

Sancheen, Kaiya, and Lucas (wife and children of Pete), along with Craig Hemmens and Emily Stohr-Gillmore (husband and daughter of Mary), deserve much credit for their forbearance and understanding of the importance of this book for their loved ones. We certainly cannot thank them, or love them, enough for it.

Finally, as with the first edition, no acknowledgement for this book on management would be complete without a nod, and really a bow, to the mentorship of Nicholas P. Lovrich, Claudius O. and Mary W. Johnson Distinguished Professor of Political Science, and retired director of the Division of Governmental Studies and Services at Washington State University – Pullman. For both of us he has modeled and taught the appropriate role of the academic as a catalyst for the development of just practices and policies in the public sector organization. His positive contributions to those organizations (including numerous police, courts, and corrections entities), and the people who encounter them and labor in them, cannot be easily tallied. As the authors labored on this book, his example of what a decent human being should be in an organizational context was never far from our minds.

Foreword

Five years ago I wrote a foreword to the first edition of this book, noting its distinctiveness, timeliness, and value for the preparation of the next generation of criminal justice practitioners and scholars. I noted that the book fills an important gap in the available literature that had to be addressed by scholars equally comfortable in the worlds of criminal justice and public administration. In the intervening years a good deal of new research has been done to add further to our insights and our collective capacity to improve both the management of our criminal justice system and enhance its effectiveness in nurturing and supporting those who work in its myriad agencies and associated community-based organizations. I can report that much of that new insight and capacity for improvement has been captured in this second edition of the Stohr and Collins book. If anything, this is a better book than the first edition from the student's perspective; the incorporation of a more light-hearted tone and the inclusion of humorous stories and telling anecdotes add importantly to the quality of this book.

As to the contents, a bit of personal reflection will prepare you well for the experience of reading this exceptional textbook. We have all had the pleasant experience of visiting a local post office or a drivers' licensing office of state government to conduct our business with an omnipresent element of our government. In one such location we encounter happy faces, a helpful "customer friendly" orientation on the part of the counter clerks, employees who know the rules and regulations that apply to our particular request for service, and staff who possess the ability and clear desire to translate those strictures into appropriate application in order to accommodate our specific request. In another local office of the *very same bureaucracy*, however, we might encounter the faces of seemingly uninspired staff, employees offering little in the way of concern for our own need for assistance, manifesting an attitude that countless rules and regulations constrain their work needlessly, and suggesting in their interactions with us that our own request for service is somewhat of an unpleasant imposition on them and their colleagues.

Why is this great disparity in how public agencies carry out their work such a common experience? Why does the same type of organization working with the same structures and system of rules and regulations produce such a different work environment for the people employed in them, and such different outcomes for the people who have business to conduct with this element of their own government? This is the first book I have encountered in over forty years of college teaching that offers direct answers to these key questions in regard to the principal agencies of the American criminal justice system. As with the fictitious local branch offices of federal and state government portrayed here, our nation's police agencies, prosecutors' offices, courts, and correction facilities range widely in their performance as places in which to work and as organizations carrying out their duties in service to a democratic society. As students in a foundational course in criminal justice you deserve a text that addresses this ubiquitous problem of highly variable public agency performance, and in the process prepares you very well for a deeper study of the many specific aspects of the criminal justice discipline. This book does precisely this! If you do your part through careful study and reflection on what you read here you will be well prepared for the more specialized courses which await you, and well prepared for the careers that lie ahead in your future.

This book reflects a commanding knowledge of the literature in the field, but the knowledge in question is presented in a student-friendly, engaging way where the approach is to put "theory into practice" through a persistent theme of translating into everyday experience the "best practices" revealed by research in the areas of policing, criminal prosecution and defense, juvenile and adult court operations, and institutional and community corrections. While historical developments and major public policy issues in these major areas of criminal justice receive proper attention, the primary focus throughout is on the *human dynamics of organizations* and how the artful management of those dynamics can lead to healthy and helpful agency settings as opposed to the dispirited and off-putting agency settings depicted above.

No other textbooks in criminal justice have attempted to capture these insights and to frame an introduction to the field in this particular way— largely because of the immense range of knowledge and experience required of authors of such a book. The authors of this book rightfully emphasize the importance for criminal justice agencies of the use of human relations management practices, the timely provision of support for professional development of staff, the consistent use of proactive, collaborative and shared responsibility forms of leadership, the development and maintenance of a deeply embedded belief in ethical practice, the implementation of evidence-based best practices in agency programming, and the building of strong bridges to an engaged and informed community. To the extent that criminal justice agencies make use of these principles and practices in the way they are managed, they are likely to be carrying out their mandates well and providing enriching jobs for their employees at the same time.

How well the criminal justice system works in any society is a telling measure of the health of democracy there. In the United States we have much of which we can be justly proud, including the dedication to the public service ethic displayed in much of our criminal justice system. We also have a great deal of work remaining to move our criminal justice system closer to what it could be *vis-à-vis* use of best practices and the creation and sustaining of enriching workplaces for the employees therein. I can't imagine a more appropriate foundational textbook than this one for preparing students to take up the challenges of making our criminal justice system the best it can be.

Nicholas P. Lovrich
Regent Professor Emeritus
Claudius O. and Mary W. Johnson Distinguished Professor
Senior Research Affiliate
Division of Governmental Studies and Services
Washington State University – Pullman

1 Criminal justice management

The big, the bad, and the beautiful

Introduction: scope and purpose of the book

The general public may not always view criminal justice agencies in a positive light, though they may admire people who labor in them. Problems with abuse of force by the police or in corrections, overcrowded courts and corrections services, lapsed supervision of clients by probation or parole officers, violence, and instances of mismanagement have been highlighted in the press and become a focus for public policy. In such instances the adjectives "big" and "bad" tend to fit criminal justice agencies, institutions, and their related management practices. But as people who work in the justice system, and those who study those organizations at any length, know, these institutions serve a vital purpose in this democracy. Namely, they not only prevent crime, respond to victims and citizens, and operate the machinery of justice; they also hold, supervise, feed, clothe, train, and rehabilitate thousands of inmates and clients daily.

The public is much safer because of the efforts of criminal justice staff who investigate crime, adjudicate cases, keep dangerous and repeat offenders incarcerated or supervised, and extract from the system innocent people inadvertently trapped there. And justice is served for both victims and offenders when the accused are given their day (or half-hour) in court, and when appropriate sentences are carried out in correctional institutions, in juvenile facilities, or in the community. Although some would argue that citizens/victims/offenders are physically or mentally harmed by their experience with the justice system, others—even those who are eventually incarcerated—if they are placed in well-managed institutions or programs, may actually benefit from this exposure. In the latter situation, one might even call that kind of criminal justice management "beautiful."

Therefore, a central theme of this book is that there are a number of paths that lead to the effective management of criminal justice organizations, and it makes all the difference which route is taken. The phrase "best practices" is often bandied about these days to describe how a correctional treatment program, a police rape investigation, or any number of other activities might be organized and implemented. We argue in this book that there are indeed "best practices," or better ways of doing things, in criminal justice management. These "better ways" are more likely to yield desirable outcomes, such as safety and security for the public, the staff, and the clientele of agencies, a skilled and involved staff, and, on balance, an enriching experience for all.

When there are problems in criminal justice, they can often be laid at the door of either public policymakers who ask too much and supply too little in the way of resources to agencies; or, in many cases, problems are the direct result of mismanagement by administrators of these agencies. Although public policy will be highlighted in a few places in this book, our primary focus is on the dynamics of organizations and how their management can be big or bad or beautiful. After a century of scholarly focus on the management of public and private sector institutions, the knowledge about how best to operate criminal justice agencies already exists and is practiced, in part or in whole, by the most successful managers. This book serves, then, to provide a theoretical, historical, and organizational context for such management practices.

To that end, this book covers a number of topics of interest to practitioners and students of criminal justice management, including organizational and environmental characteristics of criminal justice agencies (Chapter 1); distinctions between, and definitions of, common criminal justice, management, and organizational terms (Chapter 2); a discussion of the value of public vs. private service (Chapter 2); an examination of ethical issues, including official deviance, corruption, the use of excessive force, and sexual and gender harassment (Chapter 3); common management theories and their application (Chapter 4); interpersonal, organizational, and interorganizational communication and barriers (Chapter 5); the nature of the criminal justice role, socialization, and power issues (Chapter 6); leadership theories and styles (Chapter 7); personnel practices such as selection, performance appraisal, retention strategies, job enrichment, training, and related issues (Chapter 8); selection issues such as Workforce 2000, diversity and affirmative action (Chapter 9); managing and evaluating programming, accreditation, and standards (Chapter 10); and strategic planning and budgeting (Chapter 11).

Following these chapters and topics, we include a chapter devoted to the decision-making challenges faced by those who work in criminal justice agencies (Chapter 12). The final chapter encapsulates the best of management and organizational practices from the scholarly and practitioner literature in the form of an inclusive and consilient proposal of model management practices for criminal justice agencies (Chapter 13).

Chapters 3 and 6 include research instruments used to "take the temperature" of the work environment. Some chapters showcase a perspective or two on the given topic by a criminal justice practitioner, scholar, or student. Some chapters include classroom or training exercises that reinforce knowledge highlighted in the text, as well as key terms and reference tools such as web links for further investigation. Most chapters also include exercises that can be used in class to reinforce concepts and ideas. At the end of every chapter there are discussion questions to spur creative and analytical thought regarding chapter content.

One other note before we get to the "meat" of the book. The tone of the text, as reflected in our writing, is deliberately conversational at times. Research and scholarly works are highlighted in this book, but so are the experiences of people who work in, and study, criminal justice. We want to bring together the two worlds of practitioners and academe, and the best way we have found to do this while teaching is to present material in the second category in a less formal fashion.

The remainder of this chapter is devoted to setting the stage for the discussion of the management and organizational topics featured in this book. Although most students will have become acquainted with some or all of the major sectors of criminal justice (i.e., police, courts, corrections) before taking this class, the characteristics of the organizations, their staff, and their clientele bears repeating here to ensure a common understanding of them before we proceed. For example, it is important to recall that all criminal justice agencies are creatures of their environment to some extent, and that characteristic affects practice, policies, and funding. Therefore, to provide a common context from which to view the rest of the topics covered in this book, we begin with what for most students is probably a review of organizational, staff, and clientele characteristics.

Some defining issues in criminal justice: law enforcement, courts, and corrections

Police and sheriff's departments

Despite the emphasis on various federal law enforcement agencies in the media, one of the most distinguishing features of public policing is that it is local. For this reason, most of the discussions of policing in this text focus on local city and state police and sheriff's departments, with some discussion of policing agencies at the state and federal levels mixed in. Virtually every city of any size has either a local police department or contracts for such services from the county sheriff's office. Often small villages and towns also have their own police department. In fact, the sheer variety of policing and the focus of policing are enormous and complex (Langworthy and Travis 1994). The local departments, whether police or sheriff, are the most numerous law enforcement organizations and employ the most public officers.

As of 2008 there were at least 870,000 city, county, state, and federal police and sheriff's sworn officers in this country (Reaves 2011: 1). Of these, 461,000 were employed by local police departments and another 183,000 worked as sheriff's deputies; that is, 74 percent of all sworn officers work for local departments.

Duties, mission, and roles of law enforcement

The duties of officers and the mission of such departments are diverse, as they are somewhat connected to the type of community being policed (Roberg *et al.* 2011). Traditionally, that mission has been divided between order maintenance, law enforcement or crime fighting, and service delivery. Additional roles for law enforcement agencies and officers might include information gathering and acting as a protector of individual rights. "To serve and protect," the slogan of many departments, captures these duties and the overall mission of the departments, and also encompasses many separate tasks that we see officers do every day, such as investigating a crime, assisting a motorist, responding to a report of a prowler, checking the locks on a business, setting up roadside stops for drunk drivers, problem-solving with a local neighborhood group concerned about crimes in the area, and working in the local high school as a resource officer. Long ago, police scholars collapsed such tasks into service delivery, law enforcement, and order maintenance (e.g., see Goldstein 1977; Wilson 1968).

The patrol divisions perform virtually the same role—as that represents their mission—in both police and sheriff's departments. City or municipal police departments and sheriff's departments all perform basic tasks that include law enforcement, service, and order maintenance. The law enforcement tasks are the ones that come to mind when people think of the police. They include crime control activities that revolve around preventing, detecting, and investigating crime. The police or sheriff's officer in this capacity may apprehend the suspect, make an arrest, or issue a citation.

Though we think of the police as primarily engaged in law enforcement activities, for the most part they are not. In fact, the majority of their time is spent in either service delivery (e.g., unlocking car doors, assisting accident victims, locating lost children, helping the injured) or order maintenance (e.g., crowd control, directing traffic, settling disputes between neighbors, keeping an eye on vagrant youth; Travis and Langworthy 2007). The police are called to act in these capacities because they are particularly suited for them, in that they are community-wide service workers who respond to calls from citizens and have specialized training. Moreover, both service and order maintenance tasks are closely connected to law enforcement in that they may involve interpretation of, or disputes about, the law, and they could be associated with crime in some way. For instance, although in most instances the report of a lost child does not signify that an abduction, hence a violation of the law, has occurred, in some cases it does. Or, although disputes between neighbors are usually resolved amicably, the police presence may serve to calm tempers that otherwise would escalate to the point that one or more parties committed an assault or destroyed property.

We discuss the police/sheriff officer's role more in subsequent chapters, but it is instructive to note that law enforcement organizations, like the other criminal justice agencies mentioned here, determine what they do based on the demands from their environment, the type of department, and the law. As Roberg *et al.* (2011) indicate, these demands by the environment shape how the police make decisions about what they do. For example, the community environment determines whether the department is primarily engaged in service, order maintenance, or law enforcement activities (Kelling 1999). As communities become more diverse culturally, figuring out what the community wants can be daunting for the police.

Second, officers police based on perceptions of the formal and informal expectations of their department. If a supervisor wants them to concentrate on order maintenance duties at the expense of service, that is what they will do as long as the informal subculture does not discourage such prioritization (more about the formal and informal subcultures in organizations later). Therefore, the formal policies of a department and the informal culture of the department can both have an impact on how the police operate.

Finally, the law itself will shape what the police spend time on. As laws vary from state to state, and even between counties and cities in the same state, the police role will be shaped to some extent by those differences. The increasing incursion of federal law into local policing, particularly via the modern drug war, has had an impact on local policing to the extent that officers in local police and sheriff's departments are assigned to drug task forces that are often run or facilitated by federal law enforcement. While engaged in these task forces, typically in law enforcement duties involving the drug war, police and sheriff's officers may have less time to engage in service and order maintenance duties.

These diverse and sometimes competing expectations for police role activity can be "integrated" to some degree when they overlap. That is, for *mala in se* crimes (or those that are evil in and of themselves) such as murder, rape, assault, and robbery, there would be similar expectations for police behavior from the community environment, the organization, and the law. It is when the crime or disorder is less serious (*mala prohibita* crimes, or those that are defined as "evil" because they are disapproved of by society), or the service request is minor, that officers may exercise their discretion to ignore or only respond half-heartedly.

Organizational structure

Typically, police and sheriff's departments, much like jails and prisons and probation and parole departments, are structurally bureaucratic, with paramilitary regimentation, regalia, and accoutrements (more about these later), and top-down communication. They do differ in that in most cases, if a county jail exists, it is operated by the sheriff's department. Though some police departments may run a short-term holding facility, they usually do not operate a full-scale jail. State and federal law enforcement agencies do not operate correctional facilities.

Clientele

On the other hand, the clientele are generally the same for both police and sheriff's departments (and often state and federal agencies), as they are residents of the community in which the organization is located or over which it has jurisdiction. The location and type of crime or incident that compels the resident's contact with law enforcement will determine whether that contact is with a city, county, state, or federal agency. However, the clientele for those who have the most negative contact with agencies of criminal justice tends to differ in most cases from the general citizenry in several important respects. Those who have most negative contact with the police or sheriff's department tend to be male, young, uneducated, poor, and with alcohol or substance abuse problems (Roberg *et al.* 2011; Travis and Langworthy 2007). In larger cities, they also tend to be disproportionately minority group members.

Staff characteristics

Many of the officers employed in police and sheriff's departments are white males with a military background (Hickman and Reaves 2003), although the number of minorities and women employed as full-time sworn personnel in local police departments has increased from 1 in 13 in 1987 to 1 in 8 in 2007 for women and from 1 in 6 in 1987 to 1 in 4 in 2007 for minorities. After passage of the Civil Rights Act of 1964, which prohibits discrimination in hiring based on race and ethnicity, its amendment in 1972 (which prohibited discrimination based on gender), and civil suits by minority men and women and white women over the course of forty years, the law enforcement agencies have become more diverse, particularly in urban areas (Hickman and Reaves 2003). As with other sectors of the criminal justice system, the number of former military personnel involved in policing may be explained by an attraction to public sector work and the paramilitary structure of police and sheriff departments.

Location/jurisdiction

Historically, police departments were located in cities and towns and sheriff's departments were located in counties, the latter often policing rural areas. This is still true today, although some cities have grown so large in area and in population that they have expanded to encompass the same areas policed by both city and county agencies. State police departments are often headquartered in state capitals, though they usually have offices sprinkled throughout the larger cities and towns in the state. Federal agencies also tend to be located in state capitals and large cities, though they often have a home office in Washington, DC.

Public institutions

City, county, state, and federal policing and sheriff's departments are by definition publicly created and operated entities. Though there is much private policing in this country, cities, counties, and states (and the federal government) have kept and expanded their public sector agencies (Reaves 2011; Bureau of Justice Statistics 2004b, 2006; Peak 2008). Because of their standing, public agencies tend to be both politically responsive and also subject to the prevailing political winds. Which means, say in the case of a local police department, that if a mayor and the city council, who are the direct or indirect bosses of the chief, want to focus on service delivery over crime prevention, the department will shift some resources to do that: not only does the chief's job depend on it, but the departmental budget does too. But should the mayor or a majority of the city council be gone after the next election, the police department may have to reconfigure its duties based on the demands of the new mayor and council members and the local political culture.

Adult and juvenile courts

The courts as agencies act as both a stopgap and a conduit to criminal justice processing. Persons brought before the courts or reviewed by court-room actors, such as prosecutors and defense attorneys, may be sifted out of the process—say, if the evidence is not strong enough—or their case may be scheduled on the court's calendar. The courts operate at a critical juncture in the loosely connected criminal justice system in that they both control the processing valve to various correctional agencies and act as a check on police and correctional agencies. In the latter role, courtroom actors make judgments about police and correctional staff actions, including decisions regarding arrest, search and collection of evidence, use of force, and living conditions provided to inmates.

As of 2004 (the latest date for which we have statistics), there were 194 general and limited jurisdiction trial court systems in this country, including the District of Columbia and Puerto Rico (Langton and Cohen 2007: 6). In 2007 there were almost 509,000 employees involved in courts in federal, state, and local levels (Kyckelhahn 2011: 7). Most of those, or 53 percent, were employed at the local level, almost 35 percent were employed by the states, and about 12 percent worked in federal courts (Kyckelhahn 2011: 11). Adult-level courts are operated by counties, states, and the federal government, whereas juvenile courts are usually operated at the county level. As organizations, adult criminal and juvenile courts vary widely, as shown later, but there are some commonalities.

Organizational structure, the work group, and clientele

Both adult criminal and juvenile courts have an organizational structure that is regarded as "looser" than that of the typical law enforcement or correctional agency. They do not have the cohesive, single, paramilitary structure that typifies law enforcement and correctional agencies. Rather, there are two to three organizations that, when aligned, make up the courts at a given level of government, whether that be city, county, state, or federal. The two main organizations are the court organization itself and the local prosecutor's office, which has actors who regularly participate in the court "organization." In larger cities and counties there is a third organization, the public defender's office, whose attorneys fulfill the constitutional right in court for those unable to pay to have legal representation. In smaller jurisdictions, where separate public defense organizations do not exist, defense attorneys will typically be appointed to work on contract. These three actors and their organizations separately, and together, constitute the core of the courtroom work group in this country.

Courtroom work group

Other organizations have regular participants in the courtroom who might be regarded as part of the criminal justice "courtroom work group." Two of the most important of these ancillary groups are health and welfare workers—often social workers—who regularly attend to the needs of children before the juvenile court, and probation/parole or community corrections officers, who may regularly provide input to both juvenile and adult court proceedings.

Of course, each of these organizations—the court, the offices of the prosecutor and the defense attorney, probation/parole or community corrections, and health and welfare organizations—is bureaucratically structured. But the actors come together to work on cases with only a semi-powerful leader (the judge) and statutes, case law, and traditions to guide their practice as a "work group" (see Box 1.1). Unlike a police chief or a prison warden, a judge has no power to "fire" those who work "under" her in her courtroom (with the possible exception of community corrections officers in juvenile court). Nevertheless, a judge usually has the ability to sanction or to limit the practice of actors in her court. Moreover, almost all activities, except notably the plea agreement arrangements, are done in open court, are recorded, and are available for scrutiny by the public and other courtroom actors.

Box 1.1 The courtroom work group

According to Clynch and Neubauer (1981), courtrooms might best be understood as informal work groups that are bound by common attributes and goals. The following circumstances tend to bind courtroom workers to each other: the actors in these work groups (e.g., judges, prosecutors, defense attorneys) work together on a continuing basis; they possess discretion to make important decisions; they are mutually interdependent; they have similar backgrounds and tastes; and they have psychological needs (such as friendship and respect) that are met by other members of the group. The resulting work group—which ostensibly and formally should be adversarial, at least at the adult level—is instead concerned with completing the work, keeping to the work group norms for behavior, and engaging in informal arrangements (e.g., plea agreements) that are outside the official realm of the courtroom.

Clientele

Another similarity between adult and juvenile courts, and law enforcement and corrections for that matter, is that they tend to process those who have less education and money than the rest of the population. Leaving aside the middle-class and wealthy defendants who capture the media and American attention for months on end, most defendants who come before the courts are young, poor, male, and disproportionately members of a minority group with less educational achievement than is the norm for the general population (Bureau of Justice Statistics 2004c). This is not to imply that women and white people do not come before the courts; women do with increasing regularity. As white people still constitute well over half of the population in most of the country, there tend to be more of them than representatives of other racial or ethnic groups in criminal and juvenile courts. Women, too, are entering the system at an increasing rate (e.g., see Lab *et al.* 2004). However, minority group members are disproportionately represented, as are males and the poor, as defendants in courts.

The law—levels

Adult courts, which at times have accommodated some juvenile defendants, have existed for a few thousand years. By comparison, the juvenile courts were created only a century ago. As the conception of childhood changed at the turn of the twentieth century, social workers and other progressive reformers felt that children who misbehaved should be treated differently than adults and thus deserved a separate court, which would attend to their needs and act in their best interest (Empey and Stafford 1991). This ideal, of course, was not always realized. Also, some advocates for the creation of juvenile courts may have been more interested in controlling immigrant children than in any purer motives such as helping such kids. But to summarize, one can still say that juvenile courts were created to serve a different purpose and population than adult criminal courts.

In fact, for much of their history (until *In re Gault,* 1967 [387 U.S. 1] and other Supreme Court decisions changed their operation), the juvenile courts in this country operated without the traditional due process protections that are enumerated in the Bill of Rights. Juveniles, for instance, used to have no right to protection against unreasonable search and seizure (Fourth Amendment), no protection against self-incrimination (Fifth Amendment), and no right to counsel (Sixth Amendment). Today they possess these rights and more, though no right to a trial by a jury of their peers (i.e., other children) has been declared.

Of course, until recently, adults in state criminal courts did not necessarily have these rights either. Though some states provided them, the Bill of Rights (Amendments One through Ten) was "incorporated," or applied to state citizens in state courts, only incrementally, over a period of years.

What this indicates is that the law as it is applied in criminal courts has changed over time and differs by type of court (juvenile or adult), type of client (juvenile or adult), level of court (courts of limited jurisdiction, courts of general jurisdiction, intermediate appellate courts, and courts of last resort), and type of government (local, state, federal). Courtroom actors are guided by statutory law (the law on the books), case law (past judicial decisions), common law (that establishes precedents or *stare decisis*), and constitutions (state and federal level). Despite their separation, there is some overlap between state and federal courts in terms of the application of law, mostly because the federal appellate courts, with the US Supreme Court resting at the pinnacle of these, serve as the final arbitrators on some legal questions. That said, the vast majority of criminal cases are decided in state and county-level courts. Most appeals are settled in state courts. Should they be appealed to the Supreme Court, their chances of being accepted for review are small (the nine justices typically hear fewer than a hundred of the 9,000 cases that come before them every year; Walsh and Hemmens 2010). Therefore, criminal courts at the county and state level, as they are guided by state law, are *the* most important organizational unit to consider in terms of management issues in criminal justice.

The levels of these state courts are illustrated in Table 1.1. There is a clear hierarchy to these levels, with the lower-level courts (i.e., courts of limited and general jurisdiction) deferring to the decisions made in the upper-level courts (i.e., the intermediate courts of appeal and the courts of last resort). Note that the names and jurisdictions of these courts are generally the same across the states, but there is some variety too (Smith 1997). For instance, the names and responsibilities of courts of limited jurisdiction vary widely. Moreover, some states have no intermediate appellate court; rather, their Supreme Court serves in the only appellate capacity. For example, the New York court of general jurisdiction (or general trial court) is called the Supreme Court. All states, however, have a court of general jurisdiction (the trial courts) in some form, and all have a version of a court of last resort (ultimate appeals court). For our purposes we will generally be concerned with the organization and operation of the courts of general jurisdiction, as they are the most involved on a day-to-day basis in criminal matters. These are the courts that loosely supervise plea agreements, and these are the courts where criminal trials are held.

Staffing

Judges in state and local courts are either elected (in partisan or nonpartisan elections), appointed (by governors or legislatures), or selected by committee and then appointed and later elected or retained (Meyer and Grant 2003; Smith 1997). Judges in federal courts are appointed with the advice and consent of the Senate in what has become an increasingly politicized process. Students of history note that from *Marbury v. Madison* (1803) on, this process of appointment and approval of federal judges has had a political flavor; the feeding frenzy of today is a development of recent years. We will discuss the selection of judges and other court actors later in this text; suffice it to say here that no matter what method is utilized, it is hard to separate politics from a judicial position, whether it is in a local, state, or federal court. Having said this, we would also note that judges, whether selected/elected/appointed or retained, are not always concerned about politics in the operation of their courtroom or as it affects their duties on a day-to-day basis. It is when very public or infamous cases come before a judge that politics might have the most influence.

Similarly, the selection of county and state district attorneys (DAs) and United States attorneys (top federal court prosecutors in their jurisdictions) is usually by election for county and state prosecutors and by political appointment for US attorneys (Meyer and Grant 2003). In some states the DAs, however, are appointed.

Public defenders are less political in that most are not elected, but rise in their organization through appointment and performance. In large counties public defenders represent about 70 percent of felons; the rest of the defendants in these and smaller counties are represented by either private attorneys or assigned counsel (Meyer and Grant 2003). In federal district courts less than a third of defendants are represented by a public defender; the rest are served by panel or private attorneys.

However, beneath the political top dogs in the courts—prosecutor's and public defender's/assigned counsel offices—are the bureaucrats who labor in the trenches, so to speak. Assistant DAs, law clerks and bailiffs, and public or assigned defense attorneys are the people who variously prosecute the

Table 1.1 State court levels

	Common names	Jurisdiction
Courts of limited jurisdiction	County, city, municipal, probate, small claims police, justice of the peace, family, magistrate	Minor crimes, traffic offenses, misdemeanors
Courts of general jurisdiction	Superior, District, Circuit, Courts of Common Pleas or Supreme Court	Trial courts for felony cases; provide initial processing for a range of criminal and civil cases
Intermediate appellate courts	Court of Appeals, Appellate Court	Hear appeals regarding possible mistakes made during trial courts
Court of last resort	Supreme Court, Court of Appeals	Consider appeals from intermediate appellate courts or from courts of general jurisdiction

crimes (or not), record the events in a courtroom, or ensure the security of the proceedings; as noted earlier, public defenders also defend those who cannot afford a private attorney. Currently these employees across the country number in the hundreds of thousands.

Location

The county and city-level courts are located in the communities they serve. State-level appellate courts tend to be located in larger urban areas and/or in the state capital. Federal courts are also located in large urban areas that serve a region of the country.

Jail/detention and prison/juvenile facilities: how they differ

The fact that the general public, even the news media, does not make distinctions between prisons and jails as institutions is baffling. It is not unusual to hear a newscaster, or even a print journalist, refer to the recipient of a prison sentence as being "sent to jail," or vice versa (e.g., see Conover 2000). A teenager in a detention facility is inexplicably said to be "in prison." Though many readers may have a clear understanding of how adult and juvenile jails and prisons differ, others will not, so we shall note their differences and similarities. Additionally, we will discuss the nature of community corrections, also known as probation and parole, and explain how those organizations fit into the corrections picture.

Although there are some obvious similarities between adult prisons and jails and between juvenile detention and longer-term facilities, they are distinct in several ways that have a vast impact on their management. To simplify matters for this discussion, we will use "jails" to refer to both adult jails and juvenile detention centers and "prisons" to refer to adult prisons and juvenile versions of them (which are variously referred to as facilities, reformatories, ranches, or schools in other contexts). When one of the authors asks students, at the beginning of an introduction to corrections class, to list the differences between adult and juvenile prisons and jails, numerous items are typically mentioned. The most important are listed in the remainder of this section.

Conviction and sentence status

About 60 percent of jail inmates are unconvicted, whereas all prison inmates have been convicted in court and sentenced to a year or more (inmates with a sentence of less than twelve months often do their time in a jail). Notably, though, this breakdown between convicted and unconvicted inmates in jails varies to a degree from year to year (Minton 2011: 8).

Time incarcerated

Most jail inmates are released within a week, although some await trial, or sentencing, for several months. The average prison sentence is for a year or more.

Local vs. state operation

Most jails are operated at the county level, although there are some city, state (combined with prisons), and federal jails. Most prisons are operated at the state level, although there is a burgeoning federal prison system.

Size of the facility

Most jails are relatively small, holding fewer than fifty inmates, although there are jail systems in large urban areas that hold thousands of inmates: two jails alone, the City of New York and Los Angeles County, held 31,085 jail inmates in 2010, which was 5 percent of the US total (Minton 2011: 9-10). Most prisons hold 500 to 1,000 inmates or more, although some types of prisons (e.g., work releases) or juvenile facilities tend to hold fewer than a hundred inmates.

Security level of the facility

Most jails hold inmates representing a mix of security levels, from those serving their DUI sentence on the weekend to convicted murderers awaiting transfer to the state prison. Laws prevent sight and sound contact between adults and juveniles and males and females in jails. In cities of any size, there is often a separate jail facility for juveniles, but rarely a separate one for women, though some large cities (e.g., Miami, Florida, Los Angeles County, California) have women's jails. Because of the mix of security levels represented, most jails tend to operate like maximum security prisons, but with work release and trustee opportunities for the less serious offenders.

Male prisons, on the other hand, are able to specialize in the classification of security levels by considering current offense, offense history, behavior while in prison, and the needs of the inmates. So in most states there are adult male versions of maximum, medium, and minimum security prisons and work releases. Most states have only one juvenile prison and one women's prison. Yet there are likely to be halfway houses and work releases that serve men and women who have been sentenced, or juveniles who are adjudicated offenders.

Age and gender separation

As mentioned, prisons also usually separate inmates by age (juvenile vs. adult) and gender (male vs. female), though this is not always done. Sometimes teenagers are processed through the adult system for serious crimes and then do their time in adult prisons, and some states maintain co-ed prisons. Jails also generally separate adults from children and men from women; usually these subgroups are held in the same building, but with provision for sight and sound separation. Also some critics (e.g., Belknap 2001) note that when populations are combined in corrections, managers, both historically and currently, necessarily tend to focus resources and attention on the largest inmate grouping—adult males—at the expense of females and juveniles.

Location

Jails tend to be physically part of a community, usually conveniently located somewhere in the largest city in the county, whereas most prisons are located in more rural and less accessible parts of the state. The placement of jails in larger cities and towns is done to ensure close proximity to the largest police force in the county and to the county courthouse. Also, since the vast majority of inmates are in and out of jail within a week, it makes sense to have the facility closest to where they are most likely to live and work. The placement of prisons in rural areas, however, has usually been a political decision at the state level, which does not always coincide with the mission of those facilities or the original domicile of most of the inmates. In Idaho, for instance, the only women's prison per se, excepting work release facilities, is located outside the relatively remote town of Pocatello, in south-eastern Idaho, which is a four-hour drive from the largest population center, in Boise. If state policymakers had been concerned about its reintegrative function, they would have sited it outside Boise, along with the five male prisons located there; instead, political considerations determined its placement. Other states (e.g., Washington and New Mexico) also have chosen to locate their one women's prison away from the population centers. Politics affects the location decision when a community wants the facility because of the jobs it will bring and its officials have enough support at the legislative and gubernatorial levels to get what they want, despite what might best fit the mission of the prison or the circumstances of its inmates.

Jails and prisons: how they are alike

Despite all these fairly serious differences between prisons and jails, they are also quite similar. For this reason, the errant newscaster who uses "prison" and "jail" interchangeably might be forgiven, a little.

1   **Justifications for sanctioning or reasons for being** Both prisons and jails (and probation and parole) exist to punish (retribution), inca-pacitate, deter, rehabilitate, and reintegrate (see Box 1.2). Note some scholars—e.g., Cullen and Jonson (2012)—would add restorative jus-tice and saving the children to these justifications. The degree to which a prison or jail emphasizes any one of these depends on a number of factors, including the age of an inmate (juvenile or adult), the status of the inmate (i.e., convicted/sentenced or not), the type of crime the inmate has been accused or convicted of, the type of facility, the length of incarceration, the politics of the day, the availability of resources, and the proximity to rehabilitation programming in communities. Both prisons and jails have complex and multilayered missions that center on the justifications listed and restorative justice and program-ming focused on saving the children.

2   **Locus in the criminal justice system** Both prisons and jails are key facili-ties in the criminal justice system, albeit sometimes at different ends of the spectrum. Both law enforcement and the courts act to provide inputs in the form of inmates into them, either directly in the case of jails and the police and courts, or prisons and courts, or indirectly in the case of prisons and the police. Both law enforcement and the courts use the incapacitative function of prisons and jails. Judges also use both as appropriate institutions to address the retributive, deter-rent, rehabilitative, and reintegrative functions of the system, though for different types of inmates/offenders. Restorative justice is used in

Box 1.2 Definitions of police, court, and correctional justifications for sanctioning

The following justifications or reasons for the existence of criminal sanctioning are often cited.

- **Retribution (punishment):** People are in the criminal justice system, either in institutions or in the community, either to atone for their crime (retribution: balance the scales of justice) or because of the belief that they should suffer (punishment) for the crime they committed.
- **Incapacitation:** People are in the criminal justice system, either in institutions or in the community, because their engagement in criminal behavior must be stopped. To ensure that this happens, they must either be watched (community supervision) or placed in a prison or jail.
- **Deterrence:** People are in the criminal justice system, either in institutions or in the community, because that is deemed the best way to dissuade them, and others, from engaging in current or future criminal behavior.
- **Rehabilitation:** People are in the criminal justice system, either in institutions or in the community, because that experience and/or the engagement in programming and other activities is likely to lead them to rethink and desist from further criminal activity or behavior that is related to their criminal activity (e.g., excessive drinking). A related concept that is intertwined with rehabilitation is habilitation—the engagement of a person in self-change, rather than the imposition of change.
- **Reintegration:** People are in the criminal justice system, either in institutions or in the community, because that is a means of maintaining pro-social ties to the community, or gradually reintroducing them to it.
- **Restorative justice:** People in jails or prisons, or on probation and parole, are given the opportunity to recompense the victim and/or the community for the harm they have done. In turn, they are given the opportunity to gain forgiveness for their actions. "The goal is for all harms to be rectified and the injured parties to be restored" (Cullen and Jonson 2011: 10).
- **Early intervention:** The vital and unmet needs of at-risk children in correctional institutions or on probation or parole or who are in the community are satisfied so as to reduce their further or later engagement in deviant behavior (Cullen and Jonson 2011).

prisons and jails, but is more likely to be found in probation and parole programming. Efforts to save children from crime and other social maladies might exist in juvenile facilities, juvenile court, and programming for juveniles in probation and parole, but it is also likely to exist in the larger health and welfare programs for poor people in communities.

3 **Organizational structure** Typically, jails and prisons are structurally bureaucratic, with paramilitary regimentation, regalia, and accoutrements (more about these later), and top-down communication. In these ways jails and prisons are also similar to most police and sheriff's departments.

4 **Inmate characteristics** The inmates incarcerated in jails tend to be young, uneducated, poor, and disproportionately members of minority groups with alcohol or substance abuse problems (Harlow 1998; Harrison and Beck 2003; Harrison and Karberg 2003; Minton 2011). Though not as young, the inmates in prisons are, on average, younger than 35; and they are uneducated, poor, and disproportionately minority group members with alcohol or substance abuse problems. In both groups there are likely to be more members who have suffered from child abuse in all its forms than is the case in the general population, and there is likely to be a significant subgroup that are mentally disturbed (Harlow 1998; Harrison and Karberg 2003) in both types of institutions, but particularly in jails. Nearly half the women inmates in prisons and jails report past physical or sexual abuse (Harlow 1998; Harrison and Karberg 2003).

5 **Staff characteristics** A significant number of the staff in prisons and jails have a military background, and both types of facilities tend to have a predominantly white male staff (Bureau of Justice Statistics 2004a). The number of former military personnel may be explained by an attraction to public sector work and the paramilitary structure of jails and prisons. The relative lack of diversity in some facilities is tied to patterns of discrimination and cultural trends. But since the passage of the Civil Rights Act of 1964, which prohibited discrimination in hiring based on race and ethnicity; its amendment in 1972; and civil suits by minorities and white women over the course of thirty years, some real inroads have been made in the hiring of a more diverse staff (Bureau of Justice Statistics 2004a). Jails and prisons still tend to be staffed predominantly by white males, but this is much less true than even twenty years ago, particularly in urban areas. For instance, in one Florida women's jail visited by one of the authors in 1992 there was a white male administrator, but the second in command was an African American woman, and the majority of the staff were minority group members. In the twenty-first century, women and minority group men serve in all capacities of men's and women's jails and prisons, from warden or director on down, but they are still underrepresented based on

their proportion of the larger population (Bureau of Justice Statistics 2004a, 2006).

6   **Public institutions** Most prisons and jails (93 percent) are still operated by the public sector, which means that they must adhere to civil service protections of their states and communities and other laws that regulate public sector institutions (Harrison and Karberg 2003). They are in some ways more politically responsive and vulnerable as public institutions, and staff members have a service orientation that is likely to differ from that found in the private sector (more about this in the following).

Community corrections or probation and parole: how they are different and similar

The term "community corrections" is often used to refer to a more modern form of probation and parole. Both jails and prisons are tied to the respective adult or juvenile probation and/or parole system in their state or county. Probation sentences are often served before or instead of, a jail or prison sentence. A failed term on probation often precedes a prison sentence. States that still possess parole as a form of release option parole most inmates, and some jails also "parole" inmates (Glaze and Bonczar 2011).

Time sequencing

A simplistic and overgeneralized difference between adult and juvenile probation and adult and juvenile parole is that probation tends to precede prison and parole tends to follow it. The courts, instead of using incarceration, place people on probation. People on parole are released from prison by a parole board or by a mandatory conditional release after serving their time in prison. In both cases, probationers and parolees are subject to being returned to either prison or jail if they commit rule violations (are "violated") or other offenses.

Types of offenders

Another related difference, given the time sequencing of probation and parole, is that those on probation tend to be less serious offenders than those who have gone to prison and been paroled. Among adult offenders on probation at the end of 2010, only half had been convicted of a felony, 47 percent of a misdemeanor, and another 2 percent of other offenses (Glaze and Bonczar 2011: 6). In contrast, of those on parole, almost all had originally been given a prison sentence of a year or more. Probation rolls also tended to include more whites and women than those for parole.

Rules

But the similarities between probation and parole are greater than their differences. If probationers and parolees fail to adhere to certain sorts of rules, their probation or parole status will be "violated" and they may be sent to incarceration, or returned there. Moreover, the rules are usually similar (e.g., prohibition against the use of alcohol or drugs; requirements to avoid criminally engaged friends/family, to participate in programming, to get and keep employment, etc.).

Similar characteristics of staff and organizational structure

The community corrections officers who supervise probationers and parolees have similar backgrounds and training, and in small offices, they may have clients of both types on their caseloads. Probation and parole organizations are usually very similar to police and sheriff's departments and prisons and jails in that they tend to have a traditional management and bureaucratic composition. They differ in that they tend to focus more on the value of programming for their clients than is true of correctional institutions.

Juvenile probation and parole differ slightly from the adult versions in that the former officers tend to be supervised by the juvenile court, which means that they may have a more ingrained history of attending to the "best interests" of juveniles than the adult community corrections system does for men and women under its supervision.

Conclusions: the unique management milieu of criminal justice agencies

Let us begin with the ending. Bureaucrats get a bum rap. Virtually every successful presidential candidate of the past fifty years has run against big government or the Beltway (area around Washington DC) or, in essence, bureaucrats who are apparently messing everything up in America. Yet the bureaucrats in the criminal justice system—those police, probation and parole, and corrections officers; those judges, prosecutors, and defense attorneys—perform work that is of inestimable value to this country. Absent their efforts, the average citizen would not see justice done in this country, not at all. And that is what this book is about: how justice is done in this country.

Justice is "done" in large part by people in organizations. Therefore, we will study what those organizations are, who works in them, and how they are led and operated. It is our hope that when the book cover closes after that final page, the reader has a more informed, and perhaps profound, sense of the mechanics of how criminal justice is, and should be, managed.

Discussion questions

1   How are court organizations substantially different from police and corrections organizations? How might this difference affect the behavior of the actors within these organizational settings?
2   Why is policing mostly a local affair, and how is that affected by organizational and community factors? Explain your answer.
3   How is policing similar at the city, county, and state levels? Provide examples.
4   Why are courts more like informal work groups than like bureaucracies? Explain your answer.
5   How do jails and prisons differ from each other, and in what ways are they similar? Give an example.
6   What are the greatest differences between probation and parole? Give some examples.
7   What are the common characteristics of the clients in all criminal justice agencies? How might these commonalities affect their treatment by criminal justice actors?

Web link

Bureau of Justice Statistics website: www.ojp.usdoj.gov/bjs/

Cases Cited

In re Gault, 387 U.S. 1 (1967).
Marbury v. Madison, 5 U.S. 137 (1803).

References

Belknap, J. (2001) *The invisible woman: Gender, crime and justice*, 2nd edn. Belmont, CA: Wadsworth.

Bureau of Justice Statistics. (2004a) *Sourcebook of criminal justice statistics—2002*, Bureau of Justice Statistics, US Department of Justice, Washington, DC: GPO.

Bureau of Justice Statistics. (2004b) *Law enforcement statistics*, Bureau of Justice Statistics, US Department of Justice, Office of Justice Programs. Online. Available at www.ojp.usdoj.gov/bjs/ (last accessed January 31, 2013).

Bureau of Justice Statistics. (2004c) *Probation and parole statistics*. Bureau of Justice Statistics, Office of Justice Programs, US Department of Justice. Available at bjs.ojp.usdoj.gov/index.cfm?ty=pbdetail&iid=1108 (last accessed January 31, 2013).

Bureau of Justice Statistics. (2006) *Justice expenditure and employment in the United States, 2003.* Bureau of Justice Statistics, US Department of Justice, Office of Justice Programs. Available at bjs.ojp.usdoj.gov/content/pub/pdf/jeeus03.pdf (last accessed January 31, 2013).

Clynch, E. J. and Neubauer, D. W. (1981). Trial courts as organizations: A critique and synthesis. *Law and Police Quarterly*, 3(1): 69–94.

Conover, T. (2000) *Newjack: Guarding Sing Sing.* New York, NY: Random House.

Cullen, F. T. and Jonson, C. L. (2011) Rehabilitation and treatment programs. In J. Q. Wilson and J. Petersilia (eds), *Crime and Public Policy.* New York: Oxford University Press, pp. 293–344.

Cullen, F. T. and Jonson, C. L. (2012) *Correctional theory: Context and consequences.* Los Angeles, CA: Sage.

Empey, L. T. and Stafford, M. C. (1991) *American delinquency: Its meaning and construction*, 3rd edn. Belmont, CA: Wadsworth.

Glaze, L. E. and Bonczar, T. P. (2011) *Probation and parole in the United States, 2010.* Bureau of Justice Statistics, US Department of Justice, Washington DC: GPO.

Goldstein, H. (1977) *Policing a free society.* Cambridge, MA: Ballinger.

Harlow, C. W. (1998) *Profile of jail inmates.* US Department of Justice, Washington DC: GPO.

Harrison, P. M. and Beck, A. J. (2003) *Prisoners in 2002.* Bureau of Justice Statistics, US Department of Justice, Washington DC: GPO.

Harrison, P. M. and Karberg, J. C. (2003) *Prison and jail inmates at midyear 2002.* Bureau of Justice Statistics Bulletin, US Department of Justice, Washington DC: GPO.

Hickman, M. J. and Reaves, B. A. (2003) *Local police departments 2000.* Bureau of Justice Statistics, Office of Justice Programs, US Department of Justice, Washington, DC: GPO.

Kelling, G. L. (1999) *"Broken windows" and police discretion.* National Institute of Justice, Office of Justice Programs, US Department of Justice, Washington, DC: GPO.

Kyckelhahn, T. (2011) *Justice expenditures and employment, FY 1982–2007 – Statistical tables.* Bureau of Justice Statistics, Office of Justice Programs, US Department of Justice. Washington, DC: GPO.

Lab, S. P., Williams, M., Holcomb, J. E., King, W. R. and Buerger, M. E. (2004) *Explaining criminal justice.* Los Angeles, CA: Roxbury.

Langton, L. and Cohen, T.H. (2007) *State court organizations, 1987–2004.* Bureau of Justice Statistics, Office of Justice Programs, US Department of Justice, Washington DC: GPO.

Langworthy, R. and Travis L., III. (1994) *Policing in America: A balance of forces.* New York, NY: Macmillan.

Minton, T.D. (2011) *Jail inmates at midyear 2010 – Statistical tables.* Bureau of Justice Statistics, Office of Justice Programs, US Department of Justice, Washington DC: GPO.

Meyer, J. F. and Grant, D. R. (2003) *The courts in our criminal justice system.* Upper Saddle River, NJ: Prentice Hall.

Peak, K. J. (2008) *Policing America: Challenges and best practices*, 2nd edn. Upper Saddle River, NJ: Prentice-Hall.

Reaves, B. (2011) *Census of state and local law enforcement agencies, 2008.* Bureau of Justice Statistics, Office of Justice Programs, US Department of Justice, Washington, DC: GPO.

Roberg, R., Novak, K., Cordner, G. and Smith, B. (2011) *Police and society,* 5th edn. New York, NY: Oxford University Press.

Smith, C. E. (1997) *Courts, politics, and the judicial process,* 2nd edn. Chicago, IL: Nelson-Hall.

Travis, L. F. and Langworthy, R. H. (2007) *Policing in America: A balance of forces,* 4th edn. Upper Saddle River, NJ: Prentice-Hall.

Walsh, A. and Hemmens, C. (2010) *Law, justice and society: A sociolegal approach.* New York, NY: Oxford University Press.

Wilson, J. Q. (1968) *Varieties of police behavior: The management of law and order in eight communities,* Cambridge, MA: Harvard University Press.

2 Surveying the landscape of criminal justice management

Introduction: the ties that bind

The criminal justice landscape at times appears vast, stretching as far as the eye can see. In virtually every community, there is public policing, courts of one kind or another, a jail, and increasingly a prison or two. Among these distinct agencies with their unique and distinguishing characteristics, there are shared common features between them as organizations operating—for the most part—in the public sector.

In the previous chapter the focus was on the differences between and among criminal justice agencies. In this chapter we set down the markers of these common landscape features as they relate to terms and concepts, open and closed organizations, competing values of government operation, and government service. In the course of this survey of criminal justice organizations we may find that what binds organizations and their actors is more than just their mission to formally enforce and uphold the law—it is also the nature of these organizations that makes them similar.

Common terms defined

Organization, justice, bureaucracy, management, and formal and informal goals and organizations

As we explore the distinctive nature of criminal justice organizations and the characteristics of their staff and clients, there are several terms and concepts that require definition, since they will be used with some frequency throughout this text. So that there is a common understanding of language, we define a few of these terms up front.

As long as there have been organizations, or groupings of humans for a reason, there has been management. An **organization** is *a grouping of individuals with a binding purpose.* Gulick (1937: 79) first defined the theory of organization as having "[t]o do with the structure of co-ordination imposed upon the work-division units of an enterprise." For Gulick, division of work is the primary reason why an organization exists. He argues that we divide work in organizations because people have different skills and abilities, and that those attributes can be fitted to the type of work in an organization. He believes that this work in any organization must be coordinated through some sort of authority and through an understood purpose or reason for the work. Finally, he notes that organizations will develop patterns of operation whereby authority is viewed as coming either from the top down or from the bottom up.

Additionally, Selznick (1948: 125) has argued that an organizational system may have either an economic or an "adaptive social structure," both of which have "reciprocal consequences." In other words, an organizational system may exist for both economic and social purposes, as "work" (as Gulick put it) is done in that sense. In combining these perspectives, therefore, an organization could be defined as a grouping of people arranged and coordinated to accomplish some purpose.

Types of organizations might include a family, church, school, private business, country club, or political party. As mentioned, criminal justice agencies include such organizations as departments of corrections, police or sheriff's departments, state police departments, the courts (both adult and juvenile), community corrections agencies, and jails and prisons. Organizations of all these types might operate with different structures and boundaries, but they are similar in that each has a focus or goal(s), such as the administration of justice, that drives its activities and justifies its existence. Briefly, justice is defined by the American Heritage Dictionary (1992: 456) as "1. [t]he quality of being fair; fairness. 2. The principle of moral rightness; equity. 3. The upholding of what is just, especially fair treatment and due reward in accordance with honor, standards, or law." Distinctions between formal and natural justice (law and morality) and how justice is precisely and fully defined are matters best left to the philosophers. However, in this text **justice** means that those who are guilty are caught, processed, and sanctioned, as befits community, professional, and moral standards, by system actors. We think that justice exists when those who are innocent are given ample opportunity and the due process necessary to ensure they are not caught up in and sanctioned by the system. In terms of internal organizational operations, justice might also be a characteristic of a system in which employees are treated fairly and honestly by management and given the opportunity to develop and "give back" to their community. Effective or good decision making (we discuss decision making in Chapter 12) in criminal justice agencies, then, and in our view, has to do with furthering the ends of justice for those processed by and those who participate in (i.e., criminal justice actors) the system.

Some theorists on organizations (e.g., Blau and Scott 1962) argue that families are just groupings and are differentially distinct from social organizations such as police or correctional agencies or the courts. They define a formal organization as "[f]ormally established for the explicit purpose of achieving certain goals" (Blau and Scott 1962: 208). Families, for example, usually exist to provide companionship, love, and protection for their members and/or a safe harbor to raise children. The structure of a familial organization has historically been hierarchical, with an adult male head and all others subordinate. Nowadays in western cultures there is more fluidity of power, with female co-leaders and children still somewhat under their parents' control, though having certain rights of their own. Although the "traditional" family boundary could include just two parents and children related by blood, in truth families have always been much larger and more complex than that; they have often encompassed stepparents and stepsiblings, grandparents, aunts, uncles, and cousins. They also need not just be restricted to blood or marriage relations. The line where the family boundary ends and the tribe boundary begins has been determined somewhat arbitrarily among human groupings and is not always clearly defined.

A correctional facility, on the other hand, exists for the multiple and, Blau and Scott (1962) would argue, formal purposes of incapacitation, deterrence, retribution, rehabilitation, and reintegration, for example. Police and sheriff's departments were created formally to serve and protect, but also to investigate and prevent crime. Courts also act in a formal sense—to enforce the law, like the police, but also to deliberate, adjudicate, sentence, and act as brokers of support services geared toward offender reintegration (as exemplified by drug and other specialty courts). The order of the philosophical justifications of existence for all agencies varies by type of institution and by policy. For example, a jail with a shorter-term population may be more likely to focus on simply incapacitating inmates, rather than a prison setting where other overarching goals, such as rehabilitation, retribution, and reintegration likely factor in as well. By the same token, the influence of political trends that favor lengthier sentences and less rehabilitation is evident, since they have shaped the operation of courts and corrections for the last three and a half decades. Both police and corrections agencies tend to have a "traditional" organizational structure with hierarchy, specialization, and rule of law (all three attributes of a bureaucracy); top-down communication; and military accoutrements. Their organizational boundaries are set by who is employed by the institution and by who the clientele are.

Briefly, the term **bureaucracy** refers to how organizations are structured, ruled, or socially organized. According to German sociologist and political economist Max Weber, there are six main characteristics of a bureaucracy. These characteristics are presented in Box 2.1; for more about Weber himself, see Box 4.1.

Management of organizations may refer to one or more persons who have formal control over an organization, or the act or process of operating the organization. Management for our purposes will refer to both. Carlisle (1976) defined management as a process of arranging and organizing elements to achieve organizational objectives. In accordance with this definition, management does not have a set beginning or an end; rather, it is something that continues as long as the organization does. The term "management" as it is used in this text will encapsulate the more modern view that there are multiple sources of power and influence in an organization, and these are not all located at the top of the organizational chart (Micklethwait and Wooldridge 1996). In other words, in reality, management is done by all levels of the organization. Management is also goal-oriented, with a focus on achieving both the formal and the informal goals of the organization.

The **formal goals** of the formal organization are easier to discern than the informal goals of the informal organization (Blau and Scott 1962). This is true because the formal goals are those that are written down and reflected in the organization's mission statement, in the organizational chart, in the policy manual, and in training curricula. Formal goals are professed by the directors, court administrators, sheriffs, police chiefs, wardens of prisons, administrators of jails, and community corrections personnel. They are reinforced in job announcements, selection procedures, and performance appraisals by supervisors. The formal goals are concrete and often exist officially for the formal organization and for public consumption.

Box 2.1 Weber's characteristics of bureaucracy in his own words

I. There is the principle of fixed and official jurisdiction areas, which are generally ordered by rules, that is, by laws or administrative regulations.

II. The principles of office hierarchy and of levels of graded authority mean a firmly ordered system of super and subordination in which there is a supervision of the lower offices by the higher ones.

III. The management of the modern office is based upon written documents ("the files"), which are preserved in their original or draught [draft] form.

IV. Office management, at least all specialized office management—and such management is distinctly modern—usually presupposes thorough and expert training.

V. When the office is fully developed, official activity demands the full working capacity of the official, irrespective of the fact that his [or her] obligatory time in the bureau may be firmly delimited.

VI. The management of the office follows general rules, which are more or less stable, more or less exhaustive, and which can be learned.

Source: Weber (1946).

It should be noted, however, that although these goals are formally acknowledged by the organization, they are not always achievable. This is because they often conflict (e.g., for an organization tasked to simultaneously achieve both retribution and rehabilitation); there are too many of them (see, e.g., any policy manual for a large organization); and they do not always fit the informal goals or norms of behavior of organizational members.

Criminal justice employees may strive mightily to achieve these formal goals, but the fact that they are dealing with human beings and subgroupings with alternate informal goals in an informal organization hampers their progress. This occurs for several reasons. All situations cannot be covered by one general rule; instead, discretion must be exercised. Humans are also motivated by more than just organizational directives or rewards. So, for instance, they may value more time off (an informal goal of the employee) as opposed to finishing a report on time (a formal goal of the employer). In another example, the police organization itself may informally "tell" the officer, without having to state it explicitly, to ignore certain minor law breaking that clearly violates formal organizational rules, so that the appearance of peace and order in the community might be maintained. Blau and Scott (1962: 208) explain well the reasons for the **informal organization**:

> In every formal organization there arise informal organizations. The constituent groups of the organization, like all groups, develop their own practices, values, norms, and social relations as their members live and work together. The roots of these informal systems are embedded in the formal organization itself and nurtured by the very formality of its arrangements. Official rules must be general to have sufficient scope to cover the multitude of situations that may arise. But the application of these general rules to particular cases often poses problems of judgment, and informal practices tend to emerge that provide solutions for these problems. Decisions not anticipated by official regulations must frequently be made, particularly in times of change, and here again unofficial practices are likely to furnish guides for decisions... Moreover, unofficial norms are apt to develop that regulate performance and productivity. Finally, complex networks of social relations and informal status structures emerge, within groups and between them, which are influenced by many factors besides the organizational chart.

In other words, the formal organization, with its stated formal goals, does not completely describe what really happens in, and drives, the organization or its membership. This formal vs. informal juxtaposition in organizations will come up many times throughout this text because we must bear in mind that at all times there is an informal organization operating in tandem in criminal justice agencies, along with the formal one. If we pretend that the organization wholly operates along formal lines, we risk impairing our ability to understand the management of such organizations.

Street-level bureaucrats and discretion

One part of this informal organization that has often been ignored by management scholars is the importance of the line worker in determining how or whether policy is carried out. In his groundbreaking book *Street-Level Bureaucracy: Dilemmas of the Individual in Public Services*, Lipsky (1980) defines a street-level bureaucrat as someone who is a public service worker with much discretion to do their job. A key aspect of the street-level bureaucrat's job is that there are too many clients and not enough resources. Such SLBs might include police officers, teachers, public defenders or prosecutors, welfare or employment workers, juvenile or adult probation or parole officers, and jail or prison counselors or officers. SLBs have discretion to make choices about arresting offenders, helping students, defending or prosecuting cases, awarding benefits, recommending for release or parole, or identifying this or that inmate for treatment. We define (with the help of Lipsky) this **discretion** as the ability to make one or more choices and to act, or not act, thereon. The discretion possessed by SLBs allows them, according to Lipsky (1980), not only to carry out policy but to make it. The demands placed on SLBs, such as too many clients and not enough resources, mandate that they make choices about the use of their time and their efforts.

Thus the existence of SLBs and what motivates them further substantiates the existence of the informal organization at play in the operation of public sector entities such as police, courts, and corrections. For example, when one of the authors worked as a counselor in a prison in Washington State, the state wanted her and the other counselors to review inmate files and supply the department of corrections with select information about their clients for dissemination to policymakers. When told that they had to do this by their supervisors and faced with choosing this task or getting their other work done, the counselors chose informally to ignore the departmental directive. In effect, by ignoring a formal directive and thus failing to implement a policy, they as SLBs were making policy.

Ethics

The ethics of a choice that comprises an act of de facto policy making is another matter. In this instance the counselors valued their need to complete tasks more highly than the need of the larger organization to respond to designated policymakers. **Ethics** is often defined as the study of, or the act of, doing the right thing in the professional sphere (Braswell 1998). Doing the right thing in the private sphere is understood as morality. Along the same lines, **organizational integrity**, a characteristic of organizations whose actors as a whole are honest, ethical, and can be trusted by their members and the community, is also a sign of ethical operation. Suffice it to say here that a code of ethics can be a set of central guiding principles for the management of criminal justice agencies. It should also be understood that ethical decision making is entangled in the operation of both the formal and informal sides of the organization. Chapter 3 is devoted to a discussion of ethics in criminal justice organizations.

No organization is an island: open and closed organizations

In this definitional section of the chapter, we discuss the nature of closed vs. open organizations. A **closed organization** is not affected by its environment and an **open organization** is. Some scholars have noted a debate over the closed or open nature of various organizations (e.g., see Stojkovic, Kalinich, and Klofas 1998), but in truth and depending on the organization, the degree to which an organization is open or closed is relative. If any public sector organization ever fit the designation of a closed organization, then correctional organizations (prisons in particular) did, and to some degree still do today. In his classic work *Stateville,* Jacobs (1977) investigates fifty years of the history of the Stateville maximum security prison in Illinois. He describes the institution in the early 1900s as one where staff were forced to sleep at the facility, outside community contact with inmates was extremely restricted, and media involvement was limited to formal occasions when events and what outsiders saw of the inmates and the organization could be carefully orchestrated by the warden.

This type of prison is referred to as a *total institution,* in that all activities such as eating, sleeping, and working were strictly controlled and occurred under the figurative roof of the institution (Goffman 1961). The formal face of the Stateville organization was that of an ordered and frugal institution, while the informal operation included abuses of inmates and staff; however, the informal operation was allowed to continue because powerful wardens were able to control what information was available to the outside. But Jacobs (1977) notes that strict control exerted over Stateville had eroded over the years because the outside environment intruded (in terms of laws, politics, personnel, and types of inmates), which by the 1970s led to a recognition of the need to evolve in management and practice.

Most people who study criminal justice agencies today recognize their dual nature, both open and closed. Because of their organizational goals, especially incapacitation, correctional managers have a legitimate interest in restricting some access to inmates and facilities. They cannot have a facility *open* on a regular basis without impairing their ability to keep inmates in and to provide for a disruption-free workplace and living spaces. They can and must, however, allow for visits, albeit often with restrictions including appropriate friends and family, attorneys, and sometimes the media. Staff are allowed to return home after work (though a few prisons still have staff quarters), but in any event the institution's employees often bring their own beliefs and values to work. Inmates come from diverse backgrounds, and they too have some limited rights that the management must legally respect.

Police and sheriff's departments, courts, jails, and community corrections organizations have always been more "open" than prisons, for several reasons. For example, these facilities are physically located in communities, and their clients and staff move fluidly in and out of the organizations, with the staff having at least a partial mission of serving the public or the public good. The media and other community members are much more aware of, and likely to comment on, their operation. Having said this, it is clear that staff attitudes toward clients/offenders, commonly used jargon, expertise, and legal prohibitions that prevent the full sharing of information make those non-prison facilities "closed" as well. Take for instance the closed nature of some organizational police structures, such as the line-officer/squad system, which has a tendency to isolate officers from the general community while fostering a close-knit subculture within that system (Darroch and Mazerolle 2013; Crank 1998).

Another instance of the legal prohibitions that prevent the full sharing of information between criminal justice organizations and outside organizations, researchers, or the community happened when one of the authors, while working for a state department of health and welfare on a multiagency research project, was denied access to a state patrol's arrest data. Although there may have been interagency cooperation in this case, a state statute barred the sharing and use of such information by any non-police agency or personnel. The physical doors were open, but the doors leading to use of electronic information for empirical research were closed.

There are several factors that are widely acknowledged to influence criminal justice operation. These influences, though, are relative. To some degree correctional organizations of all sizes, even the notorious Stateville prison, have always been somewhat open. For example, the inmates, staff, and warden of a prison invariably import their own values and beliefs into the organizational environment, which undoubtedly has no small effect on the operation of any facility. From the beginning, even a prison as closed as Stateville was subjected to outside influences, such as the imported values and culture of its inmates and staff and the politics of budgeting of its state; one wing of the Stateville prison was not completed on time because the state's policymakers had not come up with the funding. Because of changes in law and culture over the past forty years, however, the relative openness of all criminal justice institutions and agencies—even prisons—has only increased in regard to both physical and intellectual access (such as access to data for evaluation and other empirical study, but with the exception of that state patrol's data). Common factors that influence criminal justice operation, and its relative open-to-closed nature, include the following:

Staff: their personal demographics, beliefs and values, and background.
Accused/clients/offenders/inmates: their personal demographics, beliefs and values, background, and history.
Type of agency or institution mission: as that continues to be shaped and viewed by policymakers, managers, staff, and citizens.
Engineering and architecture: the physical environment influences all aspects of the organization and, some may argue, is a manifestation of organization itself.
Community and/or state or federal political culture: as that determines practices, use of, sentences meted out, and resources given to, the organization.
Economic status of the community or state: as this determines staff hired, numbers of cases processed, what facilities can be built, how they are maintained, pay and training for staff and programs for offenders/inmates, and programming available in the facilities and the community.
Law: as that directs policing; court consideration of evidence, due process, and sentencing; supervision of clients/inmates; access to courts; and treatment of, and for, accused, clients, offenders, and inmates.
Technology: as that shapes investigations and detection of crime, behavior and accountability of staff, options for sentencing, and the supervisory capacity of staff.
Weather: as that determines when crime waxes and wanes, how agencies can respond to community crises, how correctional facilities are built and operated, and how offenders are supervised in the community.
Politics: the processes involved in decision making about organizations and within various organizations, whether they are private or public, formal or informal.

In short, because of the inherent connectivity between criminal justice agencies and their external environments, they are indeed reflections of them. To paraphrase the poet John Donne (1623), substituting the word "organization" for the word "man" in his famous Meditation 17:

> [n]o organization is an island, entire of itself. Every organization is a piece of the continent, a part of the main. If a clod be washed away by the sea, Europe is the less ... any man's death diminishes me, therefore, never send to know for whom the bell tolls, it tolls for thee.

Simply put, criminal justice organizations are what their communities make them and must be understood in that context—part of which can be understood by defining the competing public service values of democratic accountability and neutral competence.

Democratic accountability and neutral competence: the value-added difference in governmental operation

Management theories in criminal justice (which are the focus in Chapter 4) are best understood by means of contextualizing them in a discussion of the competing values of democratic accountability and neutral competence. An understanding of these two values is necessary because they have influenced the development and conceptualization of the current operation and management of justice-centered agencies.

Democratic accountability

Democratic accountability is the value in government that the public sector, or the managers and workers in government, are accountable to those who have been democratically elected and/or politically appointed. This means that those who serve in government must be responsive, via elected or politically appointed persons, to the people. Ask yourself this question: Do you believe that this is a value which should be the predominate value for government service? Inevitably, many of our students raise their hands in affirmation of this value when asked. After all, as a society (in the US) we often proclaim the merits of democracy… so, how could we not vote in support of democratic accountability?

Under the absolute version of this value's application, all workers in corrections from the warden or director or sheriff on down, would be either politically elected (as sheriffs already are, but their underlings are not) or appointed. Before the Civil Service Reform Act of 1883, also known as the Pendleton Act, all federal, state, and local public employees were likely to be beholden to a politically elected or appointed person for their job. This meant that in some counties, when a new sheriff was elected, the whole department turned over, from the lowliest staff on up (Haller 1983; Walker 1983). Wardens and heads of juvenile facilities could hire and fire employees at will, without considering either qualifications or job performance (Jacobs 1977). Probation and parole officers also served at the whim of their politically appointed department heads. Essentially, all jobs in jails, prisons, courts, and police forces were political appointments; the qualifications and knowledge of employees, or whether they had worked hard in the public's interest, was of less significance. Instead, in public service, what really mattered was "who you knew," not "what you knew."

The purest form of the value of democratic accountability occurred in nineteenth-century America and led to notable corruption and abuse at all levels of government (Van Riper 1987). During this time government employees tried to please political actors, especially those who supported them, rather than working for the public good. Therefore, government contracts were awarded based on political alliances and contacts; government workers were hired and fired based on political allegiances and public resources were exploited for private ends. Because of the high value placed on democratic accountability at this time, those who won elections (the victors) collected and awarded the patronage jobs and contracts (the spoils) to their political friends. In fact, President James A. Garfield was assassinated in 1881 by a disaffected campaign supporter who had not received the patronage job he had expected (Morrow 1987). This assassination lent support to those arguing for the passage of the Pendleton Act a few years later (see Box 2.2).

Box 2.2 The Pendleton Act and the beginning of civil service reform in the United States

The Pendleton Act of 1883 was passed in reaction to the assassination of President Garfield by a disaffected campaign supporter who did not get the patronage job he had expected (Morrow 1987). It was also passed in reaction to the general corruption in government that became apparent after fifty years (since President Andrew Jackson's administration, beginning in 1829) of over-politicization of the administration or management of government services (US National Archives and Records Administration 2005).

The act created an agency called the Civil Service Commission, which separated classified and unclassified jobs at the federal level. Those classified job applicants were to be selected based on merit. In essence, the act established a form of civil service protection for jobs (people could not be fired at will) and required that people be hired based on their qualifications or skills and abilities for the job. Initially this act applied to only 10 percent of low-level federal jobs (Cayer 1987). Eventually, its application was expanded to virtually all federal jobs, and all states passed some form of the act. The act was championed by President Chester Arthur, who succeeded Garfield. President Grover Cleveland issued an executive order in 1886 that prohibited political activities by federal civil service employees, an order that was later expanded by President Theodore Roosevelt.

It is no wonder that in 1887, Princeton professor Woodrow Wilson was arguing for a separation of politics and administration. In the same article, the future president made the case for expanding the civil service reforms begun at the federal level with the Pendleton Act to all levels of government as a moral duty; he argued that government work should

Figure 2.1 This image of Woodrow Wilson courtesy of the Library of Congress, LC-USZ62–13028, Library of Congress Prints and Photographs Division Washington, DC 20540.

be more neutral and removed from politics, and that it should be more "businesslike":

> [W]e must regard civil-service reform in its present stages as but a prelude to a fuller administrative reform. We are now rectifying methods of appointment; we must go on to adjust executive functions more fitly and to prescribe better action. Civil-service reform is thus but a moral preparation for what is to follow. It is clearing the moral atmosphere of official life by establishing the sanctity of public office as a public trust, and, by making the service unpartisan, it is opening the way for making it businesslike (Wilson 1887: 18).

Neutral competency

A competing value for government service that has existed in tandem with democratic accountability is **neutral competency**, according to which government service should be politically neutral and focused on the skills and abilities of workers to do the job at hand, rather than on their political allegiances. In essence, this value emphasizes "what you know" for government service, rather than "who you know." Do you think this should be the preeminent value for government work in criminal justice? As with democratic accountability, many if not most of our students and those reading this book may raise their hands in support of this value as well. This is of little surprise: Given the worth our society places on hard work and the attainment of knowledge, who would not want neutral competence in government service?

Since passage of the Pendleton Act of 1883, its expansion at the federal level, and passage of similar acts in the states, most jobs in criminal justice, with the exception of elective positions (e.g., prosecutors, state and local judges, sheriffs) or top jobs that are political appointments (e.g. wardens, directors of juvenile corrections, undersheriffs, police chiefs, etc.), are protected by civil service. It is because of civil service reforms that after a probationary period, most deputy sheriffs and deputy prosecutors, public defense attorneys, police officers, correctional security staff, and counselors in juvenile and adult facilities cannot be fired without cause. That cause cannot be related to political affiliation or support, which in turn means that civil servants, again with the exception of top-level positions, must be politically neutral. Not only do people in these positions enjoy some protection from arbitrary firing, under civil service requirements, they are also hired based on job-valid qualifications. We will discuss these issues more in Chapters 8 and 9, but suffice it to say that there are a series of tests that civil servants in criminal justice must pass and qualifications they must meet before they can be hired, which speaks to their competency to do the job.

Another means of reinforcing the political neutrality of government workers came in the form of the Hatch Act of 1939. This federal act, and state versions of it that followed, restricted specific forms of political activity in the workplace (see Box 2.3; Cayer 1987). According to the current version of this act, government workers at the federal level can register, vote, and campaign for their chosen candidate, among other political activities. But government workers may not run for office or campaign for others in partisan elections, among other political activities.

Box 2.3 The Hatch Act requirements

The Hatch Act contains the political activity dos and don'ts (actually, mays and may-nots) for federal employees. Essentially, covered government workers may not coerce political involvement or compliance or engage in political campaigns in an intensive way, such as by running for partisan political offices, making or handling political contributions, or managing a political campaign. A version of this act exists in all states, and most include the essential elements of the federal law. According to the US Office of Special Counsel website (2003), covered federal workers may:

- be candidates for public office in nonpartisan elections;
- register to vote as they choose;

- assist in voter registration drives;
- express opinions about candidates and issues;
- contribute money to political organizations;
- attend political fundraising functions;
- attend and be active at political rallies and meetings;
- join and be an active member of a political party or club;
- sign nominating petitions;
- campaign for or against referendum questions, constitutional amendments, municipal ordinances;
- campaign for or against candidates in partisan elections;
- make campaign speeches for candidates in partisan elections;
- distribute campaign literature in partisan elections;
- hold office in political clubs or parties;

On the other hand, they may not

- use their official authority or influence to interfere with an election;
- solicit, accept, or receive political contributions unless both individuals are members of the same federal labor organization or employee organization and the one solicited is not a subordinate employee;
- knowingly solicit or discourage the political activity of any person who has business before the agency;
- engage in political activity while on duty;
- engage in political activity in any government office;
- engage in political activity while wearing an official uniform;
- engage in political activity while using a government vehicle;
- be candidates for public office in partisan elections;
- wear political buttons while on duty.

Reconciling democratic accountability and neutral competence in government service

The cumulative effect of the civil service reforms and the Hatch Act has been to remove government workers from most of the political fray that can tend to influence their work. In its purest form, this removal can mean, however, that government is unresponsive to the democratic forces of the time. In fact, as noted in Chapter 1, virtually every successful presidential candidate since Richard Nixon in 1968 has originally run as a political "outsider" who is bent on coming to Washington DC to "fix" those supposedly lethargic and nonresponsive bureaucrats who were essentially charged with being antidemocratic for not heeding their political masters (Wamsley *et al.* 1987).

This sense that government was operating without the proper or sufficient political controls led President Jimmy Carter—who first ran as a political outsider in 1976—to use much political capital to gain passage of the Civil Service Act of 1978. This act, when implemented by the Reagan administration that followed Carter, tended to "politicize" more of the high-level federal positions (Cayer 1987). President George W. Bush—who also ran as someone "outside the beltway"—engaged in a campaign to lessen the civil service protections in all of the federal service (*New York Times* 2003). Additionally, President Barack Obama has shown evidence of further reforming or modernizing civil service in light of the many global issues that now face the United States on the home front and abroad, such as how government employees are classified and compensated (Thompson 2010). Whether these activities by American presidents signify a move back toward a greater emphasis on democratic accountability or an aim to modernize or recalibrate government service, both are key indicators of the power and influence the executive office has over federal, state, and local organizational governance.

This brief review of the competing values of neutral competence and democratic accountability indicates that either value, when rendered in its purer form, can lead to undesirable consequences. Of course, neither value has been emphasized exclusively in its "pure" form. Rather, each has enjoyed more emphasis at certain periods of our history than at others. For example, no one would argue that there was no neutrality or competence among government workers during the Jacksonian period (circa 1820s to 1880s) when democratic accountability as a value was most emphasized. Nor would any careful observer of current federal, state, or local government fail to notice the influence that political masters have on the operation of criminal justice agencies, despite the greater emphasis on neutral competence. Thus, many scholars and students conclude that both values have worth for our government, but they must be balanced to prevent the deleterious consequences of overemphasis on either.

Government service is different

One integral way in which criminal justice agencies are tied to their communities and considered open is through the service they and their employees undertake as public sector organizations. About seventy years ago the political scientist Paul Appleby (1945) argued in an often-cited article that "government is different." He noted that there were many characteristics of government work that distinguish it from work in the private sector. Before we embark on a discussion of ethics and management theories in Chapters 3 and 4, it will be useful to consider whether government service in criminal justice agencies is indeed different and, if so, discuss some reasons why.

A *higher calling* for those drawn to government service is apparent. Appleby (1945) notes that some government employees regard their work as a vocation, as something they were meant to do, and as a way of contributing to, and connecting with, their communities. In his Pulitzer Prize-winning book *The Call of Service: A Witness to Idealism*, Robert Coles (1993: 284) makes the related point that a call to service is an attempt at outreach toward others in need, but it is also inwardly motivated to bring good into our lives. He concludes his book by musing over this matter: "[a] call to oneself, a call that is a reminder: 'Watchman, what of the night?'—the darkness that defines the moment of light in us, the darkness that challenges us to shine for one another before, soon enough, we join it."

Whether motivated outwardly or inwardly, we have found this claim that some are called to service to resonate among those who are considering the broader field of criminal justice. Every semester or quarter we ask our new students to list reasons for their interest in this field. Every time, at least 60 percent of those students include a statement such as "I want to contribute," "I want to give back," or "I want to make my community safer." Of course, they say that they want steady employment, excitement, and activity in their work and a decent wage, too, but that does not negate the fact that many of them appear to be "called" to government service to some degree.

That government work focuses on such big-picture issues as the environment, waging war, defending the homeland from terrorism, maintaining the borders, maintaining transportation infrastructure, and incarcerating people accused or convicted of a crime, imparts a breadth and scope to such service that Appleby sees as another way in which government is different. As we have seen with the privatization movement over the past thirty years, there is a role that the private sector can play in some of these tasks, including in policing and corrections; for the most part, however, we have assigned these kinds of projects to government organizations because they are best equipped with the power and the resources to accomplish them.

Appleby also argues that government is different from the private sector because of the huge impact of government programs and practices and the need for organized action. Government can deny or award citizenship to non-citizens, wage war, or grant or deny liberties. The impact on justice system workers in this sense is enormous, even though for the most part, police, court, and correctional employees have little power over who each individual client is, as well as over the people who are committed to their facilities or the people in their communities that come under their supervision. However, criminal justice workers do have power over how these clients are treated, whether they are arrested or prosecuted, and at times when they are released from supervision or an institution. Again, because the public sector is still predominant in the criminal justice field, they wield much more power over citizens in this area than the private sector does or can. Currently, as a people we have determined that this power is best organized for criminal justice functions by government entities and employees.

For Appleby, government is and should be different because of the need for accountability when the issues are big and the impact is vast. Because government agencies and initiatives are created and funded in a political context, they can also be held accountable by political actors when they make mistakes. We see this in criminal justice when administrators and wardens are let go or sheriffs or prosecutors or judges are not reelected after illegal shenanigans are discovered to have taken place in their agencies or facilities. Public sector workers are ultimately held accountable when their offenses surface. The trouble is that much of what happens in criminal justice is relatively hidden because of the closed nature of those facilities, and thus accountability may be present only in an uneven fashion.

Finally, Appleby argues that government is different because it is so political. Criminal justice agencies are practically suffused with politics (the processes involved in decision making about and within various organizations, whether they are private or public, formal or informal). Political actors, whether judges, sheriffs, police chiefs, prosecutors, directors or secretaries of corrections, wardens, or even administrators of public sector juvenile facilities, usually are directly elected or appointed, or they serve at the pleasure of a politician or political appointee. Budgets for criminal justice agencies are debated in a public forum (e.g., county commission meetings or legislative sessions) and critiqued in the press. If egregious mistakes made by staff have led to a failure to arrest or prosecute, or an escape, somebody is usually going to be held politically accountable. People are hired, trained, maintained, and fired based on rules and laws that were determined in a political environment. Suspects are processed and prosecuted based on laws, crimes, and sentences that vary to some degree by community, state, and nation, which means they were politically designed. Therefore, government is different because it is all about politics, and criminal justice agencies and institutions are in the midst of this milieu.

Additionally, government is different because it both holds the ability to mandate compliance through various legal channels and, as we all know, has the power to tax and fund various public and private endeavors (Moore 1995). For example, when a city statute is passed, members of the public who fail to comply may be found in violation of the statute and therefore subject to its provisions, such as being issued a parking ticket and having to pay a fine. We as community members are forced to pay taxes, such as property tax and income tax, the proceeds of which go toward the budgets of government organizations, which in turn function to benefit our community.

Of course, the distinctions between government work and the private sector noted by Appleby and others have a defining impact on criminal justice organizations and service by their employees. If people are in part motivated to work in the justice system because of a calling to "do good" in their communities, that motivation can be fruitfully employed by managers to improve their organizations. It might be remembered that the most long-term cynical employee at one time joined the profession in part because she or he was drawn to that work. Managers and employees in criminal justice agencies can be tasked to reinvigorate that original enthusiasm for government work and its grand role in justice administration.

Conclusions: why it is important not to tell jokes about bureaucrats

"How many bureaucrats does it take to screw in a light bulb?" The answer is either "none; the requisition paperwork has not been put in yet", or "three—one to order it, another to study it, and a third to screw it in"! Yes, bureaucrats get a bum rap; some of it is deserved, but most of it is not.

What people who aspire to work in criminal justice agencies sometimes do not recognize is that they are studying and planning themselves—heck, they are paying for college so that they can be a dreaded bureaucrat, or an SLB, as Lipsky (1980) put it (we often tell our students that they're training to be SLBs, *not* SOBs!). And what people in the profession already know all too well is that their work is often not appreciated by the public, politicians, or even their own management.

Yet criminal justice agencies, both because of and in spite of their relatively closed nature (yes, environmental factors have an enormous influence, but these entities and their practices are still hidden to some degree from public view), their paramilitary and bureaucratic structure, their committed employees, and their overwhelming caseloads and overloaded cellblocks, are ripe for a paradigmatic shift in management practice. For instance, courts have adopted restorative justice approaches and mediation as means of reducing formal adjudication, clearing backlogged caseloads and increasing community involvement in processes and sentences (Bohm and Haley 2005). The paradigm for corrections is shifting back to a greater rehabilitative/facilitative focus and away from incapacitation alone (Clear 2001); and in policing, proactive and prevention/problem-oriented models have risen in popularity (National Research Council 2004; Kelling 1992).

These changes are spurred by evolving sentiments, by new research on court and police practices and strategies, by a sense that locking up people for relatively minor crimes is pointless—even immoral—and by cost considerations (see the Washington State Institute for Public Policy website for more information on cost-benefit research in criminal justice agencies). Even in flush budget years, governors and state legislators cannot ignore the escalating cost of the drug war and the bite it is taking out of other valued programs, such as schools, health care, parks, and road projects, to name a few alternative funding venues. Within these public agencies, the competing values of democratic accountability and neutral competence tend to shape the role and motivation of workers, and further influence change.

Evidence of this shift can be found in the establishment of drug courts in many states, and the resurrection of treatment in communities and corrections. States such as Michigan, which instituted one of the first and most stringent sets of mandatory sentences, repealed those laws in December 2002 and lessened the length of sentences (Families Against Mandatory Minimums 2003). Other states are also restructuring their sentencing and risk assessment instruments to allow them to reduce, or at least not increase, the use of incarceration (Van Voorhis *et al.* 2013; Wilhelm and Turner 2003).

For fifty years now the private sector has toyed with a move toward greater involvement by workers in the operation of companies (Drucker 1954, 1964; Maslow 1998). Some private sector companies have made meaningful changes in their organizational structure to reflect this change in philosophy toward more democratic participation in the workplace. Some of them have reaped positive outcomes as a result (Peters 1987; Schein 1992). It is our contention that there are very powerful reasons to move further and in a similar direction toward democratic participation. These reasons will be highlighted throughout the text and encapsulated in the management model presented in Chapter 13.

Discussion questions

1 After reviewing how public service in criminal justice might be different, list and describe the ways in which it is similar to service in the private sector.

2 If government activity is more likely to be honest when under public scrutiny, discuss the ways in which jails or prisons might become more "open" to the public.

3 Are the values of "democratic accountability" and "neutral competence" in conflict? Why or why not? What is their appeal and what is their weakness? Can you describe any current examples of either value being emphasized in public service today?

4 As mentioned in the text, criminal justice managers must confront numerous environmental factors. What, then, are some tactics those managers might employ to control their environment? How might they be proactive in this endeavor?

5 Why do you think that old modes of management, by the top only, might be outdated? Explain your answer.

6 Who is likely to know most about how the organization operates—the top-level managers or the lower-level workers? Explain your reasoning.

7 What are some ways in which SLBs make policy in police or court organizations? Give an example.

8 In addition to their shared vision to enforce and uphold the law, what drives criminal justice organizations and their actors, both formally and informally?

9 Using the web links provided following the list of key terms, analyze the various organizational mission statements and design
your own mission statement as if you were working for or managing a criminal justice agency of your choice.
10 Using the web links, choose one of the organizations and describe
the various organizational actors and the various formal and
informal goals those individuals may or may not reflect.

Web links

Corrections Corp. of America: www.cca.com/
FBI website: www.fbi.gov/quickfacts.htm
Pittsburgh Bureau of Police: www.city.pittsburgh.pa.us/police/
Seattle   Police   Department: www.seattle.gov/police/about/
mission.htm
US Department of Justice: www.justice.gov/about/about.html

Key terms

bureaucracy: refers to how organizations are structured, ruled, or
socially organized and includes hierarchy, specialization, and
rule of law.
closed/open organization: a closed organization is one that is not
affected by its environment; an open one does experience influences from its environment.
democratic accountability: the value in government that the public
sector, or the managers and workers in government, are accountable to those who have been democratically elected and/or
politically appointed.
discretion: the ability to make choices and to act, or not act, on such
selections.
ethics: the study of, or the act of, doing the right thing in the professional sphere (Braswell 1998). Morality, on the other hand, is
understood to be doing the right thing in the private sphere.
formal/informal goals: formal goals are those that are written down
and reflected in an organization's formal mission statement,
organizational chart, policy manual, memoranda, and training
curricula. Informal goals are those that reflect the norms of
behavior of organizational members.

formal/informal organization: reflects the goals, values, and beliefs that are officially acknowledged and authorized (formal organization) and unofficially sanctioned (informal organization).

justice: in this text, the term is understood to mean that those who are guilty are caught, processed, and sanctioned, as befits community, professional, and moral standards, by system actors. Justice, for our purposes, also means that those who are innocent are given ample opportunity, and the due process necessary, to ensure that they are not caught up in, and sanctioned by, the system.

management: one or more persons who have formal control over an organization; or, the act or process of operating the organization.

neutral competence: the value that government service should be politically neutral and focused on the skills and abilities of workers to do the job at hand, rather than on their political allegiances.

organization: a grouping of people arranged and coordinated to accomplish some purpose.

organizational integrity: characterizing an organization whose actors as a whole are honest, ethical, and can be trusted by their members and by the community.

References

American Heritage Dictionary. (1992) *American Heritage Dictionary*, 3rd edn. New York, NY: Delta/Houghton Mifflin.

Appleby, P. (1945, reprinted in 1987) Government is different. In J. M. Shafritz and A. C. Hyde (eds), *Classics of public administration*. Chicago, IL: Dorsey Press, pp. 158–163.

Blau, P. M. and Scott, W. R. (1962, reprinted in 2001) The concept of the formal organization. In J. M. Shafritz and S. J. Ott (eds), *Classics of organization theory*. Fort Worth, TX: Harcourt College Publishers, pp. 206–210.

Bohm, R. M. and Haley, K. N. (2005) *Introduction to criminal justice*, 4th edn. New York, NY: McGraw-Hill.

Braswell, M. C. (1998) Ethics, crime and justice: An introductory note to students. In M. C. Braswell, B. R. McCarthy and B. J. McCarthy (eds), *Justice, crime and ethics*. Cincinnati, OH: Anderson Publishing, pp. 3–9.

Carlisle, H. M. (1976) *Management: Concepts and situations*. Chicago, IL: SRA.

Cayer, N. J. (1987) Managing human resources. In R. C. Chandler (ed.), *A centennial history of the American administrative state*. New York, NY: Free Press, pp. 321–344.

Clear, T. (2001) Ten unintended consequences of the growth in imprisonment. In E. J. Latessa, A. Holsinger, J. W. Marquart and J. R. Sorensen (eds), *Correctional contexts: Contemporary and classical readings*. Los Angeles, CA: Roxbury, pp. 497–505.

Coles, R. (1993) *The call of service: A witness to idealism.* Boston, MA: Houghton Mifflin.

Crank, J. P. (1998) *Understanding police culture.* Cincinnati, OH: Anderson Publishing.

Darroch, S. and Mazerolle, L. (2013) Intelligence-led policing: A comparative analysis of organizational factors influencing innovation uptake. *Police Quarterly,* 16(1): 337.

Donne, J. (1623) No man is an island. *Devotions upon emergent occasions.* Meditation XVII.

Drucker, P. F. (1954) *The practice of management.* New York, NY: Harper & Row.

Drucker, P. F. (1964) *Managing for results.* New York, NY: Harper & Row.

Families Against Mandatory Minimums. (2003) Michigan legislature repeals mandatory sentencing laws. Available at www.november.org/razor wire/2003–01/winter/mich.html (last accessed January 31, 2013).

Goffman, E. (1961) *Asylums: Essays on the social situation of mental patients and other inmates.* New York, NY: Doubleday.

Gulick, L. (1937, reprinted in 2001) Notes on the theory of organization. In J. M. Shafritz and J. S. Ott (eds), *Classics of organization theory.* Fort Worth, TX: Harcourt College Publishers, pp. 79–87.

Haller, M. H. (1983) Chicago cops, 1890–1925. In C. B. Klockars (ed.), *Thinking about police: Contemporary readings.* New York, NY: McGraw-Hill, pp. 87–99.

Jacobs, J. (1977) *Stateville: The penitentiary in mass society.* Chicago, IL: University of Chicago Press.

Kelling, G. L. (1992) Toward new images of policing: Herman Goldstein's 'problem-oriented policing'. *Law & Social Inquiry,* 17, 539–559.

Lipsky, M. (1980) *Street-level bureaucracy: Dilemmas of the individual in public services.* New York, NY: Russell Sage Foundation.

Maslow, A. H. (1998, first published in 1967) *Maslow on management.* New York, NY: Wiley.

Micklethwait, J. and Wooldridge, A. (1996) *The witch doctors: Making sense of the management gurus.* New York: Random House.

Moore, M. H. (1995) *Creating public value: Strategic management in government.* Cambridge, MA: Harvard University Press.

Morrow, W. L. (1987) The pluralist legacy in American public administration. In R.C. Chandler (ed.), *A centennial history of the American administrative state.* New York: Free Press, pp. 161–188.

National Research Council. (2004) *Fairness and effectiveness in policing: The evidence.* Washington DC: The National Academic Press.

New York Times. (2003) Editorials/op-ed: The civil service faces an overhaul. June 12, 2003.

Peters, T. (1987) *Thriving on chaos: Handbook for a management revolution.* New York, NY: Harper & Row.

Schein, E. H. (1992) *Organizational culture and leadership,* 2nd ed. San Francisco, CA: Jossey-Bass.

Selznick, P. (1948, reprinted in 2001) Foundations of the theory of organization. In J. M. Shafritz and J. S. Ott (eds), *Classics of organization theory.* Fort Worth, TX: Harcourt College Publishers, pp. 125–134.

Stojkovic, S., Kalinich, D. and Klofas, J. (1998) *Criminal justice organizations: Administration and management,* 2nd edn. Belmont, CA: Wadsworth.

Thompson, J. R. (2010) Toward "flexible uniformity?" Civil service reform, "big government conservatism," and the promise of the intelligence community model. *Review of Public Personnel Administration*, 30(4): 423–444.

US National Archives & Records Administration. (2005) Pendleton Act. (1883). Available at www.ourdocuments.gov (last accessed January 31, 2013).

Van Riper, P. P. (1987) The American administrative state: Wilson and the founders. In R. C. Chandler (ed.), *A centennial history of the American administrative state.* New York, NY: The Free Press, pp. 3–36.

Van Voorhis, P., M. Braswell and D. Lester. (2013) *Correctional counseling and rehabilitation*, 7th edn. Cincinnati, OH: Anderson Publishing, LexisNexis.

Walker, S. (1983) *The police in America: An introduction.* New York, NY: McGraw-Hill.

Wamsley, G. L., Goodsell, C. T., Rohr, J. A., Stivers, C. M., White, O. F. and Wolf, J. F. (1987) The public administration and the governance process: Refocusing the American dialogue. In R. C. Chandler (ed.), *A centennial history of the American administrative state.* New York, NY: Free Press, pp. 291–317.

Weber, M. (1946) Bureaucracy. In H. H. Gerth and C. W. Mills (eds), *From Max Weber: Essays in sociology.* Oxford: Oxford University Press, pp. 196–198.

Wilhelm, D. F. and Turner, N. R. (2003) Is the budget crisis changing the way we look at sentencing and incarceration? New York, NY: Vera Institute of Justice Publications.

Wilson, W. (1887, reprinted in 1987) The study of administration. In J. M. Shafritz and A. C. Hyde (eds), *Classics of public administration* (pp. 10–25). Chicago, IL: Dorsey Press.

3 Managing trouble—deviance, abuse of force, and sexual/ gender harassment—using ethics

Sexual misconduct and abuse of inmates at Kansas' prison for women is "rampant throughout the facility" and persisted even as federal officials investigated problems there, according to a US Justice Department report released Thursday. ... The letter (by Thomas Perez, the assistant US attorney general for civil rights, sent to Kansas Governor Sam Brownback in September 2012) concluded that the Topeka Correctional Facility "fails to protect women prisoners from harm due to sexual abuse and misconduct from correctional staff and other prisoners in violation of their constitutional rights... The women at TCF universally fear for their own safety."

(Hanna 2012: A4)

We live in a country where the authority of the police to intervene in the affairs of the citizenry is on the ascent. Traditional due process restrictions on police authority are being relaxed. Citizens sometimes encourage illegal police behavior to "do something about crime." [A]nd with these changes, opportunities for noble-cause corruption are increasing.

(Crank and Caldero 2011: 3)

A serious impediment to the success of any anti-corruption strategy is a corrupt judiciary. An ethically compromised judiciary means that the legal and institutional mechanism designed to curb corruption, however well-targeted, efficient or honest, remains crippled. Unfortunately, evidence is steadily and increasingly surfacing of widespread corruption in the courts in many parts of the world.

(United Nations Office on Drugs and Crime 2012: 1)

Introduction

It is an axiom of criminal justice work that staff and administrators will be exposed to temptations to violate rules, procedures, laws, or standards of ethics. This is true because much of this work is hidden from public view, or ignored, and involves the secure care of people who are regarded as social outcasts and are relatively powerless. As staff possess enormous amounts of *discretion*, they become the linchpin upon which the just, or unjust, nature of their organization turns.

In fact, the history of criminal justice operations practice tells us that there have been numerous instances of corrupt and abusive individuals, institutions, or whole systems (Bennett and Hess 2001; Clear and Cole 1997; Courtless 1998; Crank and Caldero 2011; Feeley 1983; Friedrichs 2001; Gaines *et al.* 2003; Gray 2002; Holten and Lamar 1991; Mays and Winfree 2002; Silverman and Vega 1996; Welch 1996). More recent infamous instances of abuse, such as those that occurred in Texas private jails (see Box 3.1), those described by a Justice Department official in the quote that opens this chapter, the 110 documented cases of disciplinary removals of judges in the United States between 1990 and 2001 reported by the American Judicature Society (Gray 2002; see Box 3.2), or the miscarriage of justice when five African American and Latino youths were convicted of the Central Park jogger rape when there was no evidence to indicate they were involved (Burns 2011; see Box 3.3) further serve to remind us that vigilance is needed to ensure that criminal justice agencies, their actors, and their clients remain safe, secure, and just for all.

Box 3.1 Amnesty International Report on sexual abuse of inmates in the United States

The authors of a report published electronically by Amnesty International (2004: 29, 75, 211–213, 229) compiled newspaper accounts of sexual misconduct in state prison systems. The following random sample, taken by one of the authors, surveys the most egregious incidents in such accounts from Alabama, New York, Connecticut, and North Dakota.

Alabama

> A former city jailer who had quit his job the month prior was arrested for sexually assaulting inmates at the jail.
>
> (AP, December 19, 2000)

> A lieutenant in the police department resigned as his hearing began over allegations that he solicited sex from a female inmate in the city jail.
>
> (AP, April 15, 2000)

> A deputy threatened to transfer an inmate to a facility far away from her children if she did not perform oral sex, according to claims filed in circuit court.
>
> (AP, December 10, 1999)

New York

Albion Correctional Facility: A city councilman working as a prison guard was suspended for having sexual relations with a female inmate. He has not been charged with any criminal offense.

(*The Buffalo News*, August 19, 2000)

Albion Correctional Facility: Former officers sentenced to 3 years probation and fined $1,000 for having sexual relations with a female inmate.

(*The Buffalo News*, August 19, 2000)

Westchester County Jail: Officer 1 was arrested and charged with raping and sodomizing an inmate. Officer 2 was charged with raping an inmate in a supply closet. Officer 3 was charged with sexual abuse and official misconduct for forcing women inmates to strip. Officer 4 was charged with making an inmate strip for Tylenol. All the officers were released on bail. Charges were dropped against Officer 2, Officer 1 pled guilty. Charges were pending against the officers. Male officers were banned from female living quarters.

(*The New York Times*, January 27 and January 28, 2000)

Rensselaer County Jail: Officer pleaded guilty to rape and sodomy. He was sentenced to two years in jail and five years of probation. The female inmate was 16 years old at the time, and she sued the officer and the county.

(*The Times Union, Albany*, December 9, 1999)

Adirondack Correctional Facility: A former NY State prison guard was sentenced in September 1998 to three years' imprisonment after admitting he forced a male prisoner to perform oral sex. When the male inmate filed complaints with the corrections department and state police he was transferred to Clinton correctional facility. He saved the semen in a small vial, which he turned over to the correction's department inspector general's office. Tests verified the DNA matched the officer's. Faced with the strength of the DNA evidence, the officer pled guilty to the charge of felony sodomy.

(*Prison Legal News*, February 1999)

Connecticut

In March 1999, a former state probation officer pleaded no contest to 31 criminal charges including sexual assault, racketeering, kidnapping and unlawful restraint. He was originally charged with 224 counts of sexual misconduct stemming from the rape of 15 men and young boys who were on his caseload. He threatened to have the victims imprisoned if they did not submit to his attacks.

(AP, August 1999)

York Correctional Institution: A former counselor was sentenced to serve 18 months in prison for having sex with three female inmates who came to him for help with their problems.

(*The Day*, October 19, 2000)

York Correctional Institution: Prison worker convicted of sexual assault on female inmate. A jury found a food supervisor at the facility had sex with an inmate he supervised.

(AP, April 19, 2000)

North Dakota

North Dakota State Penitentiary: Former guard charged with seven counts of sexually abusing female inmates.

(North Dakota headlines, December 6, 1999)

Box 3.2 American Judicature Report: "A study of state judicial discipline sanctions"

The American Judicature Society, an independent, nonprofit organization, sponsored a study (Gray 2002) of judicial misconduct and discipline in the United States. The purpose of this discipline, as established in numerous court cases, is not necessarily to punish a judge, but to preserve "[t]he integrity of the judicial system and public confidence in the system and, when necessary, safeguard ... the bench and the public from those who are unfit" (Gray 2002: 3). In most states a reviewing court (usually the Supreme Court) hears cases regarding judicial misconduct from a judicial commission. Types of misconduct identified in the report for which judges were removed included "lack of competence," "failure to comply with a sobriety monitoring contract" (he was on probation), "failure to disqualify from a case," "misuse of powers to benefit a family member," "filing false travel vouchers," "neglect or improper performance of administrative duties," "failure to remit court funds," "abuse of contempt

powers," and "sexual harassment," among others (Gray 2002: 8–11).
Types of sanctions given for misconduct ranged in severity, from
counseling and letters of caution to suspension or outright removal
from the bench. It was established in numerous court cases that the
removal sanction was reserved only for misconduct that was "truly
egregious" or "flagrant and severe" (Gray 2002: 4).

Having said this, Gray reported that from 1990 to 2001, 110 judges
were removed owing to misconduct. As this is the most severe sanction, it can be projected that hundreds more judges may have been
given lesser sanctions for judicial misconduct during this time period.
As an indication of how widespread misconduct might be, another
625 judges resigned, retired, lost reelection, or died with a judicial
misconduct complaint pending before a reviewing court between
1990 and 1999.

Gray reported that several factors were common themes in removal
cases. Recurring factors in these cases included "dishonesty"; "a pattern of misconduct" whereby the judge was usually involved in more
than one incident of misconduct; presence of a "prior discipline
record," the claim that an established "judicial reputation" should
mitigate against any sanction; "proportionality," or ensuring that similar cases are handled similarly; and the judge's "conduct in response
to investigation" (Gray 2002: 59–66).

Box 3.3 The Central Park Five: a miscarriage of justice

In December 1989 five male teenagers were convicted of the rape and
beating of a 28-year-old woman jogger in New York's Central Park. The
woman, a white investment banker, was raped, beaten, and left for dead
in the park. Most of the male teenagers, who were African American
and Latino and were from Harlem, were in the park the night of the
crime (as were hundreds of others), but there was no evidence that
they were involved in the crime. Some of them were strangers to each
other. The police, upon learning of the presence of a few of them at the
park, brought them into the station and interrogated them for several
hours, and got them to confess to a crime they did not commit. Since
they had not committed the crime, they were completely wrong on
several factual matters (e.g., the timing of the crime, the sequencing of
the rape, who was there, and what the victim was wearing). The other

teenagers were pulled into the crime by the false confessions of the first two and through the intense interrogations of the detectives. Despite the weak case, with the confessions—which were questionable—the only evidence, the prosecutors took the case and prosecuted the teenagers. The media hyped the crime and the purported offenders, calling what the teens were doing in the park "wilding." A media circus ensued and the teenagers were convicted of rape, sexual assault, and attempted murder. They served between seven and thirteen years in prison for these crimes. It was not until a serial rapist confessed to the crime and DNA testing was done that the convictions were vacated, in 2002. Meanwhile the teenagers' lives were ruined, with their youth spent in prison and their parole as convicted felons who had to register as sex offenders. One of the original prosecutors and some of the police officers involved still argue that the teenagers, now grown men, were guilty. As Burns (2011, p. xi) writes in her book on the topic,

> The false narrative, disseminated by the police and the media, was swallowed whole by the public because it conformed to the assumptions and fears of the city and the country. *Everyone* bought the story. But the fact that so many continue to promote this narrative tells us that even though we live, as some like to say, in a "postracial" society, the racism that fueled the original rush to judgment persists, and that we have not evolved enough from the days when even the suggestion that a black man had raped a white woman could lead to a lynching.

The development of ethical codes, the professionalization of staff, and the routinization of procedural protections are often regarded as providing some protection against the temptation to engage in corrupt or unethical behaviors. These codes and processes might be seen as inoculating an organization, as if it were a living organism, against such viral infections.

In this chapter we begin with a discussion of two studies on the public image of the police and courts as social institutions and how that image is tied to ethical practices. We then discuss the explanations for, and the types of, deviance, abuse of force, and harassment problems that can plague criminal justice organizations. We will then review the concept of ethics and its philosophical underpinnings. We will also consider how ethical practice, when inculcated into the organizational structure, might serve as a partial remedy for such abuse and deviance. These topics are in sync with those covered in Chapters 7, 8, and 9, which have to do with the importance of leadership and personnel practices and the power of leaders to further professionalize criminal justice agencies.

Public distrust

In a 2010 Gallup poll about how much "trust and confidence" people have in government there were indications that trust in state and local government is up from 1973, but that it is down for the federal government (Saad 2010: 1). Trust in the legislative branch of the federal government (Congress) is down in that period by almost 30 points (from 42 in 1973 to 13 in 2010), and also down some for the executive branch (presidency) (52 in 1975 to 36 in 2010) and the judicial branch (Supreme Court) (from 45 in 1973 to 36 in 2010) (Saad 2010: 1).

The public perception of criminal justice agencies often hinges on how professional the public perceives those entities to be. In two separate studies of the courts and policing, there is some indication that those perceptions could be improved (Gallagher *et al.* 2001; Saad 2010).

In that 2010 national public opinion poll by Gallup of 1,020 randomly selected American adults, the respondents were asked to indicate their level of "trust and confidence" in several American institutions (Saad 2010: 1, 3). Only 27 percent of the respondents indicated that they had a "great deal" or "quite a lot" of trust or confidence in the criminal justice system (which is actually an increase from 23 percent in 2000), though 59 percent had this degree of belief in the police (most courts and corrections agencies were not separately mentioned; Saad 2010: 2; Sherman 2001: 6).

In their report to the International Association of Chiefs of Police on the public image of the police, Gallagher and colleagues (2001) found, after reviewing over forty years of research, that the public generally has a very positive perception of the police. However, this perception is shaped in part by one's minority/majority status, with African Americans and other racial minorities having a less positive perception than white people (Gallagher *et al.* 2001; Sherman 2001). The authors of the report also found that the public's tolerance for the use of force by the police has decreased as time has gone on. Significantly, though, "[t]he public image of honesty and ethical standards of police has fluctuated over the years, but ... improved substantially from 1977 to 2000" (Gallagher *et al.* 2001: 5). Sherman (2001) also found that compared with the past, and due to many social, legal, and economic factors, including increased expectations of equal treatment and less corruption of public figures, public confidence in the police and the rest of the criminal justice system has increased in this country, though it remains low particularly for the system as a whole.

In a study by the National Center for State Courts (1999: 7), the findings were less rosy, as indicated by the following sampling:

* Only 10 percent of the survey respondents felt the courts in their communities handled cases in an "Excellent" manner, with 20 percent indicating criminal cases and family relations cases are handled in a

"Poor" manner and nearly 30 percent indicating juvenile delinquency cases are handled in a "Poor" manner.

- The vast majority of respondents (81 percent) agree that politics influences court decisions. This pattern holds across racial and ethnic groups.
- Over 75 percent of the respondents thought that the need to raise campaign funds influences elected judges.
- Hispanic people were most positive about court performance, with African Americans being least positive and white people falling in between.

These studies clearly indicate that the public has some concerns about fair treatment at the hands of both the police and the courts, though the courts were rated higher in the NCSC study (the respondents were not queried about corrections in this study). Some of these concerns center on use of force, disparate treatment based on racial or ethnic status, and wealth as it has led to corruption of public officials and political influences, as all these factors might shape the perception that justice is or is not done in criminal justice agencies. Clearly, a low public image warps these agencies' ability to do professional work. After all, in a democracy it is only with public support and trust that the police, the courts, and correctional agencies are funded, and achieve any success. It is crucial then for criminal justice agencies to garner the trust and confidence of the people; history tells us that a critical means to this end is ethical practice.

Deviance explained

It is often assumed that staff or administrators who violate the law, rules and procedures, or ethical codes of criminal justice organizations do so for personal profit or gain or from an *egotistical* perspective. An example might be a prosecutor who accepts a bribe from the family of the accused in exchange for a reduced charge. Or we might view the exchange of sexual favors between a police officer and a prostitute hoping to avoid arrest as another example of deviance for personal gain. Or perhaps a private treatment provider might bribe a correctional administrator to ensure they get the contract to provide food services to juvenile facilities in that state.

But in actuality, *deviance* by staff in a criminal justice organization should be more broadly defined to include other *explanations* for misbehavior and abuse of authority. **Deviance by staff** might be defined as involving behavior that violates the statutes, institutional rules or procedures, or ethical codes for individual *or* organizational gain *or* even as a means of serving a "noble cause" (Bartollas and Hahn 1999; Crank and Caldero 2011; Lee and Visano 1994). Although it is difficult to determine how often staff or management deviance might be motivated by organizational or noble cause purposes, experience tells us it is likely that people misbehave in organizations for reasons other than personal profit alone.

Corruption for individual gain

But people misbehave for personal profit too! Indeed, the profit motive for corruption at the individual level in criminal justice is quite powerful, and is also easy to understand and recognize. Some people will be drawn to work in a criminal justice agency because they see the opportunity to make extra money or to get illegal services. Others might recognize these opportunities once employed. New hires might be especially tempted when they see that some colleagues are taking advantage of a situation. Because of the hidden nature of much of this corruption and the subcultural prohibition against "ratting" in most criminal justice agencies (Pollock 2010), it is difficult to determine how much deviance there is and what behaviors are involved. But stories of corruption and abuse, many much worse than those one of the authors describes from her experience in working in a prison (see Box 3.4), are rife among staff, and many agencies have had to grapple with scandals caused by the unethical or illegal behavior of their workers (see Box 3.5).

Those who have worked in or studied criminal justice agencies relate instances of parole dates being sold for political favors by board members, of FBI lab technicians misrepresenting their findings in court (Pollock 1998, 2010), of beatings of inmates by staff or inmate-on-inmate fights that are allowed by staff (Conover 2000; Marquart 1995), of sexual abuse of women inmates by staff (Amnesty International 2004; Thomas 1996), and of numerous other abuses (Crank and Caldero 2011; Muraskin 2001a, 2001b). As one of the authors has observed in visits, and as students working in criminal justice agencies have told us over the past eighteen years, juveniles in a detention center have been openly and routinely referred to as "little criminals" by some staff; police officers get overly excited and throw extra punches at resistant suspects; prosecutors who suspect police have insufficient evidence to produce an indictment overcharge to secure a plea to some crimes; prison staff regularly use foul and abusive language to address inmates; and a few jail officers in one facility routinely allowed unauthorized personnel to participate in strip searches of admittees.

Box 3.4 Personal observations of deviance in a prison setting by Mary K. Stohr

In the prison I worked at in Washington State from 1983 to 1986 there were stories of a maintenance supervisor getting his cars serviced for free and of a security sergeant with unauthorized inmate artwork in his home. I don't know if these stories were true, but staff gave them credence because the environment was so unprofessional in other respects.

For instance, a Hispanic officer told me that he was continually passed over for promotion by the warden because of his ethnicity. I found this plausible because the officer was highly qualified for positions that came open and because the warden himself told me that the Affirmative Action Committee he wanted me to be on was only a sham and he didn't really want to recruit, hire, or promote minorities. The warden also said that he had hired me, and the few other white females who worked there, only because he was forced to after five years of pressure by central office.

Other instances of unprofessional behavior by staff occurred when I worked an escape on a July 4 evening and three of the supervisors had to be driven by subordinates because they were seriously inebriated and unable to safely operate a vehicle. I also witnessed the retaliation against a female correctional officer who refused to go out with a male sergeant; she was eventually hounded out of her job by the man, who also verbally harassed all the other female staff in his orbit, including myself. This was one of two sergeants who told me, after I had just been hired, that he did not think women should work in male prisons.

Despite the reputation the harassing male sergeant had among male and female staff—most of the male staff disliked him as well because of his unprofessional behavior in other respects—and the complaints by the female staff he harassed, the man was never formally reprimanded or disciplined for his behavior. He was eventually fired, however, for an unrelated case, after he pled guilty to four counts of child sexual abuse with his preteen daughter's friend.

Box 3.5 Money and the corruption of criminal justice: the special case of private prisons

Judges accused of jailing kids for cash and *70 youths sue former judges in detention kickback case*

Two Pennsylvania juvenile court judges, Mark Ciavarella and Michael Conahan, were convicted in federal court in 2009 of wire and income-tax fraud for taking 2.6 million dollars in kickbacks from two privately run detention centers (PA Child Care and Western PA Child Care, which are sister companies; Urbina 2009). Youths accused of even minor offenses were brought before these judges, without attorneys despite the Supreme Court decision in 1967 which requires their presence, and given a hearing that lasted for only a few minutes before they were sent to these private prisons for months (Rubinkam and Dale 2009). In 2002 (now former) Judge Conahan even shut down the publicly operated county juvenile facility and helped these companies secure contracts, worth millions of dollars, to hold juveniles. The county would pay the company for each child they incarcerated and the companies paid the judges for sentencing the youths to their detention centers. As of February 2009 there were three lawsuits by private and public attorneys on behalf of the youths who had been wrongfully incarcerated. At the time the relevant newspaper articles were written (2009), the Pennsylvania Supreme Court was investigating whether hundreds and perhaps thousands of these youths' convictions should be overturned and their records expunged (Rubinkam and Dale 2009; Urbina 2009).

Proposal to buy prisons raises ethical concerns

In 2012 Harley Lappin, who was the Director of the Federal Bureau of Prisons, and who is now employed as an executive for the private prison corporation Corrections Corporation of America, made the offer to buy state and federal public prisons for $250 million (Johnson 2012: 6A). This agreement would require that the governments maintain a 90 percent occupancy rate, as that is the way the prisons would make their profit (Johnson 2012: 6A). The American Civil Liberties Union and other civil rights advocates allege that Lappin's involvement in this offer so soon after he retired as director (after being charged with driving under the influence) is ethically inappropriate. Moreover, the requirement that the prisons maintain a 90 percent occupancy rate may contribute to continued high levels of incarceration when the crime rate may not merit it.

In 2009, for the first time in twenty years, a federal judge was impeached and sentenced; he received a thirty-three-month stay in a federal prison for sexually assaulting two female staffers (*Idaho Statesman* 2009: A3). In 2009 a Mississippi state court judge was accused of bribery in federal court (Nossiter 2009). In 2009, a county jail in Texas was shut down by the incoming sheriff, who had determined that the corruption, abuse, and laxity in the enforcement of rules meant it was a dangerous place for staff and inmates and presented a security risk (Brown 2009). Almost 2000 police officers in New York City were arrested from 1992 to 2008 for drug crimes, thefts, bribery, or sex offenses (Baker and McGinty 2010). In 2010 two FBI agents, working with the North Carolina Attorney General's office, reviewed 15,000 cases and uncovered 230 cases where the evidence was tainted or withheld by the State Bureau of Investigation, resulting in the incarceration of potentially hundreds of innocent men and women (*The News Observer* 2010: 1). In 2011 the Justice Department launched an investigation into abuse-of-force and discrimination-against-minorities allegations against Seattle police officers (Yardley 2011). In 2012 a former prosecutor in Maricopa County Arizona was disbarred by the state ethics board for "bringing criminal charges against county officials and a judge in December 2009 with the purpose of embarrassing them ... for political gain and as a conflict of interest" (*New York Times* 2012: A16). A Massachusetts state drug lab chemist was arrested in 2012 for allegedly lying about some of the 60,000 drug samples, in cases involving some 34,000 criminal defendants, which she had analyzed and then providing false testimony under oath in court (*News-Leader* 2012: 7A).

Given all of these illegal acts is it any wonder that a study by the nonprofit Ethics Resource Center found a majority of local, state, and federal government workers witnessed ethical lapses? More unethical behavior was witnessed by local government workers (those who work in cities and counties), at 63 percent, than by state workers, at 57 percent, and federal workers, at 52 percent (Lee 2008). And a majority of all those workers (58 percent) who witnessed the misconduct did not report it because they thought nothing would be done.

Such unethical behavior may be committed out of stupidity, ignorance, prejudice, the desire for sex or to exert power, for convenience's sake, or to obtain some other gratification that cannot be easily quantified monetarily or otherwise by an observer or participant. The behavior might also be motivated by greed. Whereas it is fairly clear how personal profit or gratification might motivate misbehavior in criminal justice, the influence of the organization and its subculture, and of a noble cause, in motivating such behavior is less clearly understood.

Official deviance

Official deviance may be another explanation for staff corruption or abuse. Lee and Visano (1994: 203) defined **official deviance** as "[a]ctions taken by officials which violate the law and/or the formal rules of the organization, but which are clearly oriented toward the needs and goals of the organization, as perceived by the official, and thus fulfill certain informal rules of the organization." What they found in their analysis of the behavior of criminal justice actors in several agencies in Canada and the United States is that many deviant acts are not committed for personal gain; rather, the motivation is found in an organizational or subcultural end. It is believed that at times, the *informal* subculture of an organization not only encourages official deviance, but punishes or excludes those who refuse to participate. According to Lee and Visano (1994), the agencies most susceptible to official deviance are those in which decision making and practice are most hidden and the clients have the least power, as is the case in criminal justice agencies.

Examples of deviant behavior include lying in court by a police officer, withholding evidence by a prosecutor, and misrepresenting information on a revocation report by a probation officer, all for the sake of ensuring that those "presumed guilty" receive the desired verdict. The key here is that the official engaged in the unethical or illegal behavior would gain nothing beyond being a team player for the act, but the organization was seen as gaining. Official deviance also encompasses lying for, ignoring, or covering up the wrongdoing of others in an organization. Those who refuse to participate in official deviance might be shunned, or worse, by members of the subculture. Some officers might refuse to back up people who will not play along, or even harass them (Kilgannon 2010).

As remedies for official deviance, Lee and Visano (1994) recommend that criminal justice agencies open up their operations to the scrutiny and study of scholars, citizens, the media, and other interested stakeholders. They are fans of Freedom of Information Acts, assessment and evaluation of programs by outside and independent reviewers, civilianization of certain aspects of agency functioning (or fewer commissioned officers, who presumably might be more inculcated into the subculture), and investigation of wrongdoing by disinterested third parties. They warn against solutions for official deviance that include the creation of more bureaucracy and law, which would, they argue, provide more opportunities for deviance and secrecy. They also argue that those who work within the criminal justice system can neutralize the effects of official deviance by changing their language and behavior so that the system can be regarded as legitimate by those outside it. In other words, the more approachable and understandable an organization's operation is for the general public, the less official deviance will flourish there. A side benefit might be an increase in the public's trust in those organizations, as well.

Noble cause

A related concept that explains the motivation for some deviance by criminal justice staff is "noble cause" corruption. Crank and Caldero (2000: 35) define the **noble cause** for police officers as "[a] profound moral commitment to make the world a safer place to live. Put simply, it is getting bad guys off the street. Police believe they're on the side of angels and their purpose in life is getting rid of bad guys."

Crank and Caldero (2000: 35) identify two noble cause themes that explain police officer behavior: "[t]he smell of the victim's blood" and "the tower." What they mean by "the smell of the victim's blood" is that police officers are intimately aware of the suffering of the victims of crime, as symbolized by their blood. Therefore, the officers' behavior is motivated in part by the desire to see offenders "pay" for the crimes they commit, particularly against those victims who are the most defenseless, such as children.

Relatedly, Crank and Caldero (2011) and others (e.g., Bartollas and Hahn 1999; O'Connor 2001) theorize that police officers are motivated in their everyday practice by a desire to do something to make the world right. Caldero presents a scenario that illustrates this point in a police staff training session. In the scenario a sharpshooter in a university tower has already killed twelve students. Rather than running away from the tower like regular citizens, the police will literally run toward the tower, and not just because it is their job to do so. The police will "run toward the tower" because they want to actively make things right; they want to be proactive. This is, Crank and Caldero feel, yet another distinguishing motivating feature of a "noble cause" perspective for the police.

The desire by the police to defend victims and to be proactive is a laudable trait in any officer. These noble causes are corrupted, however, when the police look on these noble cause *ends* as more important than the *means* to achieve them.

According to Crank and Caldero (2011), those who engage in *noble cause corruption* are prone to see the world in black and white. They think that in their pursuit of what they perceive as just ends, they may, with impunity, use corrupt means. Therefore, a police officer might excuse excessive force, manufacturing evidence, lying on reports, or committing perjury in court if such an action were seen as serving their noble cause.

Although Crank and Caldero's book (2011) is about deviant practices of the police, the threat of noble cause corruption might be fruitfully applied to courts and corrections, since those who are drawn to other criminal justice work are just as likely to be interested in a "just end" as police officers. Though the experience of the victim is further removed from them, prosecutors, judges, and even correctional managers and staff know something of the crimes and circumstances surrounding the offenses of their clients. As with the police, their sympathies are also likely to be with the victim or potential victims, particularly for the most brutal or offensive crimes.

For example, when one of the authors was first hired to work as a correctional officer in that adult male prison in 1983, the sergeants and the other officers quickly told her who was in for "child molesting," as well as other crimes. It was implied, and at times explicitly stated, that she was to treat the child molesters—or "those scumbags," as they were often openly referred to—differently from other inmates—with more disrespect or more disdain, at a minimum. Subsequent interactions with correctional staff at other prisons and jails and in other states have reinforced the perception that correctional staff are also motivated to action by the "victim's blood," especially in the case of more defenseless victims, such as children. Although this motivation is understandable, as it is human, it also makes correctional staff, much like the police officers described in Caldero and Crank's book, susceptible to noble cause corruption.

Similarly, in McIntyre's 2004 article on criminal defense attorneys, which she provocatively titled "But How Can You Sleep Nights?," even the defenders of the accused are troubled by their concerns over what was done to the victims. If defense attorneys are attuned to the suffering of the victims, imagine how the prosecutors, whose job it is to have contact with them, may be bothered and perhaps swayed to act in an unethical fashion by the "smell of the victim's blood."

Criminal justice staff are also likely to be "doers" who are interested in rectifying wrongs and stopping criminality: in the parlance of Crank and Caldero (2011), they are the type of people who will run toward the tower. The observations of social scientists would serve to reinforce the perception that criminal justice personnel will behave in this manner. While in graduate school, one of the authors attended a lecture by an anthropology professor who had just returned from a sabbatical spent working as a correctional officer at a federal prison in California. One of the characteristics of staff that the professor remarked on was the adrenaline rush and excitement that followed an emergency summons. Whether it was to break up a fight or to deal with a lesser verbal dispute, he was surprised at the unadulterated thrill he experienced, and noticed in others, when asked to respond to an emergency situation.[1] Similarly, an older correctional officer friend of one of the authors recalled that when he was a young man working at the Walla Walla prison in Washington State in the 1960s, the most fun he had was racing to a cell to quell a disturbance or to do a cell extraction.

Conover (2000) makes the same point about correctional officers responding to a disturbance at the Sing Sing prison in New York State. Or probation officers we know relate how excited they get when going to arrest a client who has committed a new crime or has otherwise seriously violated his conditions. Or jail officers work hard to qualify so they can join the Emergency Response Team and engage in the same "fun" the Walla Walla officer had forty years ago. Or a police ombudsman noted that back when he worked as an officer, he and his colleagues were invariably excited when responding to an emergency call. Clearly, this metaphorical "racing to the tower"—which would be regarded as peculiar behavior by regular citizens, but may be one of the attractions of criminal justice work—might also lead to some abuses in the use of force.

The chances of noble cause corruption might also be heightened in the criminal justice environment because the work is often hidden from public and official view. Scrutiny by actors in the rest of the criminal justice system or by political leaders is still relatively rare and is usually isolated to infamous cases of abuse or deviance that come to public attention. What this means is that corrupt behavior and deviance are not often known of outside the institution or the agency and are sometimes easy to hide within it. For this reason, criminal justice work provides fertile ground for those who resort to illegal or unethical means, which they attempt to justify by citing a "just end."

In addition, "noble cause" staff members in criminal justice generally might view their clients, or at least some of them, as "deserving" of abuse at the hands of other staff or, in corrections, clients. Therefore, keeping the accused or offenders off the streets or away from lesser offenders, or further enhancing their punishment for wrongdoing, might inspire noble cause corruption by criminal justice staff.

Examples of noble cause corruption in criminal justice work include the same types of behaviors that constitute official deviance, but the motivation for the staff member is not to satisfy informal institutional or subcultural demands, but rather to mete out the individual's perception of a just end. This "justice" could take the form of excessive force used on a suspect, accused person, or inmate; lying in court or on reports; abusive emotional treatment; overcharging or withholding evidence by prosecutors; exceptional sentences by judges; unjustified violation/infraction resulting in the imposition of administrative or disciplinary segregation; the unwarranted loss of privileges or "good time," or any action the staff member might excuse by saying that the action would lead to a "just end," even if at the expense of "just means."

Two insidious types of abuse

Excessive use of force

One particular type of unethical behavior deserves special attention because the harm can be so serious for the person abused: The excessive use of force in the criminal justice system (also discussed in Chapter 10). Whether excessive use of force is due to a desire for personal gratification, official deviance, or noble cause corruption is rarely knowable. Moreover, the actual amount of excessive use of force in policing, courts, or corrections is difficult to determine.

An attempt was made by Hemmens and Atherton (1999) to investigate the use-of-force issue in correctional institutions. In a questionnaire sent to the fifty state corrections departments, the Federal Bureau of Prisons, US military organizations, and the Canadian provinces, Hemmens and Atherton (1999) found that about 55 percent of the US departments of correction (DOCs), 40 percent of the Canadian DOCs, 63 percent of the jails, and 45 percent of the juvenile detention facilities surveyed reported a range of 1 to 25 incidences of excessive use of force for 1997. Although there are no data available regarding the incidents themselves, the correctional agencies that responded did indicate that a range from 73 percent of the incidents (in the jails) to 33 percent (in the Canadian DOCs) resulted in disciplinary action for the correctional personnel involved.

Hemmens and Atherton (1999: 80–81) identify the key indicators of excessive use of force in corrections to which managers and staff should pay careful attention as follows:

- Staff and/or inmate rumors, incident reports, and inmate grievances;
- Unexplained injuries;
- An increase in the frequency in the overall use of force without a reasonable explanation;
- A history of burnout and no rotation of staff in facilities that contain high-risk, disruptive inmates, affording a higher potential for excessive use of force;
- Staff who fail to provide sufficient information, are clearly mimicking one another in incident reports, or are reluctant to discuss conditions surrounding use of force, signaling the possibility that excessive force is being used;
- Significant and extreme changes in inmate behavior (and in inmate group behavior).

These authors recommend a proactive use-of-force program as an effective means by which excessive use of force can be avoided. The elements of this program, which would also fit a police or court organization, involve administrative oversight; training, development, and implementation of a use-of-force policy; clear and complete documentation of incidents and training; and competency in force technology that allows for de-escalation, as well as escalation, when appropriate (see also the remedies for abuse of force, particularly in policing, as discussed in Chapter 10).

Sexual and gender harassment

Sexual and gender harassment (or just general harassment) is a particularly problematic and pernicious category of abuses practiced by a few criminal justice staff against each other and their clients. Although one might expect that it is usually motivated by personal profit or gratification, there may be official deviance both by the perpetrator of such offenses and by coworkers and supervisors, who either do nothing to stop the offenses, encourage them, or facilitate their occurrence. As the vast number of studies indicate that sexual and gender harassment in the workplace usually, but not always, involves a male perpetrator and a female target (e.g., see US Merit Systems Protection Board 1981, 1988; Erdreich *et al.* 1995), there are some who believe such behavior is really motivated by a dislike or hatred of women, or at least a distaste for working with them.

Sexual and gender harassment are defined by the US Equal Employment Opportunity Commission in the Code of Federal Regulations (2006) as:

> Unwelcome sexual advances, requests for sexual favors, and other verbal or physical conduct of a sexual nature constitute sexual harassment when: (1) submission to such conduct is made either explicitly or implicitly a term or condition of an individual's employment; (2) submission to or rejection of such conduct by an individual is used as the basis for employment decisions ... or (3) such conduct has the purpose or effect of unreasonably interfering with an individual's work performance or creating an intimidating, hostile or offensive working environment.

Behaviors that characterize sexual or gender harassment can range from unwelcome requests for dates or for personal information, to unwelcome touching (e.g., an arm around the shoulder), to stalking or physical or sexual assault. When the request for a sexual favor is tied to keeping or advancing in a job, that harassment is termed *quid pro quo* ("something for something," in Latin).

When the behavior is aimed at making the job uncomfortable for those of a specific gender, those actions are believed to create a *hostile environment* and are often more general gender, rather than sexual, harassment. Such behaviors might overlap with sexual harassment, but typically they include displaying pornographic materials in the workplace, comments about the lack of abilities of a particular gender, personal comments about the body parts of one gender, jokes that focus on the ineptitude or objectification of one gender, undesirable assignments for a particular gender, and exclusion of one gender from the more desirable assignments that lead to promotion, to name a few.

Research on sexual and gender harassment in the workplace indicates that it is not uncommon. In the three largest sampling frames of public employees ever done for a personnel issue, the US Merit System Protection Board (Erdreich *et al.* 1995; US MSPB 1981, 1988) found that the incidence of sexual harassment among federal employees remained almost identical over a fifteen-year period. In these studies of tens of thousands of clustered, randomly assigned employees, conducted in 1980, 1987, and 1994, the rate of sexual harassment among females was 42 percent (1980 and 1987) and that among males was 15 percent (1980) and 14 percent (1987); in 1994, 44 percent of the women and 19 percent of the men reported such harassment. Other studies of state government employees report similar results (McIntyre and Renick 1982). Notably, however, in a 2005 study of federal employees, only 3 percent of the participants reported that they had experienced "repeated unwanted sexual attention or harassment" in the workplace (MSPB 2005: 38). Unfortunately, in this report, the responses by gender were not separated out.

In a study of sexual and gender harassment among residents of Idaho, the researchers found that 68.8 percent of women and 31.2 percent of male respondents reported such harassment in their workplace for the year 2000 (Stohr *et al.* 2001).

Studies of sexual or gender harassment in the criminal justice workplace are less commonplace. However, the available evidence, anecdotal reports, plaintiff suits, the closed nature of some workplaces, and the tendency for such environments to be dominated by males would suggest that sexual and gender harassment is not uncommon in the criminal justice field (Amnesty International 2004; Belknap 2001; De Amicis 2005; Marquart *et al.* 2001; Martin 1980, 1990; Pogrebin and Poole 1998; Scarborough and Garrison 2006; Stohr *et al.* 1998; Thomas 1996; Zimmer 1986; Zupan 1992). The evidence does indicate that the vast majority of serious and violent sexual abuses of community members, suspects, accused persons, and inmates are committed by male staff against female victims (see, e.g., Box 3.1).

However, Marquart and his colleagues (2001: 892) found in their study of the Texas prison system that most of the staff who committed "general boundary violations" with inmates (e.g., "accepted or exchanged food products or craft work/materials with prisoners, or wrote letters to prisoners") were Anglo and female. The researchers also found that staff involved in dual relationships with the inmates were overwhelmingly female (80 percent). But they note that in fifteen cases of sexual contact between employees and inmates which involved "predatory situations," all the employees were male and all the inmates were female (Marquart *et al.* 2001). What these findings indicate is that sexual and gender harassment is not the exclusive province of men; rather, it is practiced by both male and female staff members in the criminal justice system.

The monetary costs of gender and sexual harassment are horrendous for state and local facilities and agencies. Although the charge is very difficult to "prove" in a court of law, and in most cases the plaintiff does not prevail, the court costs and staff time devoted to defending a solid case constitute a black hole of funds for a criminal justice facility or agency. One of the authors was an expert witness for the successful plaintiffs on two sexual harassment claims in the 1990s: The state of California was ordered to pay over a million dollars to the plaintiffs in each case. California is just one state; it is probable that hundreds of such cases and judgments passed through other state courts in the past two decades.

Other general forms of harassment that might be based on race, ethnicity, gender, or sexual orientation are not that uncommon in some police and other criminal justice organizations (Hassell and Brandl 2009). In a study of a Midwestern police department workplace and the experiences by police officers in terms of race, gender, and sexual orientation, Hassell and Brandl (2009) found that those of minority status *vis-à-vis* race/ethnicity, gender, and sexual orientation were more likely to have negative workplace experiences. The negative experience which was most prevalent among the study participants was "lack of support/influence/feedback" and the likely outcome of that experience was stress felt by those officers (Hassell and Brandl 2009: 416).

Box 3.6 The United Nations Report: "Strengthening judicial integrity against corruption"

In the year 2000, the United Nations convened a conference on worldwide judicial corruption. While noting that judicial corruption was a global problem, and that no country was immune from its taint, it found developing nations to be particularly susceptible. The conference attendees recognized judicial corruption and the lack of integrity as "[o]ne of the main obstacles to peace, stability, sustainable development, democracy, and human rights around the globe" (Langseth 2001: 3). "Indicators" of corruption in any given court included inefficient or overly efficient processing of bail, prisoners, or charges; suspicious treatment of cases and clients; and exceptions being made in sentences and charges.

Preliminary remedies suggested by the conferees included:

> increased pay for judicial officers so that they might be less tempted to engage in corruption; transparency in judicial appointments and case assignments to ensure that judges were selected based on merit and that cases were not assigned based on corrupt influences; the adoption of a code of conduct by judicial officers; public disclosure of officers' own and family assets; computerization court files; use of alternative dispute resolution when at all possible; use of peer pressure to encourage appropriate behavior; and punishment or disbarment of those who engage in corruption.
>
> (Langseth 2001: 3)

When we couple the monetary costs with the time commitment, emotional turmoil, and distress these experiences, complaints, and claims cause, it becomes clear that the most prudent policy for managers and staff is to try very hard to ensure that such violations do not occur. To this end, managers and staff should consider whether they need to enhance their policies, procedures, and practices in the following ways:

- Ensure that there is a formal policy specifically prohibiting behaviors of the types that comprise sexual and gender harassment and just general harassment. Ensure that this policy also includes a description of the specific disciplinary actions that violations of this policy might elicit.

- Model the appropriate and respectful treatment of all employees/clients.
- Train employees on the policy.
- Mentor employees on respectful behavior in the workplace.
- Evaluate employees based on their adherence to the policy and on their respectful treatment of colleagues and clients.
- Promote only those employees who abide by the policy and model the respectful treatment of all employees/inmates/clients.
- Provide a mechanism by which employees can complain (blow the whistle) in privacy and without retribution when the policy is violated.
- Investigate all complaints of violation of the policy.
- Discipline those who fail to abide by the policy and/or facilitate the retribution against whistleblowers.

Box 3.7 Cases in point

Albany Judge Recommended For Dismissal

A state commission has recommended that a State Supreme Court judge from Albany be removed for soliciting tens of thousands of dollars in contributions from lawyers to help pay legal bills.

According to the panel, the New York State Commission on Judicial Conduct [www.scjc.state.ny.us/], the judge, Thomas J. Spargo, had sought to stop the commission's investigation into a number of complaints by filing law suits in both federal and state courts. In the process, he incurred $140,000 in legal expenses and turned to lawyers with cases before him for donations.

Excerpt from an article by Lisa W. Foderaro, *The New York Times*, April 1, 2006. For more information on judicial corruption, see *Greylord: A Study in Judicial Corruption* (Jordan 2006).

Police Lose Badges After Sex Offenses

SALT LAKE CITY—Utah police officers most frequently lose their certification or are suspended from their jobs after sexual misconduct offenses.

Officers from agencies small and large commit sex offenses more than any other offense, including excessive force, falsifying reports or driving under the influence, according to data from the state's Peace Officers Standards and Training Council (POST) [http://post.utah.gov/index_Mash.html].

An analysis of records by The Salt Lake Tribune showed that of 94 officers whose certifications were revoked between 2000 and 2005, 42 were accused of sexual offenses. Over the same five-year period, another 22 officers were suspended for the same reason.

Excerpt from an Associated Press article in
The Idaho Statesman, October 30, 2006.

Ex-Border agents get prison for bribes.

SAN DIEGO—Two former supervisory Border Patrol agents were sentenced Tuesday to more than six years in prison for taking nearly $200,000 in bribes from what authorities say was eastern California's largest smuggling ring of illegal immigrants from Mexico.

Mario Alvarez and Samuel McClaren released smugglers and their customers from jail while working on a prisoner transfer program with the Mexican government. They released one prisoner in a Wal-Mart parking lot for a fee of $6,000, according to court documents.

The agents, based in El Centro, once smuggled two illegal immigrants across the border themselves in a government vehicle and released them for cash, according to court documents. They turned over the location of surveillance cameras and other Border Patrol intelligence to smugglers.

Excerpt from an article by Elliot Spagat, Associated Press,
The Idaho Statesman, November 1, 2006.

Ethics defined and discussed

Whether deviance in the criminal justice environment is motivated by personal gratification or gain, official deviance, or noble cause, and whether the deviance takes the form of excessive use of force, sexual or gender harassment, or some other abusive behavior, the inculcation of ethical practice into the workplace is one possible way by which the manager can focus on prevention. **Ethics** is *the study of what is right and wrong behavior in the professional sphere.* Morality is the same basic concept as ethics, but it involves the private sphere. **Ethical behavior** is action that is regarded as "right" in accordance with the ethical codes, rules and procedures, and statutes that govern the professional sphere.

Again, as stated in Chapter 2, we have both ethical behavior at the individual level and *organizational integrity*—that is, an organization exhibits integrity when its actors as a whole are honest, ethical, and can be trusted by their members and the community. In a study that examined the enhancement of police integrity, the National Institute of Justice (2005: ii) found that "[a]n agency's *culture of integrity*, as defined by clearly understood and implemented policies and rules, may be more important in shaping the ethics of police officers than hiring the 'right' people" (emphasis added).

Ethical behavior is often guided by one's own beliefs about what is right and wrong. It is possible, however, that one's ethical beliefs will conflict with organizational rules and procedures and/or with state law. This was likely a greater problem in the past, when rules and procedures were rarely written down and standardized, and the informal culture promoted or ignored unethical behavior. Where racist and other discriminatory or brutal practices were part of everyday life in some agencies, there would be general condemnation today and a sense that the condoning of such behavior was unethical, as was the action itself. In other words, most of us would say that it is understandable, even desirable, for staff to ignore agency edicts that are unethical—hence contrary to, or in conflict with, state or federal law, formal procedures and policies, or current ethical practice.

Because of court challenges to criminal justice practices and procedures over the past thirty years, however, one is less likely to find unethical behavior that is officially sanctioned or *formally* accepted; nor are rules and procedure manuals, which are much more in evidence today, likely to promote it. Of course, all of these developments tend to support organizational integrity. Nowadays when one's personal beliefs conflict with ethically acceptable behavior in a criminal justice work environment, it is more likely that the individual, rather than the organization, is dismissive of ethical behavior and so is on the wrong side of ethical practice. Of course, some criminal justice agencies might *informally* promote or facilitate official deviance, and in this case the individual staff member should choose a more appropriate ethical path (Conover 2000).

The origin of ethics

Most of the research on ethics includes some discussion of philosophical bases for decisions regarding right or wrong behavior (Braswell *et al.* 1991; Pollock 1994, 1998, 2010; Rohr 1989; Solomon 1996). Our ethical beliefs are shaped by life experiences, the prevailing culture, and important social institutions such as the family, religion, and schools, and perhaps by the work environment. The philosophical touchstones usually mentioned as guiding human decisions regarding ethics are ethical formalism, utilitarianism, religion, natural law, the ethics of virtue, the ethics of care, and egoism.

These "ethical frameworks" for criminal justice agencies are buttressed by ethical systems that are the source of moral beliefs (Pollock 1998, 2010).

There are both deontological and teleological ethical systems that shape moral behavior. **Deontological ethical systems** are concerned with whether the act itself is good, whereas **teleological ethical systems** are focused on the consequences of the act. If the act is moral or ethical, then the consequences are unimportant according to someone who is guided by a deontological system. But if an act that is immoral or unethical results in a "good" outcome, someone guided by a teleological system would be satisfied. Pollock defines the ethical frameworks that fall under these ethical systems in her book *Ethics in Crime and Justice: Dilemmas and Decisions* (1998; 2010).

She first defines **ethical formalism** as "[w]hat is good is that which conforms to the categorical imperative" (Pollock 1998: 48). There is a universal law of what is right or moral and what is wrong or immoral. One must do one's duty in order to comply with this law. According to Immanuel Kant (1724–1804), the *categorical imperative* is the requirement that each person act as the individual would wish all people to. Kant believed that people must resort to their higher reason to shape decisions. This is a deontological approach because there is a focus on the act and its rightness, rather than on the consequences of the act. Ethical formalism is an absolutist position, where all acts are either and always right or wrong. Therefore, acts such as murder, lying, and stealing are always wrong even when the end they purportedly serve might be morally good.

Utilitarianism is described as "[w]hat is good is that which results in the greatest utility for the greatest number" (Pollock 1998: 48). An individual's actions are moral if they maximize the greatest good for the greatest number of people. The British philosopher Jeremy Bentham (1748–1832) believed that because individuals will seek pleasure over pain, they will do a "utilitarian calculus" to determine what action will result in more pleasure. When an individual's pleasure conflicts with a desirable societal outcome, then the greater good for the larger number should guide behavior. This is a teleological perspective because the focus is on the good or bad end or the pleasure or pain, rather than on the good or bad means or the intent of the actor, as was the case in ethical formalism. In criminal justice work one would focus on acting so that the greatest good might be achieved for the greatest number.

A **religious perspective** would include the belief that "[w]hat is good is that which conforms to God's will" (Pollock 1998: 48). This type of perspective guides beliefs about what is right and wrong, how to treat others, and the meaning and purpose of life. Religions approach these topics in different ways with a focus on both means and ends, depending on the circumstances. Most religions have reference to a higher power—a spiritual being, or beings—as a source for the belief system. The teachings of Christianity, Judaism, Islam, Hinduism, and Buddhism also include explicit or implicit reference to a universal set of rights and wrongs. Most religions teach some form of the categorical imperative, often formulated as "Do unto others as you would have done unto you." Although there is some agreement about what constitutes right and wrong among most religions, there is disagreement about certain social practices such as drinking alcohol, dancing, foods, behavior on holy days, and the appropriateness of types of clothing, as well as the political status of women and other political minorities such as gay men or lesbians.

Someone who adheres to a **natural law** ethical framework believes that "[w]hat is good is that which is natural" (Pollock 1998: 48). Behavior is guided by a universal set of rights and wrongs that are knowable for all of us. The major difference between a natural law framework and a religious framework of moral beliefs is merely that in the former case there is no supreme being for reference. According to a natural law perspective, we know what truth and decency are; we merely have to act on our existing natural inclinations to do good. "Morality is part of the natural order of the universe." Further, "this morality is the same across cultures and times" (Pollock 1998: 41). Out of these natural laws flow natural rights, or so the authors of the US Constitution believed.

Proponents of the **ethics of virtue** ethical framework propose that "[w]hat is good is that which conforms to the golden mean [the middle ground between extreme positions]" (Pollock 1998: 48). Whether a person is good or virtuous is more important than whether an action is. The important teleological end to achieve is living a good and moral life by performing virtuous acts. "Virtues that a good person possesses include thriftiness, temperance, humility, industriousness, and honesty" (Pollock 1998: 43). Morality is learned from models or "moral exemplars" and is reinforced when the law is just. To determine what a virtuous act is, an individual must find the "golden mean." A person who develops a "habit of integrity" does not even consider acting unethically.

Box 3.8   Police ethics and public trust: getting all the systems right, by Pierce Murphy, Head of the Seattle Police Department's Office of Professional Accountability

At the beginning of 1996, the population of Boise, Idaho, stood at 140,000 and its police force employed 240 sworn personnel. Boise was a quiet city, certainly by national standards, and no one was prepared for the events of the next twenty-one months. Between January 1996 and September 1997, the Boise Police Department experienced seven officer-involved shootings. A total of eight deaths resulted, one of them the tragic death of Officer Mark Stahl, the first Boise officer killed in the line of duty. With each new shooting, more and more questions were raised in the media and on the street. By the sixth incident, the Idaho State Police were asked to jointly investigate, along with the Boise Police, in an effort to address growing questions about the police department's ability to investigate itself. Two separate citizen groups formed, each one calling for some form of police commission or citizen oversight of the police. Editorials were written demanding answers and scores of people showed up for town hall meetings. Battle lines were drawn between those calling for support of the police and others saying the police could not be trusted.

Boise's mayor and the City Council responded to these events by announcing the creation of a new position in the mayor's office: an ombudsman who would mediate between the community and the police and have a role in resolving citizen complaints. Their goal was to restore public trust and confidence in the police department; and they wanted to calm a volatile political situation. Precisely how the ombudsman's office would function and the specific duties assigned to it were not clear. These details were left to the first ombudsman to work out and recommend to the City Council.

I was appointed Boise's first ombudsman in March of 1999 and immediately began work drafting empowering legislation and detailed procedures. In July the City Council unanimously passed an ordinance specifying the ombudsman's duties and ensuring sufficient authority and independence to perform them. The ombudsman reports to both the mayor and the City Council and can only be removed for cause following a public hearing and a vote for removal by five out of six council members, or four council members plus the mayor. The independence of the ombudsman is assured by a section of the ordinance making it unlawful for anyone to undermine or attempt to undermine that independence. This same ordinance requires the ombudsman to perform the following duties: Receive and investigate complaints about law enforcement, independently investigate police incidents involving the use of deadly force or resulting in death or serious injury, audit internal affairs investigations, make policy recommendations, act as a mediator, issue public reports, and conduct community outreach.

To assure the community and the police that the ombudsman had the tools necessary to arrive at the facts and reach reasonable findings, the ordinance requires all city employees to truthfully answer questions put to them by the ombudsman and to provide him with any documents, information, and evidence he requests in the course of an ombudsman investigation. The ordinance also gives the ombudsman unfettered access to any and all police records and files. At the same time, the ordinance requires the ombudsman to respect the privacy of all parties and follow state and federal privacy laws.

I took this position because I believe that, in order to enjoy the blessings of a safe and stable community, individuals must be willing to contribute to that community in an active and even sacrificial manner. I saw how trust in the Boise Police Department had been damaged by unsubstantiated and overly generalized assertions. A serious and substantial breach of trust existed between some members of the community and the police officers serving and protecting them. There was, to borrow a phrase, an "alienation of affection" between the public and the police. However, divorce was not an option; something needed to be done to rebuild the relationship and get the partners in public safety working together again.

As the ombudsman, I share in the responsibility of maintaining public trust in the police. The public possesses a healthy suspicion of those in the government who possess the power to take away their property, their freedom, and their very lives. Trust and suspicion cannot coexist. The ombudsman's office is an objective and independent source of information about police activities. I am an advocate for accountable, professional, and ethical policing. Through my public reports and community outreach I am able to lift the veil of secrecy that often shrouds law enforcement, to open a window through which the public can view its police department. At the same time, the police receive vital feedback and learn more about the concerns of their community.

Based on my experience as a human resources professional and, more recently, as a police oversight official, I am convinced that a key strategy for maintaining the trust of the community is to take a "whole system" view of police ethics. Law enforcement agencies must hire people whose core character is inherently directed toward service and ethical behavior. Recruiting efforts and the applicant screening process should identify candidates who, given adequate encouragement and controls, will act responsibly and ethically. Investing in thorough and high-quality pre-employment background investigations will produce better officers and reduce future civil liability. The organization's culture, policies, and human resource systems must be aligned to encourage and reward behavior that rises to the highest ethical and professional standards. These systems, in addition to selection, include promotions, training, performance management, compensation, informal rewards, feedback (from both internal and external "customers"), internal audit and investigations, and complaint resolution.

Pierce Murphy earned a Master of Arts in Pastoral Studies degree from Loyola University of New Orleans, a Master of Arts degree in Counseling Psychology from Gonzaga University in Spokane, Washington, and a Bachelor of Science degree in Commerce from Santa Clara University in Santa Clara, California. He began his career in 1972 as a law enforcement officer with the City of Menlo Park in California. Prior to work in the private sector, beginning in 1994 as a manager of human resource development, he maintained a human resource management consulting practice. He served for fourteen years as the Community Ombudsman for the Boise City Police Department. He was hired in a similar position for the Seattle Police Department in May 2013.

One who believes in the **ethics of care** ethical framework subscribes to the statement that "[w]hat is good is that which meets the needs of those concerned" (Pollock 1998: 48). This perspective is focused on the feelings, needs, and care of others, rather than on whether action is, or should be, guided by universal conceptions of right or wrong. It is known as a more feminine perspective, since women are regarded as viewing the wrongness of actions undertaken to care for or nurture others as being attenuated by the human needs of those involved. Carol Gilligan (1982) found in her work on moral development that women, more than men, have a moral perspective that differs from that enunciated in western ethics. They are more likely to identify care and concern for others as more important to guiding ethical practice. Peacemaking justice and restorative justice are believed to grow from this ethical system. The goal of these perspectives is to meet the needs of all actors, while at the same time preventing further criminality.

Pollock (1998) also describes a more individualistic ethical framework titled **egoism**. Someone who believes in this framework thinks that "[w]hat is good is that which benefits me" (Pollock 1998: 48). Egoism is focused on what is best for an individual. In this framework, an individual who acts to satisfy needs or wants is acting ethically. It is believed that humans evolved and survived only because of this drive to satisfy their needs; therefore, acts in service of self are not only ethical, they are natural and the only way humans can act. A form of this system, *enlightened egoism*, predicts that even when people are acting in what appears to be a selfless manner, they are in fact acting egoistically to ensure that others treat them similarly.

A warning sign: too much focus on ends over means

Because the motivations and ethical frameworks for unethical and deviant behavior vary in criminal justice agencies, the remedies vary as well. It is relatively easy to recognize and dispense with corruption at the individual level, as the attentive manager can see that it usually involves both corrupt ends and means.

At times, however, the ends of official deviance and noble cause corruption may be good, or perceived as such by the actor and even the organization, but the means are corrupt. *One thing is certain: if staff are inordinately focused on the ends of the system and dismissive of the need to have just means, managers have a clear warning signal that staff are prone to engage in official deviance, noble cause corruption, or both.*

Of course, as with any response to wrongdoing, there are degrees of seriousness that should govern the reaction to, or remedy for, the deviance. Some research on jails and prisons does indicate that staff seems to be able to identify clear violations. In 1998 and 1999 Stohr, Hemmens, Kifer, and Schoeler (2000) administered a thirty-three-item "ethics instrument" to 467 correctional staff members at three prisons, two jails, and a jail detention academy class in a western state (see the chapter appendix for a revised version of this instrument for the jails). They found that for some types of deviance there are "bright lines" of perception for staff, or behaviors that respondents generally agree are wrong. Usually the strongest agreement was found on items that violate state laws, as well as organizational policies and ethics codes. For instance, there was a high level of agreement about the wrongness of theft or contraband smuggling by staff. But there was less certainty regarding items concerned with respect for inmates or other staff members, which are typically violations of organizational procedures and ethics codes, but not statutes.

The war on terror presents the perfect conditions for ethical abuse

After the September 11, 2001 attack by terrorists on American soil, the country experienced an understandable sense of urgency to catch and prosecute those guilty of planning the offenses. A "war on terror" was declared, and military might was exercised in pursuing terrorists around the world and at home. In democracies, however, wars can lead to suppression of speech and suspension of due process even when the battleground is not necessarily in the homeland. But when people have reason to feel threatened at home, this felt need to single out the wrongdoers takes on a whole new urgency.

Witness, for example, the suspension of due process rights by President Lincoln during the Civil War (Currie 1985). Or the internment of Japanese Americans during the Second World War (when there was the false impression that American citizens of Japanese descent were engaged in wartime espionage in the United States; Irons 1999). Or even the "war on drugs" that has led to an unraveling of some case law regarding property rights (asset seizures and forfeitures) and privacy rights (search and seizure; Cole 1999).

We do not yet know the long-term effect of the "war on terror" on criminal justice agencies at the local, state, and federal levels. Thus far, however, the war seems to have created the perfect admixture for ethical abuses to occur in agencies. First and foremost, the motivation for ethical abuses is there: What more noble cause is there than saving the homeland? What organization would not encourage deviance to catch terrorists? When matters are conducted in secrecy, with little outside review by the courts, the media, the public, or its representatives, what is to stop individual actors from profiting from this war? Second, secrecy is emphasized in this war, which would tend to provide cover for wiretapping and torture, to name a few abuses highlighted in news reports (see Box 3.9). Third, there is evidence of suppression of speech and due process rights, liberties, and protections that free peoples typically rely on to prevent the rise of tyrannical governments. Examples emerging from the "war on terror" include "legal black holes such as Guantanamo Bay and Bagram Air Force Base, where there is less judicial oversight, process, and public scrutiny due to geographical and durational logistics" (aclu.org 2009: 1). This "legal black hole" can set the stage for abuse and corruption.

At the federal level, law enforcement agencies are most susceptible to ethical abuse because of their proximity to the war and their primary responsibility for executing it. Witness, for example, the widespread secret wiretapping of American citizens without a warrant or without prior court approval—a practice that many legal scholars are calling illegal behavior (Lichtblau and Risen 2005; Strobel and Landay 2005). At this juncture, the federal courts appear reluctant to review many of the "war on terror" policies (Savage 2009). Also consider the accusation that the FBI falsified documents to cover up mistakes made in a Florida terror investigation and then punished a whistle-blower (an FBI agent himself) when he called attention to those mistakes (Lichtblau 2005: 25):

> The agent who first alerted the FBI to problems in the case, a veteran undercover operative named Mike German, was "retaliated against" by his boss, who was angered by the agent's complaints and stopped using him for prestigious assignments in training new undercover agents at FBI schools, the draft report concluded.

> Mr. German's case first became public last year, as he emerged as the latest in a string of whistleblowers at the FBI who said they had been punished and effectively silenced for voicing concerns about the handling of terror investigations and other matters since Sept. 11, 2001.

Mr. German reluctantly left the FBI even as he proclaimed his respect for the people who worked there. But he claimed his career had been ruined because he spoke out. Senator Charles E. Grassley, an Iowa Republican, agreed with Mr. German, stating in a *New York Times* article that "[u]nfortunately, this is just another case in a long line of FBI whistle-blowers who have had their careers derailed because the FBI couldn't tolerate criticism."

(Lichtblau 2005: 25)

Local law enforcement is likely to experience some of the same challenges to ethical behavior, though to a lesser degree, because of the "war on terror" as those in federal agencies. One way in which local law enforcement has become involved in this war is via the FBI-organized Joint Terrorism Task Forces (FBI 2004). The JTTFs are composed of FBI agents and state and local law enforcement and other federal agency members situated in over a hundred cities nationwide. Some JTTFs existed before September 11, 2001, and sixty-five were created afterward. The task forces collaborate on secret investigations of alleged terrorist activities in cities and states. The FBI claims that the JTTFs were involved in the identification of terrorist cells in Portland, Oregon, and northern Virginia, for example (FBI 2004). It remains to be seen how this collaboration will play out at the local and state levels. However, experience suggests that certain factors, such as secrecy, lack of review by the courts, intolerance of dissent, and the urgency that a "war" implies, will set the stage for ethical abuses motivated by personal greed/benefit, organizational deviance, and/or noble cause corruption (as indicated in Box 3.9).

Box 3.9 The *Los Angeles Times* reviews abuse of Muslim prisoners

9/11 prisoner abuse suit could be landmark: rounded up, Muslim immigrants were beaten in jail. Such open-ended detentions and sweeps might be barred.

NEW YORK—Five years after Muslim immigrants were abused in a federal jail here, the guards who beat them and the Washington policymakers who decided to hold them for months without charges are being called to account.

Some 1,200 Middle Eastern men were arrested on suspicion of terrorism after the attacks of Sept. 11, 2001. No holding place was so notorious as Brooklyn's nine-story Metropolitan Detention Center. In a special unit on the top floor, detainees were smashed into walls, repeatedly stripped and searched, and often denied basic legal rights and religious privileges, according to Federal investigations.

Now the Federal Bureau of Prisons, which runs the jail, has revealed for the first time that 13 staff members have been disciplined, two of them fired. The warden has retired and moved to the Midwest.

And in what could turn out to be a landmark case, a lawsuit filed by two Brooklyn detainees against top Bush administration officials is moving forward in the federal courts in New York.

Five investigations by the Department of Justice Inspector General's office, most of them never publicized, documented wholesale abuse of the Muslim detainees at the Brooklyn detention center. In the months after the Sept. 11 attacks, 84 men were held there. None were charged in the attacks. Most were deported on immigration infractions.

One disturbing incident, repeated over and over, is particularly haunting—inmates head-slammed into a wall where the staff had taped a T-shirt with an American flag printed on it. The motto on the shirt proclaimed: "These colors don't run." In time, that spot on the wall was covered with blood.

Guards at the detention center first denied there was any mistreatment, then slowly came forward. Finally videotapes were uncovered that showed abuse, including detainees head-butted into the T-shirt on the wall.

Traci Billingsley, a spokeswoman for the Federal Bureau of Prisons, said 13 staff members have been disciplined. Two were fired, two received 30-day suspensions and one was suspended for 21 days. Two more were suspended for four days, three for two days, and three were demoted.

Excerpt from an article by Richard A. Serrano,
Los Angeles Times, November 20, 2006.

For the full story, see http://www.latimes.com/news/nationworld/nation/la-na-jail20nov20,0,4fi83237.story?coll=la-home-headlines (last accessed January 31, 2013).

The ethical remedy to alleviate the degree of abuse, deviance, corruption, and harassment

As the preceding review of the ethical frameworks indicates, most of us derive our conception of moral behavior from several sources. Therefore, the approach used to ensure that ethical behavior is practiced in the workplace must recognize and accommodate those sources. What is clear from the discussion of official deviance and noble cause explanations for abuse and corruption is that the manager interested in inculcating ethics into the criminal justice workplace must be as concerned with just means as with just ends (Muraskin and Muraskin 2001). In addition to the solutions to alleviate abuse and corruption that have already been suggested throughout the chapter, and grievance procedures and whistleblowing mechanisms that will be reviewed in other chapters, we will also explore the inculcation of *ethics* as a preventive measure for the criminal justice environment. For the inculcation of ethics to have any effect on the workplace, however, there needs to be a level of commitment by managers to meaningfully engage their colleagues in a discussion of what an ethical work environment would be like and how to make it the reality.

As part of two ethics training exercises for thirty state probation and parole managers conducted in 1994 and 1995,[2] one of the authors, along with a colleague, explored just this topic. First, they asked the managers to identify barriers to ethical practice in their workplace. Most of the barriers identified also had been noted by Kauffman (1988: 85–112) in his study of correctional officers and included by Pollock (1994: 195) in her text on ethics, and concerned the reinforcement of negative behaviors by the subculture. The sometimes problematic behaviors identified by Kauffman, and reaffirmed as applicable by the managers, included the following:

1 Always aid your coworker.
2 Never rat on coworkers.
3 Always cover for a coworker in front of clients.
4 Always support the coworker over the client in a disagreement.
5 Always support the decision of a coworker regarding a client.
6 Don't be sympathetic toward clients. Instead be cynical about them (to be otherwise is to be naïve).
7 Probation/parole officers are the "us" and everyone else is the "them," including administration, the media, and the rest of the community.
8 Help your coworkers by completing your own work and by assisting them if they need it.
9 Since you aren't paid much or appreciated by the public or the administration, don't be a rate buster (i.e., don't do more than the minimal amount of work).
10 Handle your own work and don't allow interference.

Notably, a few of these subcultural values are positive, such as aiding your coworker or doing your work so others do not have to. But most of the values, if adopted by staff, would foster unethical work practices. In fact, most of the managers in those training sessions admitted that they regularly encountered unethical behavior on the job, from the relatively benign and more common rudeness to clients and their families to the rarer lying on reports or verbal or physical abuse of clients. In addressing these issues, the managers were stymied by the negative subcultural values that reinforced unethical behaviors by some and then prevented others from confronting or reporting it.

Of course, a number of professional criminal justice organizations have developed codes of ethics that promote an ideal workplace (e.g., see Box 3.10). Just having such codes on a wall does little to reinforce them in the workplace, though their very existence is a first step. What is really needed is some co-option and remolding of the subculture so that the ethical values an organization wants to promote are supported by most workers in the organization.

Box 3.10 The law enforcement code of ethics

As a law enforcement officer, my fundamental duty is to serve the community; to safeguard lives and property; to protect the innocent against deception, the weak against oppression or intimidation and the peaceful against violence or disorder; and to respect the constitutional rights of all to liberty, equality and justice.

I will keep my private life unsullied as an example to all and will behave in a manner that does not bring discredit to me or to my agency. I will maintain courageous calm in the face of danger, scorn or ridicule; develop self-restraint; and be constantly mindful of the welfare of others. Honest in thought and deed both in my personal and official life, I will be exemplary in obeying the law and the regulations of my department. Whatever I see or hear of a confidential nature or that is confided to me in my official capacity will be kept ever secret unless revelation is necessary in the performance of my duty.

I will never act officiously or permit personal feelings, prejudices, political beliefs, aspirations, animosities or friendships to influence my decisions. With no compromise for crime and with relentless prosecution of criminals, I will enforce the law courteously and appropriately without fear or favor, malice or ill will, never employing unnecessary force or violence and never accepting gratuities.

I recognize the badge of my office as a symbol of public faith, and I accept it as a public trust to be held so long as I am true to the ethics of police service. I will never engage in acts of corruption or bribery, nor will I condone such acts by other police officers. I will cooperate with all legally authorized agencies and their representatives in the pursuit of justice.

I know that I alone am responsible for my own standard of professional performance and will take every reasonable opportunity to enhance and improve my level of knowledge and competence.

I will constantly strive to achieve these objectives and ideals, dedicating myself before God to my chosen profession ... law enforcement.

Code provided courtesy of the International Association of Chiefs of Police website, www.theiacp.org. Reprinted here with permission from the IACP.

Here lies the difficulty for criminal justice managers and staff: How does one get all or most staff to buy into completely ethical practice when they have multiple motivations and may adhere to different ethical frameworks? Pierce Murphy, the Community Ombudsman for the City of Boise Police Department, faced just this issue when he undertook this role (see Box 3.8). He needed to first define his position and authority; then he could proceed to recommending organizational changes that were more likely to lead to an ethics-based subculture at this agency.

Relatedly, the probation and parole managers at the training sessions we conducted thought that the first step was to define what an ethical manager is.[3] The "Model of An Ethical Manager" that evolved from those discussions contained the following items.

The ethical manager

The ethical manager is:

1 "Respectful and civil in treatment of staff, clientele, the department, and community members."
2 "A person who knows that personal relationships should not be allowed to interfere with professional treatment or merit."
3 "A person who adheres to legal standards, including due process protections for staff and clientele, and works to ensure their maintenance and facilitation."
4 "A person who ensures that monies are expended in the most efficient and effective manner."
5 "A person who ensures that staff are assigned where and when they are most needed to provide the optimal program delivery."

6 "A person who ensures that program substantive content is valid."
7 "A person who ensures that staff are allocated the time, training, and the resources to successfully fulfill their assigned tasks."
8 "A person who ensures that program outcomes are measured and measurable. A person who models ethical behavior."
9 "A person who is fair and forthright in all dealings with staff, clientele, administration and community members."
10 "A person who listens empathetically."
11 "A person who is accountable for actions of self and team members in the workplace."
12 "A person who has integrity in that he or she will not be swayed by what is politically expedient, but is guided by concerns for justice and adherence to legal requirements."
13 "A person who reinforces and rewards ethical behavior by other staff in all personnel processes (selection, training, performance appraisals, promotions, and assignments)."
14 "A person who disciplines violators of ethical and professional standards of behavior."
15 "A person who provides a mechanism by which personnel can report violations."
16 "A person who ensures that whistleblowers are not punished."
17 "A person who gives employees developmental feedback so that they might know what is and isn't ethically acceptable in the department."
18 "A person who communicates openly and freely with employees."
19 "A person who values and facilitates employee input and decision making processes."
20 "A person who ensures that output from self and others is qualitatively high."
21 "A person who facilitates the growth of others."
22 "A person who is concerned with the human dignity of the clientele."
23 "A person who is concerned about the safety of the community."
24 "A person who seeks first to understand and then to be understood."

Clearly, this model reflects a number of the ethical frameworks defined by Pollock (1998) and encompasses a recognition of the influence that official deviance and noble cause perspectives can have on the subculture of any criminal justice agency. It also reflects not just what an ethical manager *should do*, but what a good manager generally *should be*. But even if managers in criminal justice adopt this model, a problem still remains: How does the ethical manager reform a subculture so that it reflects ethical values?

One possible way to reshape the subculture is to engage the workforce in an open discussion about the development of a code (using the relevant professional codes as models; Barrier *et al.* 1999; Pollock 2010). That discussion would be followed with training throughout the workplace on that code and how to implement it (use of related scenarios would be instructive).

Then the code would need to be reinforced in all selection, performance appraisal, and promotion decisions. In this way, the *formal* workplace (rules, procedures, processes) would shape the *informal* subculture of that agency, because those who bought into the ethical values would be rewarded in a number of ways.

Conclusions

In this chapter we have discussed the explanations for abuse and corruption with some focus on two particularly destructive types of deviance in criminal justice agencies—excessive use of force and sexual and gender harassment. A review of the nature and origin of ethics was included, as was the proposal that the inculcation of ethics into the workplace is one possible means management might choose in trying to improve the work environment for staff and their clients.

As was mentioned at the beginning of the chapter, and as history would instruct us, criminal justice agencies and the honorable work performed in them are particularly susceptible to corruption and abuse. But with a clear-eyed focus on "just" means and ends, and attention to the need to keep the subcultural forces on the side of the angels, the task of reinforcing ethical work behavior and creating organizational integrity in criminal justice is always doable.

Exercise: The student's ethics quiz[4]

One of the authors has conducted this informal quiz once, but with interesting and highly relevant results, so proceed at your own risk! On the single occasion of its use, the quiz was administered at the beginning of class to sharpen students' interest in a discussion of ethics.

1   Ask students to take out a blank sheet of paper and tell them they are going to take a little quiz. Once the outcry dies down, say that the quiz will not be graded and is meant only to be illustrative of ethics-related topics that were raised in the chapter.
2   Tell them not to put their names on their papers.
3   Ask them to respond to the following six questions regarding their college career:

   a   Do you know someone who has cheated on a test? (yes/no)
   b   If yes, how many times have you been aware that someone has cheated on a test? (put the raw number down)
   c   Do you know someone who has cheated on a paper? (yes/no)

d   If yes, how many times have you been aware that someone has cheated on a paper? (put the raw number down)

e   What sorts of measures do you think would keep a student from cheating on a test or paper? (list up to five)

f   What sorts of measures do you think would keep a police officer, courtroom actor, or corrections actor from engaging in corrupt behavior while on the job? (list up to five)

4   Collect the response sheets from the students.

5   Ask for six student volunteers and assign a question to each of them.

6   Line the six students up by question order and tell them how to keep track of the responses to each question (for twenty-five people in my class this took about five minutes).

7   Have each student volunteer write the class responses to his or her question on the board and discuss the findings.

Discussion questions

1   What might motivate unethical behavior by criminal justice actors?

2   What is the difference between the official deviance and noble cause motivations? Give an example.

3   How might the "smell of the victim's blood" and "the tower" be associated with unethical behavior by criminal justice actors? Give an example.

4   Under what circumstances are abuse of force and sexual/gender harassment more likely to occur and why? Explain.

5   How is ethics different from morality? Why? Explain your answer.

6   What is the difference between informal and formally sanctioned ethical lapses in behavior? Give an example.

7   What is the difference between deontological and teleological ethical systems for the control of ethical practices in criminal justice? Give an example.

8   How do the different origins of ethics affect people's view of them? What origins seem most suited for ensuring that criminal justice staff and administrators adhere to ethical codes? Why?

9   How are the means and ends of criminal justice work tied up in the discussion of ethics? What is the importance of each? Explain your answer.

10 How can we prevent the war on drugs and the war on terror from becoming a war on ethics?

Key terms

deontological ethical systems: concerned with whether an act itself is good. To someone who is guided by a deontological system, if an act is moral or ethical, then the consequences are unimportant.

deviance by staff: involving behavior that violates the statutes, institutional rules or procedures, or ethical codes for individual *or* organizational gain *or* even as a means of serving a "noble cause" (Bartollas and Hahn 1999; Crank and Caldero 2000: Lee and Visano 1994).

egoism: the belief that "[w]hat is good is that which benefits me" (Pollock 1998: 48).

ethics: the study of what is right and wrong behavior in the professional sphere; morality is the same basic concept as applied to the private sphere

ethical behavior: action that is regarded as "right" per the ethical codes, rules and procedures, and statutes that govern the professional sphere.

ethical formalism: "[w]hat is good is that which conforms to the categorical imperative" (Pollock 1998: 48).

ethics of care: "[w]hat is good is that which meets the needs of those concerned" (Pollock 1998: 48).

ethics of virtue: "[w]hat is good is that which conforms to the golden mean" (Pollock 1998: 48).

natural law: "[w]hat is good is that which is natural" (Pollock 1998: 48).

noble cause: for police officers, "[a] profound moral commitment to make the world a safer place to live. Put simply, it is getting bad guys off the street. Police believe they're on the side of angels and their purpose in life is getting rid of bad guys" (Crank and Caldero 2000: 35).

official deviance: "[a]ctions taken by officials which violate the law and/or the formal rules of the organization, but which are clearly oriented toward the needs and goals of the organization, as perceived by the official, and thus fulfill certain informal rules of the organization" (Lee and Visano 1994).

religious perspective: includes the belief that "[w]hat is good is that which conforms to God's will" (Pollock 1998: 48).

teleological ethical systems: focused on the consequences of the act. But an immoral or unethical act that results in a "good" outcome would satisfy someone guided by a teleological system.

utilitarianism: "[w]hat is good is that which results in the greatest utility for the greatest number" (Pollock 1998: 48).

Appendix The ethics instrument version for jails*

*Developed by M.K. Stohr and C. Hemmens (1997). Use of this instrument requires the permission of the authors (mary.stohr@wsu.edu or craig.hemmens@wsu.edu).

Jail staff are often faced with difficult choices that affect inmates, their job and their organization. Therefore, this instrument was developed to allow jail staff to determine which are the most pressing issues they face. Please read each question carefully and put the number that best reflects your response in the space provided in front of that question.

1 Strongly Disagree   2 Disagree   3 Neutral   4 Agree

5 Agree Strongly   6 Don't Know   7 Disagree Somewhat

8 Somewhat Agree

_____ 1. Jail staff have an obligation to report thefts by other staff.
_____ 2. The only thing that inmates respect is a show of force.
_____ 3. Special favors done for inmates by staff do not need to be taken seriously by the administration.
_____ 4. Making sexual comments in the workplace about other staff is not harassment.
_____ 5. Coworkers provide a major source of emotional and physical support on the job.
_____ 6. Inmates who have committed sex offenses deserve poor treatment in jail.
_____ 7. Most inmates, in most instances, will respond to an order with no force needed.
_____ 8. Jail administrators should provide a means for other jail staff to have input into the operation of the institution.
_____ 9. The first loyalty of jail staff is to their coworkers, not to uphold the law for the public.
_____ 10. Staff who bring in contraband should be disciplined.
_____ 11. Abusive or offensive language is sometimes appropriate when addressing inmates.
_____ 12. When staff see other staff abusing inmates they should report that abuse.
_____ 13. A jail staff member should simply listen to orders and rarely offer input.
_____ 14. An officer who reports the harassment of inmates by other staff is doing the right thing.
_____ 15. It is expected that officers on the graveyard shift will fall asleep from time to time.
_____ 16. Putdowns of people of the opposite sex in the workplace are usually meant to be funny.
_____ 17. Reasoning with inmates is usually the best way to gain their cooperation.
_____ 18. Use of stronger inmates by jail staff to control other inmates presents the potential for corruption.
_____ 19. Staff should avoid making personal comments about other staff in front of inmates.
_____ 20. Jail staff members have a duty to protect inmates.

_____21. Sexual relations between staff and inmates are sometimes acceptable.

_____22. Jail staff are the only people who can really understand why institutional rules often can't be followed by staff.

_____23. Staff who treat inmates with respect rarely get respect from inmates in return.

_____24. Jail staff at all levels have much knowledge to contribute to the operation of the jail.

_____25. Minority staff members should not be so sensitive about racial or ethnic slurs made by others in the workplace.

_____26. Hitting a disruptive inmate a few more times than is strictly necessary is understandable.

_____27. When a jail staff member is consistent and fair with inmates they are more likely to be respected by inmates.

_____28. Addressing inmates in a respectful manner may give them the idea that they can manipulate staff.

_____29. Jail staff should above all concern themselves with upholding the law.

_____30. Jail staff have the skills and abilities necessary to solve problems in the workplace.

_____31. If most of your coworkers choose to disregard policies and procedures then it is okay for you to do so as well.

_____32. Jail administrators are usually willing to listen to the concerns raised by inmates.

_____33. Minority group inmates are naturally less reliable as trustees than white inmates.

_____34. Staff should be most concerned about their duty to uphold the law, rather than about what their coworkers will think.

Notes

1   The professor was Mark Fleischer, who spoke at Washington State University in spring of 1987.

2   Drs Robert L. Marsh and Mary K. Stohr conducted two ethics training sessions for probation and parole managers in the state of Idaho in 1994 (half-day session) and a follow-up in 1995 (day-long session).

3   This model of an ethical manager was also informed by Stohr and Marsh's reading of a number of texts on ethics and/or management, our interpretation of the Idaho Code of Ethics for Field and Community Service Officers, and comments by students in Stohr's Criminal Justice Management class (Spring 1995). The last item in the model was also influenced by the "Prayer of Saint Francis." Frankly, for most of these items, it is difficult to determine who said what!

4   Some colleges and universities will expect that student surveys be subjected to institutional review because the work entails human subjects.

References

ACLU. (2009) *Obama administration continues indefinite detention policy for Bagram prisoners.* Available at http://www.aclu.org/national-security/obama-administration-continues-indefinite-detention-policy-bagram-prisoners (last accessed January 13, 2013).

Amnesty International. (2004) *Abuse of women in custody: Sexual misconduct and shackling of pregnant women, a state-by-state survey of policies and practices in the United States.* Available at http://www.amnestyusa.org (last accessed January 13, 2013).

Baker, A. and McGinty, J. C. (2010) When officers betray the badge. *The New York Times,* March 28, p. 27.

Barrier, G., Stohr, M. K., Hemmens, C. and Marsh, R. (1999) A practical user's guide: Idaho's method for implementing ethical behavior in a correctional setting. *Corrections Compendium,* 24(4): 1–3, 14–15.

Bartollas, C. and Hahn, L. D. (1999) *Policing in America.* Needham Heights, MA: Allyn and Bacon.

Belknap, J. (2001) *Invisible woman: Gender, crime, and justice,* 2nd edn. Belmont, CA: Wadsworth/Thomson Learning.

Bennett, W. W. and Hess, K. M. (2001) *Management and supervision in law enforcement.* Belmont, CA: Wadsworth Thomson Learning.

Braswell, M. C., McCarthy, B. R. and McCarthy, B. J. (1991) *Justice, crime and ethics.* Cincinnati, OH: Anderson Publishing Co.

Brown, A. K. (2009) Inmates gone wild in Texas jail. *The Idaho Statesman,* March 17, p. A7.

Burns, S. (2011) *The Central Park Five.* New York, NY: Vintage Books.

Clear, T. R. and Cole, C. F. (1997) *American corrections.* Belmont, CA: Wadsworth.

Code of Federal Regulations (2006) Title 29, 4: 198–204. Washington DC: US Government Printing Office. Citation: 29CFR1604.11.

Cole, D. (1999) *No equal justice: Race and class in the American criminal justice system.* New York, NY: New Press.

Conover, T. (2000) *Newjack: Guarding Sing Sing.* New York, NY: Random House.

Courtless, T. F. (1998) *Corrections and the criminal justice system: Laws, policies, and practices.* Belmont, CA: West/Wadsworth.

Crank, J. P. and Caldero, M. A. (2000) *Police ethics: The corruption of noble cause.* Cincinnati, OH: Anderson Publishing.

Crank, J. P. and Caldero, M. A. (2011) *Police ethics: The corruption of noble cause,* 3rd edn. Cincinnati, OH: Anderson Publishing.

Currie, D. P. (1985) *The Constitution in the Supreme Court: The first hundred years: 1789–1888.* Chicago, IL: University of Chicago Press.

De Amicis, A. P. (2005) An ethical dilemma in corrections. *American Jails,* 19(5), pp. 77–82.

Erdreich, B. L., Slavet, B. S. and Amador, A. C. (1995) *Sexual harassment in the federal workplace.* US Merit Systems Protection Board. Washington DC: GPO.

Federal Bureau of Investigation. (2004) Protecting America against terrorist attack: a closer look at the FBI's joint terrorism task forces. Available at http://www.fbi.gov/page2 (last accessed January 13, 2013).

Feeley, M. M. (1983) *Court reform on trial.* New York, NY: Basic Books.

Friedrichs, D. O. (2001) *Law in our lives: An introduction.* Los Angeles, CA: Roxbury.

Gaines, L. K., Worrall, J. L., Southerland, M. D. and Angell, J. E. (2003) *Police administration,* 2nd edn. Boston, MA: McGraw Hill.

Gallagher, C., Maguire, E. R., Mastrofski, S. D. and Reisig, M. D. (2001) *The public image of the police.* Final report to the International Association of Chiefs of Police. Available at www.theiacp.org (last accessed January 13, 2013).

Gilligan, C. (1982) *In a different voice: Psychological theory and women's development.* Cambridge, MA: Harvard University Press.

Gray, C. (2002) *A study of state judicial discipline sanctions.* Des Moines, Iowa: American Judicature Society.

Hanna, J. (2012) Sexual abuse is 'rampant': Report faults Kansas over treatment of female inmates. *The Kansas City Star,* September 7, p. A4.

Hassell, K.D. and Brandl, S.G. (2009) An examination of the workplace experiences of police patrol officers: The role of race, sex, and sexual orientation. *Police Quarterly,* 12(4), pp. 408–430.

Hemmens, C., and Atherton, E. (1999) *Use of force: Current practice and policy.* Lanham, MD: American Correctional Association.

Holten, N. G. and Lamar, L. (1991) *The criminal courts: Structures, personnel and processes.* New York: McGraw-Hill.

Idaho Statesman (2009) House votes to impeach federal judge from Texas. *The Idaho Statesman,* June 20, p. A3.

Irons, P. (1999) *A people's history of the Supreme Court: The men and women whose cases and decisions have shaped our Constitution.* New York: Viking Press.

Johnson, K. (2012) Proposal to buy prisons raises ethical concerns. *USA Today,* March 8, p. 6A.

Johnson, R. (2002) *Hard time: Understanding and reforming the prison.* Belmont, CA: Wadsworth/Thomson Learning.

Jordan, R. L. (2006) *Greylord: A study in judicial corruption.* Paper presented at the Annual Conference of Western and Pacific Association of Criminal Justice Educators, Reno, NV, October 11.

Kauffman, K. (1988) *Prison officers and their world.* Cambridge, MA: Harvard University Press.

Kilgannon, C. (2010) Serpico on Serpico. *The New York Times,* January 24, p. 27.

Langseth, P. (2001) *Strengthening judicial integrity against corruption.* Vienna: United Nations Global Programme against Corruption. Available at www.unodc.org

Lee, C. (2008) Study: Government workers at all levels see ethics lapses. *Idaho Statesman,* January 31.

Lee, J. A. and Visano, L. A. (1994) Official deviance in the legal system. In S. Stojokovic, J. Klofas and D. Kalinich (eds), *The administration and management of criminal justice organizations: A book of readings.* Prospect Heights, IL: Waveland Press, pp. 202–231.

Lichtblau, E. (2005) Report finds cover-up in an F.B.I. terror case. *The New York Times,* December 4. Available at http://www.nytimes.com/2005/12/04/politics/04fbi.html?pagewanted=print&_r=0 (last accessed January 13, 2013).

Lichtblau, E. and J. Risen (2005) Spy agency mined vast data trove, officials report. *The New York Times,* December 24, p. A1, A12.

Marquart, J. W. (1995) Doing research in prison: The strengths and weaknesses of full participation as a guard. In K. C. Haas and G. P. Alpert (eds), *The dilemmas of corrections: Contemporary readings.* Prospect Heights, IL: Waveland Press, pp. 166–182.

Marquart, J. W., Barnhill, M. B. and Balshaw-Biddle, K. (2001) Fatal attraction: An analysis of employee boundary violations in a southern prison system, 1995–1998. *Justice Quarterly,* 18(4): 877–910.

Martin, S. E. (1980) *Breaking and entering: Policewomen on patrol.* Berkeley, CA: University of California Press.

Martin, S. E. (1990) *On the move: The status of women in policing.* Washington, DC: Police Foundation.

Mays, G. L. and Winfree, L. T. (2002) *Contemporary corrections.* Belmont, CA: Wadsworth/Thomson Learning.

McIntyre, L. J. (2004) But how can you sleep nights? In S. Stojkovic, J. Klofas and D. Kalinich (eds), *The administration and management of criminal justice organizations: A book of readings.* Long Grove, IL: Waveland Press, pp. 167–198.

McIntyre, D. and Renick, J. (1982) Protecting public employees and employers from sexual harassment. *Public Personnel Management,* 11(13): 282–292.

Merit Systems Protection Board (2005) *Accomplishing our mission: Results of the Merit Principles Survey, 2005.* Available at www.mspb.gov/netsearch/viewdocs.aspx?doc number=251283andversion=25156 (last accessed January 13, 2013).

Muraskin, R. (2001a) Probation and parole officers: Ethical behavior. In R. Muraskin and M. Muraskin (eds), *Morality and the law.* Upper Saddle River, NJ: Prentice Hall, pp. 119–129.

Muraskin, R. (2001b) Corrections/punishment/correctional officer. In R. Muraskin and M. Muraskin (eds), *Morality and the law.* Upper Saddle River, NJ: Prentice Hall, pp. 140–151.

Muraskin, R., and Muraskin, M. (eds) (2001) *Morality and the law.* Upper Saddle River, New Jersey: Prentice Hall.

National Center for State Courts. (1999) *How the public views the state courts: A 1999 national survey.* Report presented at the National Conference on Public Trust and Confidence in the Justice System, May 1999, Washington, DC. Available at http://www.ncsconline.org (last accessed January 13, 2013).

National Institute of Justice. (2005) *Enhancing police integrity.* NIJ Research in Practice, December, 2005. US Department of Justice, Office of Justice Programs. Washington DC: GPO.

News-Leader. (2012) Lab chemist arrested. *News-Leader,* September 29, p. 7A.

News Observer. (2010) Scathing SBI audit says 230 cases tainted by shoddy investigations. *News Observer,* August 27, p. 1.

New York Times. (2012) Former prosecutor in Arizona is disbarred. *The New York Times,* April 11, p. A16.

Nossiter, A. (2009) Civil rights hero, now a judge, is indicted in a bribery case. *The New York Times,* February 14, p. A9.

O'Connor, M. L. (2001) Noble corruption—police perjury—what should we do? In R. Muraskin and M. Muraskin (eds), *Morality and the law.* Upper Saddle River, NJ: Prentice Hall, pp. 91–106.

Pogrebin, M. R. and Poole, E. D. (1998) Women deputies and jail work. *Journal of Contemporary Criminal Justice,* 14(2): 117–134.

Pollock, J. M. (1994) *Ethics in crime and justice: Dilemmas and decisions,* 2nd edn. Belmont, CA: Wadsworth.

Pollock, J. M. (1998) *Ethics in crime and justice: Dilemmas and decisions,* 3rd edn. Belmont, CA: West/Wadsworth.

Pollock, J. M. (2010) *Ethics in crime and justice: Dilemmas and decisions,* 7th edn. Belmont, CA: Wadsworth Thomson Learning.

Rohr, J. A. (1989) *Ethics for bureaucrats: An essay on law and values.* New York, NY: Marcel Dekker, Inc.

Rubinkam, M. and Dale, M. (2009) Judges accused of jailing kids for cash. *Idaho Statesman,* February 12, p. 15.

Saad, L. (2010) Congress ranks last in confidence in institutions. Gallup Polls. Available at www.gallup.com/poll/141512/congress-ranks-last-confidence-institutions.aspx (last accessed January 13, 2013).

Savage, D. G. (2009) A torturous process. *ABA Journal*, 95(2): 24–26.

Scarborough, K. E. and Garrison, C. (2006) Police women in the twentieth-first century. In A. V. Merlo and J. M. Pollock (eds), *Women, law, and social control*. Boston: Allyn and Bacon, pp. 91–110.

Sherman, L.W. (2001) Trust and confidence in criminal justice. Available at www.ncjrs.gov/pdffiles1/nij/189106-1.pdf (last accessed January 13, 2013).

Silverman, I. J. and Vega, M. (1996) *Corrections: A comprehensive view*. Minneapolis/Saint Paul, MN: West Publishing.

Solomon, R. C. (1996) *A handbook for ethics*. Fort Worth, TX: Harcourt Brace College Publishers.

Stohr, M. K., Hemmens, C., Kifer, M. and Schoeler, M. (2000) We know it, we just have to do it: Perceptions of ethical work in prisons and jails. *The Prison Journal*, 80(2): 126–150.

Stohr, M. K., Mays, G. L., Beck, A. C. and Kelley, T. (1998) Sexual harassment in women's jails. *Journal of Contemporary Criminal Justice*, 14(2): 135–155.

Stohr, M. K., Vazquez, S. P., Prescott, C., Green, D., Smith Daniels, S., Fellen, S., Elson, R., Gloerchinger-Granks, G., Aydelotte, J., Musser, W., Uhlenkott, R., Wulfhorst, J. D., Foltz, B. and Raschke, S. (2001) *Idaho crime victimization survey 2000*. Meridian, ID: Idaho State Police.

Strobel, W. P. and Landay, J. S. (2005) Backlash lowers spy agency morale. *Idaho Statesman*, December 25, 2001, p. 10.

Thomas, D. Q. (1996) All too familiar: Sexual abuse of women in US state prisons. Human Rights Watch. Available at www.hrw.org/summaries (last accessed January 13, 2013).

United Nations Office on Drugs and Crime (2012) Strengthening the integrity of the judiciary. United Nations. Available at www.unodc.org/unodc/en/corruption/judiciary.html (last accessed January 13, 2013).

Urbina, I. (2009) 70 youths sue former judges in detention kickback case. *New York Times*. February 27, p. A19.

US Merit Systems Protection Board, Office of Policy Evaluation. (1981) *Sexual harassment in the federal government*. Washington DC: GPO.

US Merit Systems Protection Board, Office of Policy Evaluation. (1988) *Sexual harassment in the federal government*. Washington DC: GPO.

Welch, M. (1996) *Corrections: A critical approach*. New York, NY: McGraw-Hill.

Yardley, W. (2011) Seattle police under investigation. *Idaho Statesman*, April 1, p. A9.

Zimmer, L. E. (1986) *Women guarding men*. Chicago, IL: University of Chicago Press.

Zupan, L. (1992) The progress of women correctional officers in all-male prisons. In I. L.

Moyers (ed.), *The changing roles of women in the criminal justice system*. Prospect Heights, IL: Waveland Press, pp. 232–244.

4 The administrative state and management theories in perspective

Administration is the most obvious part of government; it is government in action; it is the executive, the operative, the most visible side of government, and is of course as old as government itself.

(Woodrow Wilson 1887: 11)

[P]roper management of the work lives of human beings, of the way in which they earn their living, can improve them and improve the world and in this sense be a utopian or revolutionary technique.

(Abraham Maslow 1961: 1)

The problem is that most businesses haven't caught up to this new understanding of what motivates us. Too many organizations – not just companies, but governments and nonprofits as well – still operate from assumptions about human potential and individual performance that are outdated, unexamined, and rooted more in folklore than in science. ... For too long, there's been a mismatch between what science knows and what business does.

(Daniel H. Pink 2009: 9–10)

Introduction: a bit of background

Much of management theory regarding the operation of corrections, policing, and courts derives from the private sector. Despite Appleby's (1945) claim that government work is different from the private sector, management theories applied to the public and private sectors have usually been developed and tested in businesses. This is not to say that scholars in universities have not written extensively on public sector "administration." In fact, back when Woodrow Wilson was a political scientist at Princeton (1887), the future president wrote one of the first articles about how the administration, or management, of government is a separate issue from the politics of it. He also maintained that there should be a "science of administration" (Henry 1987).

Of course any scientific approach requires theories, and some of the first of these to develop arose from the private sector and were only later, and sometimes awkwardly, applied to public organizations. A theory is "a set of ideas, concepts, principles, or methods used to explain a wide set of observed facts" (Webster 1992: 1098). Generally, this definition suits our purposes. As we review the major theorists on management in this chapter, however, we will find that such folk often believe that theories not only describe what is, in accordance with Webster's (1992) definition, but also prescribe what should be.

As we found in the discussion of the influence of environmental factors on management practices, theories exist in a context. In Chapter 2 we saw that part of that context or overlay consists of the competing public service values of democratic accountability and neutral competence, which tend to shape the role and motivation of workers. Another key piece of that context is the extent to which the attributes of an administrative state exist. In this chapter, we discuss in detail these attributes, along with the predominant management theories that operate within this larger criminal justice framework. We end the chapter with a discussion of creativity and how that might be harnessed in criminal justice organizations to improve operations and the dispensation of justice in our communities.

The administrative state

A thorough understanding of management theories also requires some grasp of the nature of an administrative state. By "state" here we are referring generally to the government. By "administrative" we mean that part of government, usually the executive branch, which is engaged in the day-to-day operations of government. Such an understanding of the administrative state is necessary because modern management cannot exist without some sophistication in it. In other words, there needs to be a superstructure or prerequisites for democratic government to exist and for management of organizations to be at a minimum adequate. Throughout human history, the degree to which such a state existed and its level of complexity, given the time period, varied widely. Van Riper (1987: 6) notes there are six attributes of an administrative state that derive from the work of the German philosopher Max Weber (see Box 4.1). Those first six attributes are as follows:

1 A workable organization in the classical hierarchical sense.
2 The recruitment of expertise by merit.
3 Rational decision making.
4 The rule of law, with an emphasis on equality before the law.
5 Written procedures and records.
6 Not only a money economy, but also sufficient public funds to support a complex administrative apparatus.

**Box 4.1 A Brief synopsis of the life and times
of Max Weber**

Max Weber (1864–1920) was a German citizen, trained in the law, who taught at Berlin University for most of his life (Pugh *et al.* 1985). His intellectual and philosophical explorations were quite broad and included a study of the then predominant religions (i.e., Judaism, Christianity, Buddhism) and economic development. His work on organizations was focused on "authority structures" and their categorization. He observed that the dominant rational–legal institution in modern society had a bureaucratic structure. He thought that a bureaucratic structure led to greater efficiency and regularity in organizational operations, which in turn paved the way for the spread of the capitalistic economic system, the smooth functioning of which had order and objectivity as prerequisites. Most modern studies of organizations and authority begin with Weber, though his influence was not felt in the United States till after his death, when his writings were translated into English.

To these six attributes from Weber, Van Riper adds the following four:

7 At least a modest base in quantitative data and technique.
8 Adequate supporting technology, especially pertaining to records, communications, and numeracy.

9   The enforcement of responsibility and ethical standards.
10 All of the above in a moderately developed and mutually supporting arrangement.(1987: 6)

Let us review these ten attributes in order. The first attribute refers to the basic structure of the organizations in the state. For Weber and Van Riper this structure should be hierarchical, in what one might visualize as a pyramidal shape. In organizations with a hierarchical shape there is a clearly defined leader at the top who has most of the power, and the rest of the organization's members are followers. Similarly, in the larger state there are leaders who also wield most of the power and followers who abide by their decisions. Of course, this power in a democracy is far from absolute and is tempered by the electoral process, the role and mission of organizations, and the motivation of workers and citizens.

A related attribute, which illustrates a distinct preference for neutral competence on the part of Van Riper, is that of recruitment based on merit. This attribute, as well as the first, the third (rational decision making), and the fourth (rule of law and equality before the law), may provide the administrative state and the organizations that operate in that context with a degree of legitimacy. If the public believes that people are hired because of what they know, not who they know (attribute 2); that decisions are made in an explainable way with a consideration of tradition, benefits, and drawbacks (attribute 3); that the law, not a person, determines what the law is and how individuals are treated (attribute 4); and that there is someone to take responsibility for that decision (attribute 1), then people may be more likely to regard the operations of the state and its organizations as fair and just.

Written rules and procedures, as required in attribute 5, are necessary as the administrative state and its organizations become more complex. It would be impossible to operate a courtroom or a police department without such written directives, let alone the larger governmental apparatus. Such an argument also holds true for attribute 6, which requires a money economy, plus a surplus. Governmental entities—indeed, even private organizations of any size—cannot operate efficiently on a barter economy, nor can they continue to operate on a volunteer basis. Hence there must not only be a money economy, but enough money to pay for government operation to exist—even, dare we say it, flourish.

Attributes 7 and 8 are necessary to provide vital information to governmental entities. If there is no information on the number of citizens (a census), the recidivism rate, and the programs that work best, and/or the technology does not exist to collect it, then organizations operate in the dark in terms of decision making.

Attribute 9 is particularly critical if there is to be a sense of order and justice in an administrative state and among the organizations that must operate in that context. If unethical behavior is allowed to continue unchecked either in the private sector (if, e.g., some bank and investment officials had not been apprehended, tried, and punished for their crimes related to the 2007 recession), or in the public sector for the governmental officials who prosecute when there is little evidence of guilt, then people have the perception that government is not acting in a manner that is in accordance with our core beliefs. In other words, it appears that when ethical standards are ignored because of the money and power of the offender, the legitimacy of the government and its organizations (including those in criminal justice) comes into question.

Finally, the last attribute is believed to be necessary because it ameliorates all the others. For instance, and by way of example, an administrative state these days cannot operate well without a money economy, which makes it possible to attract and train qualified personnel to operate technology to determine whether the organization is applying the law in an equal fashion. In other words, all these attributes of an administrative state are interwoven and have provided the backdrop for the development of management theories and their implementation.

Management theories

Some see tracings of management theory in ancient and medieval writings on organizations and government:

> After all, it was Aristotle who first wrote of the importance of culture to management systems, ibn Taymiyyah who used the scientific method to outline the principles of administration within the framework of Islam, and Machiavelli who gave the world the definitive analysis of the use of power.
>
> (Shafritz and Ott 2001: 21)

Socrates remarks on the similarities between an organizational structure that functions as well for the public as for the private sector, and the basic structure of hierarchy and specialization is laid out by Moses in the Bible.

In the first chapter of *The Wealth of Nations*, Adam Smith discusses the value of the "division of labour." His basic contention is that an individual depends on the joint labor of any number of workers to make modern life possible:

> We shall be sensible that without the assistance and cooperation of many thousands, the very meanest person in a civilized country could not be provided, even according to, what we very falsely imagine, the easy and simple manner in which he is commonly accommodated.
>
> (Smith 1776: 12)

In other words, the production of food, clothing, housing, transportation, and entertainment for the collective good require the individual work and specialization of thousands.

For the purposes of simplification and clarity, we like to categorize management theories into two main paradigms, or ways of viewing the management world. These two paradigms are traditional (or classical) theories and human relations (or resource) theories. Some theories do not neatly fit these categorizations, and so we note at the outset that, much like the public service values of democratic accountability and neutral competency explored in the preceding chapter, few organizations in criminal justice are managed in a way that fits only one of these theories at any given time. Moreover, public administration, psychology, and business scholars describe a number of theories and philosophies that reach beyond, and improve upon, both traditional and human relations theories; examples include structural organization theory, systems theory, power and politics organization, organization culture critiques, organization culture reform movements, and the influence of the information age on organizations (Shafritz and Ott 2001). We will discuss these two sets of theories and theorists and then add some of the most influential theories, such as systems theory, which represent hybrids and extensions of traditional and human relations theories. Establishing a rough demarcation line between these theories does serve to put their more outstanding differences in sharp relief, to facilitate an analysis.

Traditional Theories of Management

Max Weber (1864–1920) and Frederick W. Taylor (1856–1917) are often thought of as the two thinkers who, when their contributions are combined, created the basis for traditional management theory. Weber's contribution is seen in his conceptualization of what a bureaucracy is. As an astute social observer of his time, Weber (2001, first printed in English in 1946) noticed that a distinct type of organization, a bureaucracy, was becoming predominant in his home country of Germany and in all of Europe. Because he described this phenomenon, some have made the mistake of believing that he advocated it, which is not true (Shafritz and Ott 2001; Weber 2001). He merely remarked on its existence and its resilience, and defined it. For Weber, there are several, but at least these three, essential components of a *bureaucracy*:

- hierarchy;
- specialization of roles;
- rule of law (including formal administrative rules).

The first term refers to a pyramidal structure of the organization whereby authority, power, and communication are centered at the top and diffused down through the organization. The second term, specialization, is important as it allows the bureaucracy to compartmentalize so that each person, rather than being a generalist, becomes an expert in a narrowly defined task. Rule of law and/or adherence to formal rules is important to ensure order and predictability of operations in the organization. Rules provide the blueprint for all workers to follow.

Frederick W. Taylor's book *The Principles of Scientific Management*, published in 1911, provided some of the other essential ingredients of the traditional management mix (see Box 4.2). As an engineer, Taylor was concerned with the mechanics of the operation of the organization. His thoughts, culminating in his book, were shaped by the great American progressive period (roughly 1880s to 1920s) and reflect the hope that many in those years placed in social engineering. He also subscribed to the idea of bureaucracy as described by Weber. That is, he clearly believed in a hierarchical structure for the private sector businesses he analyzed, and he believed in compartmentalized tasks and orderly, rule-bound organizations.

Box 4.2 Frederick W. Taylor, scientific management, and the pig iron story

Frederick Winslow Taylor (1856–1917) was trained as an engineer. He began his work as a laborer in a steel mill and eventually rose through the ranks to become chief engineer (Pugh *et al.* 1985). Later he became a consultant, as his ideas were published and gained currency. He began publication with an article in 1895, followed by a book in 1903 and, in 1911, the publication of his oft-cited *Principles*

of Scientific Management. Taylor was the founder of the scientific management movement and believed that the careful study of workers and the workplace would yield an understanding of the "one best way" to do the work and the "first rate worker" or "high-priced man" who performs it that way. He thought that management techniques could be improved to achieve the greatest profit for both management and workers. His work was often seen as controversial, even in his lifetime, and was characterized as inhumane. To be fair, Pugh and his colleagues (1985) note that one of Taylor's basic tenets, which was never implemented in American business, was unlimited earnings for the "first rate or first class man." The "pig iron story" was included in Taylor's 1911 book to illustrate how managers should interact with workers to motivate them to perform at a higher level (see the exercise at the end of the chapter).

What Taylor added was the application of the scientific method to organization study—hence the title of his book, *Scientific Management*—coupled with a theory on how best to motivate workers. **Motivation** for our purposes will be defined as "[to] impel, incite; or a stimulus prompting a person to act in a certain way" (Webster 1986: 1475). In one sense or another, all management theories are at least in part about how best to motivate workers. That motivation may come in the form of internal or external forces for the individual, depending on the theory.

In general, the scientific method is an approach to discovering the truth about phenomena. Taylor believed that if managers wanted to know the truth about how best to manage workers, they should apply this method of study. Thus, he recommended that managers study the work and the workers, formulate theories about how the work is best done and who is the "first rate worker," test those theories, and then align the information they collect as support for, or refutation of, the theory. By engaging in this scientific approach, Taylor thought that managers could identify the "one best way" of doing the work of any enterprise.

By way of illustrating the components of *Scientific Management*, one of the authors asks for volunteer actors to take on the two parts in the "pig iron story." When students act out the parts of Taylor and the hypothetical worker, "Schmidt," the class is able to discern the essential elements of Taylor's theory. Students note that this story demonstrates both Taylor's belief in the manager as "scientist" and his means of motivating workers. Taylor believed that the "first rate worker" could be motivated through a "piece rate" approach by using "money" to more efficiently increase worker output. In turn, this "first rate worker," who is receiving better pay and will become a "high-priced man," will serve as a model for other workers on how to do work "the one best way" and thus receive better pay. A worker under this theory becomes much like a machine part, which, once greased with money, functions quite predictably. To recap, the essential elements of Taylor's Scientific Management are as follows:

- use of the scientific method by managers;
- discovery of the "first rate worker";
- discovery of the "one best way";
- motivation of workers with money;
- use of a piece rate to encourage more work output;
- workers seen as machine parts.

Students also note some values that come through the "pig iron story" that Taylor did not perhaps intend. For instance, the content of the story makes clear that Taylor does not think much of the intelligence of the worker "Schmidt," who speaks broken English with an obvious German accent. Students are rightly put off by the assumption that immigrants are stupid and easily manipulated by money. Indeed, this patronizing sentiment regarding immigrants and those engaged in labor is a criticism which has been leveled at some progressives of Taylor's time (Rothman 1980). Moreover, the dictatorial approach of Taylor *vis-à-vis* Schmidt, whom he orders about, does not play well with the students either. But then, the students are part of a culture of a century away from Taylor's world, and that may make all the difference for them and for workers of today (see the discussion of the Creative Class at the end of this chapter).

Of course, the traditional management theory has been quite influential in both the public and the private sectors. Ford Motor Company's assembly line, as well as virtually any business of any size, was, and is, influenced by the bureaucratic and scientific management components of traditional theory (Kanigel 1997; Shafritz and Ott 2001). Virtually all public sector criminal justice agencies have been and are organized as bureaucracies, with some elements of scientific management embedded in their formal and informal cultures. Historically, managers treated correctional workers almost as badly as the latter treated inmates. And some managers in policing and corrections still take a dictatorial and hierarchical approach toward their workers. As with our students, however, such an approach is off-putting to modern workers and may not enhance their motivation, if it ever did (Pink 2009).

A number of scholars, both before and since Weber and Taylor, wrote about and/or supported a traditional approach to management. In France in 1916, Henri Fayol, a private sector executive engineer and a contemporary of Taylor, lauded some of the essential elements of traditional management in terms of division of labor, unity of command, centralization, rate pay, and discipline (in Shafritz and Ott 2001). He developed one of the first sets of principles of management and believed that these principles could be applied successfully in any workplace, public or private. Luther Gulick (1937), building on the work of Fayol, outlined the seven major functions of executive management, or POSDCORB(E): planning, organizing, staffing, directing, coordinating, reporting, budgeting, and (some may like to add) evaluating.

But Fayol moved beyond the traditional theorists too. He noted that in practice, hierarchy, or the "scalar chain" as he describes it, does not always work efficiently for businesses. Sometimes it is necessary for organizations to communicate horizontally, for instance, and this is not a rare occurrence in organizations, despite their formal hierarchical structure. Also, unlike Taylor, Fayol recognized the value of "equity" in the workplace—a concept that, for him, combined the use of kindliness and justice in relations between workers and managers. In fact, he finished his 1916 article on management by extolling the virtues of teams as a means of creating and maintaining an esprit de corps among workers. Although Fayol noted that it is easy to build dissension and jealousy in the workplace, such sentiments tend to hamper productivity rather than enhance it (a thought that presages the Hawthorne experiments that began a little over a decade later).

Criticisms of traditional theories of management

Critics of the traditional management theory identify several false assumptions in the approach (Kanigel 1997; McGregor 1957; Ouchi 1981; Pink 2009). For one, people at work are motivated by factors in addition to money (e.g., respect, a sense of accomplishment, social needs). The traditional approach acknowledges only the formal, and not the informal, subcultures at play in the workplace, which means that any analysis of the workplace based on a traditional approach is liable to be inaccurate.

Second, the traditional approach to management ignores all the talent, creativity, and insight found among lower level workers. Such workers and their abilities are devalued in a traditionally operated organization, which means that the business entity is not making the best use of its human resources. Since in criminal justice agencies, about 80 to 90 percent of the cost of doing business resides in personnel, this may add up to a substantial loss.

Finally, and relatedly, the traditional approach to management ignores the human needs of workers and the larger community environment. Where is the evidence of recognition of the need for kindliness and justice in relations between workers and managers that Fayol identified in 1916? In a postscript to the "pig iron story," students have wondered aloud what happened to the workers who could not carry pig iron like Schmidt? What happened when workers were sick or old? For that matter, what happened to Schmidt in his old age? Are all workers really expendable? Where, they ask, is the human care in that? And what about those workers who may be older, who cannot carry the weight of the pig iron—either literally or, when applied to other workplaces, figuratively—but who carry the traditions and knowledge vital to the work in their heads? Do not the organization and the work suffer when they are let go? What responsibilities do organizations, both public and private, have to individuals and communities beyond just the provision of jobs? In other words, the traditional theory of management is too mechanistic and cold. It makes workers expendable and the promise of the "good life" for most American workers a fable.

But the traditional approach to management has been so ubiquitous in both the private and the public sectors in part because it works for *someone* (Jaques 2001; Shafritz and Ott 2001). Though its flaws are apparent in its mechanistic, and some might say soulless, manipulation of workers, the truth is that bureaucracies exist because they can be an efficient way of organizing workers and work (Gawande 2012; Jaques 2001). A scientific approach to analyzing how the work is done and who does it best also seems to make sense. And—to a point, at least—people are mighty motivated by money; some are motivated by nothing else.

Systems theory

Although Taylor's scientific approach provided a framework for the effective measurement of workers and organizations to unearth "the one best way," the onset of the technological age brought forth more complex methods for finding out "optimal solutions" to organizational problems (Shafritz and Ott 2001). Systems theory represented a departure from classical organization theory (which viewed the closed organization as static and predictable). This is true because under systems theory the organization is considered to be open to dynamic, unpredictable environmental influences as well as to internal forces, and is viewed as much more complex and in a constant state of flux (Gordon and Milakovich 1998; Shafritz and Ott 2001). Moreover, the systems approach has provided a nice segue into the modern human relations/resources theoretical paradigm.

One way in which the difference between the two eras of scientific measurement can be delineated is simply by understanding the level of quantitative rigor used to analyze causality in organizational problem solving. With this change in rigor came the refocusing of organizational goals away from trying to control and predict everything (Gordon and Milakovich 1998). The advent of the computer made available the powerful statistical software needed to analyze increasingly large numbers of people and organizations systematically. The simple cause-and-effect statement has become infinitely complex, while numerous other variables can be added to the problem equation almost effortlessly; which means that this ability to analyze and organize a vast amount of data has impacted the way we think about organizations.

Just about every social setting can be dissected into various working components, the whole of which may be referred to as a system. Take for example, the Adam Walsh Child Protection and Safety Act of 2006, which was passed to expand the national sex offender registry, toughen federal laws against sex offenders who prey on children, and support law enforcement efforts to dampen the negative effects of child pornography on the Internet (White House 2006). We shall consider the passing of this act as an input, which may consist of demands on local police organizations to conform to the legislative requirements and may also provide support in the form of resources. The police organization as a system then reacts to these inputs and makes adjustments or outputs. For example, these adjustments may surface as new organizational goals and funding for new police training and staff. These outputs are then given environmental feedback, which then influences the inputs, and the process begins again (see Figure 4.1 for a simple schema of this theory).

Briefly, the systems perspective can be understood as an ever-changing ecosystem. According to Norbert Wiener (1948, in Shafritz and Ott 2001), there are five main active components within the model (eco)-system: the environment, the process, outputs, inputs, and feedback. Along with these components there are two main information-processing systems, the biological (human) and the mechanical (technology; Shafritz and Ott 2001). Self and organizational regulation and change can be monitored and dealt with "[t]hrough biological, social, or technological systems that can identify problems, do something about them, and receive feedback to adjust themselves automatically" (Shafritz and Ott 2001: 243). This multifaceted interplay between the environment and the organization is labeled a process, which constantly receives feedback through informed reciprocal bursts of inputs and outputs (Shafritz and Ott 2001). This pattern is absorbed and analyzed through technology and its utilization and implementation by people; this cycle, in turn, affects the processes. The acknowledgment of the workplace or organization as a complex and dynamic system of ever-changing reciprocal processes, which are interlocked in a constant battle for homeostasis or equilibrium, has forced scholars to analyze the "organization" as such.

Human relations or human resource theories

Just as the traditional theory of management gained currency in all sectors of American society, the germ for an opposite set of theories began to develop. Mary Parker Follett in 1926 was the first to recognize the value of a participatory management style for leaders that is dependent on the situation. Situational leadership will be discussed in much more detail in Chapter 7, but suffice it to say here that this precept of participatory management (which involves lower level workers in the management of an organization) flies in the face of traditional management theory, which values hierarchy and top-down, not bottom-up, communication. Parker Follett recognized that

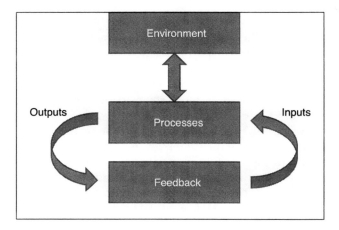

Figure 4.1 Simplified systems theory diagram

not only does giving orders rarely work practically, without the consent and involvement of people in receipt of those orders, but it is also bad business policy (Parker Follett 1926). For Parker Follett, the giving of orders will be more effective and the dignity of the worker will be maintained when all are involved in work decisions. Moreover, workers will take responsibility for their activity if they are given some say in it (this is called "ownership" today). Notably, at the time that Parker Follett wrote these words she was virtually alone in her beliefs, but that was soon to change as managers began to assimilate the findings of the Hawthorne experiments.

Box 4.3 Mary Parker Follett's pioneering work

Mary Parker Follett was born in Quincy, Massachusetts on September 3 1868. She graduated from Radcliffe College in 1898, but was denied a doctorate at Harvard because she was a woman. She worked as a social worker and by 1917 was the vice-president of the National Community Center Association. She published several books and works on politics, management, and organizations. At one point she served as a management consultant to President Theodore Roosevelt, and she was one of the first women to address the London School of Economics. Her work to humanize the workplace presaged the human relations movement and influenced the theorists who followed her. "Rosabeth Moss Kanter, of the Harvard Business School, has observed that 'many so-called new management ideas are previewed in Follett's work'" (Tonn 2003: x).

The Hawthorne Experiments

The Hawthorne experiments, which took place from 1927 to 1933 in the Hawthorne plant of Western Electric, near Chicago, were ostensibly set up to test scientific management. These experiments were conducted by Harvard professor Elton Mayo, along with his colleagues Frederick Roethlisberger, George Homans, and T. N. Whitehead. The Hawthorne experiments, and the conclusions drawn from them, set the stage for conceptualizing the management of work in an alternative fashion.

The experiments began in 1924 as a series of productivity studies, conducted from a scientific management perspective, which tinkered with environmental conditions such as lighting, room temperature, and humidity to increase worker productivity. Mayo and his colleagues were called in to take over the research in 1927 because the reasons for the outcomes were not clear (Shafritz and Ott 2001). As Roethlisberger (1941: 158) recalled later, "The purpose was to find out the relation of the quality and quantity of illumination to the efficiency of industrial workers." Experimental conditions were imposed and a "test group" and a "control group" were identified. In the initial set of studies the test group was subjected to more and less illumination by candles and they were led to believe that illumination was increased or decreased when it was not. In each of these cases, no matter what was done in terms of illumination, the workers' output in the test group remained the same as the control group whose illumination remained constant throughout these experiments. As Roethlisberger recalls, it was not until the illumination for the test group was reduced to the equivalent of moonlight—or when it became physically impossible to see—that the output of the test group declined.

The researchers were not sure what to make of these findings. Scientific management principles would have predicted a direct cause-and-effect relationship between the conditions of work and the output of workers. Thus, if lighting increased, so should productivity; if lighting decreased, so should productivity. The experimenters were not sure whether the problem lay in the workers, the experiment, or themselves. More research was planned, and Roethlisberger notes that there was some suspicion that the real culprit was an analytical approach that ignored the human situation in work: "The experimenters had obtained no human data; they had been handling electric-light bulbs and plotting average output curves. Hence their results had no human significance" (Roethlisberger 1941: 159).

So the researchers set up another set of experiments on a segregated test group of five women that lasted for five years. They varied the work breaks from one to two, they gave the women Saturday morning off (they usually worked forty-eight hours per week), they decreased the length of the working day, and they provided lunch during one break. During this whole period, productivity increased. When the researchers took all of these amenities away and productivity *still* increased, the researchers had to ask: What is going on here?

One conclusion was that what is now known as the **Hawthorne Effect** was at play. This is the belief that when humans know they are being studied or watched, they will react to that observation. In other words, the women were reacting to the presence of the experimenters, not to the experimental conditions.

Another reason for the improved output by these women may be that management practices during the experiment completely changed. The input of the women was taken into consideration in terms of experimental conditions, and the women's welfare and health was of concern. In effect, the workers received positive attention from management and their input was valued. "Inadvertently a change had been introduced which was far more important than the planned experimental innovations: the customary supervision in the room had been revolutionized. This accounted for the better attitudes of the girls and their improved rate of work" (Roethlisberger 1941: 161). The experimenters realized that worker output was tied to workers' attitudes and feelings about their labor, and workers' attitudes and feelings about their labor were affected by management.

The next stage of the research was to develop a uniform interviewing technique whereby experimenters could go into any plant and listen to the workers' concerns and complaints. Then the social behavior of a group of men was studied separately over a period of time, and it was determined that in groups, there are *norms* for worker output that operate independently of management decrees. For instance, workers were socialized to avoid being either "rate busters" (people who outperformed others by substantial amounts) or "chiselers," who worked too little. Nor should one be a "squealer," who tattles on group members, or act in an "officious" manner. From these collective efforts, the researchers concluded the following *vis-à-vis* management (Roethlisberger 1941: 162–166):

1 They found that the behavior of workers could not be understood apart from their feelings or sentiments.
2 They found that sentiments are easily disguised, and hence are difficult to recognize and to study.
3 They found that manifestations of sentiment could not be understood as things in and by themselves, but only in terms of the total situation of the person.
4 Management should listen to workers.
5 Workers operate within the accepted social standards or norms for group output. You must not be a "rate buster" or a "chiseler." Worker output will vary, but it will tend to fit within an acceptable group range.
6 People are social animals and want to be part of a group.
7 Worker output is not always directly related to intelligence or ability.
8 The social functions of the group influence worker behavior.

9   Though pay is important, it is only part of the social recognition that motivates workers.
10   Most of us want the satisfaction that comes from being accepted and recognized as people of worth by our friends and associates.
11   People want meaningful work and skills that give social recognition.
12   Management practices are archaic and need to recognize that workers are social animals and operate in that context. If this civilization is to survive, we must obtain a new understanding of human motivation and behavior in business organizations—an understanding which can be simply but effectively practiced.

The hierarchy of needs

The Hawthorne experiments set the stage for the development of a theory of human motivation, or Abraham Maslow's Hierarchy of Needs theory (also known as the actualization theory), first published in 1943 (see Box 4.4). This theory provides the framework for understanding the motivation of employees used in most of the management theories that followed it. Its importance in shaping the modern understanding of behavior in organizations cannot be overestimated.

Box 4.4 Abraham Maslow

In a description of Maslow (in *Maslow on Management*, first printed 1961, reprinted in 1998), Stephens and Heil note that Maslow taught psychology at Brooklyn College. He then worked at Brandeis University and later served as president of the American Psychological Association. In his career he published hundreds of articles and books, but he is best known for his development of the "hierarchy of needs." "Maslow believed that human beings aspired to become self-actualizing" (Stephens and Heil 1998: xx). He died in 1970 at the age of 62.

Maslow believed that there is a hierarchy of needs that motivates human beings in their lives and in their work behavior. The needs appearing at the bottom of this hierarchy were seen as the most important motivators. Those lower level needs (physiological and security-related) were "prepotent," and until they were satisfied, at least relatively, a person was not as likely to be motivated by upper-level needs. The needs in order of importance were as follows (Maslow 1943: 167–172, 1961):

- physiological needs (food, water, sex);
- security needs (physical safety, job security, provision for old age, etc.);

- love needs (need to belong, the need to give and receive love, the need to be accepted by associates);
- self-esteem needs (also known as self-respect—need for achievement, recognition, importance and for confidence in the world, the desire for a reputation or prestige);
- self-actualization needs (need to be creative, to fulfill one's potential, becoming what you were meant or fitted to be).

Maslow believed that people who were relatively satisfied in these needs were the most creative and resilient of all. A precondition to the satisfaction of these needs, he thought, was the existence of freedom (Maslow 1943: 172):

> Such conditions as freedom to speak, freedom to do what one wishes so long as no harm is done to others, freedom to express one's self, freedom to investigate and seek for information, freedom to defend one's self, justice, fairness, honesty, orderliness in the group are examples of preconditions for basic need satisfactions. Thwarting in these freedoms will be reacted to with a threat or emergency response.

Management's role was to provide a work environment where people could meet these basic needs (Maslow 1961). If management succeeded in fulfilling this role, Maslow believed, workers' motivation to produce was likely to improve.

He did note, however, that achievement of these needs was not as fixed as it might appear (Maslow 1943). For instance, he thought that for some the achievement of some needs (e.g., self-esteem) might be more important than others (e.g., love), and that some people who are driven by the need to be creative (the starving artist cliché) might bypass the satisfaction of some needs and be motivated primarily by self-actualization.

He also believed that there are others whose need for love, respect, or self-actualization in the workplace had been deadened by chronic unemployment and who are then satisfied and motivated by steady employment. Relatedly, he thought that those who were starved for love as children are not motivated by love as adults. Maslow also acknowledged that behavior is motivated or acted out for other reasons than these needs (e.g., ignorant people sometimes act stupidly), that there are multiple motivations for behavior (e.g., people eat for hunger and for love), and that sometimes people ignore the importance of their needs.

Maslow (1943: 173) states unequivocally that those who have relative satisfaction of the basic needs all their lives are the most likely to be able to withstand adversity:

> They are the "strong" people who can easily weather disagreements or opposition, who can swim against the stream of public opinion and

who can stand up for the truth at great personal cost. It is just the ones who have loved and been well loved, and who have had many deep friendships who can hold out against hatred, rejection or persecution.

Theories X and Y

A number of theories in the human relations genre followed the Hawthorne experiments and the publication and promulgation of Maslow's hierarchy of needs theory. One of the most well- known of these was Douglas McGregor's Theory X and Theory Y, as explicated in his 1957 article "The Human Side of Enterprise." (Box 4.5 supplies a brief synopsis of McGregor's life.) In that article he laid out the traditional view of management's task, or Theory X: "in harnessing human energy to organizational requirements" (McGregor 1957: 179). According to proponents of Theory X, both materials and people must be organized, controlled, and motivated by management to achieve organizational ends. The management and control of the workers is central to Theory X because people are assumed to be passive and are assumed to not like, or want, to work. McGregor (1957: 179) identifies additional beliefs that underpin the traditional Theory X:

- The average man is by nature indolent—he works as little as possible.
- He lacks ambition, dislikes responsibility, and prefers to be led.
- He is inherently self-centered, indifferent to organizational needs.
- He is by nature resistant to change.
- He is gullible, not very bright, the ready dupe to the charlatan and the demagogue.

Box 4.5 Douglas McGregor

Douglas McGregor (1906–1964) was a social psychologist who for a time served as president of Antioch College. For ten years in later life he was a management professor at the Massachusetts Institute of Technology (Pugh *et al.* 1985). McGregor is best known for explicating the traditional assumptions and style of management (Theory X) and those of human relations (Theory Y). He used the Maslowian concepts of human needs as a framework for his belief that modern organizations were those that provided a supportive environment which met the needs of workers.

McGregor (1957; Heil *et al.* 2000) believed that those who managed under the precepts of Theory X were just fundamentally wrong. He believed that they confused cause and effect in terms of motivation and thus misinterpreted the resultant behavior in the workplace. Instead he believed that a

Theory Y manager, who understood the human side of enterprise—hence McGregor's title—would build on the hierarchy of needs theory proposed by Maslow. He believed that those who did not have these needs satisfied were in effect "sick" and that this sickness would be apparent in their behavior. In fact, he believed that many negative work behaviors, such as passivity, hostility, and the refusal to accept responsibility, were symptoms of this sickness and not inherent characteristics of human nature, as those of the Theory X persuasion might think. McGregor's (1957: 183) Theory Y included the following concepts:

- Management is responsible for organizing the elements of productive enterprise—money, materials, equipment, and people—in the interest of economic ends.
- People are not by nature passive or resistant to organizational needs. They have become so as a result of experience in organizations.
- The motivation, the potential for development, the capacity for assuming responsibility, the readiness to direct behavior toward organizational goals are all present in people. Management does not put them there. It is a responsibility of management to make it possible for people to recognize and develop these human characteristics for themselves.
- The essential task of management is to arrange organizational conditions and methods of operation so that people can achieve their own goals best by directing their own efforts toward organizational objectives.

McGregor (1957; Heil *et al.* 2000) recommends that managers create these optimal conditions by decentralizing and delegating, enlarging jobs to make them more meaningful to workers, engaging in participatory and consultative management, and ensuring worker involvement in performance appraisals. He disparaged managers who only added the window dressing of participatory management or delegated tasks without truly recognizing the worth and abilities of their workers.

Other human relations-related theories

Other related theories in this genre, such as Chris Argyris's immaturity/maturity theory and Frederick Herzberg's motivation-hygiene theory, continued in a similar vein (Gordon and Milakovich 1998). In Argyris's view, subjecting workers to traditional management practices keeps them "immature," and thus management should work to develop the responsibility and skills of workers by providing the right conditions. Similarly, Herzberg noted that workers tend to be motivated by both the levels of needs identified by Maslow. For Herzberg, "hygiene factors" such as organizational policies, working conditions, interpersonal relationships, and the quality of supervision all affect job satisfaction either positively or negatively

(Schermerhorn *et al.* 1985). Herzberg hoped, though studies did not always confirm, that satisfaction in turn affected performance, hence managers needed to ensure a high level of satisfaction for workers.

Peter Drucker (1954, 1964), a contemporary of McGregor's and a management luminary, was also instrumental in spreading the human relations approach to management, both in the United States and abroad. In the context of a larger reform of the business enterprise, he cajoled executives to systematically study and research their businesses (a scientific management approach), but to be cognizant of the needs and wants of their staffs and the effect that a business has on the larger community (Drucker 1954, 1964). Drucker, in effect, bridged the gap between the traditional and human relations theories of management and between the first version of the latter and all subsequent versions.

Criticisms of early human relations theories of management

Of course, human relations theories have had their share of critics (Gordon and Milakovich 1998). One weakness that is identified is that the democracy assumed under human relations is excessive and may lead to inefficiencies. Jaques (2001) remarks that hierarchy in organizations tends to "work" because it makes the lines of command and tasks explicit. If there are too many people involved in making decisions, then it is difficult to accomplish much.

Some have critiqued the suppression of individuality that might occur when people are urged to always work in groups or teams. In his seminal book *Victims of Groupthink*, Irving Janis (1972) outlines the dangers of "groupthink" for organizations that put too high a premium on group engagement at the expense of individual thought and critique.

A third criticism is that there is an overemphasis on employee happiness and wellbeing. After all, it is the first responsibility of an organization to get the job done, not to fret about whether the workers are content.

And, finally, some have argued that Theory Y-ers' assumption that people are generally kind and naturally exercise self-control is false. This assumption is part of the larger belief system that people are good at heart and should be given freedom, as opposed to the assumption that human nature is basically evil and in need of control. These opposing assumptions lie at the heart of the centuries-old debate about the nature of human nature, and for the more traditional manager the belief that people need no control is just plain false.

Despite these criticisms and concerns about human relations theories, most modern management theories advocate a version of them. Theory Z, teams, total quality management, management by objectives, and learning organizations theories all hold as their basic premise a human relations approach to management. But what is interesting is that in practice such an approach is often still carried out within an organizational structure that is bureaucratic and includes other elements of traditional theories. In other words, modern management in practice, whether in a computer chip manufacturing firm or a police department, is really an amalgamation of traditional and human relations theories.

Modern human relations theories and techniques: Theory Z, TQM, MBO and learning organizations

The **Theory Z management** approach advocated by Ouchi (1981) and others represents a conscious choice to combine some of the important elements of both traditional and human relations theories of management. It also recognizes the importance of the larger environment in influencing and motivating human behavior at work. In fact, Theory Z is distinguished from Theories X and Y because Ouchi centers the organization in the context of the larger social, political, and economic environment. Other social institutions such as schools, families, and religious organizations also influence the work setting for Z proponents.

Theory Z is also a "bridging" theory between Theories X and Y because it recognizes the production needs of X along with the human needs of Y (Klofas *et al.* 1990). To summarize, Theory Z management is concerned with the production needs of X, the human needs of Y, and environmental impact and influence—the unique contribution of Z. Ouchi (1981) highlights the team approach to work in organizations, a concept that he believed distinguished the Japanese workplace from the American workplace of the 1970s. Other attributes included the shared decision making central to other human relations theories, but combined with a distinct career path to motivate workers up the organizational ladder (both X and Y theories).

The logical extension of Theory Z was **total quality management** (TQM), or the idea that the greater the involvement of workers or teams in developing and delivering on organizational goals, the higher their level of commitment to achievement of those goals. When you review the key elements of TQM (see below), you also see remnants of traditional theories or the assumption that people can be motivated by rewards, and that both workers and management must be held accountable for productivity. The key elements of TQM (Gordon and Milakovich 1998: 374) are as follows:

- top-level support and commitment;
- focus on customer satisfaction;
- written productivity and quality goals and an annual improvement plan;
- productivity and quality measures and standards that are consistent with agency goals;

- use of the improvement plan and measurement system to hold managers and employees accountable;
- employee involvement in productivity and quality improvement efforts;
- rewards for quality and productivity achievement;
- training in methods for improving productivity and quality;
- retraining and out-placement for any employees who might be negatively affected by improvement efforts;
- reducing barriers to productivity and quality improvement.

Another derivative of the human relations approach, which was key to Theory Z, was the advent of **quality circles** in American management practice of the 1980s. Developed in the 1960s in Japan by an American (W. Edwards Deming), quality circles are just groups of workers who consider all the data available to them and make decisions. Such circles, in all-important respects, closely resemble the team approach to management and worker engagement that has been popular since the 1980s, in both the public and private sectors (Fink, Jenks, and Willits 1983; Larson and LaFasto 1989). In quality circles and teams we see the full recognition of the importance of the work group and its dynamics as first documented in the Hawthorne experiments some fifty years beforehand. There is also a clear and obvious link between quality circles/teams and TQM (Gordon and Milakovich 1998). In all such practices and philosophies, including management by objectives (MBO), there is an emphasis on employee involvement and empowerment in the workplace as an integral piece of the successful management puzzle.

Management by objectives is a philosophy of management that also contains elements of both the traditional and human relations theories, with particular emphasis on the latter in terms of employee relations. It really caught fire in the private sector in the 1970s and 1980s, but was developed by Drucker (1954) almost twenty years earlier. It is a collaborative approach by all members of the organization to achieve objectives. Fink and his colleagues (1983: 36) note:

> [MBO] says, in essence, that commitment to organizational goals can best be achieved by allowing and encouraging members of the organization to play an active role in setting their own work objectives [through a collaborative process in which superiors and subordinates jointly articulate work objectives, with mutually agreed upon targets and timetables.] This approach to management keeps all members focused on the achievement of specific outcomes, which converge over time toward general goals and purposes.

Another, more recent, innovation in the application of human relations theories has been the conceptualization of organizations as living, evolving, and learning entities (Kaufman 1985; Gordon and Milakovich 1998). The **learning organization** is believed to be one that operates in an open environment, as defined in Chapter 1. For an organization to be effective in such a dynamic milieu, its members must learn from that environment. Because the environment of the organization is continually changing, the organization members must grow, learn, and adapt as well. "Learning organizations are built on many of the same assumptions as those of earlier theories, including shared vision, consistent values, dedication to customer service, and competence" (Gordon and Milakovich 1998: 137).

A related concept that has gained credence in the management literature and that has been particularly espoused by management guru Tom Peters (1987, 1992) is the expectation that organizations and their members will have to take risks and make mistakes to learn. Under traditional management systems, Peters claims, people are punished for their mistakes; so, as rational beings, when they make mistakes they hide them. The problem is that those hidden mistakes do not provide any opportunity for learning. Instead, other organizational members continue to make the same mistakes, and hide them. Moreover, it is only through the taking of some risks that innovation and growth can be achieved. Though under this perspective some mistakes are expected—even welcomed, as they provide a learning opportunity—they make innovation and growth possible for the organization.

Taken in tandem, all the more recent organizational theories and practices require some semblance of the following:

1   A fatter and flatter organizational structure, or a less pyramidal shape to the organization than is traditional.
2   Shared decision making by all sectors of the organization.
3   A mechanism or mechanisms for sharing those decisions.
4   Empowered employees who are willing and able to participate fully in decision making that affects their workplace.
5   Enhancement of top-down communication with bottom-up, horizontal, and diagonal communication avenues.
6   Acceptance and expectation that the organization and its members must adapt, grow, and even take risks, if they hope to achieve objectives.

Of course, any organization wishing to shift from a more traditional format to become a TQM, MBO, or learning/risk-taking organization has much work in front of it. Change of this magnitude takes time, patience, commitment, and persistence over a period of years. Such a change requires a paradigm shift that affects all aspects of management.

Motivating the creative class

In his book *Drive: The Surprising Truth About What Motivates Us*, Daniel Pink (2009) discusses research on what motivates people today. Rather than extrinsic rewards such as money or rewards, or the traditional management approach to motivation, Pink argues that people are instead motivated for the long-term by intrinsic rewards. He admits that in order for workers to be motivated they need a base pay (extrinsic reward) that is fair and that reflects their skills and abilities, but beyond that, people are motivated in workplaces which foster and value their natural creative urges (which are intrinsic). According to the studies and research on motivation which Pink (2009) cites, people excel at work when they are given some autonomy, when they can strive toward mastery, and when their work has purpose.

In tandem with Pink's thesis that people at work, at least in westernized countries, are motivated differently in the creative economy, the idea of a "creative class" has arisen and has begun to influence how people think about work, their lives, and their communities (Florida 2002). The **creative class** has been defined as an economic class which "consists of people who add economic value through their creativity" and who "create meaningful new forms" (Florida 2002: 68). This class includes those who make their living through knowledge, art, or the creation of new ideas or products, but also professional and technical workers who analyze those things. They are a class not because they own property necessarily, but because they tend to group together socially and their cultural, consumption, and social identities are similar to each other.

A discussion of the creative class makes sense here because it provides a modern justification for moving more in the direction of human relations management. Increasingly people who work in policing, courts and corrections are asked to analyze, to problem solve, and to think up new ideas—to be creative—in order to face the challenges of their work. Problem solving policing, drug/mental health/veterans' courts, restorative justice initiatives, therapeutic communities, and just evidence-based practices in all sectors of criminal justice are all dependent on the creative engagement of motivated workers. Yet, the thinking goes, traditional forms of management or the corporatized organizational age spawned by traditional management serve to stifle creativity and to crush innovation. The question then is: How can criminal justice organizations, which tend to be traditionally managed and which need to be operated based on the law and accountability to the law, respond to this need to foster creativity among their workers?

This is not an easy question to answer, nor is there a clearly prescribed path that criminal justice organizational managers might take. Certainly a greater move to human relations management, where that is possible in criminal justice organizations, is a big part of that answer. People who work in criminal justice agencies, almost by definition, have a purpose; it is whether their agency can provide the autonomy and the room to strive toward mastery of their tasks that is in question (see Box 4.6 for an example of creative work in a police department). Key to the management of the creative class, whether in business or criminal justice organizations, is giving them "solid values, clear rules, open communication, good working conditions and fair treatment. People don't want to be abandoned and they don't want to be micromanaged. They don't want to take orders, but they do want direction" (Florida 2002: 133).

Box 4.6 Two examples of creative work in the Springfield, Missouri police department

The city of Springfield, Missouri is located in south-west Missouri, with a growing population of about 160,000 people. At the time of writing (spring 2013), Chief Paul Williams of the Springfield police has been on the job for about three years. In the following he identifies two initiatives by his staff that represent "creative class"-type work in a police department.

1 The Crime Prevention Unit officers knew that research has indicated Neighborhood Watch programs, as usually operated, do not result in definitive reductions in crime. So they came up with a new approach based on studies that indicate that if a "set of eyes" are watching (even in a passive way) there is less likelihood that people will engage in thefts. So, with the involvement of several neighborhoods in town, the team created signs to put at the entrances of neighborhoods which had a photo of a police officer and two neighbors watching entrants, with the legend underneath: "See Something, Say Something." Then the department trained people about what to watch for in their neighborhood to prevent crime. The department also pledged to provide, maintain, and replace the signs as needed if enough neighbors were involved in the training. Since this is a recent initiative, we are waiting to see if crime goes down. In addition, we plan to survey the residents of these neighborhoods about their perceptions of safety and security after the first full year of operation.

2 There has been a problem in Springfield, as in other communities, with mentally ill people being dumped into the jail when they really don't always need to be. About 10 percent of the officers in Springfield receive forty hours of Crisis Intervention Training (CIT), which is devoted to how to deal with the mentally

ill; they know from this training that outside services instead of jail are often called for in such cases. Therefore, the department changed policy and gave officers the autonomy, in cases involving the mentally ill when only a misdemeanor offense had been committed (e.g. urinating in public or disturbing the peace), to divert those cases from the jail to outside mental health services. Working in conjunction with the Green County Sheriff's Office, a federal grant allowed officers to provide services to mentally ill substance abusers who have committed only a minor crime and who are in need of treatment, not incarceration. The effect of this policy is that officers are able to assess the best likely outcome for people in need of services, the jail is not crowded with people who do not need to be there (thus saving money), and people get the services they need to stay out of the criminal justice system. In the past year we were able to divert 25 percent of those who were identified as frequently incarcerated mentally ill offenders, who were also suffering from substance abuse problems, from the jail to treatment and services.

Conclusions: the application of management theories to criminal justice agencies

Some writers on organizations have been skeptical regarding the application of old and new human relations theories to criminal justice. They think that although agencies of criminal justice would undoubtedly benefit from greater sensitivity to employee wellbeing, their organizational missions preclude them from adopting a modified, "fatter and flatter structure." Moreover, greater employee engagement in decision making is impractical for organizations that must react to emergencies, adjudicate difficult matters, and house and supervise people who sometimes have little concern for the niceties of behavior. Such skepticism may be misplaced, however, for two reasons: First, criminal justice organizations have as great a need for effective management as any other private or public sector organization, and second, human relations management practices are already ubiquitous in criminal justice organizations, as elsewhere. *It is not a matter of whether criminal justice organizations will adopt human relations practices, but how much they will adopt them.* Therefore, our focus for the management of criminal justice should center on the latter issue, as the former is already settled.

As a case in point, consider the existence of inmate team unit management in corrections. Since the 1970s and continuing into the 2010s, many prisons, jails, probation and parole departments, and juvenile facilities have implemented a team process for classifying and managing inmates/offenders. We can also include police and sheriff's departments that engage in team policing in neighborhoods. What is this process but a replication of quality circles?

Or consider most performance appraisal systems in courts, corrections, and police departments. Most supervisors ask employees for their input before, during, or after an appraisal. Oftentimes a supervisor will sit down with the employee beforehand and develop appropriate goals for that person. What is this engagement but a version of MBO?

Training in criminal justice often includes recognition of the importance of employee participation and shared leadership and decision making. Because human relations practices have become so ingrained in the thinking on management, leaders in such agencies will often claim they are transparent or open even if they are not.

That said, there is much that can be done to move criminal justice organizations further toward the adoption of modern management principles and practices, as represented by Theory Z, TQM, MBO, and learning organizations. There are some areas and instances when these principles will not or cannot apply, but for the most part, they can and do. Much of the rest of this book will be concerned with the application of modern human relations theories and practices to management of criminal justice organizations. Suffice it to say that as all management thought on organizations has made the shift to a human relations perspective, criminal justice agencies and institutions will inevitably move in that direction to a greater extent as well.

Exercise: Taylor's pig iron story[1]

Ask for two student volunteers. If more than two students volunteer, choose the pair who seem to have a flair for drama. Go into the hallway so that the class cannot hear the discussion and brief them on their roles. One is to adopt the role of "Schmidt," aka "the high-priced man," a worker who speaks broken English with an exaggerated "foreign" accent. The other is to adopt the role of the industrial engineer and theorist Frederick Taylor. Taylor should speak with forceful authority and Schmidt should be just a bit clueless. Hand the volunteers a copy of the script and have them read over it once and then run through it together (this takes at most five minutes).

After briefing the student volunteers, return to the classroom and explain to the class that pig iron is a kind of metal that has been produced by American companies since the turn of the nineteenth century. Taylor (point to the student representing him) is involved in a discussion regarding the loading of pig iron with a worker in the factory named Schmidt (point to the student representing Schmidt). This dialog was printed in Taylor's 1911 book *Scientific Management* as a way of illustrating the author's approach to management, workers, and motivation. Ask the class to be careful observers of the interaction between Taylor and Schmidt.

Then, without further ado, the students should stand in front of the class and perform/read from the script. Afterward, the class discusses what they noticed about the dialog and the two characters. The two student performers also remark on what they noticed about the dialog and how they felt about their characters. The collective observations provide a very nice rampart from which to discuss Taylorism and traditional management theory. Depending on the acting ability of the respective students and the liveliness of the audience, this exercise is usually fun as well as instructive.

The dialog

T: Schmidt, are you a high-priced man?

S: Vell, I don't know vat you mean.

T: Oh, come now, you answer my questions. What I want to find out is whether you are a high-priced man or one of these cheap fellows here. What I want to find out is whether you want to earn $1.85 a day or whether you are satisfied with $1.15, just the same as all those cheap fellows are getting.

S: Did I vant $1.85 a day? Vas dot a high-priced man? Vell, yes, I vas a high-priced man.

T: Oh, you're aggravating me. Of course you want $1.85 a day— everyone wants it! You know perfectly well that has very little to do with your being a high-priced man. For goodness sake answer my questions, and don't waste any more of my time. Now come over here. You see that pile of pig iron?

S: Yes.

T: You see that car?

S: Yes.

T: Well, if you are a high-priced man, you will load that pig iron on that car tomorrow for $1.85. Now do wake up and answer my question. Tell me whether you are a high-priced man or not.

S: Vell—did I got $1.85 for loading dot pig iron on dot car tomorrow?

T: Yes, of course you do, and you get $1.85 for loading a pile like that every day right through the year. That is what a high-priced man does, and you know it just as well as I do.

S: Vell, dot's all right. I could load dot pig iron on the car tomorrow for $1.85 and I get it every day, don't I?

T: Certainly you do—certainly you do.

S: Vell, den, I vas a high priced man.

T: Now, hold on, hold on. You know just as well as I do that a
high-priced man has to do exactly as he's told from morning
till night. You have seen this man here before, haven't you?

S: No, I never saw him.

T: Well, if you are a high-priced man, you will do exactly as this
man tells you tomorrow, from morning till night. When he
tells you to pick up a pig and walk, you pick it up and you walk,
and when he tells you to sit down and rest, you sit down. You
do that right straight through the day. And what's more, no
back talk. Do you understand that? When this man tells you
to walk, you walk; when he tells you to sit down, you sit down,
and you don't talk back at him. Now you come on to work here
tomorrow and I'll know before night whether you are really a
high-priced man or not.

Discussion questions

1   Why does Van Riper argue that an administrative state is more
sophisticated and functional if there is a money economy and at
least a modest semblance of quantitative data and technique? Do
you think that an administrative state existed before the computer, at the turn of the twentieth century, or at the founding of the
country? Why or why not?

2   What portions of traditional management theory apply to the
operation of courts? Explain your answer.

3   How do the five major components of a system work together?
Give an example of a system and explain your answer.

4   What portions of human relations theories apply to the operation
of police and corrections? Explain your answer.

5   How would Maslow's Theory of Human Needs apply in explaining the behavior of staff and inmates in a juvenile correctional
institution? Give an example.

6   What motivates you? Is there a difference between short and long-
term motivation for you? If so, what would that difference be?

7   What kind of workplace, one based on traditional management
theories or one based on human relations theories, is most attrac-
tive to you? How would you justify your answer to this question?

Key terms

bureaucracy: includes hierarchy, specialization of roles, and rule of law (including formal administrative rules).

creative class: defined as an economic class which "consists of people who add economic value through their creativity" and who "create meaningful new forms" (Florida 2002: 68). This class includes those who make their living through knowledge, art, or the creation of new ideas or products, but also professional and technical workers who analyze those things. They are a class not because they own property necessarily, but because they tend to group together socially and their cultural, consumption, and social identities are similar to each other.

Hawthorne effect: the belief that when humans know they are being studied or watched, they will react to that observation.

Hierarchy of needs: The needs in order of importance were as follows (Maslow 1943: 167–172, 1961): physiological needs (food, water, sex), security needs (physical safety, job security, provision for old age, etc.), love needs (need to belong, the need to give and receive love, the need to be accepted by associates), self-esteem needs (also known as self-respect—need for achievement, recognition, importance and confidence in the world, the desire for a reputation or prestige), self-actualization needs (need to be creative, to fulfill one's potential, becoming what you were meant or fitted to be).

learning organization: one that operates in an open environment. For an organization to be effective in such a dynamic milieu, there must be learning from that environment. Because the environment of the organization is continually changing, the organization must also grow, learn, and adapt.

management by objectives: a philosophy of management that also contains the elements of both the traditional and the human relations theories, with particular emphasis on the latter in terms of employee relations.

motivation: (for our purposes), "[to] impel, incite; or a stimulus prompting a person to act in a certain way" (Webster 1986: 1475).

quality circles: worker groups whose members consider all the data available to them and make decisions.

scientific management: includes use of the scientific method by managers, discovery of the "first rate worker," discovery of the "one best way," motivation of workers with money, use of a piece rate to encourage more work output, workers seen as machine parts.

systems theory: five main active components within the model (eco)-system include the environment, the process, outputs, inputs, and feedback.

theory: "a set of ideas, concepts, principles, or methods used to explain a wide set of observed facts" (Webster 1992: 1098).

Theory X: The management and control of the workers is central because people are assumed to be passive and are assumed to not like, or want, to work. McGregor (1957: 179) identifies additional beliefs that underpin the traditional Theory X: The average man is by nature indolent—he works as little as possible; he lacks ambition, dislikes responsibility, and prefers to be led; he is inherently self-centered, indifferent to organizational needs; He is by nature resistant to change; he is gullible, not very bright, the ready dupe to the charlatan and the demagogue.

Theory Y: McGregor's (1957: 183) Theory Y included the following concepts: Management is responsible for organizing the elements of productive enterprise—money, materials, equipment, and people— in the interest of economic ends; people are not by nature passive or resistant to organizational needs; the motivation, the potential for development, the capacity for assuming responsibility, the readiness to direct behavior toward organizational goals are all present in people. It is a responsibility of management to make it possible for people to recognize and develop these human characteristics for themselves; the essential task of management is to arrange organizational conditions and methods of operation so that people can achieve their own goals best by directing their own efforts toward organizational objectives; managers should create these optimal conditions by decentralizing and delegating, enlarging jobs to make them more meaningful to workers, by engaging in participatory and consultive management, and by ensuring worker involvement in performance appraisals.

Theory Z: management is concerned with the production needs of X, the human needs of Y, and the environmental impact and influence—the unique contribution of Z.

total quality management: (TQM): the idea that the greater the involvement of workers or teams in developing and delivering organizational goals, the higher their level of commitment to achievement of those goals.

Note

1 The idea for this exercise was suggested many years ago by Dr. Tara Gray of New Mexico State University.

References

Appleby, P. (1945, reprinted in 1987) Government is different. In J. M. Shafritz and A. C. Hyde (eds), *Classics of public administration*. Chicago, IL: Dorsey Press, pp. 158–163.

Drucker, P. F. (1954) *The practice of management*. New York, NY: Harper & Row.

Drucker, P. F. (1964) *Managing for results*. New York, NY: Harper & Row.

Fayol, H. (1916, reprinted in 2005) General principles of management. In J. M. Shafritz, S. Ott and Y. S. Jang (eds), *Classics of organization theory*. Belmont, CA: Thomson/Wadsworth, pp. 48–60.

Fink, S. L., Jenks, R. S. and Willits, R. D. (1983) *Designing and managing organizations*. Homewood, IL: Richard D. Irwin.

Florida, R. (2002) *The rise of the creative class*. New York, NY: Basic Books.

Gawande, A. (2012) Annals of health care: Big med. *The New Yorker*, August 13, August 20.

Gordon, G. J. and Milakovich, M. E. (1998) *Public administration in America*, 6th edn. New York, NY: St. Martin's Press.

Gulick, L. (1937, reprinted in 1978) Notes on the theory of organization. In J. M. Shafritz and A. C. Hyde (eds), *Classics of public administration*. Chicago, IL: Dorsey Press, pp. 79–95.

Heil, G., Bennis, W. and Stephens, D. C. (2000) *Douglas McGregor revisited: Managing the human side of the enterprise*. New York, NY: Wiley.

Henry, N. (1987) The emergence of public administration as a field of study. In R. C. Chandler (ed.), *A centennial history of the American administrative state*. New York, NY: Free Press, pp. 37–85.

Janis, I. L. (1972) *Victims of groupthink: A psychological study of foreign policy decisions and fiascoes*. Boston, MA: Houghton Mifflin.

Jaques, E. (2001, first printed in 1990) In praise of hierarchy. In J. M. Shafritz and J. S. Ott (eds), *Classics of organization theory*. Fort Worth, TX: Harcourt College Publishers, pp. 152–157.

Kanigel, R. (1997) *The one best way: Frederick Winslow Taylor and the enigma of efficiency*. New York, NY: Viking Press.

Kaufman, H. (1985) *Time, chance, and organizations: Natural selection in a perilous environment*. Chatham, NJ: Chatham House Publishers.

Klofas, J., Stojokovic, S. and Kalinich, D. (1990) *Criminal justice organizations administration and management*. Pacific Grove, CA: Brooks/Cole.

Larson, C. E. and LaFasto, F. M. J. (1989) *Teamwork: What must go right/What can go wrong*. Newbury Park, CA: Sage.

Maslow, A. H. (1943, reprinted in 2001) A theory of human motivation. In J. M. Shafritz and J. S. Ott (eds), *Classics of organization theory*. Fort Worth, TX: Harcourt College Publishers, pp. 152–157.

Maslow, A. H. (1961, reprinted in 1998) *Maslow on management*. New York, NY: Wiley.

McGregor, D. (1957, reprinted in 2001). In J. M. Shafritz and J. S. Ott (eds), *Classics of organization theory*. Fort Worth, TX: Harcourt College Publishers, pp. 152–157.

Ouchi, W. (1981) *Theory Z: How American business can meet the Japanese challenge*. Reading, MA: Addison-Wesley.

Parker Follett, M. (1926, reprinted in 2001) The giving of orders. In J. M. Shafritz and J. S. Ott (eds), *Classics of organization theory*. Fort Worth, TX: Harcourt College Publishers, pp. 152–157.

Peters, T. (1987) *Thriving on chaos: Handbook for a management revolution*. New York, NY: Harper & Row.

Peters, T. (1992) *Liberation management: Necessary disorganization for the nanosecond nineties*. New York, NY: Knopf.

Pink, D. H. (2009) *Drive: The surprising truth about what motivates us*. New York, NY: Riverhead Books.

Pugh, D. S., Hickson, D. J. and Hinings, C. R. (1985) *Writers on organizations*. Beverly Hills, CA: Sage.

Roethlisberger, F. J. (1941, reprinted in 2001) The Hawthorne experiments. In J. M. Shafritz and J. S. Ott (eds), *Classics of organization theory*. Fort Worth, TX: Harcourt College Publishers, pp. 158–166.

Rothman, D. J. (1980) *Conscience and convenience: The asylum and its alternatives in progressive America*. Glenview, IL: Scott, Foresman.

Schermerhorn, J. R., Hunt, J. G. and Osborn, R. N. (1985) *Managing organizational behavior*, 2nd edn. New York, NY: Wiley.

Shafritz, J. M. and J. S. Ott (eds) (2001) *Classics of organization theory*, 5th edn. Fort Worth, TX: Harcourt College Publishers.

Smith, A. (1776, reprinted in 1937). *The wealth of nations*. New York: Random House.

Stephens, D. C. and Heil, G. (1998, in reprinted text by Maslow, 1961) *Abraham Maslow: The man and his work. Maslow on management*. New York, NY: Wiley.

Taylor, F. W. (1911) *The principles of scientific management*. Norcross, GA: Engineering and Management Press.

Tonn, J. C. (2003) *Mary Parker Follett: Creating democracy, transforming management*. New Haven, CT: Yale University Press.

Van Riper, P. P. (1987) The American administrative state: Wilson and the founders. In R. C. Chandler (eds), *A centennial history of the American administrative state*. New York, NY: Free Press, pp. 3–36.

Weber, M. (2001, first printed in 1946) Bureaucracy. In J. M. Shafritz and J. S. Ott (eds), *Classics of organization theory*. Fort Worth, TX: Harcourt College Publishers, pp. 152–157.

Webster. (1986) *Webster's third new international dictionary*. Springfield, MA: Merriam Webster.

Webster. (1992) *Webster's new world encyclopedia*. New York, NY: Prentice Hall.

White House. (2006) Fact Sheet: The Adam Walsh Child Protection and Safety Act of 2006. Office of the Press Secretary, July 27, 2006. Available at www.whitehouse. gov/news/releases/2006/07/20060727-7.html (last accessed January 31, 2013).

Wilson, W. (1887, reprinted in 1987) The study of administration. In J. M. Shafritz and A. C. Hyde (eds), *Classics of public administration*. Chicago, IL: Dorsey Press, pp. 10–25.

5 Communications

What you say and do is what they think you mean

... the idea of fairly ambitious partnerships between a range of practitioners, community members, researchers, etc. has taken root and is developing a promising track record in practice. The core intervention framework, the Ceasefire "model," clearly works across various settings and is increasingly being implemented.

> (Interview with David Kennedy [2010: 60] regarding problem solving used in Boston by the police and researchers, and along with community members, to successfully reduce gang violence and achieve the purported "Boston Miracle" in that regard)

A successfully functioning jail environment is one where good communications are the basic requirement. ... Good communications flow in both directions—from the top to the bottom of the organization and vice versa.

> (Kerle 2002: 5)

Changes in response to the growing workload demands have negatively affected communication between judges and probation officers ... the independent voice probation officers can provide to judges is in jeopardy.

> (MacDonald and Baroody-Hart 1999: 49)

What was going on with this team? ...Virtually every one of them was uncomfortable with interpersonal disagreements. ... Suddenly the reason for the team's inability to make decisions was obvious. It had never come to the collective realization that open discussion and disagreements about ideas – as opposed to attacks on people who hold disparate views – sharpen decision making. Instead, the team had adopted the habit of avoiding all disputes.

> (Goleman *et al.* 2002: 171–172)

Introduction: the message and the medium

Some criminal justice managers may think that if their intent is pure and their ideas are superior, positive change is inevitable in their organization. They could not be more wrong. If we have learned nothing else in the past century, it is that effective communication abilities and techniques, whether in a more sophisticated web conferencing format or in an informal tête-à-tête at lunch, are key to moving a management agenda. It is not just the message that is important when communicating; it is the medium.

But, of course, for the receivers of your message, what they think you mean is what you both say and do. Thus, communication is often defined as a sharing or exchange of information, via a medium, between a sender and a receiver (McLuhan 1964). As indicated by this definition, information is not just shared; it is at times exchanged for something from the receiver. In other words, communication can be tied to expectations within the organization that the process will entail a *quid pro quo* (something for something).

Obviously, the medium of communication can be accomplished verbally, in writing and other nonverbal forms (e.g., body language, symbols, etc.), or electronically (McLuhan 1964). Moreover, the message in organizations is sent and received through both formal and informal channels, and sometimes the latter can be as important as the former. Formal communications are usually found in the policies and procedures, the mission statement, training sessions, and the training manual, and in official communiqués or memorandums. Informal communications, on the other hand, are found in the one-on-one conversations, the asides, and the jokes that permeate the workplace (Morash and Haarr 1995). These informal communications can even come across in formal training venues as examples or tropes ("stories, ironies, and metaphors") that are used to illustrate how criminal justice works in the real world, as opposed to training situations (Crank 1996: 265).

In this chapter we discuss the multiple purposes of communication, the types of communication within, between, and across organizational boundaries, the barriers to effective communication, and some means by which they might be tackled. Since both formal and informal communications occur in the organization and shape its operation, both will be discussed in this chapter.

We note at the outset that in criminal justice organizations that have adopted a human relations management perspective, there is a greater need to understand the techniques that enhance communication. Under traditional theories, formal communications are presumed to move from the top down, although informally there is much unrecognized activity. In contrast, in organizations focused on human relations, there is formal recognition that communications should come from and move in all directions: From the top down, from the bottom up, horizontally, diagonally, within a group, between groups, and so on. As most modern organizations have moved to some extent in the human relations direction, a thorough discussion and understanding of communication becomes even more paramount for managers and workers in criminal justice agencies.

The purpose and modes of communication

People undertake communication in criminal justice for any number of reasons. Each of these purposes for communication is tied in some way to multiple missions of those organizations. For example, communication is used differently when the "protect" mission of policing is the primary focus as opposed to when "service" has taken center stage. Typical purposes of communication that are mentioned by the current authors and others (e.g., see Klofas *et al.* 1990; Peters 1992; Souryal and Killinger 1985) include the following:

- to solicit information;
- to train;
- to explain/inform;
- to command or give an order;
- to reassure;
- to educate;
- to stimulate;
- to motivate;
- to facilitate;
- to understand;
- to listen;
- to unite;
- to persuade;
- to mediate;
- to reduce anger or stress;
- to debilitate/harm;
- to denigrate;
- to problem solve;
- to brainstorm;
- to empower;
- to confess;
- to document.

The "how" of communication, or the medium for communication, can be as simple as a conversation between friends and as complex as a webinar delivered from one site to several via satellite and computer. These days public organizations, along with private individuals, have adopted multiple methods of communicating their message to their members, their stakeholders, and the general public. Increasingly that medium is electronic, computer, smartphone, or tablet-based and less likely to be in hard copy.

For instance, when a correctional officer in a prison is supervising inmate workers, she might communicate to motivate, to persuade, or to command. In other circumstances, when explaining the rule regarding use of art supplies, she might be communicating to solicit information about the use of these materials, to educate people regarding any applicable rules, and to explain expectations concerning compliance with the rules. At another point in the day she might communicate to mediate a dispute between two inmates, or to avert violence by working to reduce an inmate's anger or stress. Managers, in turn, might train that same officer on supervision techniques and practices, anger/stress management, and how to spot non-verbal preparations for a riot, or the body language of inmates who are on the brink of violent behavior. The inmates might educate each other about what the best job assignments are, who the best staff supervisors are, how hobby work is done, and how to defend themselves in the event of attack.

Police officers and court personnel also use communication during all aspects of their work. During a domestic violence call, an officer may communicate to solicit information, to mediate, and to problem solve. Later, that same officer will most likely document what he observed during the call, both to describe the situation and to inform others of the incident. He may be summoned to court to testify to the facts of the case.

These illustrations of the purposes of communication in corrections, policing, and courts indicate that there are multiple reasons or motives for communication. These reasons vary by the situation, as well as with the role of the sender and the receiver (Hassett-Walker 2012). Communication can be either formal or informal. People engage in communication for many reasons, most of which are tempered by each person's intent, his or her place in the organization, the type of organization (its mission), the medium available, and the situation existing at that point in time.

For instance, in a study of the victimization of youthful prison inmates, Maitland and Sluder (1998) found that the most common form of victimization by inmates of other inmates was verbal harassment. Here communication was used to debilitate or harm a group of younger and more vulnerable inmates in a setting where they felt particularly threatened. In a related study, Belknap, Holsinger, and Dunn (1997) used a particular communication/research device, the focus group, to listen to both young female inmates and correctional personnel so that the latter might better understand the lives of incarcerated girls in Ohio. In both cases, the type of communication used, its intent, and its effects were situation-based and dependent on the particular senders and receivers.

The decision whether to confess to a crime during a police interrogation can also be affected by the situation in which suspects find themselves. In a study by Deslauriers-Varin *et al.* (2011: 5) on why 21 percent of 211 incarcerated offenders changed their mind about confessing, the researchers found that those with a lengthy record, those who were advised by an attorney, those who were accused of a drug crime and those involved in cases where there was weak evidence against them were less likely to confess to the police.

Such situations, for instance, sometimes drive the formal responses of agencies to public or media inquiries. Motschall and Cao (2002) found from a convenience sample survey of public information officers (PIOs) for police departments that PIOs primarily see their role as media-oriented and reactive to inquiries. They communicate to inform the community and to reassure people regarding police activities. But communication from the police to the public sometimes reverses direction. The researchers noted that PIO personnel also bring information into the organization from the public and the media; in this sense they act as a "liaison" between the public and the police (Motschall and Cao 2002: 175). Related to this organizational-level communication with the public, in a national study of municipal police websites, Rosenbaum *et al.* (2011: 25) found that departments who had adopted a community policing mission were more likely to have a website and to "exhibit greater transparency in the display of data and provide more opportunities for citizen input."

Communication within and across organizational boundaries, and complaints

In any organization, both the sender and the receiver may be participants in communication within a group, between groups, or across groups or organizational boundaries. In any of these instances, the sender and the receiver might engage in either formal or informal communications.

Communication within and between groups

As the Hawthorne experiment findings indicated (see Chapter 4), the communication that occurs within and between groups is vital not only to those groups but also to the organization. The researchers at the Western Electric plant found that they themselves both set the pace and moderated it, in terms of work produced. Likewise, and more recently, Ouchi (1981), the proponent of Theory Z, sees work groups, as they function internally and in their interactions with others, as important incubators of ideas and solvers of puzzles. In fact, the fascination with grouping and teaming concepts as a means of problem solving has become quite popular as organizations have evolved (Gordon and Milakovich 1998; Kennedy 2010; Larson and LaFasto 1989; Lipnack and Stamps 2003; Peters 1992, 1995; Wageman 2003). Witness, for instance, the adoption of quality circles and teams in both the public and private sectors since the 1980s. In police, probation and parole, institutional corrections, defense, and prosecutorial agencies some form of teaming is often used to target crime, provide services, or process cases.

In criminal justice over the past thirty years, we have seen the proliferation of classification teams, policy and procedure development teams, prosecution and defense teams, crime task forces, informal courtroom work groups, training teams, neighborhood policing teams (as part of community policing and problem solving efforts), organizational change teams, emergency response teams, treatment teams, and selection teams, among many others (Bennett and Hess 2001; Clear and Cole 1997; Gaines *et al.* 1991; Kennedy 2010; Goleman *et al.* 2002; Meyer and Grant 2003; Phillips and Orvis 1999; Pollock 1997; Seiter 2002; Stojokovic and Lovell 1997; Swanson *et al.* 1998; Tewksbury 1997; Thibault *et al.* 1998; Whisenand and Rush 1998). The very existence of these teams and their viability over time in criminal justice organizations signals the importance of their communication function. Depending on their mission, their role in the organization, and the team members, such teams can be a vital means of both sending and receiving communications.

By classifying juveniles in a given way, the team sends a message to detainees that the youths' current behavior and criminal history determine their living unit placement, or not, in the detention center. By formalizing policies regarding the respectful treatment of others in the workplace, a policy and procedures team at a police department puts on notice those who are inclined to abuse force in the workplace. In other words, the concepts of teams and within-group communication are so compelling and so pervasive in the workplace now because they can be used as tools to enhance communication there (Wageman 2003). Teams can generate information by problem solving and brainstorming, and they can convey it by educating their members and others about organization policies and practices. As indicated by the quote from Goleman and colleagues (2002) which appears at the beginning of this chapter, however, team communication does not always flow smoothly. Sometimes it needs to be assessed and improved so that irrelevant disputes between members and petty problems do not prevent the team from functioning well together.

Teams might also serve the purpose of empowering workers who do not feel they have enough say in the workplace (Wageman 2003). Not only may those who feel they have a say in the development of policies and plans in the organization be more likely to engage in the implementation of those ideas, but they may also try to convince others (Ouchi 1981). In this sense, teaming can be an effective management tool for enhancing communication in the workplace.

Box 5.1   Teaming to create an ethics code

In a western state prison, one of the authors witnessed the use of teaming to assist management and staff in getting buy-in on an ethics code (Barrier *et al.* 1999). A medium security prison wanted to open a discussion among staff regarding ethical and unethical behavior in the prison. The author and a colleague were called in to facilitate staff training on the current procedures and policies that existed regarding ethical behavior. The management staff required that this training was attended by all staff, including managers, support, treatment, and security. We used a mix of lecture, exercises, and surveys to elicit information from and among attendees. The open nature of these sessions provided a forum for staff to vent about ethical violations they had observed and about the general inadequacy of the policy manual *vis-à-vis* ethical violations.

As an outgrowth of those sessions, management decided to create a team to develop an ethics code for the institution. A progressive associate warden was given the task of creating this team. He asked that the author serve as a consultant to the team, and declined to participate himself, though he did observe team operation. To his credit, the associate warden selected team members who were representative of all facets of the prison (medical, kitchen supervisors, security, treatment), from different levels (supervisors, line staff, sergeants, and lieutenants), and who represented multiple perspectives (both those who were enthusiastic and those who were skeptical). During the first meeting the group vented their frustrations and concerns and chose a chair (a young officer who was well respected). During the second meeting there were some continuing complaints and venting, but mostly there was a sense that we should get on with the task. Thus information was collected and disseminated to group members regarding other state codes and those of the American Correctional Association and the American Jails Association. The team also reviewed the comments of their fellow staff members, which had been provided anonymously on the surveys gathered by the trainers.

From this information, over a period of a couple of months, with weekly meetings, an ethics code was developed for this prison. Once there was consensus regarding the code, the members engaged in a campaign to promote it among their colleagues. To do this they placed the code in several issues of the institution newsletter and promoted it by providing examples of its application. The group leaders also met with the warden and the associate wardens to emphasize the importance of allowing code compliance to guide selection, but particularly performance appraisal and promotion decisions. In other words, if management truly believed in the process and wanted staff buy-in on the values expressed in the code, then those who abided by it should be rewarded, to send the message that the ethics code values were an integral part of the organization. Management agreed enthusiastically, and the author received reports later indicating that promotion and performance appraisals had been affected by this code and relative adherence to it. But the best indication of success of this teaming exercise occurred when one of the more curmudgeonly members of the team, who had been a complete skeptic about the code and the process at the beginning, told the group in a later meeting that he had defended both the code and its development process to coworkers.

Communication across organizational boundaries

Communication between organizations—say between the local police department and the prosecutor's office, or the courts and the parole board, or the detention facility and the juvenile court—can be tricky. As with communications that occur within the organization, there are both formal and informal communications between organizations and their members. The difference is that people within an organization have at a minimum a shared mission, enabling legislation and statutory requirements, leadership, culture, and traditions in common to at least loosely bind them with others in their organization, consequently forging a collective understanding. Although a cooperative spirit might pervade communications between organizations, the differences between them, on so many levels, may present an obstacle to effective communication. Some have argued that such organizations, while still part of the criminal justice system, are only "loosely coupled" in terms of their communication and shared goals (King Davis *et al.* 2003: 23).

The difficulties inherent in establishing open lines of communication between criminal justice organizations can lead to any number of problems, such as duplication of efforts and cost overruns. Giacomazzi and Smithey (2001) found just such problems as they chronicled an effort by several diverse agencies (including a large police department and relevant service provider agencies) to collaborate on solutions to problems stemming from violence against women in one metropolitan area. They noted that organizational factors sometimes hampered communication and collaboration, while at other times personnel's unwillingness to engage created difficulties. Disputes over turf, philosophy of approach (e.g., preventive vs. law enforcement), and disorganization were just some of the obstacles to effective collaboration and communication.

Coleman (1998) describes a different experience with interagency collaboration, one that involved the King County Jail in Seattle, Washington, in the 1990s. As in the rest of the country, jail populations in Seattle were exploding.

When the relatively new jail was filled only shortly after it was opened, the manager of the facility knew he had to do something. That something involved engaging the major actors from other organizations in a discussion of the best means of addressing the overuse of jail facilities. So he developed a monthly interagency meeting over dinner: The participants, who went Dutch, included representative and influential judges, police officials, prosecutors, public defenders, jail administrators, and other relevant stakeholders. The agenda for these meetings was both to educate members about the limited jail resources and to engage them in a problem solving discussion, with the goal of developing an informal plan for limiting use of the jail. The jail manager reported that as a direct result of these discussions over dinner, use of the jail dropped or remained steady for several years and the building of another jail was temporarily averted (Coleman 1998).

This example demonstrates that inter-organizational communication is as important to the effective operation of some criminal justice agencies as is intra-organizational communication. Other examples of inter-organizational teaming between criminal justice organizations abound: Drug task forces, community policing teams that include other stakeholders besides the police, youth councils, and many more. These groups exist and flourish because they play a major role in enhancing communication between organizations and allow those organizations, in turn, flexibility in meeting the demands of their environment.

Complaints

Another important element of the enhancement of both inter-organizational and intra-organizational communications is embedded in how these organizations deal with complaints from the community and other organizations. First, it is important to note that there are several sources and outcomes of complaints. For example, police respond to a complaint of loud noise originating from a party near campus, or to a victim's complaint of an assault. In these examples, the complaints could result in drunken underage partygoers being cited as MIPs (minors in possession), or the assault victim's attacker being identified and arrested. However, here the focus is on complaints directed at the police, court, or correctional agency from within, or originating from, the community. There are several issues within the realm of intra-agency and community complaints, especially when it comes to police use of excessive force, correctional officers' misuse of power (inmate coercion), or arbitrary sentencing practices (such as those based on race), and whether such conduct is intentional or negligent (De Angelis 2009; Langworthy and Travis 1994; Smith and Holmes 2003).

In each of these scenarios the criminal justice agency (or community ombudsman) must effectively field and deal with citizen complaints and assess whether each one is founded. A complaint filed against a police, court, or corrections officer may spur an internal investigation, which may include assessment of criminal or civil liability, as well as disciplinary action, and may also address some form of restitution (individual and/or community; Smith and Holmes 2003; Smith 2004).

Complaints filed from within a criminal justice agency are ideally treated in similar ways. However, because of "office politics," power differentials between managers and staff, and close personal ties—not always amicable—among and between various employees, some form of complainant anonymity must be allowed. One way to curb the arbitrary backlash that may arise when an employee reports abuse (whether physical, emotional, or financial) has been the implementation of "whistleblower" programs, which are described shortly. When one considers that most criminal justice agency mission statements purport some form of "service to the community," it is easy to see why effectively dealing with citizen and employee complaints becomes paramount to public relations and the success of the agency (De Angelis 2009).

Barriers to effective communication

Effective communication, which has occurred when the receiver comprehends the message sent by the sender, is often stymied by intentional or unintentional barriers. As noted in the discussion of inter-organizational communication, different organizations may be prevented from engaging in productive communication by their formal and informal policies, procedures, missions, politics, turf, and traditions (Giacomazzi and Smithey 2001; King Davis *et al.* 2003). But barriers for organizations exist at both the interpersonal and organizational levels (Klofas *et al.* 1990). Some common barriers at the interpersonal level or in the communications between individuals which are identified by Klofas *et al.* (1990: 66–67), Wallace and Roberson (2013: 52–58), Whisenand and Rush (1998: 102), and the authors include the following:

- preconceived ideas;
- denial of contrary information;
- filtering;
- emotionality;
- noncredibility of the source;
- personality differences;
- use of personalized meanings or semantic barriers;
- use of complex channels;
- lack of motivation or interest;
- lack of communication skills;
- nonverbal signs;
- poor organizational climate;
- information overload;

- fear of embarrassment;
- fear of reprisal;
- time pressures.

When people have "preconceived ideas" about others or deny "contrary information" or information that conflicts with preconceived beliefs, it is more likely there will be a breakdown in communications. These conditions can in turn lead to a belief that the source is not credible. All these perceptions might be conveyed both verbally and nonverbally. Of course, as with all organizations in which there are regular interactions among individuals, these barriers are common. Categorizations based on personal characteristics, family and friend associations, income, role, and any number of other factors would appear to be common among humans. The bias and prejudicial attitudes that result, however, can lead to an inability, and even an unwillingness, to communicate with people unlike you: the "other" or "outsider." Such attitudes can also lead to discriminatory behavior. For instance, it is not uncommon for inmates to claim that staff look down on them, ignore them, and treat them with disrespect in large part because of their inmate status (Belknap *et al.* 1997; Johnson 1996). Some police officers may claim that their race, age, or gender is the basis for discriminatory behavior by colleagues (Morash and Haarr 1995). The preconceived ideas about others that result, or those regarding projects or policies, can also hamper communication in the workplace. Relatedly, filtering of information can result from deliberate twisting of information by either the sender or the receiver. Perhaps the best management remedy is to ask staff to have an open mind and then to train them on diversity issues and organizational initiatives as a means of overcoming these communication barriers.

A related barrier, but one that is less obvious, may be the clash that comes from divergent personalities working together. Emotions might also get tangled up in this delivery of information when people do not understand each other. For instance, an extroverted probation officer and an introverted supervisor will act differently in the workplace. These differences may lead to a breakdown in communication, as the introvert prefers a quiet workplace where she can reflect on written material and the extrovert is most comfortable with dialog and diversions in the workplace. The measurement of personality types in the workplace has become popular management practice (see Box 5.2) and may serve to enhance communication and understanding between these divergent personality types.

Box 5.2   The Myers–Briggs Personality Test and the workplace

Isabel Myers and her mother, Katharine Cook Briggs, developed the instrument called the Myers–Briggs Personality Type Indicator to enhance learning and understanding of personality types in all kinds of venues (for more information and recommended Internet, or in-person, providers of the test, log on to www.myersbriggs.org). The Indicator is based on the work of Carl-Gustav Jung and his book *Psychological Types*. Myers, influenced by both her mother's and Jung's work, began devising the Indicator in 1942.

The Myers–Briggs personality test helps to identify which of sixteen personality types a person tends to fit into. The original short form of the test includes seventy questions, which are used to diagnose whether a person is an extrovert or an introvert (E/I) and has a preference for intuition or sensing (N/S), for thinking or feeling (T/F), and for judgment or perception (J/P). There are no preferred or superior personality types, just different ones. Some types are much more common in the population than others.

In the workplace, the Indicator has been used in a number of ways to improve understanding and matching of personality types. For instance, if you Google "MyersBriggs" you will find there are numerous business entities promising to use the tests, or a version of it, to assist organizations in teaming, diagnosing communication styles, career planning, pre-employment testing, turning managers into coaches, and improving sales, among other things. Myers–Briggs has also been put to use in the social and familial spheres in the matching of dates and mates and as a means of improving understanding between parents and children. Over the years, millions of people have taken the personality test.

The use of personalized meanings as a barrier to effective communication is also common to criminal justice agencies. The police, with their coded designations of criminal events, but particularly the legal profession and their use of Latin (lawyers resuscitate this "dead" language throughout their careers!), to all intents and purposes limit the number of people who can understand them. Though corrections is not quite as esoteric in its use of language, the slang and abbreviations used throughout the system create barriers to effective engagement with others not on the inside, so to speak. What is a kite, a shank, or a rap in a correctional setting? (Answer: a grievance, a knife, and a charge, respectively.)

Relatedly, the need to use complex channels of communication makes it difficult to convey information from the bottom up. It also makes the accurate transfer of information from the top down questionable. Often a simple communication must pass through several layers of bureaucracy—a problem that is particularly acute when the bureaucracy has not been flattened in terms of levels of supervisors.

Interpersonal communications can also break down when there is little motivation to communicate and/or either sender or receiver has poor skills in this area. The latter problem can usually be addressed with training. But lack of motivation is a more difficult issue and may be related to a poor organizational climate that neither fosters communication nor rewards its effective use. This climate might further hamper communication when there are time pressures. Again, the remedy is to provide open and accessible lines that allow for the ready communication of ideas and information.

College students, particularly before an exam, often remark that they are overloaded with information, and they are. Police staff faced with tome-like policy and procedures manuals and weekly, if not daily, memorandums regarding initiatives and policies are likely to feel the same way. The solution, of course, requires that college teachers and police administrators limit the test or training to a review of the most relevant topics. But it also means that the students and policing staff, given the complexity of the information and their role in the processing of it, engage in a continuous course of learning. For students this means they study much and often throughout the term, not just before an exam. By the same token, police staff, including administrators, must take on the role of "learner" throughout their careers.

Some staff and clients/inmates may be reluctant to communicate in corrections because they fear either reprisal or the embarrassment that might result from the disclosure of certain information. In the depositions of female and male staff who had witnessed sexual harassment, one of the authors has seen both these fears expressed as motivators for keeping quiet and not confronting the harasser, or reporting the improper behavior. Likewise, inmates sometimes express the fear that they will be punished if they report the wrongdoing of staff (Belknap *et al.* 1997). Wells *et al.* (2005) found in their study of citizen responses to an audit on police practices in Lincoln, Nebraska that, even when given performance feedback by community members, officers might not alter how they interact with the public.

Given these difficulties in communicating problems for clients, one solution of long standing that enhances the reporting of more egregious abuses of management or staff is the development of "whistleblower" programs in government. Many states have such programs because there is a recognition of the reluctance of staff to report wrongdoing when punishment might result (Hananel 2002). The best of such programs allow the whistleblower to remain anonymous. Although this must surely invite abuse and vindictive behavior by some who make spurious claims, it also means that people who previously would not report real abuses will now do so.

There are similar barriers to communication at the organizational level, including the checks and balances between organizations, the personalized meanings of words as discussed earlier, the fact that agencies will intentionally withhold information because they are in competition with each other or because they are required to by statute, and built-in conflict between the roles of the actors (Klofas *et al.* 1990). The checks and balances between organizations—for instance, the courts monitoring police searches or overseeing consent decrees in jails—can stymie communication between organizations. This is not to say, of course, that these checks and balances are wrong; just that they may hamper communication. Similarly, the formal adversarial role of the actors in criminal justice (e.g., the prosecutor and the defense attorney and the need for the judge to remain objective) can lead to a breakdown in communications. This would certainly be true when attorneys for plaintiff inmates are advocating before the courts for improvement in conditions of confinement. It is unlikely in this instance that communications between the plaintiff's attorney and the warden or director of the correctional facility would be warm and friendly, if even allowed.

Improving communications

Several authors of texts on criminal justice, police, corrections management have proposed solutions to the communication barriers that bedevil all criminal justice organizations (Champion 2003; Klofas *et al.* 1990; Seiter 2002; Souryal and Killinger 1985; Wallace and Roberson 2013; Whisenand and Rush 1998). These authors provide some solutions for overcoming the barriers to communication that occur at both the individual and organizational levels. It is worth noting, however, that some barriers are beneficial to our system of governance and are constitutionally mandated, such as the checks and balances between the branches of government (e.g., the courts reviewing the actions of the police and corrections).

Having recognized this, though, we will discuss the solutions to overcoming the illegitimate barriers that are offered by other authors and then mention a few of our own. Klofas *et al.* (1990) propose organizational change as a means of improving communication. These authors believe that the change to a more participatory form of management along the lines of Theory Z is most likely to lend itself to open lines of communication and more avenues of communication.

Champion (2003) details the functional and dysfunctional aspects of communication in organizations, especially as it occurs in informal and formal groups. His message, like that of Whisenand and Rush (1998), is that despite the pitfalls of over-reliance on either informal or formal communications, both should be recognized and utilized by managers. Whisenand and Rush also emphasize the need for greater clarity in the message and the medium. Repeating the message, delivering it verbally as well as in written form, and reducing ambiguity are some of the suggestions they provide.

Seiter's (2002) and Souryal and Killinger's (1985) suggestions are more situationally based, but also indicate a bias toward organizational change. They recommend that managers who are interested in improving communications should consider the situation and tailor their communication style and message to it. Souryal and Killinger also suggest emphasizing requests and de-emphasizing orders in interactions with staff. They argue that managers should be respectful of staff and avoid threats; in addition, they should "avoid excessive solicitousness" but focus on cooperation. Seiter would have the supervisor be interested in positive verbal communication, be knowledgeable about the subject, and know the facts and the background of the recipient. He would ask that senders keep their remarks specific and use language that is clear.

Seiter (2002) and Wallace and Roberson (2013) go further, however, to recommend an active listening process for those who work in criminal justice as a means of enhancing communication. They believe that two-way communication in corrections and policing is sometimes stymied because supervisors view questions by the public or staff as a threat to their authority or because they (the supervisors) are ill prepared to provide adequate information to their supervisees or to the general public. Ironically, Seiter notes that the same person who will be held responsible if an inferior job is done by those under his or her supervision often ignores vital information from subordinates. His prescription for effective listening is as follows (Seiter 2002: 356):

- ask questions;
- concentrate;
- listen for main ideas;
- listen for the rationale behind what the other person is saying;
- listen for key words;
- organize what you hear in your own mind in a way that is logical for you;
- take notes if the issue or request is complex.

An additional prescription for communication enhancement

Clearly, as indicated by the suggestions of other authors, the secret to enhancing communication in an organization and to overcoming barriers is more communication. How more communication is achieved depends on the situation, and the sender and the receiver involved in it. Fortunately, there are techniques and processes that can be used in the criminal justice workplace to improve communication.

Training

One method of transmitting the formal message of the organization is to TRAIN, TRAIN, and TRAIN. Consult any successful manager, management text, or text on organizational change and the importance of training will be prominently featured. Training is used to inform, to prevent mistakes, and to address misconceptions. In a sense, it levels the playing field of knowledge and empowers workers to negotiate in their workplace more effectively: The old cliché is true: "Knowledge is power."

Teaming

To achieve positive change in any organization, training is one part of the solution, and teaming is another (see Box 5.3). Teams perform collective problem solving, solution-building, and even implementation-monitoring functions that are vital in the twenty-first-century workplace. They de-structure the hierarchy of the organization by opening up avenues of communication that are too narrow in traditional organizations (Lipnack and Stamps 2003; Peters 1992; Wageman 2003; Zhao *et al.* 2010). Teams also lend credibility to the process and make employees feel that they have a voice in organizational operation. They can provide a mechanism for bridging the divide between organizations within the same system that may have interests in common.

Listening

Seiter (2002) makes an excellent point, and one echoed in some fashion in many management texts: If you want to know your organization and your workers, develop effective listening skills. Perhaps because they think they must, managers may propose initiatives or support programs without first taking the temperature of the organization or, for that matter, truly knowing the organization. It is the height of arrogance for a new manager to come in and propose changes without knowing why or how the current policies or practices work. Such managers, who are more inclined to tell or sell their initiative without listening first, risk losing not only the chance to successfully implement their own ideas (because people will sabotage them), but the allegiance of the workers. We will discuss leadership issues much further in Chapter 7. One last point here: Sometimes "listening" means paying attention to the nonverbal communication as much as the verbal (see Box 5.4).

Newsletters

It is a given that written communications of all kinds proliferate in bureaucratic organizations. Formal communiqués flutter down from the top and incident reports filter up through the ranks, while more informal e-mails zigzag throughout the organization. The value of departmental newsletters is that they can be used to cross hierarchical lines and capture the most salient of both the formal and informal information filtering through the organization. At their best, they can serve the purpose of training, passing along general staff information while also influencing the subculture. They are more likely to be seen as a means for input if all levels and types of staff have a say in their content. In other words, if newsletters are produced by the top for the bottom, they will be viewed as merely a more developed memorandum rather than as a vehicle for interactive communication between ranks and roles.

Box 5.3 Leadership teams at the Ada County sheriff's office, by Sheriff Gary Raney, Ada County, Idaho

As I rose through the ranks, I so often thought to myself, "If only they would have sought input from those of us who are doing the job, we could have offered some good ideas." Even as a deputy I wanted to see things run well across all of the organization. Often when I felt we had good ideas, I was frustrated that there was no mechanism to share them other than the chain of command, who were often wrapped up in their own issues and didn't want to take on more.

When I became sheriff, I was convinced that forming focus groups to provide feedback from within the agency presented many benefits. I wanted to offer that attentive ear to my employees that I wished I could have had. I also wanted to make changes in the organization. I knew that a feedback loop would be necessary to monitor those changes, and what better feedback loop than the front line? Lastly, I also knew that I wanted employees to feel engaged with management and that a great instrument for that would be the honest and open, but respectful, discussion of how supervision and management were doing from a front-line perspective.

I assembled focus groups, later to be called leadership teams, and intentionally sought a cross-section of employees within each major area of the agency. I included them all—young and old, males and females, new and veteran, happy and unhappy. Mostly, I tried to identify the employees who had the personal maturity to think outside their own agendas and to be honest with me.

Some executives insulate themselves to only listen to upper management. I have to ask if they think they'll actually hear the bad news from the person in charge of it. It's doubtful. That said, I also set ground rules for the leadership teams to qualify that these meetings were not a "bitch session" or a convenient opportunity to circumvent the chain of command with personal agendas, but an opportunity for employees and management to work together.

I think success requires that someone at the top listen to the bad news, filter out what's accurate, and act upon it. The outcome of these groups has been as simple as getting many small, irritating issues taken care of (from regular inspections of laptops in patrol cars to replacement of missing keys). More significantly, the open dialog brought forward some specific examples of supervision and management inconsistencies in policy and practice, and it was ultimately the catalyst for some sound operational changes such as how we deliver medication in the jail—a high liability and time-consuming issue—and our patrol training program. Last but not least, rumors can drag an organization down. Each time we met I solicited the rumors from out of the group and addressed them very directly, which both greatly decreased the negative rumors and reinforced the idea that people should verify what they hear.

This process really helped me know what reality was at the line level. Equally, it became very meaningful to them when they could see something happen as a direct result of their discussion and conclusions. I think it was the realistic application of the buzzwords we like to use: Empowerment, participative leadership, buy-in, etc. I believe an organization can operate by completing necessary tasks, but an organization can only run well when communication becomes more important than the tasks. The leadership teams have bridged that communication gap better than anything else I know of, and they have made the whole system work better.

Gary Raney began his career with the Ada County Sheriff's Office in 1983, rising through the ranks to become sheriff in 2005. The agency, based in Boise, Idaho, has 530 employees and provides full-service law enforcement, jail, and support services.

Grievance procedures and whistleblowing programs

Although grievance procedures and whistleblowing programs tend to engender negative communications within the organization, they are central to preventing abuses by employees. To enhance legitimacy, they need to be handled in the most professional, objective, and formal way possible. The programs should afford anonymity to whistleblowers, and provisions for punishing retaliation against whistleblowers should be in place (Hananel 2002).

Technology

It is well known that technology has revolutionized communication in so many aspects of our lives, including in the criminal justice arena. It is also a truism that telephones, cars, radios, and computers have all made the management of staff and clientele more efficient and effective in criminal justice organizations (Langworthy and Travis 1994). In a more recent example of the powerful effect of technology on improving communications, appellate decisions, previously available only through private companies, are now published widely on the Internet for free (Shelton 2000). Furthermore, through the use of e-mails, listservs, and web pages, courts and the police and correctional agencies are able to provide information to the public that was heretofore difficult or impossible to access.

Inside and outside research

Even the best manager in the world may lack workplace information that workers are afraid to report, purposefully withhold, do not know they know, or do not consider relevant; still other information is not self-evident to the manager. Several states and localities have research entities in their criminal justice organizations (usually in state-level or large metro-area agencies), but unfortunately most small municipalities and states have little or no research capacity. Yet there is no substitute for a fresh and unbiased eye for examining any phenomenon, and the criminal justice organization is no exception. To the extent that a criminal justice entity can embrace the value of research and encourage it, the validity of the information cycling through the communication channels will improve (Fleisher 1996; Kerle 2003). A related point is that even if the criminal justice agency cannot initiate its own research, there are studies in both the professional and academic press that should be regularly accessed by the savvy manager and staff. Professional magazines should be subscribed to and passed around the workplace, as they often feature relevant research. Managers should also subscribe to, read, and make available to their employees the relevant academic journals. Not all the articles in these journals will be directly related to a particular workplace, but many of them will. However, even articles without direct application can be used to broaden the understanding of research, functions, and innovations in other criminal justice agencies.

Organizational change

Underlying most prescriptions for the improvement of communications in organizations (e.g., Champion 2003; Klofas *et al.* 1990; Peters 1992, 1995; Seiter 2002; Whisenand and Rush 1998) is the belief that we must move beyond the natural constrictions placed by a bureaucratic organization on people's ability and willingness to communicate (Stohr *et al.* 1994). Many modern observers of organizations also argue for a more human relations-oriented management style (see Chapter 4).

As discussed previously in this chapter and others, bureaucracy and a traditional management perspective favor communication from the top down and provide no formal mechanism for bottom-up or horizontal—or, for that matter, diagonal—communication. As bureaucracy is here to stay in terms of the basic shape of most criminal justice organizations (although they can definitely get fatter and flatter—see Chapter 4) and courts are a notable exception, there can and must be some change in traditional management if we are to see measurable improvement in communications in such organizations. In fact, a basic assumption of our prescription for improving communication is that criminal justice organizations will further move to embrace a human relations perspective on management.

From such a perspective, the knowledge and skills that workers bring to their jobs are recognized, and managers who do not value that information or provide vehicles for its transmission are seen as handicapping their organization. There is also clear evidence that criminal justice workers will be more committed, more satisfied, less stressed, and less likely to quit if they are given the chance to meaningfully develop and participate in workplace decision making (Alarid 1999; Brody *et al.* 2002; Kiekbusch *et al.* 2003; Lipnack and Stamps 2003; Slate *et al.* 2001; Stohr *et al.* 1994; Witte *et al.* 1990; Wright *et al.*1997; Wageman 2003).

Box 5.4 Nonverbal communication

In a training session for prison classification counselors that one of the authors attended in the mid-1980s in Washington State, the facilitators had attendees engage in a group problem-solving process. Those present were given a problem to tackle and the circumstances surrounding it, and told to discuss solutions among themselves. Unbeknownst to the participants, the trainers used this exercise as an opportunity to diagnose the interpersonal and team communication styles within each group by focusing on the nonverbal communication that was exhibited.

When the discussion of the problem was complete, the facilitators asked the groups to identify who in each group had been most engaged, most disengaged, and most thoughtful in their interactions in the group. Many times, but not always, the group perceptions of an individual member's activity conformed to the observers' perception of the nonverbal communication which was occurring in the groups. They found that those who were leaning forward toward the group, with arms somewhat loose and open, or leaning on elbows and maintaining eye contact with other group members, were also those identified by team members as most involved. Likewise, those who sat back away from the group and had their arms folded, legs crossed, and eyes anywhere but on other group members, were, of course, identified as disengaged. The training facilitators also noticed that some group members exhibited a mix of these behaviors, depending on what part of the exercise the group was engaged in. The explicit and verbal message at the time by the facilitators was to pay attention to the nonverbal communications by both coworkers and clients/inmates in the workplace, as these behaviors include a message as well.

Relatedly, Brougham (1992), in an *FBI Law Enforcement Bulletin* article, discusses the importance of nonverbal communication in his work as a police sergeant in Chicago. He notes that attention to body movements (movement of feet and hands, folded arms, etc.), personal distance (increasing and decreasing proximity from other people), facial expressions (asymmetry in the face that occurs when people lie, increased eye blinking, etc.), physiological symptoms (perspiration, flushing, etc.), and paralanguage (the pitch and rate of speech, etc.) all convey an involuntary message about the truth to the astute observer of nonverbal communications.

Conclusions

Communication in criminal justice organizations is formal and informal, verbal and nonverbal; it is rarely as straightforward in delivery or interpretation as we might like. People and their jobs, roles, and organizations differ, and this makes communication problematic. Yet there is plenty of evidence that effective communication is key to organizational success and positive work perceptions (Flanagan *et al.* 1996). As discussed in the chapter, there are techniques and processes that can serve to improve the amount of communications and their accuracy. Though there is nothing particularly new about the prescriptions for improving communication in criminal justice that are offered by ourselves and others, these measures are likely to provide the kind of environment in which communications flow most freely.

Exercise: the space invader

Just for fun, we include a version of a communication exercise that is ubiquitous in classroom and training environments. The exercise has no clear author that we are aware of, and the name invented for it here is not to be confused with the video game. We have found the exercise useful in the classroom and in training as a means of conveying the nuances in communication. Without giving the game away, so to speak, we note that the exercise usually yields interesting insights from participants about the nature of communication. It also serves to liven up lecture or training sessions on communication in a way that mere lecturing cannot always accomplish.

The space invader

1   Ask the group to form two facing lines about five feet apart; it works best if there is enough room so the lines do not have to double over or twist around. You can have men in one line and women in the other, or use another criterion than gender to separate people.

2   Ask everyone to identify a specific person in the other line as a point of reference.

3   It is okay if every woman is not matched with a man and vice versa, as it actually is interesting to have a mix of male/female, female/female, and male/male matchings for comparison (which means you may have to move some of the excess males to the female line or some of the excess females to the male line; you could do this even if there is the same number of males and females).

4   Ask all to pay careful attention to their own reaction, and that of their point-of-reference person in the other line, during the exercise.

5   Ask the people in one line to walk slowly toward their respective point-of-reference partners and ask the people in the other line to put one hand forward (palm facing the point-of-reference person) when they are starting to feel uncomfortable (we usually have the male line walk and give the female line the power to stop them—the reason should become obvious as you complete this exercise!).

6   When all in the "walking" line have been stopped, ask the members of both lines to note mentally, and WITHOUT SPEAKING, the distance they are from their point of reference and then glance around the room to see how far other people are from their points of reference.

7   You could stop here and ask for observations by people regarding the different amounts of space between given individuals and why that might be so, or you could delay the observations until after the group has repeated the exercise with the opposite line walking toward their point-of-reference people.

8   Inevitably, the observations include some discussion about how people react differently to the proximity of others based on the personal characteristics of those in the "walking" and the "stopping" lines (gender is an important variable here, but so are many others).

9   Participants are asked how these differences in proximity comfort levels might affect and color communication interactions in the workplace.

Discussion questions

1   Why and how would the style of communication vary when the issue is service vs. protection in policing? Explain your reasoning.
2   Why are barriers to communication within and between organizations sometimes a good thing? Explain your answer.
3   What are the best methods for surmounting organizational barriers to communication within the organization? List and explain your answers.
4   What are the best methods for surmounting the organizational barriers to communication between organizations? List and explain your answers.
5   What is an approach to improving the flow of "negative" communications within the organization? Give a real-world example of this method.
6   What set of organizational theories serves as the underpinning for many recommendations for improvements in communications? Why is this so?
7   If you had to devise a "system" for enhancing communication within a given criminal justice organization, what would be its components?

Web link

Myers–Briggs Personality Test website: http://www.myersbriggs.org

Key terms

communication: often defined as a sharing or exchange of information, via a medium, between a sender and a receiver (McLuhan 1964). As indicated by this definition, information is not just shared; it is at times exchanged for something. In other words, communication can be tied to expectations within the organization that there will be a *quid pro quo* (something for something) in the process.
formal communications: usually found in the policies and procedures, the mission statement, training sessions, and the training manual, as well as in official communiqués or memorandums.
informal communications: the one-on-one conversations, asides, and jokes that permeate the workplace.

References

Alarid, L. F. (1999) Law enforcement departments as learning organizations: Argyris's theory as a framework for implementing community-oriented policing. *Police Quarterly*, 2(3): 321–337.

Barrier, G., Stohr, M. K., Hemmens, C. and Marsh, R. (1999) A practical user's guide to ethical practices: Idaho's method for implementing ethical behavior in a correctional setting. *Corrections Compendium*, 24(4): 1–12.

Belknap, J., Holsinger, K. and Dunn, M. (1997) Understanding incarcerated girls: The results of a focus group study. *The Prison Journal*, 77(4): 381–404.

Bennett, W. W. and Hess, K. (2001) *Management and supervision in law enforcement*, 3rd edn. Belmont, CA: Wadsworth/Thomson Learning.

Brody, D. C., DeMarco, C. and Lovrich, N. P. (2002) Community policing and job satisfaction: Suggestive evidence of positive workforce effects from a multijurisdictional comparison in Washington State. *Police Quarterly*, 5(2): 181–205.

Brougham, C. G. (1992) Nonverbal communication: Can what they don't say give them away? *FBI Law Enforcement Bulletin*, 61(7): 15–18.

Champion, D. J. (2003) *Administration of criminal justice: Structure, function and process.* Upper Saddle River, NJ: Prentice Hall.

Clear, T. and G. F. Cole. (1997) *American corrections*, 4th edn. Belmont, CA: Wadsworth.

Coleman, R. J. (1998) A cooperative corrections arrangement: A blueprint for criminal justice in the 21st century. *Corrections Now*, 3(1): 1.

Crank, J. P. (1996) The construction of meaning during training for probation and parole. *Justice Quarterly*, 13(2): 265–290.

De Angelis, J. (2009) Assessing the impact of oversight and procedural justice on the attitudes of individuals who file police complaints. *Police Quarterly*, 12(2): 214–236.

Deslauriers-Varin, N., Beauregard, E. and Wong, J. (2011) Changing their mind about confessing to police: The role of contextual factors in crime confession. *Police Quarterly*, 14(1): pp. 5-24.

Flanagan, T., Johnson, W. W. and Bennett, K. (1996) Job satisfaction among correctional executives: A contemporary portrait of wardens of state prisons for adults. *The Prison Journal*, 76(4): 385–397.

Fleisher, M. S. (1996) Management assessment and policy dissemination in federal prisons. *The Prison Journal*, 76(1): 81–91.

Gaines, L. K., Southerland, M. D. and Angell, J. E. (1991) *Police administration.* New York, NY: McGraw-Hill.

Giacomazzi, A. L. and Smithey, M. (2001) Community policing and family violence against women: Lessons learned from a multiagency collaboration. *Police Quarterly*, 4(1): 99–122.

Goleman, D., Boyatzis, R. and McKee, A. (2002) *Primal leadership: Realizing the power of emotional intelligence.* Boston, MA: Harvard Business School Press.

Gordon, G. J. and Milakovich, M. E. (1998) *Public administration in America*, 6th edn. New York: St. Martin's Press.

Hananel, S. (2002) Whistle-blower report cites abuser. *Washington Post.* Available at www.washingtonpost.com. (last accessed January 31, 2013).

Hassett-Walker, C. (2012) Race, social class, communication, and accusations: The Duke University Lacrosse Team party. *Journal of Ethnicity in Criminal Justice*, 10: 267–294.

Johnson, R. (1996) *Hard time: Understanding and reforming the prison.* Belmont, CA: Wadsworth.

Kennedy, D. (2010) Interview. In A. Fox and E. Gold (eds), *Daring to fail: First-person stories of criminal justice reform.* New York, NY: Center for Court Innovation, pp. 58–62.

Kerle, K. (2002) Editorial: Communications. *American Jails,* 15(6): 5.

Kerle, K. (2003) Editorial: Keeping your best employees? *American Jails,* 17(4): 5.

Kiekbusch, R., Price, W. and Theis, J. (2003) Turnover predictors: Causes of employee turnover in sheriff-operated jails. *Criminal Justice Studies,* 16(2): 67–76.

King Davis, R., Applegate, B. K., Otto, C. W., Surette, R. and McCarthy, B. J. (2003) Roles and responsibilities: Analyzing local leaders' views on jail crowding from a systems perspective. *Crime and Delinquency,* 49(10): 1–25.

Klofas, J., Stojokovic, S. and Kalinich, D. (1990) *Criminal justice organizations.* Pacific Grove, CA: Brooks/Cols.

Langworthy, R. H. and Travis, L. F., III (1994) *Policing in America: A balance of forces.* New York, NY: Macmillan.

Larson, C. E., and LaFasto, F. M. J. (1989) *Teamwork: What must go right/What can go wrong.* Newbury Park, CA: Sage.

Lipnack, J. and Stamps, J. (2003) Virtual teams: The new way to work. In J. S. Ott, S. J. Parkes and R. B. Simpson (eds), *Readings in organizational behavior.* Belmont, CA: Wadsworth/Thomson Learning, pp. 297–303.

MacDonald, S. S. and Baroody-Hart, C. (1999) Communication between probation officers and judges: An innovative model. *Federal Probation,* 63(1): 42–51.

McLuhan, M. (1964, reprinted in 1994) *Understanding media: The extensions of man.* Cambridge, MA: MIT Press.

Maitland, A. S. and Sluder, R. D. (1998) Victimization and youthful prison inmates: An empirical analysis. *The Prison Journal,* 78(1): 55–73.

Meyer, J. F. and Grant, D. R. (2003) *The courts in our criminal justice system.* Upper Saddle River, NJ: Prentice Hall.

Morash, M. and Haarr, R. N. (1995) Gender, workplace problems, and stress in policing. *Justice Quarterly,* 12: 113–140.

Motschall, M. and Cao, L. (2002) An analysis of the public relations role of the police public information officer. *Police Quarterly,* 5(2): 152–180.

Ouchi, W. (1981) *Theory Z: How American business can meet the Japanese challenge.* Reading, MA: Addison-Wesley.

Peters, T. (1992) *Liberation management: Necessary disorganization for the nanosecond nineties.* New York, NY: Knopf.

Peters, T. (1995) *Two complete books: Thriving on chaos and a passion for excellence (with Nancy Austin).* New York, NY: Random House.

Phillips, P. W. and Orvis, G. P. (1999) Intergovernmental relations and the crime task force: A case study of the East Texas Violent Crime Task Force and its implications. *Police Quarterly,* 2(4): 438–461.

Pollock, J. M. (ed.). (1997) *Prisons: Today and tomorrow.* Gaithersburg, MDA: Aspen Publishers.

Rosenbaum, D. P., Graziano, L. M., Stephens, C. D. and Schuck, A. M. (2011). Understanding community policing and legitimacy-seeking behavior in virtual reality: A national study of municipal police websites. *Police Quarterly,* 14(1): 25–47.

Seiter, R. P. (2002) *Correctional administration: Integrating theory and practice.* Upper Saddle River, NJ: Prentice Hall.

Shelton, D. E. (2000) Communicating with lawyers on the Internet. *The Judges Journal*, 39(1): 26–27.

Slate, R. N., Vogel, R. E. and Johnson, W. W. (2001) To quit or not to quit: Perceptions of participation in correctional decision making and the impact of organizational stress. *Corrections Management Quarterly*, 5(2): 68–78.

Smith, B. W. and Holmes, M. D. (2003) Community accountability, minority threat, and police brutality: An examination of civil rights criminal complaints. *Criminology*, 41(4): 1035–1063.

Smith, G. (2004) Rethinking police complaints. *British Journal of Criminology*, 44(1): 15–33.

Souryal, S. and Killinger, G. G. (1985) *Police organization and administration.* Cincinnati, OH: Pilgrimmage.

Stohr, M. K., Lovrich N. P., Jr., Menke, B. A. and Zupan, L. L. (1994) Staff management in correctional institutions: Comparing DiIulio's 'control model' and 'employee investment model' outcomes in five jails. *Justice Quarterly*, 11(3): 471–497.

Stojokovic, S. and Lovell, R. (1997) *Corrections: An introduction*, 2nd edn. Cincinnati, OH: Anderson Publishing.

Swanson, C. R., Territo, L., and Taylor, R.W. (1998) *Police administration structures, processes, and behavior*, 4th edn. Upper Saddle River, NJ: Prentice Hall.

Tewksbury, R. A. (1997) *Introduction to corrections*, 3rd edn. New York, NY: Glencoe.

Thibault, E. A., Lynch, L. M. and McBride, R. B. (1998) *Proactive police management*, 4th edn. Upper Saddle River, NJ: Prentice Hall.

Wageman, R. (2003) Critical success factors for creating superb self-managing teams. In J. S. Ott, S. J. Parkes and R. B. Simpson (eds), *Readings in organizational behavior*. Belmont, CA: Wadsworth/Thomson Learning, pp. 285–296.

Wallace, H. and Roberson, C. (2013) *Written and interpersonal communication: Methods for law enforcement*, 4th edn. Boston, MA: Pearson.

Wells, W., Horney, J. and Maguire, E. R. (2005) Patrol officer responses to citizen feedback: An experimental analysis. *Police Quarterly*, 8(2): 171–205.

Whisenand, P. M. and Rush, G. E. (1998) *Supervising police personnel: The fifteen responsibilities*, 3rd edn. Upper Saddle River, NJ: Prentice Hall.

Witte, J. H, Travis, L. G., III and Langworthy, R. H. (1990) Participatory management in law enforcement: Police officer, supervisor and administrator perceptions. *American Journal of Police*, 9(4): 1–24.

Wright, K. N., Saylor, W. G., Gilman, E. and Camp, S. (1997) Job control and occupational outcomes among prison workers. *Justice Quarterly*, 14(3): 525–546.

Zhao, J., Ren, L. and Lovrich, N. P. (2010) Police organizational structures during the 1990s: An application of contingency theory. *Police Quarterly*, 13(2): 209–232.

6 Socialization, roles, and power issues

Power corrupts and absolute power corrupts absolutely.
(Lord Acton 1887, in a letter to Bishop Creighton)

This analysis argues that, instead of being a simple matter of putting on a uniform and learning about schedules, becoming and being a prison officer is a complex process. Behind the walls, through constant interaction that is typically informal and subtle, yet sometimes frighteningly bold and sudden, the recruit learns the contours of the prison world and his place in it...
(Crouch and Marquart 1994: 327)

Not only does justice require the prosecutor to "weed out" cases where the evidence is weak, but the practical need to conserve scarce legal resources for only the most serious cases demands this...
(Meyer and Grant 2003: 116)

Cops are selecting modes of adaptation that they prefer, that they sometimes, to use a term uncommon to scholarly studies, simply like ... they make choices that are pleasing to them, that make them feel good, or that at appropriate times make them angry.
(Crank 1998: 21)

Introduction: what is my job and how do I do it?

The topics of socialization, roles, and power issues in criminal justice organizations are really concerned with what the job of the professional is (roles), how people learn about it (socialization), and how they exercise one of the most important tools at hand (power). In the multicontextual environment of criminal justice organizations, where politics, economics, crime levels, and stakeholder expectations all affect the operation of the multilayered agency, the answers to our questions (what is my job and how do I do it?) may not be as clear in practice as they are in the formal job announcement.

In this chapter we discuss the criminal justice workers at the base of the management chart. They, like managers and others within their larger organizations, are professionals who are often asked to do too much with too little. Recall that these types of workers, such as police and correctional officers, counselors, probation and parole officers, prosecutors, and defense attorneys, fit the description given in Chapter 2 of street-level bureaucrats (SLBs; Lipsky 1980). Again, these are public service workers who have more demands on their time and agency resources than they can meet, and who also have the discretion to make choices about their work.

This chapter is framed with a focus on SLBs because how they are socialized into the role they adopt essentially defines criminal justice policy in practice. As all who are likely to read this book know, work in the criminal justice field is fascinating because of the human element that defines it. The roles of detention officers, prosecutors, and counselors are diverse, but bound by the nature of the socialization into those roles, including the presence of power. How socialization is accomplished and the choice of roles adopted really defines criminal justice agencies, and the dispersion of "justice" in the United States.

Socialization

Occupational socialization, like any form of socialization, involves learning and teaching. A child in school is taught what and how to learn by teachers and fellow classmates. A new member of a book club is initiated into the ways of the club operation and focus by the other members. Likewise, the new police recruit learns from organizational members and others who teach her or him the job, including how to do it. But recruits don't just learn the particulars of the job itself; they learn what the organization's prevailing and conflicting values and beliefs are. This learning curve is steepest at the beginning and will likely begin to level, but as each officer gains more knowledge and experience, they often relearn their role, likely many times over the course of their career.

Therefore, according to Klofas *et al.* (1990: 150), **occupational socialization** is "[t]he process by which a person acquires the values, attitudes, and behaviors of an ongoing occupational social system." Socialization is a process and it is ongoing. What is not said here, but is implied, is that socialization is not done by organizational members only; rather, as we will discuss later in the chapter, clients and other stakeholders also teach the criminal justice worker about the job (Collins *et al.* 2012; Stohr *et al.* 2012; Crank 1998; Lipsky 1980; Lombardo 1989). The socialization process may also vary based on individual personal characteristics; for instance, the gender and race/ethnicity of the jobholder have been shown to influence how criminal justice staff view and perform their jobs (Griffin *et al.* 2012; Camp *et al.* 2001; Haarr 1997; Jenne and Kersting 1998; Morash and Haarr 2012, 1995).

This socialization process is believed to take place in three stages: *anticipatory*, *formal*, and *informal*. Each stage entails learning, but the first and the third particularly involve some socialization by others outside the organization.

Anticipatory socialization

The **anticipatory socialization** stage begins before the criminal justice worker even starts the job. It occurs as the person *anticipates* perhaps someday working in law, police, or corrections. Those involved in anticipatory socialization for this prospective criminal justice recruit could include family, friends, teachers, and the media. In fact, this process may begin in childhood as a person is influenced by friends and family who are employed by or in contact with the relevant agencies, or by popular media depictions of that kind of work. Although family and friends who work in corrections may be able to supply important and relevant information about work in corrections, depictions of such work in the popular media are usually grossly inaccurate and almost uniformly misleading (e.g. *Dexter*, the *"CSI effect,"* *Law and Order SVU*, etc.).

The same holds true, of course, for policing and legal work. Though many of us might be aficionados of the various *Law and Order* series, the reruns of the *NYPD Blue* drama, or even the comical *Reno 911*, someone unacquainted with actual police or legal work may be led to believe by these shows that detectives and prosecutors have the luxury to pursue every lead and to prosecute every case to the fullest extent of the law—or in contrast, as is depicted on *Reno 911*, that the police are hilariously incompetent. Moreover, the defense of cases in such programs is usually vigorous even if the defendant is poor and socially powerless. Although, of course, police, prosecutors, and defense attorneys do at times behave in accordance with the TV dramas, these descriptors hardly represent every case (but see *The Wire* as an example of a more realistic portrayal of work in the CJ system). As Ford (2003: 87) writes regarding the "media tales" told about policing: "Gleaned from the epic stories recounted in police lore, media tales take rare events and magnify and describe heroic stories as the everyday grist of police work." But once on the job, those new recruits "[s]ense that what they will be doing is a far cry from the media's promise" (Ford 2003: 87).

Just as misleading, if not more so, are the depictions of corrections in the movies and on television. The inmates, most of whom are murderers and rapists, are invariably housed in dirty large city jails or in maximum security prisons overseen by guards who are uncaring and sarcastic in their demeanor.

A related problem with anticipatory socialization and the criminal justice system is that much of the work is done outside the view of the public.

This heightens the (in)credibility of justice-related media depictions, since those are often the only intimate exposure people have to criminal justice agencies. It is somewhat rare to find a community member who has taken a tour of the local jail, has sat through a trial, or knows how the parole office supervises parolees. Because of this general lack of knowledge and because many people do not know anyone who works in the criminal justice system and have not taken related classes in college, those who anticipate working in criminal justice-related positions tend to be most influenced by inaccurate media depictions, which do not give a complete or true picture of the work.

College students considering a career in criminal justice are also socialized into the nature of the work when they take courses or are assigned coursework related to the criminal justice system. An introductory survey class on the system (police, courts, and corrections) and a research methods class (Southerland 2002) are included by 40 percent (if not more) of criminal justice or criminology programs and departments. Fewer, but still a significant number, require law, juvenile justice/delinquency, and policing courses. Not as many programs, however, require a corrections class. These classes may or may not include much discussion of the actual work done in the field, but to the extent that they do, anticipatory socialization occurs through classroom lectures, readings, criminal justice professionals who give guest lectures, or visits to local work sites. Inevitably, many students note that they find guest speakers and on-site visits to be the most enlivening parts of our criminal justice classes.

Perhaps because of the media depictions, a lack of knowledge, and some notable abuses of power that tend to make the headlines, some types of criminal justice work today (e.g., that of correctional officers) have not achieved the professional status enjoyed by police, lawyers, teachers, and firefighters. Criminal justice will have arrived as a profession when a little boy or girl responds to the ubiquitous adult question, "What do you want to be when you grow up?", with "I want to work in a prison" or "I want to work with kids at the detention center." When children begin to provide such responses, the popular image of corrections will have changed to reflect an understanding of the work and recognition of its professional status. At this point anticipatory socialization may more accurately reflect the positive side of work in corrections. Because of generally higher educational and training requirements, not to mention pay for policing and law, workers in those organizations are more likely to be regarded as "professionals."

Formal socialization

Formal socialization occurs when a worker is exposed to the legal or officially sanctioned requirements of a job. Formal socialization can begin in the job interview and, in criminal justice agencies, usually occurs in the initial on-the-job training conducted by a designated official, during the academy training (for corrections and policing), and in ongoing training sessions throughout the career of those workers.

The amount of academy training received by corrections and police workers varies widely across job types, between the states, and between positions at the federal, state, county, and city levels. The average length of a police recruit training program is 640 hours (Thibault *et al.* 2004), although a number of agencies provide far less. For instance, according to their respective websites (accessed spring 2013), the Michigan State Police Training Division provides 594 hours for law enforcement basic training and the Georgia State University Police Department provides only 335 hours. On the other hand, the websites of the police departments of Tulsa, Oklahoma, and Mobile, Alabama (accessed spring 2013) indicate that new recruits receive up to twenty-five weeks, or between 600 and 920 hours, of training.

Required recruit training for corrections jobs is usually far less. Unfortunately, there is no easily accessible national compilation of training requirements for corrections work, as there is for policing in the *Criminal Justice Statistics 2002* Sourcebook (Maguire and Pastore 2004). However, individual states and organizations do publish their entry-level training requirements.

For instance, the private Corrections Corporation of America (CCA) provides all staff with forty hours of training; correctional officers get an additional 120 hours of training during their first year (CCA website 2013). Those first forty hours of training include such topics as corporate history and practice, facility and personnel policies and procedures, employee standards of conduct, communicable diseases, institutional safety, special management of offenders, suicide prevention, unit management, use of force, emergency procedures, and sexual harassment. The 120-hour specialized training course for correctional officers includes such topics as count procedures, cultural diversity, defensive tactics, direct supervision, emergency procedures, facility policy and procedures, firearms training, hostage situations, first aid/CPR, and inmate disciplinary, grievance, and classification procedures.

Though they do not indicate what the training topics are, the Maine Criminal Justice Academy (MCJA) website notes that eighty hours of academy training in a two-week period are provided for correctional officers (MCJA 2013). The Maine officials also do not indicate on their website what training is required for probation and parole or juvenile justice workers. In Delaware, a nine- or twelve-week basic training program is required for either correctional officers (nine) or probation and parole officers (twelve). The state website include the general training topics, but does not indicate whether the training is at forty hours per week; but if so, then Delaware requires 360–480 hours of entry-level training for these officers (Delaware Department of Correction 2004).

In contrast, in California, probation officers and parole agents are treated somewhat differently. Counties in California hire the probation officers and the state hires the parole agents, who work for either the Department of Corrections or the Youth Authority (California Employment Development Department 2004) Both positions, as is often true for adult and juvenile probation and parole officers, require a four-year degree. Probation officers in California must also complete 200 hours of basic training within their first year, and parole agents must complete four weeks (possibly 160 hours) of training in the same time period. In Nevada, the probation and parole officers are afforded 480 hours of training in their first year of employment, but that includes both classroom and field training hours (Nevada Department of Public Safety 2004)

Attorneys laboring in the criminal courts usually get on-the-job mentoring by more experienced colleagues, much like those in policing and corrections who participate in training in the field, through a field training officer (FTO). Of course, three years of law school, particularly if a clinic (or clerking) is required, might be regarded as providing some formal training, in addition to education. Smith (1997) notes that law school students often do not enroll in clinical programs, though such programs might help them become better lawyers, because they are not tested on bar exams. The stark truth is law students feel the need to focus on those courses that will help them pass the bar exam and the bar exam is not based on clinical practice. In fact, the bar exam tends to be preoccupied with business law (Smith 1997). Therefore, some might argue that ironically, the profession with perhaps the highest regard in the criminal justice system, and which arguably exerts the most power, has the least practical training.

Reddington and Kreisel (2003) found in their research on training requirements for juvenile probation officers that thirty-six states mandate some form of training, which varies widely in amount and type. They noted that one to two weeks of fundamental skills training was typical for most of these states. They note that "[t]his average amount of training for juvenile probation officers is somewhat lower than the average for adult probation officers, which is 125 hours, or for law enforcement officers" (Reddington and Kreisel 2003: 45).

Needless to say, the amount of training for entry-level positions varies widely by position and organization. But generally correctional workers get less formal socialization via training at the beginning of their career than do police officers, and much less anticipatory socialization via education than attorneys (particularly those who take a criminal law clinic) working in the criminal court system.

Ongoing training offered by criminal justice agencies also varies widely by jurisdictions and jobs. Some workers are required to take 10–20 hours per year to remain current in their field, while others may be offered little or no training, or participation is viewed as entirely optional. We will discuss training more in subsequent chapters, but clearly the extent to which training is provided and required for criminal justice workers is a measure of the professional stature that a field has acquired.

In addition to the academy and ongoing training that police and corrections workers are exposed to, they, and new prosecuting and defense attorneys, are often also formally socialized by an on-the-job trainer/mentor or a field training officer, either before or after their initial training. The FTOs, who often have years of tenure in the job, are tasked with teaching the relatively new employee how things are "officially" done in the organization. If selected correctly, the trainer/mentor/FTO can impart valuable knowledge about how to translate formal education and training to actual job practice. They can both model professional work and allow the new employee the opportunity to learn and practice skills while gradually transitioning into full practice on the job (Sun 2003).

The policing field first adopted FTO programs in the 1970s (Thibault *et al.* 2004). Critics of these early programs noted that instead of being the water walkers of the organization, too often FTOs are those who get stuck with the extra task of on-the-job training without instruction in how to do it, without the necessary time to do it right, and without any particular predilection to teach on the part of the officers. Hence, recommendations for current programs hinge on training for the trainers or FTOs and adherence to official policies, procedures, review, and evaluation requirements (Thibault *et al.* 2004). Bradford and Pynes (2000) also note that police academy training has not kept up with changing focuses in police work. Specifically, they note that few academies provide training in problem solving or interpersonal and decision making skills, though such knowledge is key to working in an organization that is focused on community policing.

Informal socialization

Informal socialization is teaching and learning that takes place on the job. It is outside the official strictures of law and procedure and away from the officially recognized instructors. It is learning how the job is actually done, and many times that means learning the official and the unofficial versions. The divide that sometimes separates the official and unofficial versions of how the job is done is represented by the experience of many correctional and police practitioners upon finishing the academy: They were taken aside by an old-timer and told something like "Okay, now forget that bullshit you heard at the academy, I'll show you how we REALLY do things around here." This happened to one of the authors after a week with an FTO when she first started as a correctional officer, and she saw it happen to correctional officers returning from academy training. Our students report having had the same experience when they began work in corrections and policing after academy training.

The means of transmitting this informal socialization can take many forms. In his study of community corrections, Crank (1996) noted that it may happen under the guise of "official" training when stories or "tropes" are told to illustrate how "real" work is done. In Crank's observation of training for probation and parole officers in Nevada, commonsense advice about how to do the job was transmitted to new hires via a linguistic device he termed a *trope*, which he defines as a "[s]tory, an irony, a metaphor, or some combination of these, constituted from everyday experience" (Crank 1996: 271). For example, one instructor was trying to illustrate the importance of body searches and the inherent danger if they are not done correctly:

> This is the place [the groin area] where people hide all kinds of stuff. There was a case in California where a guy was up for parole. He went before the board, and they turned him down. He bent over and pulled a stabbing tool out of his anal cavity. He jumped over the desk and stabbed a parole board member that he didn't like in the shoulder a couple of times.
>
> (Crank 1996: 227)

A different instructor uses a trope to illustrate the understandable sympathy probation and parole officers have when their clients cannot meet their P and P conditions because they are too poor:

> We have a bad situation in our country. A lot of times it is impossible to find work for an unemployed mother. There's no way minimum wage can provide the support she can get from unemployment and ADC. However, a condition of parole is employment. You may have to talk to your supervisor. A low-skill offender with three children, her children will literally starve if she has to take a minimum-wage job. They can't afford childcare. You can write it up so that they have to work, but you can write it up so that they can take care of their children at home.
>
> (Crank 1996: 282)

In both instances the academy instructors for probation and parole are informally socializing the new recruits to the nature of the work. In the second trope, the instructor is even advocating that the officer ignore a formal condition out of compassion for the circumstances some clients face.

Greenhorn criminal justice workers are also informally socialized by their colleagues. They observe what common practice is within given situations/contexts and they sometimes model that (Pollock 2004). If juveniles in the detention center are treated with respect in speech and deed by the majority of the other counselors, then the new counselor understands that this is the norm for behavior. If, however, the kids are referred to as "little criminals" or worse by staff, if their requests for assistance and information are ignored and their privacy is repeatedly violated for no purpose, then new counselors will detect a conflict between the official version of their job and the informal socialization being provided on the job.

In addition to the stories or tropes and observations of common practice, informal socialization may occur when clients train workers. Lipsky (1980) noted that clients will tell SLBs what behavior they expect either directly or indirectly. They might do this with intent or inadvertently. It is possible that the more prolonged and intense the contact with clients, the more likely they are to be able to "shape" the behavior of the workers. If this is true, those who work in corrections are probably more likely to experience the influence of the client than are police officers or criminal attorneys, whose exposure is likely to be short-term and more remote. For instance, an inmate in a prison or jail might shape the behavior of the correctional officer by refusing to follow an order, by following the order, or by just ignoring it. If the same person refused an order by a police officer, the officer would handle it as she does all such circumstances, without the constraint of knowing that she will have to deal with the person over and over again over a span of days, months, or years.

Even so, repeated exposure to the same victims and offenders, or persons in similar circumstances, surely shapes the reactions of both the police and criminal attorneys. It is often noted in the police literature, for instance, that officers can become cynical about domestic violence because they are called to the same house to mediate the same disputes again and again. Likewise the literature on sentencing indicates that criminal attorneys and judges will develop "norms" for sentencing, or alike sentences for similar offenders and offenses even when the law allows a wide range of sentencing options. In both the domestic violence and sentencing examples just given, it is possible that coworkers and supervisors are also shaping the behavior of the police and attorneys; but we must not forget that the clients in these circumstances may also be exerting some influence (Lipsky 1980).

In corrections, a counselor is subtly reminded to hurry up with the current client by the line of inmates waiting outside the office. Repetitive requests from a juvenile's parents for an alcohol or drug program placement may persuade a probation officer to be a particular advocate for that child's case. A defense attorney may be persuaded by a client's fervent claims of innocence to allocate more time for that case. The point is that clients, and their friends and family, can also serve in a socialization capacity *vis-à-vis* the criminal justice worker.

Crouch and Marquart (1994: 303), in their classic article "On Becoming a Prison Guard," note that the decision to work in institutional corrections comes later in life for many, and it "[o]ften appears to be somewhat accidental, a rather unplanned response to a fortuitous opportunity or a need for immediate employment." Once on the job, the authors found that the inmates and the "guard" subculture were central components to the socialization of the new recruit.

The new officer reacts to and is shaped to some degree by the inmate subculture, which may be foreign to him, as the inmates react to his official status and authority (Crouch and Marquart 1994). Some officers are tested by inmates and some who fail the test are then corrupted in ways that Sykes (1958) identified a half-century ago: officers become too friendly with inmates, they engage in reciprocity with inmates (such as ignoring enforcement of one rule to secure inmate obedience in another matter); officers concede some tasks to inmates (such as mail delivery), and inmates use the officer's transgressions to blackmail them.

In the prison at which one of the authors worked in the 1980s, a sergeant she admired told her to ignore the bulldogging by one powerful inmate. This inmate, whom we'll call Jim, coercively collected soda and potato chips and other store items from inmates in a dorm room one Saturday. The sergeant wanted his younger colleague to ignore the bulldogging because the inmate was an important ally for staff in keeping younger and rowdier inmates in line. Greatly influenced by the wisdom of this sergeant, the new officer did not infract Jim for the prohibited behavior; it was a decision she later came to regret. Eventually, the bulldogging inmate was infracted and transferred out, but only when he went too far in his collection and enforcement efforts—he was involved in a serious assault on an inmate that could not be officially ignored.

Crouch and Marquart also note the influence of the correctional subculture in informally socializing the new officer: "The recruit learns how to be a guard most directly by observing, listening to and imitating the veterans with whom he works" (1994: 312). This subculture teaches the officer how to perceive and manage inmates and how to anticipate and handle trouble. Old-time officers tell the newer officers that if they heed such advice they are less likely to find themselves in a bad spot with inmates and more likely to garner the respect of other officers.

In addition to the circumstances of the job and the socialization that criminal justice workers receive from clients and coworkers, there is evidence that other factors influence socialization. For instance, the personal characteristics and framework that criminal justice workers bring to their jobs have been found to influence how they feel about the work and how they behave in their role. Martin (1990) was one of the first to note that men and women police officers experienced their jobs differently. Jurik and Halemba (1984) and Jurik (1985) also noted this difference between the genders in their research on job perceptions and performance of correctional officers in Arizona in the 1980s. Notably, since that time, and building on Jurik and Halemba's research, others have found both similarities and differences between the genders in how they experience and perform corrections and police work (Daniello 2011; Farkas 1999; Lutze and Murphy 1999; Lawrence and Mahan 1998; Pogrebin and Poole 1997; Belknap 1995; Martin 1990; Zupan 1986). Research has also documented that people of diverse races and ethnicities and/or with diverse backgrounds (e.g., military service) may differ in their views of the work and how they perform it (Stohr *et al.* 2012; Hemmens *et al.* 2002; Van Voorhis *et al.* 1991). When there are differences between groups, however, it is not always clear whether they are the result of a framework people bring to the job or the result of socialization on the job (Ford 2003): Is it nature or nurture? The perennial question indeed—which has no clear answer yet!

The criminal justice role

Anticipatory, formal, and informal socialization in the workplace are geared toward defining what the job is for the criminal justice worker or what his or her role is. According to Katz and Kahn (1978), role behavior is essentially what people do over and over on the job. What you do on the job is your role, be that officially outlined by statutorily defined tasks, position descriptions and policies, and procedural requirements, or unofficially defined by the actual work that is done and required. As we have seen from our discussion of socialization, the criminal justice role is both officially and unofficially defined in the organization (Purkiss *et al.* 2003). But oftentimes those official requirements for the role are in conflict with unofficial requirements.

Role conflict: the service vs. security/serve vs. protect dichotomies

Role conflict occurs when there are competing expectations for the role that are difficult to fulfill. A related concept is **role ambiguity**, which occurs when expectations for the role are not clear or are confusing. In corrections and policing there is a classic dichotomy of roles for workers between the informal and formal demands of service work and rehabilitative tasks and the competing requirement that they always be attentive to security, protection, incapacitative, and even punitive requirements (Buerger *et al.* 1999; Cullen and Gilbert 1982; Johnson 1996; Lombardo 1989; Maahs and Pratt 2001).

Prosecutors and defense attorneys have clearer roles, formally speaking, than their sisters and brothers in policing and corrections. Nevertheless it can be said of them, as is true of the police and corrections, that organizational demands on their time, such as caseloads, can serve to informally reduce their ability to perform their defense or prosecutorial roles adequately (Hemmens *et al.* 2010; Smith 1997). According to Smith, lawyers must both defend the rights and interests of the client (in the case of prosecutors this would be the state) and serve as gatekeepers to the court system, keeping out complaints that do not merit prosecution and pursuing those that do. Their role also includes the ability to transform grievances into legal claims, develop new legal theories and arguments, serve as decision makers, exert influence over public policy, and control entry into the legal profession (Hemmens *et al.* 2010; Smith 1997). In the larger sense lawyering includes these grander activities, but down in the trenches of the criminal court the role of the defense or prosecuting attorney is primarily to advocate for the client or case and to get through the caseload.

Lombardo (1989) found in his research on officers working in the state prison in Auburn, New York, in the 1970s and 1980s that institutional rules sometimes prohibited an informal role that was weighted toward rehabilitative services. The roles for corrections workers are often in conflict and at times ambiguous. Similarly, Buerger *et al.* (1999: 125) note the difficulties that arise when police officers who are more traditional in their expectations for law enforcement (e.g. "favoring confrontation, command, and coercion") are suddenly working in a community policing-based organization where interactions with citizens might be expected to include more "participation, promotion, and persuasion."

Role conflict occurs because of the differing expectations for corrections and policing work. Past research shows that the general public and many system actors strongly supported punishment as the primary goal of corrections, which was reflected in how inmates were dealt with within the system, as well as how they were treated once released back into their communities (Norman and Burbridge 1991; Zimmerman *et al.* 1988). More recently, however, several studies indicate a shift to support for rehabilitation among the general public and correctional actors (Collins *et al.* 2012; Cullen *et al.* 1988; Flanagan and Caulfield 1984; Gordon 1999; Kifer *et al.* 2003; McCorkle 1993; Moak and Wallace 2000; Moon *et al.* 2000). The result is that in correctional settings, role conflict is more common because of slow systemic change and the bifurcated interests in rehabilitation and punishment that have resulted.

In an analysis of the statutorily defined role for probation officers, Purkiss *et al.* (2003) found that state legislatures required officers to perform twenty-three tasks in 2002. These tasks included a mix of law enforcement, rehabilitative, and other requirements. The authors note that a comparison of 1992 through 2002 statutes in the states clearly shows that the law enforcement role for probation officers gained primacy in the early 1990s, whereas rehabilitation and a restorative justice focus became more popular as the decade ended and the new century began.

The service or rehabilitative role, also known as the human service role, requires a trust relationship between correctional worker and client and a willingness of the worker to advocate for the client. On the other hand a security or punitive role, also known as the custodial role, requires for the correctional worker distrust and suspicion of clients and the need to maintain distance from them. Johnson, in his important book *Hard Time: Understanding and Reforming the Prison*, starkly defines these two roles, first describing the custodial officer working in prisons as follows (see also Box 6.1):

"Smug hacks" ... typically account for about a quarter of the guard force. They are custodial officers in the pejorative sense of the term. They seek order at any price, and violence—their own or that of inmate allies—is one of the tools of their trade. Their stance of toughness is exalted in the guard subculture, and is the public image (though not the private reality) adopted by most officers. Smug hacks find their counterparts in the convicts of the prison yard. The combative relations that ensue between these groups account for much of the abuse and even brutality that occurs in the prison.

(Johnson 197: 1996)

In contrast, Johnson defines human service officers as those who:

Use their authority to help inmates cope with prison life; they provide human service rather than custodial repression. They do the best they can with the resources at their disposal to make the prison a better place in which to live and work. In contrast to their merely custodial colleagues, these officers cope maturely with their own problems as well as with the problems experienced by prisoners. They serve, by their helping activities and by example, as true correctional officers.

(Johnson 223: 1996)

Clearly, there cannot always be an obvious demarcation in these roles. Police and correctional staff often adopt one role or the other depending on the situation. Sometimes police officers need to exercise a law enforcement role to maintain the safety of the community. Sometimes a human service role might be misinterpreted by inmates and/or might compromise the ability of the correctional officer to objectively supervise. Certainly mindless brutality is never called for in policing or corrections, but an emphasis on protection, security, and order often is. It is the degree to which criminal justice staff fall on one or the other end of this continuum of roles, and how they respond to a given situation, that should be of interest.

Box 6.1 The human service and custodial roles for corrections

Johnson in *Hard Time* (1996) and Lombardo in *Guards Imprisoned: Correctional Officers at Work* (1989), both following in the footsteps of Toch (1978), discuss the human service and custodial roles for correctional officers. The primary attributes of each are as follows:
Custodial officer

* mindless
* brutal
* custodian
* emphasis on order maintenance

Human service officer

- provider of goods and services
- referral agent or an advocate
- assistance with institutional adjustment

Both men thought that human service work was common practice for most correctional officers and that the custodial officer role was the exception rather than the rule.

Whereas Johnson (1996) and Lombardo (1989) each developed an understanding of these roles from studies of adult prisons, similar distinctions have been made officially and unofficially for other sectors of criminal justice. Juvenile justice has traditionally had the greatest focus on a service or rehabilitative role for its staff (Rothman 1980). As the juvenile court, juvenile probation and parole programs, and detention and prison facilities were established to function formally in "the best interest of the child," there has naturally been a greater focus on rehabilitation.

In research on the attitudes of juvenile correctional facility directors, Caeti *et al.* (2003) administered a questionnaire measuring role orientation, job satisfaction, and stress to the 406 facility directors across the nation. They had a 63.5 percent response rate and found that most directors (61.2 percent) ranked rehabilitation as the number-one goal of juvenile corrections, with deterrence (25.6 percent), incapacitation (12.0 percent), and retribution (0.4 percent) following. In that same publication, Caeti and his colleagues compared these responses to those by prison wardens (to a questionnaire administered in the early 1990s). The wardens' ranking was in the following order: retribution, deterrence, rehabilitation, and incapacitation.

Not surprisingly, then, there tends to be a more formal orientation toward a rehabilitative role for criminal justice workers who have juvenile clients or who work in that system. Informally, however, the actual role that the police, attorneys for juveniles, and their probation and parole officers or detention workers or prison counselors adopt is shaped by their roles as SLBs (with too many clients and not enough resources) and by the clients themselves, the ambient subculture, and the political winds. In his book describing the work of juvenile probation officers, Jacobs (1990) notes that because of the crushing pressure of young clients on the caseload, the officer often has to make a King Solomon-like choice—whether to focus their energies on those who need them most, or on those who show the most promise.

As with criminal justice workers who labor in the juvenile justice system the traditional role of probation and parole officers who work with adults has also differed somewhat from that of adult correctional institution workers. Probation and parole departments were established based on the belief that clients were in need of a helping hand to settle into a job and put a roof over their heads (Rothman 1980). Probation and parole officers were expected to help and counsel their clients. In reality, probation and parole officers, termed community corrections officers now in some states also function as SLBs, with too many demands on their time and too many clients. Their role is also shaped by their clients, by the subculture, and by the politics of the day (Lipsky 1980).

For both the juvenile justice system and adult probation and parole, there has been a move toward a more custodial role. This is due in large part to a shift in the political winds toward a more conservative approach to criminal justice in general (Benekos and Merlo 2001; Seiter 2002). Crowded correctional institutions and crowded caseloads for court personnel and probation and parole officers at both the adult and juvenile levels are a direct consequence of the greater willingness to punish by putting more and more people under some kind of correctional supervision in the past thirty years (e.g., King Davis *et al.* 2004). Until recently this also meant that the dollars available to fund correctional programming were scarce in most states and communities. In the late 1990s, as governments were flush in terms of tax dollars and as there was a dawning realization that the cost of locking so many people up would eventually claim any extra revenue, there was renewed interest in rehabilitation programming in many states and at the federal level. Unfortunately, funding was uneven and sometimes inadequate at all levels in the first decade of the 2000s.

Moreover, and relatedly, juvenile and adult probation and parole officers lament their client overload and the lack of programming options for the indigent clients they supervise (Jacobs 1990; Seiter 2002). What this means is that even if they were inclined to perform a more rehabilitative or service-oriented role, their efforts would be stymied by the nature of the work and the lack of funding in their communities.

Seiter (2002), in a survey and interviews of adult parole officers in Missouri, found that despite the crowding and despite political pressures to focus on the security/surveillance and control role, many officers thought that the most important aspects of their job involved helping and assisting parolees. When officers were asked to identify the most important aspects of reentry programs for parolees they listed employment, treatment, and support from loved ones first, second, and third, and supervision/monitoring and controlling and holding offenders accountable fourth and fifth. Likewise, when parole officers were asked to identify the most important aspect of their job that leads to successful completion of parole, they provided similar responses. Specifically, they listed the supervision/monitoring and controlling activities first, but the assessment of needs and referral to agencies and the support for employment second and third, with accountability fourth.

Criminal justice workers at both the juvenile and adult levels are faced with similar limitations on their ability to adopt a service or rehabilitative role. There is little rehabilitative programming in adult corrections in many states and facilities. What does exist is too often delivered in a non-structured way, by volunteers or by staff who have received little training to conduct it. Moreover, the programming is rarely subjected to rigorous evaluation. The "best practices" research provides some hope for improvement in this area, but funding, delivery, and evaluation of programming in correctional institutions and in the communities is problematic, though not hopeless. In policing, and as indicated earlier, the training for officers has not kept up with the move to a more service and problem-solving role for officers working in community policing-oriented organizations.

Not surprisingly, role conflict and ambiguity have been tied to several negative (and in some ways interrelated) outcomes for workers in the criminal justice system, including alienation from their work, cynicism, lowered job satisfaction and commitment, a less favorable attitude toward service and treatment, and stress and turnover (Bennett and Schmitt 2002; Brody *et al.* 2002; Crouch and Marquart 1994; Lombardo 1989; Maahs and Pratt 2001). For the criminal justice manager interested in minimizing role conflict, the answer may lie in greater clarification of the role and reinforcement of the appropriate role both officially and unofficially. Personnel practices such as selection, training, performance evaluation, and promotions should reinforce the expectations for the role. Bennett and Schmitt (2002) find that cynicism among police officers is intimately tied to job satisfaction. In turn, in the other studies just mentioned, levels of job satisfaction have varied depending on role conflict and ambiguity. Johnson (1996) argues that officers who adopt a more human services role in corrections have a more enlarged and enriched job, and are more likely to gain satisfaction from it. Also Lombardo (1989) argues that human service work in corrections reduces the alienation that officers feel from their work. Relatedly, Brody and colleagues (2002) found that police officers report more job satisfaction when they work in agencies most supportive of a community policing role.

An alternative perspective is that criminal justice workers *integrate* the roles of security/law enforcement and service/rehabilitation/treatment, rather than experiencing role conflict as a result of the existence of different sets of requirements. In a study of two probation-intensive supervision sites, one in Ohio and the other in Georgia, Clear and Latessa (1993) found that individual officers' behavior was influenced by the policy of each person's organization. They also found that within the same organization some officers may display an interest in one role over the other, but that the roles were not incompatible, as "[a]n officer's preference for one attitude will not cause avoidance of tasks consistent with the other" (Clear and Latessa 1993: 457).

Our colleague Craig Hemmens and one of the present authors (Stohr) developed the "correctional role instrument" as a means of diagnosing role preference in jails and prisons (see Box 6.2 and Section 2 of the chapter appendix). This instrument, or a version of it, might be used by correctional managers to research which role preference tends to predominate in their facility. We think that most of these instrument items could be reworded to fit the work of those in probation and parole and the juvenile justice system.

Box 6.2 A discussion of the correctional role instrument
By Mary K. Stohr

We developed the thirty-six-item "correctional role instrument" for several reasons (Stohr *et al.* 2012; Hemmens and Stohr 2000; 2001; Hemmens *et al.* 2002). First, we wanted to measure the extent to which correctional staff in jails and prisons identified with either a human services or a custodial role for corrections. We were also interested in perceptions of the use of force by staff and perceptions of male and female staff of the work of women as correctional officers. We were measuring perceptions, not actual behavior.

The instrument items were developed based on a review of the relevant literature and prior work experience (by Stohr), and on comments provided by a correctional role scholar (Robert Johnson). After face validity analysis by a warden and a deputy warden in a medium security prison (Barrier *et al.* 1999; Stohr *et al.* 2000), the items were rewritten and the instrument was pretested at a medium security prison in fall 1997, then refined in 1998 in response to those findings, and used once again in 2007 (Stohr *et al.* 2012; Hemmens and Stohr 2000, 2001). The questionnaire and the research process were subjected to Human Subjects Review before the instrument was pretested and administered.

Respondents were asked to indicate their level of agreement or disagreement with each given statement. Responses could range from 1 (strongly disagree) to 7 (strongly agree). Respondents also had the options of answering "don't know" or leaving a particular item blank. A number of items were reverse coded. This was done to ensure that staff completing the questionnaire were truly reading the questions and responding with some degree of consistency. As recoded, for all items, the higher the mean, the greater the agreement with the human service role.

The studies were conducted in 1998, 1999, and 2007. At each institution, including male minimum and male maximum security prisons, a female prison (combined minimum, medium, and maximum security), two mixed-gender jails, and a jail training academy, the research teams administered and collected the questionnaires. Facility administrators scheduled training or meetings at different times of the day, so that all shifts were given the opportunity to complete the questionnaires. Attendance at the meeting was mandatory, but completion of the survey was entirely voluntary. For most of the facilities, the research team returned on different days and at different times to complete administration of the questionnaire.

The findings are more fully summarized in the publications cited earlier, but here are the basics: Most correctional staff tended to favor a human service role orientation; women were less likely to value the use of force in their work; men and women tended to positively perceive the work of women in corrections, but women had a higher regard for their ability to do corrections work than men; military service tended to have a negative effect on the perception of abilities of female staff; and, as other research has determined regarding cynicism and alienation (see Toch and Klofas 1982), those in midcareer (6–10 years) tend to be less human service-oriented than those at the beginning and end of their careers.

The jail version of the instrument is provided in the appendix at the end of this chapter. Readers may use it, the cover page (without our names!), and the demographics sheet. We would caution anyone who uses the instrument to closely follow the data collection procedures outlined in the cited publications and to secure human subject approval by an accredited university or institution prior to administration of this questionnaire. We would also urge users to abide by accepted methodological practices in terms of questionnaire administration and data analysis. Item means might be compared with those in the publications, though we made slight changes in a few items over the course of the instrument development and testing. Please notify Hemmens and Stohr if you intend to use the instrument, and share your methodology and findings with us afterward.

The popular perception of criminal justice employees is that their role is heavily invested with power, and to some extent this is true. Such employees do have the ability to limit the liberty and freedoms of those they are entrusted to investigate, hold, try, sentence, watch, supervise, treat, and care for. These are awesome powers when situated in a democracy such as ours, where regular citizens are guaranteed a certain level of protection from their government via the Constitution and the Bill of Rights. Given how important power is to the role of criminal justice workers, especially in a democracy, some discussion of its nature is warranted.

Power *is the ability to get others to do what they otherwise wouldn't* (which is very close to Dahl's 1957 definition). This definition works at the individual level, but it does not encompass the power that organizations wield in their environments. In other words, power is exerted at the individual level and at the organizational level in criminal justice agencies and of course within the organization. There is power that attaches to individuals because of their charm, charisma, or other personal abilities. There is power that attaches to a given job or project or team, and supervisors and staff have the power to wield raw coercion over suspects, accused persons, inmates, and clients.

Weber (1947) noted that there were three types of **authority**, a term formally defined as "[t]he right and power to enforce laws, exact obedience, command, determine, or judge," which he equated with *legitimized power* (American Heritage Dictionary 1992: 56). The first type of authority he identified is **traditional**, or the power held by royalty or a head of state, or power that is vested with a sense of tradition and history. The second type is **charismatic**, or based on the personal charm and leadership qualities of the individual. The third type of authority is **legal**, or that based in laws and rules that are generally accepted. These three types of authority give those who wield them the legitimized power to operate without resort to the other types of power.

Relatedly, French and Raven (1959) identified the following five types or bases of power (along with legitimized power):

- *Reward* (or the perception that the power holder can give some kind of reward). In criminal justice agencies actors have the power to decline to arrest, investigate, or prosecute; they can prefer charges or grant sentence reductions; they can secure better housing or job placement, direct that someone receive a positive write-up, or decline to infract or violate a person's probation or parole.
- *Coercive* (or the perception that the power holder can use force to get what he or she wants). In criminal justice agencies this can range from the threat of force if the power recipient does not comply with commands to the actual use of force.
- *Legitimate* (or the perception that the power holder has legal or official status). In criminal justice agencies this means a position as an attorney or officer or counselor or work supervisor or health care provider is recognized as empowering the holder.
- *Referent* (or the perception that the power holder is a reference for the power recipient). In criminal justice agencies this means that the worker is looked upon as a model for the power recipient, which in turn empowers the worker.
- *Expert* (or the perception that the power holder has qualifications that confer this status). In criminal justice agencies this means that the power holder is recognized as possessing experience or knowledge that makes him or her qualified to exert power.

Hepburn (1985) studied each of these bases of power in the correctional environment in the 1980s. He administered questionnaires that included five items related to each type of power. Officers in five prisons in four different states were asked to indicate, by ranking these items, why inmates obey the correctional staff. In the same study, Hepburn collected background information on the officers, as well as their attitudes toward work and toward inmates. What he found was that the officers thought that inmates did what they otherwise would not do because of the legitimate and expert power of the officers. "Legitimate power was ranked first by over one-third of the guards, and three of every five guards ranked legitimate power as either the first or second most important reason why prisoners did what they were told" (Hepburn 1985: 291). The types of power were ranked as follows: legitimate, expert, referent, coercive, and reward. This ranking was relatively stable across the different institutions and states. Hepburn notes that Lombardo (1981) also found that 44 percent of the prison officers he interviewed attributed their base of power to legitimacy.

Hepburn did find that the more experience an officer had, the more likely he or she was to rank expert power as more important and coercion and legitimacy as less so. He found little effect for education, formal contact with inmates, or attitudes toward work. He also found that the higher the custody orientation of the officer, the more likely the officer was to see coercion as an important power base.

Hepburn (1985) explains these findings by drawing attention to the regular duties of correctional staff. On a day-to-day basis and in the context of the normal operation of the institution, officers give direction to inmates based on their legitimate role. Rarely do they need to give orders that are starkly coercive. Rare too are the rewards they can give for ordinary compliance with rules and requirements. Hence, there is little need for reliance on coercion or rewards as bases for power in the usual operation of institutions.

Moreover, the use of coercion on a day-to-day basis would be highly inefficient and disruptive in corrections work. If a correctional officer was continually having to use force or its threat, it would be very difficult to get through the day and hard feelings and resistance would accumulate among the inmates (experiment with the role exercise at the end of the chapter to see how this dynamic might play out). As an officer is usually outnumbered by at least 30 to 1 when out and about with inmates, he could easily be overpowered if the inmates were to choose to cooperate in such a maneuver. Calling for backup continually to get inmates to comply with basic rules would throw the whole institution into disarray and would not be positively viewed by coworkers or administration. The ability to supervise of an officer who makes frequent calls for backup will very quickly be called into question.

On the other hand, corrections work is inherently coercive inasmuch as those who are supervised or incarcerated rarely volunteered for this status. Instead, the state in the form of criminal justice actors like the police, prosecuting attorneys, and correctional workers uses the threat of or actual force to gain compliance (Hemmens and Atherton 1999). Yet it is curious that in the day-to-day relations with inmates, the officers do not perceive coercion as the reason for inmates' general compliance with institutional rules and directives. One wonders whether inmates would respond in a similar manner to the ranking of power bases by Hepburn. Would they mark "legitimacy" as the primary power base for correctional officers?

In policing, the use of force or coercive power has been the subject of much scholarly discussion and study (Alpert and Smith 1999; Crank 1998; Griffin and Bernard 2003; Kaminski *et al.* 2004; Terrill *et al.* 2003). In their discussion of the police use of extra-legal force, Griffin and Bernard (2003) argue for the salience of the angry aggression theory. They posit that officers who do not learn coping mechanisms to handle the multiple sources of stress that are inherent in police work (e.g., citizen hostility, danger) are physiologically aroused by this stress, which tends to lead to more fear of threats and eventual aggression. A feedback loop develops (as in systems theory) whereby this chronic physiological arousal leads to the perception of more threats, then to aggression and the development of an "authoritarian" personality, back to still more perceived threats and more aggression. Other related negative outcomes, which only serve to reinforce the perception of threats and the concomitant aggression, are social isolation and displaced aggression (Griffin and Bernard 2003).

Another angle to the discussion of power is the fact that some criminal justice employees feel relatively powerless in their jobs. For instance, in his research on prisons Lombardo (1989: 145) noted frequent job dissatisfaction among correctional staff because officers had a perceived "[i]nability to influence [their] work environment in an effective manner." He found that the most mentioned reason for this feeling was a "lack of support" by administrators, supervisors, and coworkers, who not only were not always helpful but also sometimes worked at cross-purposes with the officer. The officers thought that they were too often obliged to work short-handed; that administrators tended to resolve problems by focusing on short-term rather than on long-term solutions; that officers were not always backed up regarding inmate discipline; and that the behavior of other officers was at times "lax and non-cooperative." Griffin and Bernard (2003) also mention the helplessness that police officers feel *vis-à-vis* their inability to change aspects of their job, a condition that adds to their stress and ultimately, for some, leads to the abuse of coercive power.

Sometimes it is not just the criminal justice actor who feels powerless in the system. Smith (1997) notes that though 13 percent of the American population falls below the poverty line, less than 2 percent of lawyers do legal work for agencies representing the poor. Clearly this highly skewed distribution of legal resources has led to an imbalance of advantages when the poor are drawn into the criminal courts.

For workers however this sense of powerlessness is to some degree attached to the type of management theory practiced in particular institutions, as was discussed in Chapter 4. If criminal justice workers had the opportunity to participate to a greater degree in decisions affecting their workplace, it is unlikely that they would feel so powerless.

Conclusions

Criminal justice work is composed of complex tasks requiring multiple skills and favoring those with certain propensities. The criminal justice organization has the opportunity to shape the outlook and habits of workers through both informal and formal socialization. The role such workers adopt is determined to a large extent by the emphasis that managers place on it. People generally will do what they are rewarded for. To the extent that a service or security or advocacy role for staff is acceptable to, and supported by, management, organizational members will recognize this fact and respond accordingly.

How criminal justice workers wield power is also shaped by the socialization process and the role the workers have adopted. Officers in Hepburn's study were quite clear in their belief that legitimacy, followed by expertise, constituted their main bases of power. The bureaucratic nature of the job and the inefficiency of force usage preclude the regular use of force to gain compliance. Thus almost by default, criminal justice workers are more likely to need human service role skills to maintain the daily routines of their work. Studies of power in police organization confirm that the organizational culture, along with stressors inherent to the job, can lead to the routinized abuse of power by officers.

Exercise: the role—ordering people about

One of the authors first observed and participated in a version of this exercise in a mandatory anger-management training session for correctional staff. She saw another version of it done in a training session with the state police years later. The purpose of this kind of exercise is to illustrate different styles of supervision and their relative success, or lack of it.

1　Select 6–10 people (you need a minimum of three pairs) and pair them off without respect to demographics. Ask the rest of the class to observe the proceedings.
2　Ask one person from each pair to be "the inmate" and the other to be "the correctional officer."
3　Have the inmates and officers meet separately to discuss their approach to being supervised (inmates) or their approach to supervision (officers).
4　Have the pairs meet up again and have the "officer" direct the "subject" to simulate sweeping the floor. The "inmates" may respond as they will (within reason!).
5　Stop the action after a few minutes and ask the "inmates" and "officers" to recount their experiences. Ask for audience comments. There should be obvious tie-ins with the role and power discussions in this chapter. Perhaps some linkage may be made to socialization and training (or lack thereof).

Discussion questions

1 How does socialization affect the role that criminal justice workers adopt? Give an example.
2 What are the main components of the human service and the
  custodial roles for corrections?
3 What are the main components of the service and the protection
  roles for policing?
4 Why would the use of coercion be inefficient in most situations
  encountered in the criminal justice environment? Explain your
  answer.
5 Which types of power tend to fit into the roles? Why would this
  be so?
6 How is the socialization for lawyers in the criminal courts substantially different from that for the police and corrections workers?
7 Do you think that inmates would rank legitimacy first and coercion next to last if they were asked what is the most important
  basis for correctional power? Why or why not?
8 Do you think that probation and parole officers would respond
  similarly to the correctional officers in Hepburn's study? Why or
  why not?
9 How do you think police officers can reduce stress to prevent themselves from engaging in angry aggression? Give an example.

Key terms

anticipatory socialization: begins before the criminal justice worker
  starts the job. It occurs as the person anticipates someday working
  in law, police, or corrections.
authority: "[t]he right and power to enforce laws, exact obedience,
  command, determine, or judge" (American Heritage Dictionary
  1992: 56).
charismatic authority: based on the personal charm and leadership
  qualities of the individual.
formal socialization: occurs when the worker is exposed to the legal
  or officially sanctioned requirements of the job.
informal socialization: the teaching and learning that take place on
  the job. It is outside the official strictures of law and procedure
  and occurs away from the officially recognized instructors.
legal authority: based in laws and rules that are generally accepted.

occupational socialization: "[t]he process by which a person acquires the values, attitudes, and behaviors of an ongoing occupational social system" (Klofas *et al.* 1990: 150).

power: the ability to get others to do what they otherwise wouldn't (Dahl 1957).

role: what you do on the job, be it officially outlined by statutorily defined tasks, position descriptions, and policies and procedural requirements, or unofficially defined by the actual work that is done and required.

role ambiguity: occurs when expectations for a role are not clear or are confusing.

role conflict: occurs when there are competing expectations for a role that are difficult to fulfill.

traditional authority: the power one holds in a position (e.g., as royalty or an elected head of state) or which is vested with a sense of tradition and history.

Appendix

Feel free to contact Mary Stohr to inquire about acquiring a digital version of this survey for research purposes:

THE CORRECTIONAL ROLE INSTRUMENT: JAIL RESEARCH DESCRIPTION SHEET

Dear Jail Staff Person:

This questionnaire was developed by Mary K. Stohr and Craig Hemmens, professors in the Department of Criminal Justice at Washington State University. WSU students are also assisting in this research. Information obtained from responses to the questionnaire will be kept COMPLETELY CONFIDENTIAL and PARTICIPATION IS COMPLETELY VOLUNTARY. No names should be mentioned on this questionnaire, and all responses will be combined by the research team so that it will be impossible to identify specific persons. We developed this questionnaire so that staff perceptions of jail roles might be better understood by people working in the field and by researchers. In essence, we are trying to determine what people think about their work in jails and why. We would really appreciate it if you would take the time to complete this questionnaire (it should take about 15 minutes).

You may keep this sheet for reference if you like. All responses to this questionnaire will be kept completely confidential and participation is voluntary. There is no reason to provide your name. Questionnaires should be returned directly to: _____. All responses will be grouped together in any report or publication produced using these data. Thanks so much for your participation.

SECTION ONE: Demographics

Please provide us with some general information about yourself.

1   Position:
2   Years of service:
3   Military service:
        Yes   No
4   Age:
5   Education (circle one)
        Less than GED
        GED
        High school graduate
        Some college
        BA or BS degree
        Master's degree or more
6   What is your current shift? (i.e., night, day, swing, other)
7   Did you choose your current shift?
        Yes   No
8   Gender:
        Male   Female
9   Race:
        White
        Black or African American
        Asian
        Other
        Multiracial
10   Ethnicity:
        Hispanic   Non-Hispanic

SECTION TWO: Jail Role Instrument

The role of jail staff presents many challenges and opportunities. This instrument was developed so that the various parts of that role might be identified by staff. Please read each question and using the agreement scale below, place the number that best reflects your level of agreement with the statement in the space provided in front of that question.

Scale (format for survey):

Strongly Disagree = 1
Disagree Slightly = 2
Slightly Disagree = 3
Neutral = 4
Slightly Agree = 5
Agree = 6
Strongly Agree = 7
Don't Know = 8

_____1. Jail staff should make an effort to answer the questions of inmates.

_____2. Jail staff should do what they can to make sure inmates have reasonable access to counselors.

_____3. Jail staff should ignore most inmate complaints.

_____4. Inmates should receive their store/commissary goods on time.

_____5. When an inmate doesn't get the correct medication, a staff member should contact medical staff.

_____6. Anyone who would visit an inmate is likely to be engaged in illegal activity.

_____7. Staff should ensure that inmates have the appropriate access to legal material they have a right to.

_____8. Ensuring that inmates have reasonable access to visitors is a responsibility of jail staff.

_____9. Using force is usually the best method to get inmates to follow orders.

_____10. Most inmates are trying to manipulate staff.

_____11. Explaining the reason for an order will usually gain inmate cooperation.

_____12. Inmate access to medical personnel should be limited to emergency situations.

_____13. When staff members make a mistake, they should admit it.

_____14. Promises made to inmates by staff are promises made to be broken.

_____15. Mail service should be regularly provided to inmates by staff.

_____16. Sometimes a little extra physical force is needed to let inmates know they can't get away with things.

_____17. Providing a set of written rules (dos and don'ts) to inmates at the beginning helps to avoid problems and misunderstandings later.

_____18. An inmate who fails at one task is likely to fail at another.

_____19. Helping inmates to find a suitable work situation is a responsibility of jail staff.

_____20. Inmate complaints are often just whining about nothing in particular.

_____21. Inmates usually choose to attend religious services, not because they have any faith, but so that they can appear to have changed.

_____22. Staff should assist inmates in gaining access to educational, drug/alcohol, and other programming.

_____23. It is part of the jail staff's job responsibilities to provide important information to inmates.

_____24. Staff should rarely have friendly conversations with inmates.

_____25. Use of physical force is not the easiest way to get an inmate to obey an order.

_____26. Staff should act how they want inmates to act.

_____27. It is okay if staff bend the rules every now and then, given that they have to supervise criminals.

_____28. Inmates often claim they are sick just to get out of school or work details.

_____29. When inmates succeed in jail, staff should be happy for them.

_____30. Jail staff should not guide or mentor inmates during their incarceration.

_____31. Staff are in part responsible for whether inmates "succeed" while incarcerated.

_____32. Female staff are as capable in working with inmates as male staff.

_____33. Inmates who complain about their medication are usually trying to get access to more drugs than they need.

_____34. Jail staff should have a voice in determining how their workplace operates.

_____35. Problem inmates can be more effectively handled when staff communicate and work as a team.

_____36. Female jail officers can carry out their duties just as well as male officers.

SECTION THREE: Additional Comments

Please feel free to provide additional information or to comment on all or part of this questionnaire in the space provided below or on the back of this sheet (or contact the researchers):

References

Alpert, G. P. and Smith, M. R. (1999) Police use-of-force data: Where we are and where we should be going. *Police Quarterly*, 2: 57–78.

American Heritage Dictionary (1992) *American heritage dictionary*. New York, NY: Houghton Mifflin.

Barrier, G., Stohr, M. K., Hemmens, C. and Marsh, R. (1999) A practical user's guide to ethical practices: Idaho's method for implementing ethical behavior in a correctional setting. *Corrections Compendium*, 24: 1–12.

Belknap, J. (1995) Women in conflict: An analysis of women correctional officers. In B. R. Price and N. J. Sokoloff (eds), *The criminal justice system and women: Offenders, victims and workers*. New York, NY: McGraw Hill, pp. 195–227.

Benekos, P. and Merlo, A. V. (2001) Three strikes and you're out: The political sentencing game. In E. J. Latessa, A. Holsinger, J. W. Marquart and J. R. Sorensen (eds), *Correctional contexts: Contemporary and classical readings*. Los Angeles, LA: Roxbury, pp. 454–463.

Bennett, R. R. and Schmitt, E. L. (2002) The effect of work environment on levels of police cynicism: A comparative study. *Police Quarterly*, 5: 493–522.

Bradford, D. and Pynes, J. E. (2000) Police academy training: Why hasn't it kept up with practice? *Police Quarterly*, 2, 283–301.

Brody, D. C., DeMarco, C. and Lovrich, N. P. (2002) Community policing and job satisfaction: Suggestive evidence of positive workforce effects from a multijurisdictional comparison in Washington State. *Police Quarterly*, 5, 181–205.

Buerger, M. E., Petrosino, A. J. and Petrosino, C. (1999) Extending the police role: Implications of police mediation as a problem-solving tool. *Police Quarterly*, 2: 125–149.

Caeti, T., Hemmens, C., Cullen, F. T. and Burton, V. S., Jr. (2003) Management of juvenile correctional facilities. *The Prison Journal*, 83(4): 1–23.

California Employment Development Department. (2004) *Probation officers and parole agents*. Employment development department: Labor market information. Available at www.calmis.cahwnet.gov (last accessed January 31, 2013).

Camp, S. D., Saylor, W. G. and Wright, K. N. (2001) Research note, racial diversity of correctional workers and inmates: Organizational commitment, teamwork and workers' efficacy in prisons. *Justice Quarterly*, 18(2): 411–427.

CCA. (2013) Careers. Corrections Corporation of America website. Available at www.correctionscorp.com/training (last accessed January 31, 2013).

Clear, T. R. and Latessa, E. J. (1993) Probation officers' roles in intensive supervision: Surveillance versus treatment. *Justice Quarterly*, 10(3): 441–462.

Collins, P. A., Iannacchione, B. Hudson, M. Stohr, M. K. and Hemmens, C. (2012) A comparison of jail inmate and staff correctional goal orientations: Results from across the line. *Journal of Crime and Justice*, 36(1): 100–115.

Crank, J. P. (1996) The construction of meaning during training for probation and parole. *Justice Quarterly*, 13(2): 265–290.

Crank, J. P. (1998) *Understanding police culture.* Cincinnati, OH: Anderson Publishing.

Crouch, B. and Marquart, J. (1994) On becoming a prison guard. In S. Stojkovic, J. Klofas and D. Kalinich (eds), *The administration and management of criminal justice organizations: A book of readings.* Prospect Heights, IL: Waveland Press, pp. 301–331.

Cullen, F., Cullen, J. and Wozniak, J. (1988) Is rehabilitation dead? The myth of the punitive public. *Journal of Criminal Justice*, 16: 303–317.

Cullen, F. T. and Gilbert, K. E. (1982) *Reaffirming rehabilitation.* Cincinnati, OH: Anderson Publishing.

Dahl, R. (1957) The concept of power. *Behavioral Science*, 2(3): 201–215.

Daniello, R. J. (2011) *Police officer stress awareness and management: A handbook for practitioners.* Lanham, MD: Hamilton Books.

Delaware Department of Correction (2013) Probation and parole officer 1. Available at www.doc.delaware.gov/EDC/InitialTraining.shtml (last accessed January 31, 2013).

Farkas, M. A. (1999) Inmate supervisory style: Does gender make a difference? *Women and Criminal Justice*, 10: 25–46.

Flanagan, T. and Caulfield, S. (1984) Public opinion and prison policy: A review. *The Prison Journal*, 64: 31–46.

Ford, R. E. (2003) Saying one thing, meaning another: The role of parables in police training. *Police Quarterly*, 6, 84–110.

French, J. and Raven, B. (1959) The bases of social power. In D. Cartwright (ed.), *Studies in social power.* Ann Arbor, MI: University of Michigan, pp. 150–167.

Gordon, J. (1999) Do staff attitudes vary by position? A look at one juvenile correctional center. *American Journal of Criminal Justice*, 24(1): 81–93.

Griffin, M. L., Hogan, N. L. and Lambert, E. G. (2012) Doing "people work" in the prison setting: An examination of the job characteristics model and correctional staff burnout. *Criminal Justice & Behavior*, 39(9): 1131–1147.

Griffin, S. P. and Bernard, T. J. (2003) Angry aggression among police officers. *Police Quarterly*, 6: 3–21.

Haarr, R. (1997) Patterns of interaction in a police patrol bureau: Race and gender barriers to integration. *Justice Quarterly*, 14(1): 53–85.

Hemmens, C. and Atherton, E. (1999) *Use of force: Current practice and policy.* Lanham, MD: American Correctional Association.

Hemmens, C., Brody, D. C. and Spohn, C. (2010) *Criminal courts: A contemporary perspective.* Thousand Oaks, CA: Sage Publications.

Hemmens, C. and Stohr, M. K. (2000) The two faces of the correctional role: An exploration of the value of the correctional role instrument. *International Journal of Offender Therapy and Comparative Criminology*, 44(3): 326–349.

Hemmens, C. and Stohr, M. K. (2001) Correctional staff attitudes regarding the use of force in corrections. *Corrections Management Quarterly*, 5: 26–39.

Hemmens, C., Stohr, M. K., Schoeler, M. and Miller, B. (2002) One step up, two steps back: The progression of perceptions of women's work in prisons and jails. *Journal of Criminal Justice*, 30(6): 473–489.

Hepburn, J. R. (1985) The exercise of power in coercive organizations. In S. Stojkovic, J. Klofas and D. Kalinich (eds) (1990), *The administration and management of criminal justice organizations.* Prospect Heights, IL: Waveland Press, pp. 249–265.

Jacobs, M. D. (1990) *Screwing the system and making it work: Juvenile justice in the no-fault society.* Chicago, IL: University of Chicago Press.

Jenne, D. L. and Kersting, R. C. (1998) Gender, power, and reciprocity in the correctional setting. *The Prison Journal*, 78(2): 166–186.

Johnson, R. (1996) *Hard time: Understanding and reforming the prison*, 2nd edn. Belmont, CA: Wadsworth.

Jurik, N. (1985) Individual and organizational determinants of correctional officer attitudes toward inmates. *Criminology*, 23: 523–539.

Jurik, N. and Halemba, G. (1984) Gender, working conditions and the job satisfaction of women in a non-traditional occupation: Female correctional officers in men's prisons. *Sociological Quarterly*, 25: 551–566.

Kaminski, R. J., DiGiovanni, C. and Downs, R. (2004) The use of force between the police and persons with impaired judgment. *Police Quarterly*, 7: 311–338.

Katz, D. and Kahn, D. (1978) *The social psychology of organizations*, 2nd edn. New York, NY: Wiley.

Kifer, M., Hemmens, C. and Stohr, M. K. (2003) The goals of corrections: Perspectives from the line. *Criminal Justice Review*, 28(1): 47–69.

King Davis, R., Applegate, B., Otto, C., Surette, R. and McCarthy, B. (2004) Roles and responsibilities: Analyzing local leaders' views on jail crowding from a systems perspective. *Crime and Delinquency*, 50(3): 458–482.

Klofas, J., Stojkovic, S. and Kalinich, D. (1990) *Criminal justice organizations administration and management.* Pacific Grove, CA: Brooks/Cole.

Lawrence, R. and Mahan, S. (1998) Women correctional officers in men's prisons: Acceptance and perceived job performance. *Women and Criminal Justice*, 9: 63–86.

Lipsky, M. (1980) *Street-level bureaucracy: Dilemmas of the individual in public services.* New York, NY: Russell Sage Foundation.

Lombardo, L. X. (1981) *Guards imprisoned: Correctional officers at work.* New York, NY: Elsevier.

Lombardo, L. X. (1989) *Guards imprisoned: Correctional officers at work*, 2nd edn. Cincinnati, OH: Anderson Publishing.

Lutze, F. E. and Murphy, D. W. (1999) Ultramasculine prison environments and inmates' adjustment: It's time to move beyond the 'boys will be boys' paradigm. *Justice Quarterly*, 16: 709–734.

Maahs, J. and Pratt, T. (2001) Uncovering the predictors of correctional officers' attitudes and behaviors: A meta-analysis. *Correctional Management Quarterly*, 5(2), 13–19.

Maguire, K. and Pastore, A. L. (eds) (2004) *Sourcebook of criminal justice statistics.* Available at www.albany.edu/sourcebook.

Martin, S. E. (1990) *On the move: The status of women in policing.* Washington DC: Police Foundation.

McCorkle, R. (1993) Research note: Punish and rehabilitate? Public attitudes toward six common crimes. *Crime and Delinquency*, 39: 240–252.

MCJA. (2013) Basic corrections training program. Maine Criminal Justice Academy website. Available at www.state.me.us/dps/mcja/training (last accessed January 31, 2013).

Meyer, J. and Grant, D. R. (2003) *The courts in our criminal justice system.* Upper Saddle River, NJ: Prentice Hall.

Moak, S. and Wallace, L. (2000) Attitudes of Louisiana practitioners toward rehabilitation of juvenile offenders. *American Journal of Criminal Justice*, 24(2): 272–284.

Mobile Alabama Police Department. Training information. Available at http://www.mobilepd.org/training.php (last accessed January 31, 2013).

Moon, M., Sundt, J., Cullen, F. and Wright, J. P. (2000) Is child saving dead? Public support for juvenile rehabilitation. *Crime and Delinquency*, 46(1): 38–60.

Morash, M. and Haarr, R. N. (2012) Doing, redoing, and undoing gender variation in gender identities of women working as police officers. *Feminist Criminology*, 7(1), 2–23.

Morash, M. and Haarr, R. N. (1995) Gender, workplace problems, and stress in policing. *Justice Quarterly*, 12: 113–140.

Nevada Department of Public Safety. (2004) Officer training. Available at http://dps.gov/pandp/training.htm (last accessed January 31, 2013).

Norman, M. and Burbridge, G. (1991) Attitudes of youth corrections professionals toward juvenile justice reform and policy alternatives—A Utah survey. *Journal of Criminal Justice*, 19: 81–91.

Pogrebin, M. R. and Poole, E. D. (1997) Women deputies and jail work. *Journal of Contemporary Criminal Justice*, 14: 117–134.

Pollock, J. M. (2004) *Prisons and prison life: Costs and consequences.* Los Angeles, CA: Roxbury.

Purkiss, M., Kifer, M., Hemmens, C. and Burton, V. S. (2003) Probation officer functions—A statutory analysis. *Federal Probation*, 67(1): 12–33.

Reddington, F. P. and Kreisel, B. W. (2003) The basic fundamental skills training for juvenile probation officers—Results of a nationwide survey of curriculum content. *Federal Probation*, 67(1): 41–46.

Rothman, D. J. (1980) *Conscience and convenience: The asylum and its alternatives in progressive America.* Boston, MA: Little, Brown.

Seiter, R. P. (2002) Prisoner reentry and the role of parole officers. *Federal Probation*, 66(3): 50–55.

Smith, C. E. (1997) *Courts, politics, and the judicial process*, 2nd edn. Chicago, IL: Nelson-Hall.

Southerland, M. D. (2002) Presidential address: Criminal justice curricula in the United States: A decade of change. *Justice Quarterly*, 19(4): 589–601.

Stohr, M. K., Hemmens, C., Marsh, R. L., Barrier, G. and Palhegyi, D. (2000) Can't scale this: The ethical parameters of correctional work. *The Prison Journal*, 80(1): 40–56.

Stohr, M. K., Hemmens, C., Collins, P. A., Iannacchione, B. and Hudson, M. (2012) Assessing the organizational culture in a jail setting. *The Prison Journal*, 92(3): 358–387.

Sun, I. Y. (2003) A comparison of police field training officers' and non-training officers' conflict resolution styles: Controlling versus supportive strategies. *Police Quarterly*, 6: 22–50.

Sykes, G. (1958) *The society of captives*. Princeton, NJ: Princeton University Press.

Terrill, W., Alpert, G. P., Dunham, R. G. and Smith, M. R. (2003) A management tool for evaluating police use of force: An application of the force factor. *Police Quarterly*, 6: 150–171.

Thibault, E. A., Lynch, L. M. and McBride, R. B. (2004) *Proactive police management*, 6th edn. Upper Saddle River, NJ: Prentice Hall.

Toch, H. (1978) Is a correctional officer, by any other name, a screw? *Criminal Justice Review*, 2: 19–35.

Toch, H. and Klofas, J. (1982) Alienation and desire for job enrichment among correctional officers. *Federal Probation*, 46: 35–44.

Tulsa Oklahoma Police Department. Training information. Available at https://www.tulsapolice.org/join-tpd/faq-recruiting.aspx#How long academy (last accessed January 31, 2013).

Van Voorhis, P., Cullen, F. T., Link, B. G. and Wolfe, N. T. (1991) The impact of race and gender on correctional officers' orientation to the integrated environment. *Journal of Research in Crime and Delinquency*, 28: 472–500.

Weber, M. (1947) The theory of social and economic organization. New York, NY: The Free Press.

Zimmerman, S., Van Alstyne, D. and Dunn, C. (1988) The national punishment survey and public policy consequences. *Journal of Research in Crime and Delinquency*, 25: 120–149.

Zupan, L. L. (1986) Gender-related differences in correctional officers' perceptions and attitudes. *Journal of Criminal Justice*, 14: 349–361.

7 Leadership and criminal justice organizations

To some men the matter of giving orders seems a very simple affair; they expect to issue their own orders and have them obeyed without question. Yet, on the other hand, the shrewd common sense of many a business executive has shown him that the issuing of orders is surrounded by many difficulties; that to demand an unquestioning obedience to an order not approved, not perhaps understood, is bad business policy.

(Parker Follett 1926: 152)

The manager is the dynamic, life-giving element in any business. Without his leadership the "resources of production" remain resources and never become production. In a competitive economy, above all, the quality and performance of managers determine the success of the business, indeed they determine its survival.

(Drucker 1954: 3)

When approaching team leadership, however, many [supervisors] revert to their underlying beliefs about control and direction. They argue that leadership can be taught and learned, but team leadership is suspected of being a fleeting fad. ... Team leaders instill heart, passion, spirit, and vision in the work group.

(Whisenand 2004: 115)

The key, of course, to making primal leadership work to everyone's advantage lies in the leadership competencies of *emotional intelligence*: how leaders handle themselves and their relationships. Leaders who maximize the benefits of primal leadership drive the emotions of those they lead in the right direction.

(Goleman *et al.* 2002: 6)

Introduction: after you've worked for "bad" leaders, you begin to appreciate the importance of "good" leadership

It is really true: People rarely appreciate competent, caring, and effective leaders until they are saddled with the opposite. During their teen and college years, both authors worked in orchards or berry fields, for fast food restaurants, in the business office of a resort, and as security guards in an art museum and a silicone wafer plant. Of course, in these experiences we could not help but notice how our supervisors and bosses behaved, which management practices seemed to work, and which did not. But at that time it did not matter much because we were not going to make a career in any of these enterprises. If we liked a supervisor or if we did not, if a boss seemed effective or not, was of no long-term consequence since we were going to be gone soon.

After college, however, one of the authors was hired as a correctional officer and then a counselor—because she was considering a career in corrections—and leadership began to matter a great deal. While working in the prison, she noticed that the supervisors displayed a number of leadership styles and abilities. When she worked a shift with a supervisor who was corrupt, and after she had had many opportunities to observe how the warden and some of his minions led, she began to appreciate the value of the well-intentioned leadership of most of the other supervisors. Integrity, intelligence, vision, and the ability to connect with people in a meaningful way, all of a sudden were vitally important as attributes of a leader. She also began to appreciate from that prison work, research, and her later jobs in academe that an organization is successful as a result of the efforts of all its members, but that a "bad" leader or two can quickly sour the culture and productivity of the best of work units.

The role of the leader in a criminal justice organization has always been pivotal. In part because much of the work proceeds outside the public eye, and because of the nature of the clientele, criminal justice leaders have enjoyed more power and latitude to shape their domains than is true for other public or private sector leaders. Some criminal justice agencies in the past operated as mini-kingdoms, with the police chief, prosecuting attorney, judge, warden, juvenile facility, jail or probation and parole administrators functioning with little or no oversight by the rest of the legal system, the media, or the public. At times, this lack of oversight led to notable abuses.

Since the civil rights movement and Supreme Court decisions of the 1960s and 1970s, with the cycles of riots that heighten media attention, the court interventions, the growth in the number of professionally trained administrators entering criminal justice positions, in concert with the professional movement by practitioner organizations, criminal justice leadership has moved closer to the principles governing other public sector leaders. In this chapter we define leadership and discuss its theoretical bases. This definition and these theories will be fleshed out to include such topics as leadership styles, techniques, responsibilities, roles, teaming, shared leadership, and the role of emotion in the act of leading. We will also discuss research on the relative satisfaction of criminal justice leaders and two possible pitfalls for them and their organization: Organizational decline and groupthink. All these topics, of course, are shaped by the human relations perspective of who leaders are and what they should be in criminal justice organizations.

Leadership defined

Leadership has been defined in a number of ways. For instance, oftentimes leadership and management concepts are combined as expectations for leaders of public organizations. Peter Drucker (1954) tended to mix the conceptions of public sector leaders with those of managers in the private sector. He highlighted the skills of the leader or manager as "organizer of resources," "manager of the organization (rather than as a politician)," and "decision maker."

Maslow (1976: 82) argued that "enlightened management" or leadership was necessarily concerned with the "[p]roblems of human beings, with the problems of ethics, of the future of man." He stated unequivocally that enlightened management in the workplace was the only patriotic way for leaders to behave, as it was prodemocracy. Stojkovic and his colleagues (1998) note that leadership is not static, but is a process (like management) that can be learned and must be keenly attuned to the accomplishment of organizational goals. In his book *Organizational Culture and Leadership*, Schein (1992) describes the central role of leaders in "creating, embedding, and transmitting culture." He argues that leadership is intimately tied up with culture making and sustenance in organizations.

In their book *Correctional Leadership: A Cultural Perspective*, Stojkovic and Farkas (2003) also recognize the "cultural creating function" of leadership, and their definition encompasses the cooperative nature of leadership (involving line and management staff) in modern correctional organizations. These authors argue (2003: 7) that leadership is "[f]undamentally a process by which an organizational culture is engendered such that tasks, objectives, and goals are achieved through the coordinated efforts of supervisors and subordinates." Whisenand, who further adds to our understanding of leadership, links being a leader in policing to team building or being one who creates, empowers, and maintains teams. In *Supervising Police Personnel: The Fifteen Responsibilities*, he lists (2004: 124) "seven common traits and practices" that a team leader is born with or acquires over time:

1 Accentuate the positive.
2 Know what's going on.
3 Rivet one's attention through vision.
4 Create meaning through communication.

5   Build trust through positioning.
6   Deploy themselves through positive self-regard and trying.
7   Master change.

Relatedly, Gordon and Milakovich (1998) distinguish between political and administrative leadership. A political leader is someone who is either elected or appointed by elected individuals. Such leaders in criminal justice typically include sheriffs, prosecuting attorneys, and sometimes judges. In this book we are concerned with both political and administrative leadership. It should be recognized that even heads of criminal justice agencies who are typically not elected (e.g., police chiefs, wardens, public defenders, many judges, directors of probation and parole or juvenile facilities) necessarily have a political component to their work; as, for instance, they must garner resources from—and some are appointed by—politicians. Gordon and Milakovich (1998: 231–238) also identify several critical activities for the leader, including the following:

- leader as director: Reconciling personal and organizational goals;
- leader as motivator: The carrot or the stick?;
- leader as coordinator/integrator: Meshing the gears;
- leader as catalyst/innovator: Pointing the way;
- leader as external spokesperson—and gladiator;
- leader as manager of crisis in the organization.

What is notable about all these definitions and descriptors of leadership is that they tend to mesh what a leader is and what a leader does. For the purposes of this book and in the interest of being somewhat comprehensive in the consideration of criminal justice leadership's past, present, and future, we define *leadership* as an ongoing process of activity involving organizing, decision making, innovating, communicating, team building, culture creation, and molding that is engaged in by workers and supervisors to achieve organizational goals. Note that this definition borrows, and combines concepts about, leadership from the work of others (those cited earlier and many more). It also is value-neutral in the sense that someone who operates according to this definition of leadership in criminal justice is not necessarily a likable leader, though he or she may be an effective one. And an effective leader is not necessarily one whose practices are regarded as moral or decent (as will become evident in our discussion of "born vs. made" leaders).

Our definition is not value-neutral in some respects, though, because it encompasses the human relations perspective of criminal justice management. Although the tertiary head of the agency and the supervisors under her are typically regarded as "leaders" for the organizations, this definition recognizes that those on the line and in support activities are necessarily involved in leadership activities. Of course, it is another matter whether the leadership of those at the lower levels of the organization is widely recognized in the organization or outside it. Moreover, the greater this involvement by all who perform meaningful leadership activities, the less likely it is that the decision making process in the organization will degrade into a "group-think" situation (more about this concept at the end of the chapter).

Are leaders born and/or made?

Are leaders born with all the traits that make them effective, or do they learn them over time? Many administration and management scholars in criminal justice and public administration tend to think that this matter is settled: Leadership skills can be learned, and so leaders are "made" (Gordon and Milakovich 1998). Certainly the assumption that workers can be molded into leaders fits the treasured American value of equality. It also provides the rampart upon which many management training programs in the public and private sector stand. After all, if the traits of effective leaders are innate, there would be no sense in trying to develop leadership skills through training. Instead, if leaders were born, those who happened to possess the requisite leadership traits/skills—whatever those were determined to be—would merely assume the mantle of leadership.

But it is hard to believe that just any of us can be, or want to be, leaders. Let us assume that courage, gregariousness, thoughtfulness, intelligence, wisdom, and candor are desirable leadership traits. Can any or all of these traits be taught? Or are some people more inclined toward them?

Let us also assume that communication techniques (e.g., verbal or written), time and resource management, planning and policy development, and "walking-around management" are some desirable leadership skills. Again, can these skills be taught? Or are some people just better at these activities both because they have received appropriate training and because they have some innate ability in these areas?

In other words, the research on leaders and leadership in organizations has not established that leaders are born or made. The assumption, of late, has been that they are made. Again, perhaps current scholars accept the "made" theory of leadership because organizations have no ability to influence the innate leadership skills that a person might possess. But both cases might be true. The best leaders, and most of us have a few people in mind as "American (or Foreign) Leadership Idols" (see the exercise at the end of the chapter), may have a combination of desirable leadership traits and skills, some innate and some gained through experience or training.

Leadership theories

The first theories regarding leadership focused on the "traits" that a leader was assumed to be born with (Gordon and Milakovich 1998). Such traits were linked to the leader's personality and what were thought to be innate abilities and included courage, intelligence, ability to motivate, interpersonal skills, and drive. Yet whether a person was born with such traits or gained them from life experience was difficult to establish with research. Therefore, the *traits theory* of leadership was essentially abandoned in the 1950s, and the research shifted toward situational characteristics that were related to how a leader did or should behave. Notably, the conventional wisdom has continued to support the belief that at least some critical leadership skills are heritable, and the recent (past twenty years') interest in personalities and their relationship to leadership smacks of the old trait theory too (note the discussion of the Myers–Briggs personality test in Chapter 5). Some personality types identified by such indicators as the Myers–Briggs test would appear to better fit the typical requirements of a political or administrative leader (as well as many other roles and professions in organizations).

An alternative way of viewing leadership is the *behavioral model* (Stojkovic *et al.* 1998). Under this model it is believed that the most effective leaders are those who balance concern for the needs of the people they supervise with concern for getting the mission accomplished, or production. One critique of this model offered by Stojkovic *et al.* (1998) is that it fails to take into consideration the situation that the leader is facing. Would the concern for the needs of the employees be the same, for instance, if the leader was faced with a budgetary shortfall and the need to make staff cuts? On the other hand, would the need for production be paramount for leadership when people were demoralized, and thus less motivated to produce, by a lack of pay rises during a recession?

Therefore, a new set of theories regarding leadership that builds on the behavioral theory surfaced on the academic plain. Despite the sidelight interest in personality traits as related to leadership and other roles, and the behavioral study of leaders themselves, much of the interest in the study of leadership has shifted toward *situational leadership theories*. These theories focus on leader–member relations, the needs presented by the group, organizational circumstances, and the skills and abilities of the followers. The belief is that different situations require different leaders or leadership skills.

Situational leadership theories are popular because it is obvious that in the normal course of events in an organization the leader is called upon to shift to varying skill sets based on what is happening at the time. The juvenile probation officer must use different skills with those he supervises in an emergency—say, a child on a serious crime spree—than when he is leading the members of the work unit in development of their component of the county's five-year plan. Likewise, the police officer on the beat must use different leadership skills when one juvenile is threatening others with a knife and when she is training school children on bicycle safety. Similarly, the district court judge is likely to view the recommendations of an experienced probation officer differently from the opinions of one who has just started the job. In all these situations, the theory goes, the leadership skills and techniques, not to mention decision making ability, need to fit and adapt to the situation.

Change, maintenance leadership and leadership styles

Some believe, for instance, that the leaders and leadership skills required when an organization is involved in change are different from those needed in a more status-quo mode. A "change" leader must know how to marshal enthusiasm, assemble and redirect resources and, perhaps most damaging of all to his survival in that organization, be willing to upset some people, who are perfectly satisfied with the status quo and may even benefit from it. Once the change process has been completed, the leader will need to shift gears to focus more on stability and order in the organization and the routinization of practices. To effect this change—that is, to become a "maintenance leader"—requires a whole different skill set and maybe a whole different leader from those who are engaged in change and innovation.

Participants at the leadership conference of the International Association of Chiefs of Police (IACP) presented a radical view of the leader as responsible for change (IACP 1999). As the chief of police for Marietta, Georgia—past president of IACP, Bobby Moody—wrote, the participants "recognized the emerging potential, need for, contribution, and acceptability of the 'transition chief'—a comparatively 'short tenure' executive to engineer painful and radical organizational transformation" (Moody 1999: ii). Not only would "change leaders" develop in the organizations that needed them, but the IACP members recognized that they should develop. They also realized that there would be repercussions for such leaders in the form of shortened tenure in office and greater conflict while there. But the point of such change leaders would be to move the organization in a more professional direction.

Perhaps predictably, a "change leader" who tries to move into a "maintenance leader" role will find it difficult or impossible to mend fences with those he has upset previously. He also may not be as comfortable in exercising the skills needed for the sedate and orderly operation of the organization as he was in moving it in a new direction. This is why one of the authors often tells students that "change leaders" typically *die*—organizationally, of course. A case in point: Jerome Miller, supervisor of the Department of Youth Service in Massachusetts in the early 1970s, closed most of the large training schools in that state. He did so in response to numerous reports of abuse of juveniles at the hands of staff and other incarcerated youth (Welch 1996). In the face of resistance by the bureaucracy to change, and political pressure, he resigned. Notably, the long-term effect of his action was the decreased use of incarceration for delinquent youth. But Miller suffered an organizational "death" to achieve this feat.

Another case in point is fictional Brubaker, from the movie of the same name, who agitated for reform of a prison in Arkansas in the 1970s. This

1980 Robert Redford movie includes a synopsis of what happened to Thomas Murton, the practitioner/academic after whom Brubaker was largely modeled, when he tried to change the backward Arkansas prison system in the 1970s (see also Murton 1976). He too died, organizationally. In both cases political and organizational force was applied to remove a leader of reforms. Some such change leaders, even should they not suffer an organizational death, may find that they do not fit the new situation for their organization, or are unwilling to adopt the skill set needed to be a "maintenance" leader (e.g., see Box 7.1).

Fred Fielder and his colleagues (1969) developed a form of situational leadership theory called *contingency theory*. This theory is based on the consideration of three situational dimensions: Leader–member relations, task

---

Box 7.1 Leadership styles in policing and management as seen by a local police manager, by Chief Paul Williams, Springfield, Missouri

Although I believe in and practice situational leadership, my leadership style tends to be participatory. I see myself as a relationship builder, as someone who wants to involve people in decisions, to solicit input and get them to buy into changes. For instance, I felt we needed to change the disciplinary process in the department. We changed it so that once a complaint is sustained, but before the discipline is decided, the person who is due to be disciplined gets to plead their case at a pre-disciplinary hearing and their chain of command is there too. As Chief, I get a transcript of that hearing and am able to make a more informed decision because there is full involvement by all parties.

Another example of participatory leadership is the Leadership Council I've established in the department. The Leadership Council is made up of eleven people in all areas and all ranks of the department (including support personnel). Participation on the Council rotates so that people are on it only for a couple of years. I will give them an issue to discuss and ask for their input. Once they decide I go by the Council's decision unless I am prohibited by law or it would bust the budget. So far the Leadership Council has created a new award/recognition program, they have made decisions on changing the cars and uniforms, and they have had input on the new promotional system. The Leadership Council gives people in the department the feeling that they have a great deal of input into how the department operates.

structure, and the position power of the leader. According to this theory, the leadership style employed should adapt to, or be contingent on, these three considerations: Whether the leader and the members have positive relations (or not), whether the task structure (what to do and how to do it) is clear and set (or not), and whether the leader is powerful (or not). Another dimension of this theory is that the leader is believed to have a more "human relations" orientation to management depending on how he describes his least favorite worker. If that worker is described unfavorably, the leader is believed to have a more traditional approach to leadership and management; if the opposite is true, then his management and leadership styles will be less traditional. Notably, this theory encompasses the trait theory in that it recognizes the attributes of the situation (e.g., the relations, the task, the power of the leader) that can be manipulated, but the leader is understood to react to a situation based on his or her personality (Gordon and Milakovich 1998).

Box 7.2 The leadership skills needed for the change process from a traditional to a new generational jail

One of the most notable changes to occur in corrections in the last two decades of the twentieth century and the first decade of the twenty-first century was the transformation of traditional jails to "new generation" or podular/direct supervision jails. A number of jails made this move; many are still implementing it, and some have claimed to have made the switch even when they had not or could not. Even some prisons have adopted forms of the supervision and architecture that distinguish new-generation jails from traditional facilities.

A traditional jail is one that has intermittent or remote supervision and linear architecture. What this means is that the correctional officer sees the inmates by walking by their cells or looking through a window, or via an electronic device (camera), only about once per hour. The rest of the time the straight lines of the architecture and the windows, doors, and bars that separate inmates from staff prevent the staff from supervising. These architectural obstructions also allow the more powerful inmates to fill the leadership void created when staff are not physically around. As the jail-building boom exploded over the past thirty years, many counties and cities replaced old jails or added new jails.

Some of these newly constructed jails were new-generation jails with distinct characteristics, the two most important of which were direct supervision by staff and podular architecture. Direct supervision means that the officer joins the inmates in the living unit (which ideally houses from forty to sixty inmates). The architecture is podular (think pea pod and modular) in that it is open and rounded. The officer in the living unit should ideally be able to stand in the middle of the unit and see all that is going on, with only a few architectural obstructions (shower rooms, etc.). In new-generation jails the architecture complements the supervision, or makes direct supervision possible.

As jails began to engage in this huge change, many of the staff accustomed to little, and often brief, contact with inmates were very concerned about the change to podular/direct supervision facilities. Many were not just apprehensive but downright fearful of how they would handle themselves and inmates when they were face-to-face with the inmates for the duration of a shift. Clearly, the correctional officers supervising inmates in these jails were going to need a whole different skill set to be able to operate effectively. In some of the jails making this change in the early 1980s and 1990s, and particularly before the benefits of podular/direct supervision jails had become established in the literature, staff quit or openly rebelled against this change.

While in graduate school one of the authors had the opportunity to observe a western state county jail involved in this change. The savvy jail manager was very cognizant of his staff's concerns regarding the move. In addition to having to sell the local political leaders and the community on the virtues of this jail (he liberally used the media and media events—such as a jail sleepover for community members before its opening), he needed to "sell" the idea to his staff. This "selling" involved sending key staff to other such jails already in operation, distribution of the current research on podular/direct supervision jails that was emanating from the National Institute of Corrections, and training staff not just on the concept, but on the leadership and interpersonal communication skills that would be needed to run the pods. Despite his efforts, some of the correctional officers quit and others never "bought" the idea until they had actually worked in the facility for a time and had their fears and concerns allayed. A very few never got used to the change.

Once the change was complete and the kinks had been worked out organizationally, the jail manager noticed that his leadership style did not fit the maintenance phase the organization had entered. Moreover, the correctional officers, who now exercised more developed leadership and interpersonal skills during their workday with inmates in the pods, were less amenable to the traditional management that had fit the old traditional jail. In other words, the jail administrator needed to adjust his style not only to the new maintenance phase of his facility, but to the new "mature" style of the staff. The jail manager retired from his position after a few years and a newer manager came in with a leadership style that fit the new reality of that jail.

Under Fielder's contingency theory, the leader should be more "directive" when leader and member relations are positive, task structure is clear, and the leader is positive. In other words, the leader has high situational control when these factors are present (Stojkovic *et al.* 2003). But if these circumstances do not obtain, the leader's behavior should reflect concern with keeping or enhancing relationships, clarifying the task, and sharing or building the power. Proponents of this theory seem to assume that leaders tend to be either task-oriented or human relations-oriented, but not both. When the leadership moves to a greater consideration of the members, Gordon and Milakovich (1998) and Goleman *et al.* (2002) would describe this as a new model of relational and emotional leadership that better fits the evolving learning organization described in Chapter 4.

A problem with Fielder's contingency theory is that the three factors identified as enhancing the situational control for the leader often are not present in criminal justice organizations. The tasks and roles in criminal justice work are very complex and are often unclear (e.g., see the discussion of roles in Chapter 6). Moreover, leadership styles are often mutable in that some leaders do switch from a task focus to a concern for the workers, depending on the situation; they are not necessarily rigidly married to one style or the other in every situation. It is also hard for the public sector leader who has only limited ability to hire and fire people (recall those pesky civil service rules) to exert much position power. Finally, leadership styles may lie on a continuum, with style use varying by situation; dichotomies involving only a production or task-driven style and a human concerns style may be inadequate to describe leadership in an organization.

A second contingency theory that appears to address these concerns about the need for congruence, or a fit, between leader style and the situation is *path–goal theory* (House and Mitchell 1982). Leadership behavior under path–goal theory includes the following four styles: directive, supportive, participative, and achievement-oriented. The directive style focuses on the task and the need to get the job done. Rules and regulations are valued under this style and are cited to subordinates as a means of increasing job performance. The supportive style combines the task orientation of the directive style with a concern for employees. This concern manifests itself in an open and friendly approach to workers. A participative style emphasizes the engagement of the leader and workers in organizational decision making; here the workers' input and standing in the organization are valued. Under the achievement-oriented style high goals for production are set for the workers, and the leader expects that those goals will be met when the workers are motivated.

These four styles vary and are contingent on the characteristics of the workers and on environmental factors (House and Mitchell 1982: 522). The subordinates' locus of control (are they self-motivated or do they need direction?), orientation to authoritarianism (do they like to be told what to do or would they like to participate in decision making?), and ability (how competent are they to do the job?) determine the appropriate leadership style. Environmental factors also determine which leadership style might be appropriate to a given situation, including such variables as the nature of the task (is it clear and understood?), the formal authority system (does it reward accomplishment of goals or serve as a barrier to it?), and the primary work group (can coworkers serve as a catalyst for the accomplishment of tasks or do they comprise another barrier?). Stojkovic and his colleagues note that the path–goal theory is particularly useful for the administration of criminal justice organizations because it delineates a way in which leaders can shape the organizational environment that makes the accomplishment of tasks more likely.

> First criminal justice administrators need to spell out clearly the types of rewards that subordinates can receive if and when they follow specific paths designed and structured by the organization. ... Second, path–goal theory suggests, correctly, that no one style of leadership is sufficient for all the situations faced by criminal justice administrators and supervisors. This point cannot be stated too often. ... Third, path–goal theory requires that criminal justice administrators design paths and goals for criminal justice employees that are reasonable and attainable. Path–goal theory assumes active leadership on the part of supervisors.
> (Stojkovic *et al.* 2003: 176–178)

The difficulty, as Stojkovic and his colleagues admit, is that administrators in the criminal justice system cannot always make the changes necessary to ensure effective leadership. For instance, they cannot always control the linkage between performance and rewards. Performance measures and expectations are sometimes confusing and contradictory, and administrators do not always have ready control over the rewards. Nevertheless, the path–goal theory does provide a means of matching style to situation and improving the situation.

A related leadership instrument, known as the LEAD (leader effectiveness and adaptability description) was developed by Hersey and Blanchard (1972, 1974) and is based on the contingency theories of leadership. This instrument is situation-based and measures leaders' style range, or "[d]ominant style plus supporting styles," and style adaptability, or "[t]he degree to which leader behavior is appropriate to the demands of a given situation" (Hersey and Blanchard 1974: 28). While style range indicates a willingness to use multiple styles, it is less related to leader effectiveness than is style adaptability. Style adaptability was determined based on which of the four alternative actions a leader might choose in twelve different situations. Each alternative action was "weighted" by Hersey and Blanchard (1974) based on theory, concepts, and research in the behavioral sciences.

Those responding to this instrument were thought to adjust their leadership style based on the situation, whether the case at hand required task or relationship behavior, and the maturity of the followers. Task and relationship behavior by the leader are juxtaposed in the LEAD instrument (Hersey and Blanchard 1972). Task behavior is much like the directive style discussed under the path–goal theory: The leader is focused on getting the job done and keeping production up. Relationship behavior is also much like the supportive leadership style under the path–goal theory; here the leader is concerned about the well-being of the followers. Effective leaders will vary their style based on what the situation requires (e.g., Farkas 1999; Murataya 2006).

The maturity of the followers refers to their psychological age or their knowledge base and performance in the past, rather than their chronological age. Thus a 16-year-old McDonald's worker can be "mature" in her job if she has been at the shop for a time and has a history of displaying competence in required tasks.

The four styles of leadership measured by the LEAD instrument are *telling* (high task/low relationship), *selling* (high task/high relationship), *participatory* (low task/high relationship), and *delegating* (low task/low relationship). A leader should adopt a style on the basis of what the situation requires. For instance, the first of the twelve situations included in the LEAD instrument and the alternative actions are as follows (Hersey and Blanchard 1974: 30):

1   Subordinates are not responding lately to the leader's friendly conversation and obvious concern for their welfare. Their performance is in a tailspin.
2   Alternative actions:

The leader would...

   a   emphasize the use of uniform procedures and the necessity for task accomplishment.

    b   be available for discussion, but do not push.
    c   talk with subordinates and then set goals.
    d   intentionally not intervene.

Hersey and Blanchard (1974) ranked the effectiveness of responses to this situation in the following order: a, c, b, d. They rated action (a) highest because they thought the situation required directive (or telling) leadership, and they also gave the (c) response a positive weight—albeit less than (a)—because this response is also directive, but it recognizes the value of relationship concern if the followers are mature enough (something we can't determine from the short description of the situation). Taken in tandem and once tallied, all the responses indicate whether a given respondent has a proclivity for telling, selling, participatory, or delegating leadership styles (most people have at least a couple of strong style preferences), and how effective that person is in adapting to the given situations.

    Hersey and Blanchard administered this instrument to over 20,000 middle managers in all kinds of organizations (Kuykendall and Unsinger 1990). They found that a participatory–selling style combo is the most prevalent among leaders in the United States.[1] Kuykendall and Unsinger (1990) also administered the LEAD instrument to police managers in the early 1980s. They found at that time that 155 police managers tended to prefer a selling style, with about 80 percent rating "somewhat effective" to "very effective" on the instrument. The selling style is regarded as the "safest" by Kuykendall and Unsinger (1990), because it allows police managers to focus on the task, while not ignoring the relationship needs of workers. Of course, in policing, as in corrections and courts, with high-accountability situations, rare but important emergency situations, and due process requirements, a directive style does appear to be called for at times. But what about when the "maturity" of the workers increases or the situation is more routine, rather than an emergency? What leadership style of criminal justice managers would best fit these instances? Hersey and Blanchard (1974) would argue that there are consequences for the leader and the organization when the leader fails to recognize the need to shift from telling to selling, to participatory, or even to delegating styles when the maturity of the workers or other attributes of the situation merit it. One consequence they mention is that the inflexible leader will be less effective in accomplishing goals.

Leadership styles vs. techniques

Leadership styles are not the same as techniques. A criminal justice manager might employ several techniques at the same time. Techniques are subsumed under styles in that any given style might include several techniques. For instance, a leader might use some of the techniques identified by Yukl (1981: 12–17), such as reminding followers that a request is legitimate, while also trying to persuade them of the rationality of a given action.

Or a police chief may try to indoctrinate followers regarding acceptable behavior *vis-à-vis* relationships with suspects while also threatening his people with suspension and/or firing should they cross that line. Thus, either singly or in combination, the following are some techniques which Yukl (1981: 12–17) identified: "legitimate request, instrumental compliance, coercion, rational persuasion, rational faith, inspirational appeal, indoctrination, situational engineering, and personal identification."

The responsibilities of leadership

Criminal justice leaders and managers, much like their comrades in the public and private sector, are faced with a myriad of responsibilities and duties that make the roles very challenging. Ultimately, as they usually work in traditionally structured bureaucracies, the buck stops with them: that is, they are accountable for the work done by those they supervise. In the state of Idaho in the mid-2000s we saw a salient reminder of this fact when the director of corrections resigned under pressure after an inmate work program was found to be seriously mismanaged (inmates assigned to deliver furniture in the community were making personal stops, with staff knowledge). Although there was no indication that the director knew about these activities, there was an expectation that he should have. Because of this belief that leaders are accountable for what happens in the facilities for which they are responsible, and as our definition of criminal justice leadership indicated, they often have a diverse stewardship role that spans the breadth of the organization or organizations (Boin 2001; Carlson and Simon Garrett 1999; Giever 1997; Higgs 2009; Huang *et al.* 2011; Metz 2002; Schein 1992; Seiter 2002; Stojkovic and Farkas 2003; Thibault *et al.* 2004; Webb and Morris 2002; Whisenand 2004; Zupan 2002).

Typical responsibilities for this role include the following:

- community relations;
- internal communications;
- maintenance of professional standards;
- conflict resolution;
- control of violence and deviance;
- human resource management;
- training management;
- collective bargaining;
- suspect/client/inmate management;
- planning, policy implementation, and budget oversight;
- culture creation and maintenance;
- employee empowerment;
- team building and team facilitation;
- change agent and innovator.

Of course, in all these tasks, the criminal justice leader works with others in the organization. For some tasks the leader has a role that is merely supervisory; for others the leader's involvement is very hands-on. The extent to which criminal justice leaders are actually involved in the activities just listed depends on the type of organization, the level of government in which it functions (city, county, state, or federal), the size of the organization (whether it is large enough for staff specialization in these tasks), and the supervisory style of the leader (hands-on, intermediate involvement, or removed; Zhao *et al.* 2010).

The role of leader as communicator to a large extent shapes all the other activities in which he is involved (for a review of the importance of communication, see Chapter 5). For example, the director of a halfway house for troubled youth may be actively engaged with governmental entities that oversee the institution and have ultimate responsibility for the youth. He will also be cognizant of the need to communicate with employers, family members, school officials, the police, the juvenile court, and others who are connected with, and have concern and responsibility for, those youth. He might also be in close contact with the city council or county commissioners and local zoning officials about the placement and continued existence of his facility. Of course, and in general, as with all public sector leaders of organizations that create public concern over safety, he will have a broad public relations responsibility to build and keep support for his facility.

Clearly, the criminal justice leader has a central role in shaping and maintaining internal communications. At a minimum, such a responsibility encompasses supporting open communication throughout the organization in any number of ways, including newsletters, transparency in administration, grievance procedures and whistleblowing, training, promotion of research, and teaming. Of course, communication flows more freely internally when the organization and its leaders tear down barriers to its transmission. In this sense, an organization that is focused on human relations management and has a learning focus is an organization that is more likely to promote positive internal communication.

Criminal justice leaders often serve as the symbolic and literal model of professionalism for their organization. They set the tone for the organization in what they say but, more importantly, in what they do. If the sheriff upholds standards of professional conduct herself, it is more likely that her deputies will follow suit. She also needs to ensure that personnel and other practices in the organization reinforce the value placed on professional behavior. Thus, those who behave professionally are also those who get positive performance evaluations and promotions.

The criminal justice leader is also apt to be engaged in the role of mediator between conflicting interests within the organization. Whether the prosecuting attorney for the county resolves conflicts over issues, such as resources, will determine how other staff experience their work. Most conflicts in the organization are resolved at its lower levels informally and, more rarely, formally; for the big-picture issues, however, the prosecuting attorney may be the only person who has the stature and the authority to meaningfully intercede in some conflicts in his office.

The criminal justice leader is also engaged as the controller of violence and deviance by both staff (see Chapter 3 for a more detailed discussion of this) and those they process. Adult jail and prison administrators are more likely to have to grapple with problems of violence, although other correctional entities in the community, and the police, are afflicted with similar issues of deviance by staff and clients.

Jails and prisons—but particularly prisons—perhaps more than any other social institution contain the ingredients for the use of excessive force and other forms of deviance. The institutions themselves are total and removed from public view much of the time; they house unhappy people, many of whom are prone to violence; and the staff are often stressed by the attributes of the work. Ironically, given public indifference to the existence of these factors and efforts to ameliorate them, nothing catches the attention and disturbs the public more than the use of excess force in public institutions like prisons and jails. Again, the warden, administrator, or sheriff, as the head of the organization, is ultimately responsible for ensuring that the amount of violence and deviance is under control in his or her facility, bearing in mind that given the clientele and the need to control them, there is little hope of completely eliminating all violence and deviance in correctional institutions.

The criminal justice leader is also engaged as the human resource manager, the training manager, and the collective bargainer (in agencies where staff are unionized). Of course, if the organization is of any size, there are separate people assigned as the formal managers of these tasks. But in the end, how these areas are managed is the responsibility of the leader. Such tasks will be discussed in much more detail in later chapters; at a minimum, they involve selection, performance appraisal, promotion, disciplinary actions, firing, mediation, negotiation, and training activities of all kinds. In smaller court jurisdictions, staffed by fewer than fifty, the judge may make these decisions personally and sometimes will participate in the delivery of training. In such instances, he will be shaping the organization with his own hands, so to speak. But whether directly involved or not, the judge acting as an administrator is best situated to influence human resource, collective bargaining, and training management.

Similarly, the criminal justice leader has some responsibility as the manager of suspects/clients/inmates, though except in the very tiniest of facilities and programs (say in a home for troubled youth), this responsibility is rarely direct. For instance, how juvenile inmates are managed in a detention facility is determined by the leadership-sanctioned policies, procedures, and practices. If the leader is not concerned about ensuring privacy for the youth, then staff are likely to be lackadaisical in this area. If the leader insists on the provision of high school-level classes for the detention inmates, then the schools and the school board are more likely to find a way to support that programming. Again, the leader sets the tone and has enormous influence over how clients and suspects are treated in the system.

Planner, policy implementer, and budget manager are also responsibilities of the criminal justice leader (these topics will be discussed in greater detail in Chapter 11). Though criminal justice policies are often set these days by statute and the mission statements of the organization, the extent of their adherence in practice can be greatly influenced by the leader or manager. The budget process necessarily involves and overshadows both the planning and policy implementation considerations for organizations of any size. The criminal justice leader needs to take an active part in this role, since it is intertwined with just about everything else in the organization.

The criminal justice leader is a central figure in empowering employees and as a team builder and facilitator in her organization. She is the one who ensures there are avenues for input, and she gives the go-ahead for team creation, viability, and relevance. For instance, the manager of a drug court program can ensure that employees involved in case management teaming have the opportunity to meet and that their decisions are respected by other team members and the court.

Finally, the criminal justice leader has the pivotal responsibility as change agent and innovator (or at least facilitation of innovation) for the organization. Though these responsibilities might be shared formally or informally with others, it is the criminal justice leader who must buy into the need for change and supply the resources for it to actually happen. Without this buy-in and support, change may still occur, but it will be stymied as long as the leader does not engage fully in the enterprise.

Teaming as a means of sharing group leadership responsibilities

Teaming presents one way of sharing and channeling the leadership responsibilities in an organization. Criminal justice organizations, like most other public and private sector organizations of the twenty-first century, tend to dabble in the use of teams. Some criminal justice agencies are particularly adept in their use; others use them only in a rudimentary and perfunctory fashion. Giber *et al.* (2000) argue that the most important of leadership competencies is the ability to build teamwork. In their research in the private sector, they found that this competency of leaders had the most impact on the leadership development program in the corporations they studied. Lambert *et al.* (2002) found that the organizational commitment and job satisfaction of correctional officers increased when the work environment had greater group cohesion and cooperation.

Larson and LaFasto (1989) synthesized some of the research on the effectiveness of all manner of teams from public, nonprofit, and private sector organizations. They then did a series of interviews of leaders and members of a sample of teams that they deemed noteworthy for their achievements or for insights they could provide regarding successful teams. In their book *Teamwork: What Must Go Right/What Can Go Wrong*, Larson and LaFasto (1989: 19) defined a *team* as "[t]wo or more people; (with) a specific performance objective or recognizable goal to be attained ... coordination of activity among the members of the team is required for the attainment of the team goal or objective." So on the basis of this definition, we could say that criminal justice *teams* are groups of people whose activity is coordinated to achieve objectives and goals of the organization.

Larson and LaFasto (1989: 26) posit that teams need some key ingredients to be successful:

- Not just a clear goal, but one that inspires passion and action.
- The team must be structured so that it can achieve results.
- The team members need to have the competency that befits the type of goal or objective the team must address.
- The team needs to be unified in their commitment to the achievement of the goal or objective or they need that elusive quality of "team spirit."
- For the team to function effectively there needs to be a collaborative and supportive climate in the organization.
- High standards of excellence need to guide the team's work.
- External support and recognition make the success of team activity more likely.
- Leadership of the team is principled and "transformative" and creates other leaders.

The authors found that the most common reason for team failure was the inability to stay focused on a clear performance goal. Perhaps because of concern over control issues, or because of personal or organizational political factors, team members sometimes get sidetracked and are rendered incapable of attending to their goals. Of course, in criminal justice, as has been emphasized throughout this text, the definition of clear goals can be problematic for organizations that have multiple missions. However, if the goal can be stated in a clear declarative sentence or two, and if focus on goal attainment can be maintained, the team is less likely to succumb to failure from this source.

Relatedly, Larson and LaFasto (1989) found that if the goal itself was inspiring or "elevating," as they put it, team members were more likely to be focused on its attainment. Of course, teams in criminal justice, much like other bureaucratic organizations in the public sector, do not have the luxury of dealing with only "elevating" goals, a fact that the authors acknowledge. To the extent that it is possible, however, they think that teams handling matters of some import are more likely to be focused on, and successful in, goal attainment.

Larson and LaFasto (1989) also found that team structure and competent team members were key to team success in achieving its goal. They describe a "results-driven" structure for the team that has clear communication lines, division of tasks, and assigned authority for team members. They also found that opportunities for feedback among team members and a rule that judgments are based on facts reinforces a collaborative environment and allows for the exercise of all members' competencies. "Competency of members" describes an attribute of people who are best equipped in terms of knowledge and skills to perform in the structure and to achieve the goal of the team. Larson and LaFasto were referring both to skills and abilities related to technical aspects of the job and getting along well with others.

Team members need to be unified in their commitment to achievement of the goal, and the environment should be collaborative. Larson and LaFasto (1989) found that a sense of enthusiasm, dedication, and loyalty to the team would bind individual members with others and to their collective purpose. All these aspects should also allow team collaboration on projects. Rather than competition with each other, the prevailing objective in team operation should be the welfare of the group and group work. Teams that were most successful were guided by high standards of excellence: That level of excellence was also supported by the organization with the necessary resources and time to get the job done.

Finally, Larson and LaFasto (1989) discuss the importance of "transformative" leadership in teams and organizations as central to the success of any endeavor. Such leaders, who were first identified by Bennis and Nanus (1985: 3) and others, are those who not only "commit people to action" but transform "followers into leaders" and "leaders into agents of change." In essence, Larson and LaFasto (1989: 121) conclude that the effective leader in a team and an organization should do the following:

- establish a vision;
- create change;
- unleash talent.

Of course, to accomplish these tasks, the leader of a team must have all the other criteria in place (e.g., a clear and elevating goal, competent team members, etc.). Wageman (2003: 285) argues that a self-managing team in private and public organizations would ensure that these key ingredients are acquired and maintained; she defines self-managing teams as those that "take responsibility for their work, monitor their own performance, and alter their performance strategies as needed to solve problems and adapt to changing conditions." The benefits of employing such teams for the organization are potentially heightened performance, more learning and flexibility *vis-à-vis* the environment, and employees' greater commitment to the organization.

The role of emotions in leadership

Leaders in criminal justice organizations, including those who work at all levels and specializations, are often called upon to hold in their emotions, to not express them openly. This is understandable given some of the traumatic experiences they encounter and the need to think objectively and rationally in response to them. The police officer arriving on the scene of a car accident which resulted in fatalities as a result of a drunk driver crossing the center line and hitting another car head on, for instance, must contain his emotional reaction to the drunk driver so that he can see to the injuries of all parties and conduct a thorough and unbiased investigation. Because of situations like these, which workers in the criminal justice system encounter regularly, we can certainly understand the need to contain one's emotions on the job. However, there is research which indicates that when one is a leader of an organization, emotions are necessary to motivate and to connect with others in a meaningful way (Goleman *et al.* 2002).

The contention of Goleman and his colleagues, authors of the book *Primal Leadership: Realizing the Power of Emotional Intelligence* (2002), is that leaders are great when they can inspire passion in their followers and when they can steer that emotion in the right direction. They base this argument on research on the brain which indicates that humans' brains respond to the emotions, both negative and positive, of others. Anger, along with other negative emotions and much like a cold, can be "caught" from those closest to us, just as happiness and laughter can be spread from person to person. In fact, according to the authors, the research indicates that the human brain is more likely to respond to positive emotions than negative ones. Which is why they argue that leaders who primarily employ *resonant* leadership styles (i.e., visionary "moves people toward shared dreams," coaching "connects what a person wants with the organization's goals," affiliative "creates harmony by connecting people to each other," and democratic "values people's input and gets commitment through participation") are more likely to be effective in the workplace than *dissonant* styles (i.e. pacesetting "meets challenging and exciting goals" and commanding "soothes fears by giving clear direction in an emergency"; Goleman *et al.* 2002: 55); though they acknowledge that some situations might call for dissonant styles, most situations which a leader encounters in the workplace are better suited to a resonant style.

According to these authors, leaders who seek to change the organization in a positive way need to signal that to their followers and to use emotion while they do it. Training workers on the change, without clear commitment by the top echelons of the organization and a clear sense of the emotional value of such change, will be ineffective. Moreover the leader of an organization must understand its culture if it hopes to change it. *Organizational culture* is, according to Schein (1992), the norms, values, beliefs, traditions, and history of a workplace which make it distinct. Goleman *et al.* (2002)

believe that the leader needs to have a clear understanding of this culture before it can be changed. One attribute of the culture has to be how satisfied he is with his job.

The relative satisfaction and status of criminal justice leaders/managers and supervisors

In several studies of relative job satisfaction, stress, and performance among wardens and police chiefs' (Caeti *et al.* 2003; Flanagan *et al.* 1996; Rainguet and Dodge 2001), some common themes emerge. Personnel issues and the work climate, stress from the responsibilities of the role, and political pressures are all tied into satisfaction levels and the likelihood of an extended tenure as a leader in a given organization.

Flanagan *et al.* (1996), in their study of 641 wardens of state prisons for adults, found that wardens as a group are quite satisfied with their work. But they found that the level of satisfaction may have decreased from 1980 to 1995. They also found that racial and ethnic minority wardens tended to be more satisfied than whites; a warden's age, gender, education, military service, and experience were unrelated to job satisfaction, however. The political ideology or political party affiliation of the wardens was also not associated with job satisfaction. Nor did the authors find any relationship between job satisfaction and the size of the institution or the gender of the inmates supervised. What they did find, however, was that relationships with colleagues at the prison had an effect on the wardens' job satisfaction. Satisfaction increased when the wardens had "positive relationships" with their coworkers. "The direction of these relationships suggests that supportive, trusting, and professional relationships with the staff of the prison are a more important correlate of wardens' job satisfaction than other organizational attributes such as population size" (Flanagan *et al.* 1996: 393).

Caeti and his colleagues (2003) conducted a national survey of juvenile correctional facility directors to determine how they felt about a number of individual, managerial, and organizational matters, including their level of job satisfaction. What they found from the 258 respondents (they had a 63.6 percent response rate) was that on a scale of 1–10, the facility directors had an average job satisfaction level of 8.48, with a range in scores from 3.6 to 10. In other words, and in general, they are a very satisfied group. In comparisons with similar studies in and outside corrections, Caeti *et al.* (2003: 397) found that "[j]uvenile facility directors were a little less satisfied than prison wardens, more satisfied than correctional officers, and much more satisfied than the general public." They also found that salary, stress, years as a director, and level of support for rehabilitation all affected reported job satisfaction. The greater the salary and the less the stress, the higher the job satisfaction. The longer the service as director, however, the less the job satisfaction. Also, interestingly enough, the more emphatically a director supported rehabilitation as a primary goal for corrections, the higher his or her level of job satisfaction appeared to be.

Rainguet and Dodge (2001), in their in-depth interviews of ten former and incumbent police executives, found that the major reasons reported for police chief turnover could be collapsed into a few categories. The authors found that stress due to long hours and worry, the resultant health concerns, human resource issues (including unethical behavior of personnel and disciplinary actions), and political pressures exerted by local officials all contributed to the early exit of police chiefs. It did not appear from the interviews that these chiefs were satisfied with their work.

Studies of lawyers indicate that they are a relatively satisfied lot (Dinovitzer and Garth 2007). Those who work in the public sector, such as in criminal justice agencies, and those who work in smaller organizations tend to be more satisfied than those who labor in the private sector and larger organizations, even despite the generally higher salaries of the private sector group. Among judges, some research indicates that those who work directly with clients over a period of time and in a therapeutic capacity, such as judges in drug courts, may be more satisfied with their work than regular criminal court or family court judges (Chase and Hora 2009). In their study of 355 judges, Chase and Hora (2009: 209) found that these "problem-solving" court judges were more likely to believe the litigants wanted to change and were more respectful and grateful for help, as well as to feel that their role was to help them. Interestingly enough, one of the expectations of the researchers was that problem-solving judges "[w]ould feel more strongly that their assignments have had a positive emotional effect on them personally" (Chase and Hora 2009: 210). What they found was that 85 percent of the problem-solving judges, as opposed to 58 percent of the other judges, did report such an effect and within the problem-solving group, 91 percent of the drug court judges felt this way (Chase and Hora 2009: 228).

In general, these findings for all criminal justice managers might be summarized in the following way: The greater the salary, autonomy from political control, and resources to do the job, the less stressed and more satisfied a leader will be. Moreover, public sector work may provide more satisfaction for lawyers than private sector work. And those who have direct contact with clients, in a therapeutic capacity, might be the most satisfied of the lot.

Criminal justice leaders: success, failure, and the dangers of groupthink

Organizational and leader success and measurement

The relative satisfaction of criminal justice leaders and managers is one measure of organizational success. A few other measures of organizational and leadership success, named in no particular order, might include the satisfaction of the other workers, low levels of stress and turnover for staff, fewer complaints from the community about police/courts/corrections personnel, greater satisfaction with services by community members, the prevention of escapes, reduction or elimination of assaults between inmates/clients and community members or between inmates/clients and staff, reduction in use-of-force incidents involving community members, numerous and valid programming options for clients, successful completion of programs, an abundance of training opportunities for staff, criminal justice managers who encourage input and engagement by staff (and to a limited degree community members and clients) in the operation of the organization, and resource acquisition that allows for the normal operations of the organization. Unfortunately, in the criminal justice organization, many of these measures of success are rarely taken, and some defy true estimation.

For instance, and notwithstanding the studies cited earlier regarding criminal justice leaders and satisfaction, managers in most organizations have little idea whether staff are truly satisfied with their work. Few engage in regular assessment over enough time to allow for comparisons. Rather, they might note the turnover of staff (whether high or low) and use that as a rough barometer of staff sentiments regarding job satisfaction. But turnover (and stress if measured) are only approximately related to organizational operation because these variables might be influenced by opportunities for employment elsewhere (in the case of turnover) or family and work responsibilities (in the case of stress). Although a lack of escapes or people jumping parole/probation to a lesser extent might be validly aligned with prevention efforts, it is difficult to know how much of this activity is averted because of organizational efforts. This is true because we cannot know or measure what did not happen. For instance, over a four-month period in a correctional institution, the sergeant and one of the authors had no escapes during their shift, but the same shifts during the other half of the week had two. The successful officers attributed their good result to incessant and unpredictable bed and perimeter checks during the shift, but they could not know for sure that those efforts had prevented escapes in the period in question.

Can we use the lack of community complaints regarding court personnel as a real measure of success? Perhaps no good mechanisms for complaining exist. Perhaps court personnel actively discourage complaints or obstruct the process. Maybe the courtrooms that receive more complaints about their personnel are actually providing better service to their communities because the people feel free to complain and are given the opportunity to do so.

Nor is it always possible to know how many assaults occur between juveniles in a training school. Given the informal organizational cultural prohibition against "ratting" on others, and perhaps fear of retribution, most detainees (of any age) will not report the wrongdoing of others. As juveniles are not likely to advertise assaults, staff are not always aware of their occurrence either. Rather, blood on the sidewalk or in the bed sheets may be the first, only, and purely accidental indication that an assault may have occurred. This is not to say that prevention efforts should not be aggressively pursued to forestall efforts to escape, jump supervision, or assault others. We say simply that one can't always know whether prevention measures are working, and hence whether the organization is successful in this regard.

In other words, some measures of success of the organization, and indirectly leadership, can be counted—for example, escapes, official assaults, turnover, official use of force, programming options and training opportunities, avenues for input, and whether the budget increases to cover rising costs from year to year. But the intangibles such as satisfaction and stress levels; unofficial assaults and use of force; whether programming, training, and prevention efforts work; and whether people feel comfortable communicating openly and honestly with the leader and in the organization are not always known and sometimes are not knowable. Of course, this does not mean that a criminal justice leader should or can abandon her responsibilities in these areas, but it does mean that measuring the success of the efforts by her and by the organization is not always possible.

Two leadership pitfalls: organizational decline and failure and groupthink

Organizational decline and failure

Another measure of the success of an organization and, indirectly, of a leader, is the organization's continued existence and its ability to garner more resources (Kaufman 1985). Meyer and Zucker (1989), in their book *Permanently Failing Organizations*, observed that the mortality of organizations actually declines with age (the longer an organization exists, the longer it will continue to exist) and that the performance of organizations generally does not improve with age. They argue that when the performance for the organization is high, there is agreement between the two groups that control the organization: Group 1, the politicians and top-tier managers and those who benefit from organizational existence; and group 2, managers, employees, community members, clients (though no suspects, inmates, or supervisees), and other stakeholders. But when performance for the organization is low, those who control the organization, who also usually wield the most power, are apt to want to change it or even end it. In contrast, those who benefit from its existence will fight to keep it or even increase its resources (Jacoby 2002). The longer an organization exists, the more groups and individuals—the group entities—are likely to benefit from its continued existence. Group 2 power grows as the organization ages. Hence, self-interest keeps some organizations in operation even though they are "permanently failing," as Meyer and Zucker (1989) put it. Jacoby (2002: 169) explains this dynamic in his article on the "endurance of failing correctional institutions":

> Any given criminal justice agency established to fulfill a stated purpose ... evolves and survives by serving a variety of other purposes. Among these would be providing patronage opportunities, providing construction and maintenance contract opportunities, providing jobs, and controlling potentially troublesome segments of the population. The participants who depend upon these latent functions of a criminal justice agency and the degree of consciousness of this dependency vary enormously.

Meyer and Zucker (1989) believe that the longer an organization persists, the less likely it is to be "high performing." They note that this is true because efforts at innovation are resisted by those who benefit from the status quo. Also, in the public sector, there are competing goals for the organization, which often conflict and are difficult to quantify (how does one measure "justice," for instance?). Because of this goal focus and conflict problem, it is almost impossible to demonstrate that the status quo is not working just fine, and thus the organization and its leaders find it difficult to make the case that change is needed.

Of course, the leadership role is key to preventing this slide into a "permanently failing" organization. The leader(s) are positioned in the organization to connect the followers with the political masters. They have the means both formally and informally to ensure high performance by staff (Goleman *et al.* 2002). As management and staff's self-interest is only natural as a motivator, one way of maintaining high performance is to make it in the employee's best interest to excel. One way of accessing the power of this motivator is by evaluating, training, and promoting with high-performance criteria in mind. We will discuss personnel practices more fully in Chapters 8 and 9 as both motivational and culture-shaping tools.

Groupthink

The groupthink phenomenon represents another type of organizational pitfall that is best addressed by a leader. Irving Janis, in his well-known 1972 book *Victims of Groupthink*, described the phenomenon at work in decision making in the executive office of the president during the Franklin D. Roosevelt, Truman, Kennedy, and Johnson administrations, as a means of understanding some major policy fiascoes. But "groupthink" as a concept can be fruitfully applied in other organizational contexts that involve group processes. Borrowing from the type of speech that George Orwell used in *1984*, Janis (1972: 9) defined groupthink as "[a] mode of thinking that people engage in when they are deeply involved in a cohesive in-group, when the members' strivings for unanimity override their motivation to realistically appraise alternative courses of action." Janis (1972: 9) believed that groupthink results in a "deterioration of mental efficiency, reality testing, and moral judgment that results from in-group pressures."

Groupthink does not occur, say, in a policing context, because the leader does not appreciate critical thinking. The leader may genuinely wish for the group members to question and critique his decisions. Instead, groupthink is an invidious, subtle process that occurs because of at least six defects in group decision making (Janis 1972: 10):

1   The group considers only a few alternative actions (usually just two).
2   The group does not always consider the "non-obvious risk and draw-backs" of the course of action preferred by the majority.
3   The members ignore courses of action that are not popular with the majority.
4   Members do not seek out expert advice on courses of action.
5   Members filter out the facts and information that do not support their preferred course of action.
6   Members do not consider how the implementation of the decision might be stymied by common obstacles such as bureaucratic inertia, sabotage by political opponents, or temporary derailment by the common accidents that beset the best-laid plans.

Finally, Janis found in his analysis of fiascoes resulting from groupthink that another danger is the members' high level of group loyalty: "in a sense, members consider loyalty to the group the highest form of moral-ity. That loyalty requires each member to avoid raising controversial issues, questioning weak arguments, or calling a halt to softheaded thinking" (Janis 1972: 12). This group loyalty, along with group cohesion and con-formance to group norms, are only reinforced when the group can identify an "enemy" or "opponent(s)."

In criminal justice, as in other public and private organizations, there is a continuing interest in maintaining and even accelerating the use of groups and group decision making (more on decision making in Chapter 12). For instance, see the earlier discussion of teaming as a responsibility of leader-ship. Some criminal justice actors may also have an "us vs. them" attitude toward suspects/clients/inmates, as well as toward groups or organizations that are considered "outsiders." Decision making is often the province of cohesive groups who, given the hierarchical nature of the organizations and the deference to authority, may self-police out any dissent from the party line. Hence, the danger that groupthink represents for criminal jus-tice decision making is real. Janis's message to us is that without the proper safeguards and vigilance, groups can and do descend into groupthink, sometimes with disastrous results.

Therefore, Janis recommends that preventive measures can be taken to forestall the development of groupthink within group processes. Needless to say, the leader's role in preventing groupthink is key. Specifically, Janis (1972: 209–216) offers eight prescriptions for healthy group decision making:

1   The leader needs to ensure that each member takes on the role of critical evaluator and that the group allows for and airs their doubts and concerns. This means that the leader needs to be ready to accept and process any criticisms of his own judgments as well.
2   The leader of the organization should be objective and refrain from expressing any preferences for action or decisions at the outset of the group's formation. Group members should not be swayed before they have had a chance to deliberate by the leader's stated or inferred preferences.
3   On matters of some moment, independent parallel groups with different leaders should be formed to simultaneously consider the same issues.
4   As part of the group process, the main group should subdivide when necessary to work on particular problems and then re-form to work out any differences.
5   Members of the group should talk out group decisions with others in the organization, as well as people outside the group, and then take their input back into the group.
6   Outside experts or "qualified colleagues" should be asked to attend pertinent group meetings and encouraged "to challenge the views of the core members."
7   One member at every meeting should play the role of devil's advocate.
8   When the matter under consideration is in opposition to another organization or entity, at least one of the group's meetings should be devoted to considering "all the warning signals" from that "rival" and "constructing alternative scenarios of the rival's intentions."

Janis (1972) believes that if the organization and leader proactively engage in these preventive measures, they have a chance of avoiding the fiascoes that sometimes result from groupthink. If they do not, they risk making and abiding by decisions that may be disastrous for the organization and for those who are affected by its operation.

Conclusions

Criminal justice leaders occupy a linchpin and pivotal position in their organizations. As such, they can wreak havoc or be the harbingers of change, progress, and stability for the organization. Leadership in organizations, whether it is recognized or not, is performed by members at the top, on the bottom, and throughout its structure. It is not just a static act, but an ongoing process of organizing, decision making, innovating, communicating, team building, culture creation, and molding to achieve organizational goals. We also need to be cognizant, though, of the individual and group goals that leaders pursue both formally and informally under the aegis of the organization.

In this chapter we discussed the contention that leaders are born and made, though we can really test only the latter, and so that is where the research is focused. Most current writers on leadership tend to see the appropriate style and techniques as tied to the situation faced by the leader. If the followers are well versed in their work and have a history of high performance, it would not be productive for the leader to continue to "tell" them what to do; in fact, that might breed resistance and resentment and lead to a decline in morale and productivity. Likewise, the leader of a group that is apathetic and unskilled, or that faces an emergency situation, should not be delegating tasks. Leadership, it is believed, is contingent on the situation.

As was also discussed in this chapter, leadership carries with it several responsibilities. These responsibilities might be shared to some degree among organizational members, but formally the fame or blame for their accomplishment resides at the top tier of the organization. One means of sharing responsibilities and building the competence of organizational members, and in the process helping them to "mature organizationally," is to engage in shared problem solving and decision making, or "teaming" in the organization. It is thought that teaming promotes individual and group communication, development, and innovation by using the human resources and leadership capabilities of all organizational members. Those capabilities are best inspired by a leader who taps into the positive emotions of his followers.

The satisfaction of criminal justice managers is typically high. Research indicates, however, that job satisfaction is contingent on characteristics of the leader and the job.

One pitfall that confronts organizations is their tendency toward decreasing effectiveness over time, even as support for their continued existence grows. In addition to recognizing this phenomenon, the criminal justice leader should actively work to prevent the organization from sliding into a state of "permanent failure."

The criminal justice leader must also be mindful of the tendency of management groups to fall into "groupthink" in matters of decision making. The danger of such a phenomenon may be doubly likely in organizations that are most hidden from the community and whose decisions are most removed from critical review. Remedies to prevent the occurrence of groupthink in criminal justice have been offered and discussed.

Exercise: the American (leadership) idols

This discussion helps to illuminate the two sides of the debate over whether leaders are "born" or "made." Usually, we like to do this in-class exercise before the students have had a chance to read the chapter—for instance, at the end of the lecture on roles and socialization. Despite the name of the exercise, no singing is required, though the instructor or students may be inspired to break into song should their favorite singer make the list as an important leader!

1 Ask class members to identify some of the most important American (or foreign) leaders (their idols and others). The leaders may be from any time period.
2 Write the leaders' names on the board as they are mentioned in class.
3 Tell students to note the demographics of the leaders mentioned and ask them to explain why persons of certain races, ethnicity, gender, occupations, and so on tend to prevail as choices (if such a pattern appears).
4 Ask students: If these are our idols, what does that say about societal values?
5 Probe students to discover why they identified a particular leader as important. What were the particular skills and abilities that made that person stand out as a leader?
6 In a separate column, list those skills and abilities.
7 Then ask students whether they think important leaders were born with those skills or at some point learned them.
8 Reexamine the list of leadership idols on the board. Ask students to make judgment calls about whether a given leader accomplished good or evil in this world. (Note: We've had students mention some really morally abhorrent leaders.) All the leaders listed on the board may be "important," but were they all "good"?
9 Ask students if the same skills and abilities are necessary for an "important" leader as for a "good" one. The difference between such leaders is not always readily apparent, so ask what it is.
10 Ask students to discuss how leaders in a given field of criminal justice might acquire the necessary skills of both an important and a good leader.

Discussion questions

1 What theory of management is in sync with the behavioral model of leadership? Why?

2   How are leadership styles tied to management theories? Explain your answer.
3   Which of the four leadership styles would (or do) you use in a criminal justice setting? Why have you chosen this style? In what situations do you think this style best fits? Are those situations common or uncommon in criminal justice settings?
4   How does "teaming" affect leadership decisions in organizations? Who is best equipped to make leadership decisions in organizations?
5   Explain how "permanent failure" in organizations occurs. How would we know if a criminal justice agency was sinking into this state?
6   What is groupthink? List and explain five reasons why it might be more likely to happen in criminal justice organizations versus other public or private sector organizations.

Key terms

behavioral model: under this model it is believed that the most effective leaders are those who balance concern for the needs of the people supervised with concern for getting the mission accomplished, or production (Stojkovic *et al.* 1998).

contingency theory: based on the consideration of three situational dimensions: leader–member relations, task structure, and position power of the leader. According to this theory, the leadership style employed should adapt to, or be contingent on, three considerations: whether the leader and the members have positive relations (or not), whether the task structure (what to do and how to do it) is clear and set (or not), and whether the leader is powerful (or not).

groupthink: "[a] mode of thinking that people engage in when they are deeply involved in a cohesive in-group, when the members' strivings for unanimity override their motivation to realistically appraise alternative courses of action" (Janis 1972: 9).

leadership: an ongoing process of activity involving organizing, decision making, innovating, communicating, team building, culture creation, and molding followers and coworkers that is engaged in by workers and supervisors to achieve organizational goals.

path–goal theory: leadership behavior incorporating the following four styles: directive, supportive, participative, and achievement-oriented leadership.

political leader: influential person who is either elected or appointed by elected officials. Such leaders in criminal justice typically include sheriffs, prosecuting attorneys, and sometimes judges.

relationship behavior: characteristic of a leader who is concerned about the well-being of his or her followers.

situational leadership theories: focus on leader–member relations, the needs presented by the group, the organizational circumstances, and the skills and abilities of the followers. The belief is that different situations require different leaders or leadership skills.

task behavior: describes the actions of the leader who is focused on getting the job done and keeping production up.

Note

1   If you are interested in learning more about the LEAD instrument and would like to use it in your classroom or work situation, see the website for the Center for Leadership Studies (established by Dr. Paul Hersey in the 1960s) at www.situational.com. You might also consult the original Hersey and Blanchard (1974) article published in the *Training and Development Journal* and cited in the references. A more recent source is the 1988 book by Hersey and Blanchard, also cited in the references for this chapter.

References

Bennis, W. and Nanus, N. (1985) *Leaders: The strategies for taking charge.* New York, NY: Harper and Row.

Boin, A. (2001) *Crafting public institutions: Leadership in two prison systems.* Boulder, CO: Lynne Rienner Publishers.

Caeti, T., Hemmens, C., Cullen, F. T. and Burton, V. S., Jr. (2003) Management of juvenile correctional facilities. *The Prison Journal,* 83(4): 1–23.

Carlson, P. M. and Simon Garrett, J. (eds). (1999) *Prison and jail administration: Practice and theory.* Gaithersburg, MD: Aspen Publishers.

Chase, D. and Hora, P. F. (2009) The best seat in the house: The court assignment and judicial satisfaction. *Family Court Review,* 47(2): 209–238.

Dinovitzer, R. and Garth, B. G. (2007) Lawyer satisfaction in the process of structuring legal careers. *Law and Society Review,* 41(1): 1–50.

Drucker, P. F. (1954, reprinted in 1993) *The practice of management.* New York, NY: HarperBusiness.

Farkas, M. A. (1999) Inmate supervisory style: Does gender make a difference? *Women and Criminal Justice,* 10(4): 25–45.

Fielder, F. E. (1969) Style or circumstance: The leadership enigma. *Psychology Today,* 2: 39–43.

Flanagan, T., Johnson, W. W. and Bennett, K. (1996) Job satisfaction among correctional executives: A contemporary portrait of wardens of state prisons for adults. *The Prison Journal,* 76(4): 385–397.

Giber, D., Carter, L. and Goldsmith, M. (2000) *Linkage Inc.'s best practices in leadership development handbook.* San Francisco, CA: Jossey-Bass.

Giever, D. (1997) Jails. In J. Pollock (ed.), *Prisons: Today and tomorrow.* Gaithersburg, MD: Aspen Publishers, pp. 414–465.

Goleman, D., Boyatzis, R. and McKee, A. (2002) *Primal leadership: Realizing the power of emotional intelligence.* Boston, MA: Harvard Business School Press.

Gordon, G. J. and Milakovich, M. E. (1998) *Public administration in America*, 6th edn. New York, NY: St. Martin's Press.

Hersey, P., and Blanchard, K. H. (1972). *Management of organizational behavior: Utilizing human resources*, 2nd edn. New York, NY: Prentice Hall.

Hersey, P., and Blanchard, K. H. (1974) So you want to know your leadership style? *Training and Development Journal*, 28(2): 22–37.

Hersey, P., and Blanchard, K. H. (1988) *Management of organizational behavior: Utilizing human resources*, 5th edn. Englewood Cliffs, NJ: Prentice Hall.

Higgs, M. (2009) The good, the bad and the ugly: Leadership and narcissism. *Journal of Change Management*, 9(2): 165–178.

House, R. J. and Mitchell, T. R. (1982) Path–goal theory of leadership. In H. L. Tosi and W. C. Hammer (eds), *Organizational behavior and management: A contingency approach.* New York: Wiley, pp. 517–526.

Huang, C-M., Hsu, P-Y. and Chiau, W-L. (2011) Perceptions of the impact of chief executive leadership style on organizational performance through successful enterprise resource planning. *Social Behavior and Personality*, 39(7): 865–878.

IACP. (1999) *Police leadership in the 21st century: Achieving and sustaining executive success. Recommendations from the president's first leadership conference, May 1999.* Alexandria, VA: International Association of Chiefs of Police.

Jacoby, J. E. (2002) The endurance of failing correctional institutions: A worst case scenario. *The Prison Journal*, 82(2): 168–188.

Janis, I. L. (1972) *Victims of groupthink: A psychological study of foreign-policy decisions and fiascoes.* Boston, MA: Houghton Mifflin.

Kaufman, H. (1985) *Time, chance, and organizations: Natural selection in a perilous environment.* Chatham, NJ: Chatham House.

Kuykendall, J., and Unsinger, P. C. (1990) The leadership styles of police managers. In S. Stojkovic, J. Klofas and D. Kalinich (eds), *The administration and management of criminal justice organizations: A book of readings.* Prospect Heights, IL: Waveland Press, pp. 162–175.

Lambert, E. G., Hogan, N. L., Barton, S. M. and Clarke, A. W. (2002) The impact of instrumental communication and integration on correctional staff. *The Justice Professional*, 15(2): 181–193.

Larson, C. E. and LaFasto, F. M. J. (1989) *Teamwork: What must go right/What can go wrong.* Newbury Park, CA: Sage.

Maslow, A. H. (1976, reprinted in 1998) *Maslow on management.* New York, NY: Wiley.

Metz, A. (2002) Life on the inside: The jailers. In T. Gray (ed.), *Exploring corrections: A book of readings.* Boston, MA: Allyn and Bacon, pp. 64–68.

Meyer, M. W. and Zucker, L. G. (1989) *Permanently failing organizations.* Newbury Park, CA: Sage.

Moody, B. (1999) *Police leadership in the 21st century: Achieving and sustaining executive success.* Alexandria, VA: International Association of Chiefs of Police.

Murataya, R. (2006) An examination of the leadership style of the chief of police of a small town in central Washington. *Police Forum: Academy of Criminal Justice Sciences Police Section*, 15(2): 4–13.

Murton, T. O. (1976) *The dilemma of prison reform*. New York, NY: Praeger.

Parker Follett, M. (1926, reprinted in 2001) The giving of orders. In J. M. Shafritz and J. S. Ott (eds), *Classics of organization theory*. Fort Worth, TX: Harcourt College Publishers, pp. 152–157.

Rainguet, F. W. and Dodge, M. (2001) The problems of police chiefs: An examination of the issues in tenure and turnover. *Police Quarterly*, 4(3): 268–288.

Schein, E. H. (1992) *Organizational culture and leadership*, 2nd edn. San Francisco, CA: Jossey-Bass.

Seiter, R. P. (2002) *Correctional administration: Integrating theory and practice*. Upper Saddle River, NJ: Prentice Hall.

Stojkovic, S. and Farkas, M. A. (2003) *Correctional leadership: A cultural perspective*. Belmont, CA: Wadsworth/Thomson Learning.

Stojkovic, S., Kalinich, D. and Klofas J. (1998) *Criminal justice organizations: Administration and management*. Belmont, CA: West/Wadsworth Publishing Company.

Stojkovic, S., Kalinich, D. and Klofas, J. (2003) *Criminal justice organizations: Administration and management*, 3rd edn. Belmont, CA: Wadsworth/Thomson Learning.

Thibault, E. A., Lynch, L. M. and McBride, R. B. (2004) *Proactive police management*, 6th edn. Upper Saddle River, NJ: Prentice Hall.

Wageman, R. (2003) Critical success factors for creating superb self-managing teams. In J. S. Ott, S. J. Parkes and R. B. Simpson (eds), *Readings in organizational behavior*. Belmont, CA: Wadsworth/Thomson Learning, pp. 285–296.

Webb, G. L. and Morris, D. G. (2002) Working as a prison guard. In T. Gray (ed.), *Exploring corrections: A book of readings*. Boston, MA: Allyn and Bacon, pp. 69–83.

Welch, M. (1996) *Corrections: A critical approach*. New York, NY: McGraw-Hill.

Whisenand, P. M. (2004) *Supervising police personnel: The fifteen responsibilities*, 5th edn. Upper Saddle River, NJ: Pearson/Prentice Hall.

Yukl, G. (1981) *Leadership in organizations*. Englewood Cliffs, NJ: Prentice Hall.

Zupan, L. L. (2002) The persistent problems plaguing modern jails. In T. Gray (ed.), *Exploring corrections: A book of readings*. Boston, MA: Allyn and Bacon, pp. 37–63.

Zhao, J., Ren, L. and Lovrich, N. (2010) Police organizational structures during the 1990s: An application of contingency theory. *Police Quarterly*, 13(2): 209–232.

8 Personnel processes and practices

Selection, performance appraisal, training and motivation principles
are four key systems necessary for insuring the proper management of
an organization's human resources.

(Latham and Wexley 1981)

What's not important is the [appraisal] form or the [measuring] scale.
What's important is that managers can objectively observe people's performance and objectively give feedback on that performance ... [says]
Ronald Gross, a Maitland, Florida industrial psychologist and human
resources consultant.

(Wessel 2003: CB 1)

Introduction: you've got to protect your investment!

Criminal justice agencies are labor-intensive enterprises. People do virtually
everything. Personnel costs, then, are by far the greatest expense for criminal justice organizations. Depending on the type of agency, the selection,
training, pay, performance appraisal, promotion, disciplinary, stress, and
turnover costs or operating expenses can eat up most of the budget of a
criminal justice organization and much of the time of employees (Austin
and Irwin 2001; Mays and Winfree 2002; Thibault *et al.* 2004). For this reason
alone, criminal justice organizations, managers, and members need to make
sure their investment in personnel is well placed and well protected.

By "well placed" we mean that the best people are selected, promoted,
and retained in the organization. By "well protected" we mean that employees are prepared adequately to do their work (trained) and supported by
the organization in their efforts to excel (mentored and provided with
resources); in addition, the best of these workers are encouraged to pursue
a career with the agency (via performance appraisals and promotions).

Of course, the opposite is true as well. As with other public and private
agencies, once a selection mistake has been made, poor performers in criminal justice need to be remotivated and, if that does not work, encouraged to
leave the organization.

The point is that mistakes in areas of personnel processes are extremely costly financially. But there are also less tangible costs for the criminal justice organization with "flawed personnel processes." There are human costs for the organization in terms of morale, stress, and overwork when the organization cannot retain competent staff. Clients also suffer when valued staff leave or become demoralized. There are also human costs for employees and community members and clients when staff are selected who are unwilling or incapable of doing their jobs. Such employees can truly wreak havoc in the workplace. Corruption, abuse, harassment, and the resulting complaints and lawsuits are just some of the behaviors and their consequences that can be visited on the organization, coworkers, and community members/clients when personnel processes fail to keep the best and weed out the worst.

In this chapter we review the personnel processes at play in criminal justice agencies. These processes, and the practices that emanate from them, present a real opportunity to shape the organization using human capital. Since the success of criminal justice organizations, holding environmental factors constant, depends to a large degree on who works there, managers and policymakers would do well to ensure that such processes are valid, cost-effective, and just.

Selection

Job-valid qualifications

Typical qualifications for criminal justice work revolve around personal characteristics such as age, height, weight, physical ability, eyesight, and hearing, among other attributes. What people often do not understand is that discrimination based on some job-valid characteristics is perfectly legal. For instance, in most states a person under the age of 18 cannot be hired to work in any criminal justice facility, even though this age requirement discriminates against capable 17-year-olds. Indeed, we shall see in Chapter 9 that in Illinois and North Carolina, prospective criminal justice employees cannot be younger than 18 and 20, respectively.

A qualification is job-valid if it is related to attributes or abilities that are needed to get the job done. The word validity simply means truth. A qualification is job-valid, which means that those who do not have it can be eliminated from the candidate pool, if it is truly related to what is to be done on the job. Being a legal adult (18 or older) is a job-valid qualification for some jobs and for virtually all criminal justice jobs. In fact, the law enforcement agencies in the federal government have established in court cases that being younger than 37 when first hired is a job-valid qualification for them, because they want to retire agents at a fairly young age (usually within 20–25 years). They want to hire before age 37 because they have argued that they need people at the peak of their physical ability, which for most of us, sadly, declines with age.

Being too short or too tall or too overweight might also be job-valid qualifications if these characteristics prevented people from fitting into standard-issue uniforms or using existing equipment or facilities. Being in shape might also be a job-valid qualification if one could not otherwise engage in regular required aspects of the job. Having a known history of drug use or alcohol abuse are job-valid disqualifiers, as may be a serious (sometimes any) criminal history or a record of several traffic offenses. As you might expect, most of these determinations of job-validity of requirements have been established over a period of time through practice, by means of adjustment, and in the courts. Criminal justice agencies have to establish that any skill or attribute they require is one that is regularly exercised on the job. If it is not, then that skill or attribute cannot be required of applicants.

In this regard, we like to ask our older students who have worked in law enforcement for years how many times in their career they have been required to jump and pull themselves over an eight to ten-foot fence? Typically, they say never. Yet until the 1990s, the state police academy in a western state required that applicants be able to do this as part of the test for new recruits. If you could not perform this feat, you were out. Many women, and some men, failed at this task, perhaps because they did not have enough upper-body strength or perhaps because they were short (Lonsway 2003). Since such fences usually do not exist in the real world, and since police officers claim they have rarely, if ever, had to try to scale one, this would not be a job-valid requirement. (A seasoned male officer who had never faced this dilemma in police work told one of the authors that if he had, he would have gone around it!)

But what of other physical agility and ability tests? Is it reasonable to expect that a person applying for a police position be able to run a mile in twelve or thirteen minutes? If you might need to chase down juvenile suspects on the street, maybe it is. Is it reasonable to expect that people be able to complete twenty-five sit-ups or push-ups in a certain amount of time as a measure of general physical fitness? If you need to be able to engage in the occasional physical altercation with inmates in a jail, perhaps it is. Do such requirements discriminate more against women than men? Yes they do (Lonsway 2003). But the courts have said, and probably most reasonable people would agree, that if a requirement or attribute is actually related to real work on the job, or job-valid—and then even if it discriminates against certain groups disproportionately—it is allowable because the ability to do the job is more important (but see Box 8.1).

Job-valid qualifications that have less to do with one's physical attributes and more to do with one's achievements might include educational level attained (almost always a high school diploma and often some college or a college degree for criminal justice jobs) and special certificates or qualifications (e.g. substance abuse training or graduating from law school and passing the bar or graduating from the police or corrections academy). Whether one can read and write at an elevated level, understand and evaluate complex situations and think critically about solutions—as these abilities are developed and honed in an educational environment or by experience—is certainly related to the more professional-level jobs available in criminal justice. In a study of police recruit performance in the Academy, those with an elevated reading level (also likely associated with better writing and communication skills) did better than those without this ability (White 2008).

Box 8.1   The Americans with Disabilities Act (ADA): a brief summary, by U.S. Equal Employment Opportunity Commission

Barriers to employment, transportation, public accommodations, public services, and telecommunications have imposed staggering economic and social costs on American society and have undermined our well-intentioned efforts to educate, rehabilitate, and employ individuals with disabilities. By breaking down these barriers, the Americans with Disabilities Act (ADA) will enable society to benefit from the skills and talents of individuals with disabilities, will allow us all to gain from their increased purchasing power and ability to use it, and will lead to fuller, more productive lives for all Americans.

The Americans with Disabilities Act gives civil rights protections to individuals with disabilities similar to those provided to individuals on the basis of race, color, sex, national origin, age, and religion. It guarantees equal opportunity for individuals with disabilities in public accommodations, employment, transportation, State and local government services, and telecommunications.

Source: U.S. Equal Employment Opportunity Commission, U.S. Department of Justice, May 2002. http://www.usdoj.gov/crt/ada/ q%26aeng02.htm (last accessed January 31, 2013).

Legal disqualifiers

Most criminal justice agencies, but not all, will not hire applicants with felony convictions (Vohryzek-Bolden and Croisdale 1999). Most agencies also do drug tests at some point in the hiring process, and if illegal drugs are detected, they will not hire the applicant. A pattern of traffic offenses or serious traffic offenses may also disqualify an applicant. The appearance in a background check of a known and recent history of alcohol abuse will usually suffice to disqualify an applicant.

All these reasons—criminal history, illegal drug use, alcohol abuse, and traffic offenses—are either prohibitions established in state or local statutes or practices developed by criminal justice agencies to avoid legal liability problems with new hires (and old hands). But there are exceptions to these rules. In 2007 the FBI even relaxed its policy on the history of marijuana use by applicants, although what it now allows for is experimentation in the past, not regular or current use (Johnson 2007). For instance, in Idaho one of the authors has seen several students hired as substance abuse counselors in public correctional agencies and in human services private sector-type agencies despite a history of drug use or alcohol abuse; these individuals had successfully completed treatment and had been clean and sober for a number of years. That author also knows of a manager of treatment programs for a state department of corrections who had a known history of extensive use of illegal drugs, including heroin. In these instances, a history of abuse, with an emphasis on *history*, is sometimes seen as a *qualification* for a treatment position and may not limit a person's career options, particularly in the treatment field.

Moreover, there is a real variation among agencies within and across the states. For instance, one of the authors knows of a college student with a juvenile history of robbery who was not hired by a jail facility in a small rural state. The same young man was told that this history would be overlooked, in light of more recent accomplishments (completing college, success on the football field), by an urban sheriff's department in a larger state.

Cost

Another major consideration in the devising of a selection process is cost. If you review the typical steps in this process, as we will shortly, you will note that the process for hiring staff for criminal justice agencies is usually geared toward reducing the cost and ensuring the effective management of time. As the number of applicants is largest at the beginning, and as many applicants will not be suited for criminal justice work, the task in selection is to weed out most of the applicants at the beginning and middle stages of the process. Cost and time considerations also dictate that the most expensive portions of the selection process, such as medical exams, psychological exams, and individual oral interviews, are reserved for the applicants who survive the weeding-out process.

Typical selection practices

The selection process for criminal justice positions varies widely by type of position, locality, and qualifications (see Tables 8.1 and 8.2). Generally speaking, the jobs that required more education and experience are less likely to require a lengthy selection process and training period afterward. In other words, jobs with a more "professional" mantle are more likely to

Table 8.1 The selection process typical for law enforcement and some corrections jobs

---

Application form: if you meet the qualifications, have filled out the form completely, and submitted it on time, then proceed; otherwise you're out)

Written test: if you pass, then proceed; otherwise you're out

Medical exam: if you pass, then proceed; otherwise you're out

Physical ability/agility test: if you pass, then proceed; otherwise you're out

Background investigation: if you pass, then proceed; otherwise you're out

Psychological test: if you pass, then proceed; otherwise you're out

Polygraph test: if you pass, then proceed; otherwise you're out

Oral interviews: if you pass, then proceed; otherwise you're out

Ranked on hiring list/register: if you are selected when a position opens, you may be hired conditionally or unconditionally, but it doesn't stop here...

Probationary period and/or graduation from the academy: the process continues

Training/continual education: the process continues

Performance appraisals and evaluation: the process continues

---

depend on the applicant's extant qualifications rather than on tests of suitability for the job. Since the length and content of a selection process for any given criminal justice job depends on such factors as educational and experience qualifications the following discussion of typical selection components should be considered with that in mind.

The application form

As public sector entities that are guided by civil service requirements, criminal justice agencies typically have applicants fill out a form listing personal data (name, address, social security number, etc.). Applicants might be asked to provide information about their education and degrees, current or past employment, and where they have lived over the years. Because some application forms are very detailed, covering virtually the person's whole life, it is important for potential applicants to keep organized and accurate records of where they have worked and lived, along with the names and phone numbers of supervisors and apartment managers. They will be grateful to have such information if it is required.

As a starting point in the selection process, the application form serves at least two purposes. It allows the agency to eliminate applicants who do not meet the minimum job requirements as outlined in the job announcement. It also allows the agency to eliminate those who do not fill out the form correctly or completely and those who fail to turn in the application on time. Because the selection process is guided by concerns about job validity and cost, as well as selecting the best applicants, the application form is perfect for fulfilling these multiple purposes.

It is worthy of note that for prosecuting attorney and public defender offices, the selection process typically skips over the other steps and moves straight to the personal interview. For such jobs, then, and as an indication of their "professional status," past work-related experiences, academic success (particularly in law school), and good recommendations/references become paramount. Judges are "selected" either by the voters through the election process or "appointed" through other means entailing varying degrees of political influence. Bailiffs, court recorders, and other support personnel usually fill out application forms and are interviewed, but are unlikely to have to submit to all the other steps described in the sections that follow.

The written test

Written tests are commonly used in selection processes for police officers, probation and parole officers, and officers for correctional institutions. This portion of the process is also geared toward ensuring that those who do not have the minimum qualifications for the job are eliminated early so that no more organizational money is expended on them. To that end, written exams typically include standardized multiple-choice questions that can be easily graded and short answer and essay portions.

The written test may also test analytical skills, math ability, and reading comprehension. The written tests sometimes include situational questions that tend to favor those who have already done the job or are familiar with how the job is done in this particular agency. Such questions also allow the agency to screen out those who would be unsuited for police, community corrections, or correctional institution work—for instance, those who might favor the overuse of force in certain situations. A sample of the California State written test for correctional officers includes questions devoted to spelling, punctuation, and grammar; reading comprehension; basic math skills; and logic (California Department of Corrections 2013; a sample copy of the 2013 test is available online at: http://www.cdcr.ca.gov/Career_Opportunities/POR/docs/COYCOYCC%20Sample%20Test.pdf, last accessed January 31, 2013). But obviously, the content and use of such tests varies to some extent. For example, some tests include a short essay question that allows the examiner to quickly note deficiencies in relevant areas.

The variability in content creates a need for the criminal justice agency to validate the testing tool. Test validation is done to ascertain the neutrality (e.g., race/ethnicity, gender) of content, with a view to thwarting any possible discrimination lawsuits. Validation can be outsourced to another public or private vendor that specializes in testing, or an agency can develop and validate its test in-house. Both methods are acceptable; however, there are pros and cons for both. Keep the test in-house, and the agency accepts more responsibility for validation but has more control and may save some expense. Outsource the test, and the possibility of the agency falling under a discrimination lawsuit lessens, but the agency may lose some control over the process, and expenses may rise.

Table 8.2 Interviews, tests and examinations used (%) in selection of new officer recruits in local police departments, by size of population served, 2007

Population served	Personal interview	Medical exam	Drug test	Psychological evaluation	Physical agility test	Written aptitude test	Personality inventory	Polygraph exam	Voice stress analyzer	Second language ability test*
All sizes	99	89	83	72	60	48	46	26	5	1
1,000,000 or more	100	100	100	100	100	100	85	77	0	0
500,000–999,999	97	100	100	100	97	90	68	74	13	11
250,000–499,999	96	100	91	100	96	96	67	83	7	2
100,000–249,999	98	100	95	99	86	88	64	77	13	1
50,000–99,999	99	100	96	100	89	87	66	63	13	3
25,000–49,999	100	100	97	98	90	83	64	51	9	2
10,000–24,999	100	99	94	94	78	76	57	42	11	1
2,500–9999	100	95	87	82	65	56	44	26	5	—
Under 2,500	98	76	73	48	41	20	38	10	2	—

Note: List of selection methods is not intended to be exhaustive. Dash—indicates less than 0.5%.

Adapted from Bureau of Justice Statistics, US Department of Justice (2010) Law Enforcement Management and Administrative Statistics: Local Police Departments, 2007

*Second language ability test adapted from Bureau of Justice Statistics, US Department of Justice (2006) Law Enforcement Management and Administrative Statistics: Local Police Departments, 2003. May 2006, NCJ 210118, Washington DC: Office of Justice Programs.

A western state's written test for adult probation and parole officers includes a self-assessment of skills and abilities for the job. The problem with such a self-assessment is that some applicants are too modest about their accomplishments and some less qualified applicants provide an inflated evaluation of their skills and experiences. In other words, the agency using such a self-assessment test may be compromising its ability to select the best applicants.

Since all portions of the written exams for criminal justice jobs must be job-valid, the components of this test need to measure, at least indirectly, skills and abilities that would be required on the job. Cost considerations also determine to some extent the content and use of this test.

Medical exam

Most agencies require that applicants be drug-tested as part of the selection process. Several agencies will also ask about any current or past drug use (North Carolina 2013). Some agencies also require that the hearing, eyesight, and general physical health of the applicant be assessed before a hiring decision is made. Sometimes people do not realize that certain physical ailments may prevent them from gaining employment in criminal justice agencies. For example, although color blindness is usually not assessed for jobs in institutional corrections, students should be aware that color blindness may prevent them from working in most police departments and some probation and parole jobs, where operation of a vehicle is a job requirement (though not all agencies test for this).

Physical ability/agility tests

Only some correctional agencies have these tests, but they are de rigueur for police officer positions. Their purpose is to weed out those who do not meet basic fitness levels and to keep those who meet those requirements. Some states and counties may reserve these tests for the academy, recognizing the decreased emphasis on this ability for institutional and community corrections. One critique of such tests in the past has been that they discriminate against women without measuring job-valid qualifications. Because such tests have been debated in the courts, they now tend to measure just the basic fitness of individuals to do the job, including such measures as timed runs, sit-ups, and push-ups. Since such tests can be administered en masse, they are usually relatively low cost and tend to weed out those who would not have the physical capabilities to be able to complete job tasks.

Background investigation

Once an agency gets to the background investigation, the cost of the selection process begins to escalate, although the cost of the investigation varies in accordance with its thoroughness. It is expensive to review current employment, living arrangements, references and social relationships, and credit history, let alone those going back a few years. Generally speaking, those who apply for federal positions are most extensively investigated, but some counties and states do an in-depth job here too. The most important issue from the agencies' perspective is the criminal history of the applicant. Agencies will also check the driving record of the applicant, their work history, and personal references, and will review a credit/financial history report to look for irregularities such as bankruptcies or bad checks/credit.

A thorough investigation proceeds in "snowball" fashion: References listed on the application form constitute only the starting point for the investigator. Past and present employers, landlords, family members, friends, teachers and professors, roommates, coworkers, clerks at an applicant's neighborhood video store (just kidding)—virtually anyone with significant contact with the applicant will be contacted. And this includes people beyond those listed on the application form, because the investigator will ask who else the applicant was friendly with or who else the person liked or disliked and then talk to them. Investigators will ask questions relevant to a person's relationship with the applicant; for example, landlords will be asked if the applicant paid her rent on time. There will also be questions about what was observed or known about the applicant: Did you ever see the person engage in unethical behavior or know of it? Did you ever know the person to lie? Do you have any concerns about this person working with children? Do you have any concerns about this person working with vulnerable populations at all? Have you ever seen the person use illegal drugs or known of it? Did you ever see the person drunk? In other words, thorough background investigations can be quite time-consuming and costly, but they can also be very effective in weeding out those who might not be suited for work in criminal justice agencies.

Psychological test

Psychological exams take many forms. Some include the use of the Minnesota Multiphasic Personality Inventory (commonly known as the MMPI), to screen out those who are obviously unsuited for criminal justice work. Responses on the MMPI and other forms of such tests are usually analyzed by a trained psychologist. Other forms of such exams include writing a story in response to a fairly innocuous picture. An applicant whose story features a violent or deviant theme presumably would be rejected. Sometimes applicants are interviewed by an actual psychologist who asks standard questions about their childhood and perceptions of the world. Other versions of psychological exams are also employed. Typically, however, since these tests are time-consuming and must be evaluated by a skilled professional, they are costly. Unfortunately, it is not always clear how effective psychological tests are in terms of targeting future employees. They are probably better at screening out obviously psychotic or antisocial applicants who are not crafty enough to figure out why. For example, if applicants are asked if they like to see small animals suffer, they should not answer yes!

Polygraph testing

Although polygraph exams are not admitted as evidence in courts, police and corrections agencies are allowed to use them as a means of assessing applicants. If done correctly, they are time-consuming, complex, and costly. The applicant is hooked up to several monitors that record his physiological responses to questions. The polygraph or lie-detector test is done to determine whether the applicant exhibits physical reactions to questions that may not be consistent with honest answers. The accuracy of the assessment to the responses depends to some extent on the training and ability of the examiner. Examiners should be highly skilled practitioners with hundreds of hours of training to ensure professional assessment of responses. Typically, the applicant is told the questions beforehand. To establish a baseline for responses, the applicant will be asked innocuous questions first. The primary questions, however, will touch on legal issues, criminal involvement, relationships, and any ethical lapses that may lie in the applicant's background.

But sometimes polygraph exams include outrageous and unrelated questions. (The students of one of the authors have told of being asked about sex with animals and whether they have ever engaged in homosexual acts in the course of applying for jobs as police officers.) Clearly, not all criminal justice managers use these tests responsibly.

The professional examiner will ask the primary questions while the applicant is hooked up to the machine. Should there be an aberrant response, the examiner usually explores this with the applicant, who is allowed to respond again. If it is the assessment of the examiner that the applicant has answered truthfully on all the questions, then he will have passed the polygraph.

Oral interviews

Usually, but not always, the oral interview falls at the very end or toward the end of the selection process. Because these interviews may include an oral board, usually consisting of three or four high-ranking staff members with years of experience, they can be quite costly for the organization to administer. If used at the beginning of the selection process, the sheer number of applicants should be daunting and could be unnecessarily disruptive for the organization.

The types of questions asked at these interviews are usually standardized at the beginning, though follow-up questions may explore the specific responses of individuals. Applicants are usually asked to respond to questions regarding situations they might encounter on the job. Possible responses may be provided to the applicant, and/or he or she may be asked to formulate a response. Applicants may be asked not only how they would respond to a given situation, but also why they would respond that way. They may also be asked to explain why they did not choose an alternate response. Sometimes oral board members will play "good cop" or "bad cop" as a means of throwing people off and seeing how they respond to stress.

Oral interviews are also likely to include questions that are commonly asked in other job interviews: Why do you want to work here? What skills do you bring to this job? What was the biggest mistake you ever made in your life? What are your greatest strengths and weaknesses? The applicant may also be asked to provide an example of a difficult situation she handled well and then another instance in which the opposite was true. She may then be probed about why she thinks she was successful or unsuccessful in handling these situations.

In addition, the applicant may be asked about her perceptions of the client population she would be working with. Would she be comfortable working alone in a patrol car? What, if any, concerns would she have about working in a male prison? Does she have any qualms about going into the shower room, should this be necessary? What is her attitude toward juvenile offenders? What would she consider the appropriate relationship between the public and the police? She may also be asked to provide examples of her experiences supervising the relevant population.

Finally, the oral interviewers may ask the applicant about her personal habits and likes as a means of getting a sense of who she is. When does she get up in the morning? What kind of music does she like? Who serves as a model for her life and why?

Selection from the applicant's perspective

As our discussion of the selection process indicates, it can be an arduous affair. It is often said that looking for a job *is* a full-time job, and there is some truth to that claim. If you are a student reading this book and are interested in working in corrections, policing, the legal field, or some other public sector job, consider applying for such jobs early in your senior year of college or in your last year of law school. It takes at least six months to a year to get a job in the public sector, and some agencies advertise only once per year. Of course, if a degree is required of all who submit applications, then you will have to wait until you have one. But some agencies do not require a degree (though it is likely desired) or allow employees to complete degree requirements while they are on the job.

Therefore you may want to consider applying for jobs before you graduate. Do this because of the length of most selection processes, but also because it is good practice. People who have taken written tests or have been before oral boards may be more likely to do better the second or third time around. The whole selection process for agencies can be intimidating, but it will be less so for the experienced applicant.

Another point for students and/or prospective criminal justice employees to consider is that employers are more likely to look favorably on applicants who have experience (Vohryzek-Bolden and Croisdale 1999). Too often students get to the point of graduation with little real-world experience related to their profession. To build your résumé and contacts in the community, consider doing volunteer, internship, or part-time work in the agency you want to work for. If it is not possible to work for that agency, consider doing volunteer/internship or part-time work with a similar agency. Or consider doing volunteer work that builds up your human service experience and prepares you for the kind of work you expect to be doing. For instance, if you are interested in working with juveniles, consider volunteering or part-time employment at the local Boys and Girls Club, or do an internship with the juvenile court, detention center, or drug court.

A final piece of advice is to apply widely for jobs. It is rare for college graduates to get the exact position they want right out of school. Therefore, consider applying for the job you want, should it be open, but also for jobs that might be your second or third choices. Such jobs are likely to be more plentiful and less sought after by skilled applicants. It is possible you will get your dream job right away, but it is more likely that you will have to take something else until you can build your résumé to be more competitive. Besides, applying for several jobs gives you more options for employment and more experience with the application process. The whole idea is to have employment options after graduation and/or soon thereafter.

On the job, the selection process continues

Once hired, the applicant is in a sense still just that—an applicant—as tenure in the job is usually contingent on successful completion of a probationary period (typically six months to a year) and, for newly hired police or corrections officers, graduation from the agency's academy (we will discuss the content of the academy training more shortly). The ordering of these experiences is not always uniform. Many correctional agencies will not spend thousands of dollars to send a new hire to an academy setting until they are sure that the person is going to work out. So in corrections you often have people who have not completed any training course working for up to a year in jails, prisons, and juvenile facilities, and in community corrections (e.g., Ruddell and Main 2006). In policing there is a greater concern regarding liability. As a police lieutenant once put it, "It is scary and dangerous to give an inexperienced person a gun and a car and send them out on the street with no training." Therefore, other than very small rural departments in financially straitened circumstances, most police recruits complete the academy after they are hired, but before they are sent on patrol alone.

Most police and correctional agencies also pair up the new hire with one or more on-the-job training (OJT) officers to show them around and to evaluate their performance on the job. The skills and abilities of such field training officers (FTOs) vary widely, but the best, obviously, are those who have many years of experience in the job and are the most professionally oriented toward the work. The cliché, as noted in Chapter 6 in our discussion of socialization, is for an old hand to take the new hire aside and say, "Forget what you learned in the academy (or from administration), I'm going to show you how it is really done." Of course, and again obviously, and assuming that the academy training or any other preliminary training befits the organizational mission and priorities, an FTO who delivers this message to trainees is not the right person to socialize new hires.

Training

The importance of training in socializing and instilling values in new hires (recall this discussion in Chapter 6) and in reorienting in-service workers should not be underestimated. Training represents the most common and official means of transmitting the organizational mission and socializing new hires and old hands (Ford 2003). It is also the best way to "professionalize" the workforce and to thus prepare people for all the challenges they will inevitably encounter in the workplace.

Historically, those who worked in criminal justice received little more than OJT, and sometimes not even that (Thibault *et al.* 2004). Law school was not required for attorneys to practice in many states until the twentieth century; instead, novice attorneys were given the option of serving as an apprentice for an older hand for a number of years. Likewise, most police and corrections departments did not have academies for their recruits until later in the twentieth century. It is still true that some corrections departments and jails, even smaller police departments, do not send their recruits to academies until they have been on the job as long as a year.

Back in the early 1980s, when one of the authors was hired as a correctional officer, she received one week of OJT and then was put on a regular shift in the prison. She never did attend the academy for correctional officers, but probably would have if she had not been promoted to the counselor position after eight months. After several months in that role she was sent to a two-week academy. Recently (in 2013) she discussed academy attendance with a relatively new jail employee at a medium-sized jail in a Midwestern state and found out that after a year of actual work, this correctional officer was just now being scheduled for the academy. So the problem of training—especially in corrections, but also in some smaller police departments—coming too little and too late is still true today in some jurisdictions.

The offices of prosecutors and public defenders often regard law school as one long training academy and couple that experience with on-the-job mentoring by skilled attorneys. Many state bar associations promote or require ongoing training for practicing attorneys, and some states provide formal annual training for judges and court administrators (National Center for State Courts 2013).

Today police agencies typically require 600–800+ hours of training (this includes field training or OJT), whereas prisons, jails, juvenile facilities, and probation and parole agencies have a mix of training requirements. Table 8.3 gives a breakdown of average number of new police officer training hours required by population size. In an analysis of 1993 Bureau of Justice Statistics data, Gaines *et al.* (2003) found that the larger the population served (and presumably the larger the agency itself), the longer the classroom and field training hours required for police recruits.

The training required and provided varies widely in the criminal justice system. For instance, Utah's Weber County Jail requires that correctional officers complete twelve weeks of academy training, or 480 hours (Weber County Sheriff's Office 2013). In contrast, the Utah State POST Academy for law enforcement requires fifteen weeks, or 600 hours, of training for new hires in police departments (Utah Department of Public Safety 2013). Correctional officers hired by the federal government undergo only 120 hours of initial training, which they need to have completed within sixty days of joining the Bureau of Prisons (Federal Bureau of Prisons 2013). The New Agents' Training Unit for FBI agents requires twenty weeks, or 800 hours, of instruction at the FBI Academy in Quantico, Virginia (FBI Academy 2013).

Correctional officers in New York State are required to complete eight weeks of training, or 320 hours, and probation officers for the state have to complete a total of three weeks or 120 hours of initial training (New York State Department of Corrections and Community Supervision 2013; New York State Division of Criminal Justice Services 2013). Yet in New York, the state troopers take twenty-six weeks, or 1,040 hours, of basic training (New York State Police 2013).

In a quick survey of 150 directors and staff trainers, with responses received from thirteen states or agencies in April 2004, the Juvenile Justice Trainers Association found that about 140 to 180 hours of preservice, academy-like training is required for most new hires in juvenile facilities.[1]

In yet another survey of all states regarding adult and juvenile correctional academy training requirements, researchers for the state of California found that the range of hours required for those correctional officers working with adults was 120–640, for parole agents it was 40–440, and for correctional officers working with juveniles it was 54–450 (Vohryzek-Bolden and Croisdale 1999). Moreover, probation, staff, parole officers, and counselors in adult prisons and juvenile facilities may or may not be required to complete a formal academy training course. This may be partly because these employees are required to have more college education (Vohryzek-Bolden and Croisdale 1999). But in that case, they are likely to have to take a test to become "certified" at the end of that training (Bureau of Labor Statistics 2004b).

This difference in training provided to those who work as adult and youth officers in corrections versus those who work in policing or as attorneys (if we regard law school as training-oriented) reflects the lack of professional status accorded some parts of correctional work. Another reason for decreased requirements is probably that different populations are served by correctional staff, versus the police or even the courts. There may be less concern about correctional populations from the general public and funding bodies such as state legislatures and county commissions than there is about the people who come in contact with the police or in the courts, all of whom are innocent until/unless proven guilty. Most people in the community and the courts can also vote, and they have more access to the courts in the event of real or perceived improprieties on the part of the police or prosecutors.

Yet there is research that indicates training is key to building the skills of staff, maintaining staff, and delivering services for all persons served by the criminal justice system, including inmates and supervisees. For example, in a small study of probation and parole officer attitudes, Fulton *et al.* (1997: 295) found that training made a difference in how officers related to those they supervised. They concluded that "[a] comprehensive approach to training and development can effectively instill in officers the supervision attitudes that are most conducive to promoting offender change."

Academy training

Academy training typically includes a mix of topics (Bennett and Hess 2001; Corrections Compendium 2003a, 2003b; FBI Training Academy 2013; Ford 2003; Gaines *et al.* 2003; Haberfeld 2002; Jordan 2003; Vohryzek-Bolden and Croisdale 1999). Typically emphasized are first aid, CPR, interpersonal

Table 8.3 Training requirements (average number of hours required) for new officer recruits in local police departments, by size of population served, 2007

Population served	Total	Academy	Field
All sizes	922	613	309
1,000,000 or more	1,700	1,033	667
500,000–999,999	1,783	1,063	720
250,000–499,999	1,542	906	636
100,000–249,999	1,463	809	654
50,000–99,999	1,341	731	610
25,000–49,999	1,241	698	543
10,000–24,999	1,101	666	434
2500–9999	979	634	345
Under 2,500	691	538	153

Bureau of Justice Statistics, US Department of Justice (2010). Law Enforcement Management and Administrative Statistics: Local Police Departments, 2007 skills, communication skills, writing, legal issues and restrictions, firearms proficiency, self-defense and physical tactics, and supervision techniques. More specialized courses are provided for positions with counseling, addictions, investigative, interrogation, treatment, or tactical team responsibilities (Bureau of Labor Statistics 2004a; FBI Training Academy 2013; e.g., Peak *et al.* 2006).

Especially prevalent in the latest Corrections Compendium (2003a: 11) survey of institutional corrections' academy training was the presence of the following topics: Inmate manipulation, report writing, and self-defense. In 100 percent of the responding facilities, these three topics were covered in the academy. Next important—covered by 90 percent or more of the responding agencies in their academies—were communicable diseases (93 percent), communications (98 percent), CPR (96 percent), crisis management (98 percent), ethics (98 percent), fire/safety (96 percent), first aid (98 percent), hostages (93 percent), inmate classification (98 percent), inmate gangs (91 percent), race relations (91 percent), security devices (96 percent), stress reduction (91 percent), suicide prevention (93 percent), and use of force (98 percent).

In that survey of all states on amount and type of correctional training undertaken for the state of California, Vohryzek-Bolden and Croisdale (1999) found that only eighteen states had training academies for parole agents who supervise adults. Of those, eight states provided training curricula to the researchers. The researchers (1999: 12) found that the training topics could be divided into the following categories: "overview, narcotics issues, use of force, firearms training, legal, communications, departmental, parole process, community resources, health issues, computer training, academy, and other." Of course, there was some variation in topics included and excluded from these academies. For instance, some states included extensive training on legal issues, while others barely touched on the topic. Other states included officer survival training; training on how to manage habitual offenders; sex offenders and offenses; defensive driving training; and courses on sexual harassment, stress management, ethics/professionalism, personnel, and cultural diversity (Vohryzek-Bolden and Croisdale 1999: 12–13).

Only one state (California) provided information to the researchers regarding the training curriculum for parole agents who work with juveniles. The courses offered in California include the following topics: legal issues, use of force, firearms, planning arrests and arrests, search and seizure field exercise, crisis intervention/communication, sexual harassment, labor union, mission/values, intake procedures, revocation and writing violations, and training on the California Law Enforcement Telecommunications Systems.

In the same survey, the researchers were able to determine that sixteen states had an academy for correctional officers who work with juveniles (Vohryzek-Bolden and Croisdale 1999). Of those states, ten provided training curricula to the researchers, who divided those courses into the following fifteen categories: "correctional issues, law enforcement, safety procedures, staff/ward relations, security operations, ward control, use of force, firearms training, communication, departmental, academy, ward rights, health and welfare, on-the-job training, and other" (1999: 14). Again, the responding states varied greatly in the amounts and types of training provided. Moreover, the quality of the training provided is another matter entirely; it is not addressed by information on types and amounts.

In her book-length review of police training, Haberfeld (2002) found that academy training typically included the following general categories: "administrative procedures" (academy skills), "administration of justice" (history of the police and other affiliated agencies), "basic law" (types of law that affect policing and police practices), "police procedures" (the whole range of what the police do and confront), "police proficiency" (firearms and other skills and techniques necessary for success), and "community relations." Some agencies, she found, delivered their academy training in-house (e.g., Washington, DC; Charlotte, North Carolina; Indianapolis, Indiana; New York City), while others sent their new recruits to a regional academy (e.g., the police departments of St. Petersburg, Florida, and Northern Virginia), and still others sent their new officers to the state academy (e.g., Charleston, South Carolina).

The FBI "New Agents' Training Unit" includes four components in its curriculum: "academics, case exercises, firearms training and operational skills" (FBI Academy 2013: 1). Under these components are concentrations in "academics, firearms, operational skills" and what is called "the integrated case scenario" (FBI Academy 2013: 1). New agents need to pass their academic exams with a score of 85 percent or better in such subjects as behavioral science, ethics, forensics, and interrogation. Physical training is also quite rigorous and requires that new recruits pass both physical agility and defensive tactics exams (see the FBI Academy website: http://www.fbi.gov/about-us/training/sat).

> Agent trainees study a broad range of subjects that grounds them in the fundamentals of law, ethics, behavioral science, interviewing and report writing, basic and advanced investigative and intelligence techniques, interrogation, and forensic science. Students learn how to manage and run counterterrorism, counterintelligence, weapons of mass destruction, cyber, and criminal investigations—so they are flexible and well rounded and able to handle any case upon graduation. Trainees must score 85 percent or better on exams in three legal disciplines, interviewing, national security investigations, criminal investigations, and interrogation. As part of their ethics training, students tour the U.S. Holocaust Memorial Museum in Washington, D.C. to learn what can happen when law enforcement loses its core values.
>
> (FBI Academy 2013: 1).

Beyond academy training, almost all criminal justice agencies require some form of OJT with an experienced coworker or supervisor. As with initial training at post academies, OJT is usually of longer duration for those working in policing and law than it is for correctional staff.

Ongoing training

In addition to OJT training, many criminal justice agencies require that their employees be trained as they progress through their career (Bennett and Hess 2001; Haberfeld 2002; FBI Academy 2013; National Center for State Courts 2013; Stohr *et al.* 1996; Vohryzek-Bolden and Croisdale 1999; Utah Department of Public Safety 2013; Weber County Sheriff's Office 2013). Sometimes particular training is required, such as use of new equipment, restraint techniques, and training on sexual harassment or ethics, and sometimes it is optional. Some agencies require that their employees complete a requisite amount of training per year. Obviously, the more training required and offered, assuming that most of it is useful, the more opportunities there are for the employee to develop and to further the aims of the organization to be a "learning organization," as was discussed in Chapter 4. Training subjects offered depend to a large degree on the position one occupies and the resources of the organization. Such training might include the following:

- first-line supervisor training;
- dealing with special populations (e.g., mentally ill, aged, gangs);
- interpersonal communication skills;
- building of counseling skills;
- interviewing and interrogation;
- treatment best practices;
- terrorism/homeland security;
- community relations;
- diversity training;
- sexual harassment;
- firearms;
- anger management and de-escalation;
- report writing;
- security techniques;
- use of technical equipment;
- data management;
- evaluation techniques;
- supervision and management theory and techniques.

Common deficiencies in training

The substance and relevance of training varies widely from jurisdiction to jurisdiction and from job to job (Bennett and Hess 2001; Bradford and Pynes 1999; Cornett-DeVito and McGlone 2000; Gaines *et al.* 2003; Haberfeld 2002; National Center for State Courts 2013; Vohryzek-Bolden and Croisdale 1999). Often a correctional officer at a jail will receive more or less training than a correctional officer in a juvenile facility in the same state. Larger police departments may be able to fund more ongoing training than smaller jurisdictions. Probation departments may value a more human service curriculum for training than is the case at maximum security prisons for men. The prosecutor's office may be able to fund more training than the public defender organization, should it exist. It is natural, then, for training levels and content to vary depending on the mission, available funding, and size of an organization.

It is safe to say that in too many organizations, the training for some staff is insufficient. As we have discussed throughout this book, the roles for those involved in criminal justice are complex, at times contradictory, and very challenging. The work is often hidden from public view. Therefore, the best organizations provide the training necessary to do the work in the most professional manner. Until funding bodies such as state legislatures and county commissions acknowledge the need to provide professional-level training, however, the amount of training is not likely to increase. We are not saying that simply throwing money at the problem will fix everything, but addressing serious deficiencies calls for resources (both monetary and human capital) to be directed toward this issue.

Other problems associated with the training offered in criminal justice are concerned with the trainers and the training facilities. Concerns have been raised about the qualifications and teaching skills of trainers, both at academies and on the job, and about the lack of adequate and well-maintained facilities. The content of training offerings is not always of the best quality, either. Given the paucity of training offered to staff in some jurisdictions, there is sometimes a tendency to focus on "security" and "control" topics that, while necessary, do not provide the other skills that staff need daily; often lacking, for example, are training in ethics and opportunities to acquire interpersonal, anger management, or problem-solving skills (Bradford and Pynes 1999). If managers of criminal justice agencies truly want to engage staff in meaningful dialog and receive useful input, training must precede such engagement, both for staff and for management.

One last point regarding deficiencies in training has to do with the fact that training is not a cure-all for anything that might ail an organization. As Buerger (1998: 52) writes regarding police training "as a Pentecost," police managers too often rely on training for "[m]iraculous transformations on the basis of too little [words alone], too late [well after the audience is already steeped in police culture]."

Performance appraisals

Performance appraisals are typically administered formally and informally in most criminal justice and other types of agencies (see Box 8.2). The "Atta Boys" or "Atta Girls" used by the affirming manager, or the "You'd better shape up" or "Let's reconsider that decision" lectures that managers must use from time to time, are very important. Such feedback is central to maintaining productivity, morale, and enthusiasm and, in the latter case, instilling discipline. The provision of regular and mostly positive, or at least supportive, feedback on the job—when that is warranted—cannot be overestimated. The research indicates that there are numerous beneficial outcomes that derive from the provision of regular feedback (Brody 2004; Hackman and Oldham 1974; Zupan and Menke 1988). Such positive outcomes might include increased productivity, enriched jobs for staff, the recognition that what people are doing and how they are doing it is important, the confidence to continue to strive, and/or the corrective action needed to get employees back on the right track.

Performance appraisals serve the same function of affirming good work, noting any areas that might need improvement, and setting goals for the next appraisal period. Performance appraisals also serve as formal departmental documents that can be used to establish a track record of work, whether outstanding or dismal or, more likely, somewhere in between. The performance appraisal may stay in the employee's file throughout his or her entire tenure. Thus, performance appraisals are often reviewed when promotions are discussed and referenced when disciplinary action is being considered.

Typically, performance appraisals are done by one's immediate supervisor after the first six months for new employees and then at, or near, the yearly anniversary of hiring. They take many forms, sometimes involving self-appraisal by the employee and then comments by the supervisor, or appraisal by the supervisor with meaningful input from the employee. At the other end of the spectrum, appraisal by the supervisor with little or no input from the employee is sometimes the norm.

The types of items included in the appraisal form also vary; some are general statements about performance, others are related to actual job behaviors and sometimes, as mentioned in the foregoing, they encompass larger categories. General areas of evaluation might include whether the supervisee "was supportive of coworkers" and "responded appropriately to directives," among other items. Or the items might be anchored to actual job behaviors, such as "employee conducts four treatment groups per week" or "employee provides medications to inmates in a timely fashion" or "employee made ten traffic stops per week." Some instruments assess only general dimensions of behavior like "communication" or "use of resources," with sub-questions that are addressed by either the supervisor or the supervisee. Or, again, the appraisal form may include general areas, which have no set response categories but instead are completed by the supervisor or the supervisee in a more free-form manner.

The responses allowed on the appraisal can take many forms as well. There may be multiple-choice questions requiring a yes or no answer. Or the possible responses might have a range of 1–5 or 1–7, covering "strongly agree" to "strongly disagree" as responses to the given statements.

In sum, performance appraisals take many forms in terms of employee involvement in the process, content of the form, and response categories. The different facets of the form tend to reflect the management style preferred by leaders and supervisors in the organization. A more traditional manager would believe in supervisor evaluation and perhaps little input— an opportunity provided at the end of the process—by the employee. A human relations or learning-oriented manager, on the other hand, would opt for greater involvement by staff in their own evaluation. Such a manager might encourage an initial self-evaluation, followed by review by the supervisor and then joint evaluation in a face-to-face interview.

The form of the appraisal instrument and its type of questions also reflect organizational traditions. Older performance appraisal instruments tend to have generalized statements about job performance that could apply to several positions. But since the 1960s and 1970s and the movement to remove bias in hiring and promotions, there has been a parallel movement to ensure that the items one is evaluated on in a performance appraisal are actually related to the job one is doing (Latham and Wexley 1981). We might label these efforts as attempts to increase the validity of performance evaluations. What a novel idea! So, for instance, if a major task for a counselor at a Boys' Ranch is to facilitate groups on substance abuse, several items on the evaluation must be actually related to this central part of the role.

Job analysis represents one approach to increasing performance appraisal validity. A job analysis allows the employer to determine what tasks are routinely required for the job and to ensure that those are then evaluated on the performance appraisal instrument (Latham and Wexley 1981). One version of a job analysis is the Critical Incident Technique (see Box 8.2). The advantages inherent in the development of the instrument in this manner are that employees are intimately engaged in deciding the content of the evaluation. Thus, since they developed the instrument, a general sense of fairness and ownership attends the process. Moreover, should a performance appraisal be challenged in an administrative proceeding, it is more likely to be seen as fair if the items are job-valid. The disadvantage of developing such an instrument is that it can be time-consuming to work through each major job category. Notably, some items on this instrument could be shared by several jobs when there are responsibilities and tasks that are shared across roles (e.g., security), thus obviating the need to develop wholly different instruments for each job.

Box 8.2 Using the critical incident technique to develop a job-valid performance appraisal instrument

Typically, this technique, which is also used to develop selection instruments, requires that several people who actually do the job, and those who directly supervise them, describe situations in which they witnessed job behavior that they regarded as particularly effective (Latham and Wexley 1981). Then those people are asked to describe situations that afforded examples of particularly ineffective job behaviors. From these examples, items are developed that reflect actual job behaviors associated with dimensions of that job. These behaviors are reviewed by the jobholders and their supervisors for validity purposes and then pretested in an appraisal process. Once the bugs have been worked out, an appraisal form emerges that actually measures real job behaviors (Latham and Wexley 1981). The advantage of developing the instrument this way is that the instrument is job-valid. However, this technique is time-consuming if it must be applied to every position in the institution.

Best practices in performance appraisal

All this discussion of the performance appraisal instrument and its validity presupposes that the knowledge level about job performance is sufficient to permit a valid appraisal. But sometimes it is not. Sometimes supervisors and managers are too busy to pay attention to what their supervisees are doing. When this happens, there can be no valid evaluation. Therefore, in the interest of establishing and reiterating some basic parameters for performance appraisals, or best or optimal practices, the authors, along with others (Coutts and Schneider 2004; Latham and Wexley 1981; Wessel 2003; see also Box 8.3), offer the following:

1 Allow high involvement of subordinates in the whole process; this will enhance their satisfaction with the appraisal process, and consequently their productivity.
2 Supply supportive supervision throughout employment; this will increase the employee's satisfaction with the appraisal.
3 Engage in joint problem-solving about specific goals with the employee; this will increase productivity in those areas.
4 In the evaluation of high-performing individuals, minimize critical comments on the performance appraisal.
5 For those who are struggling in the workplace, provide feedback on problem behavior that is clearly documented in the performance appraisal.

6   Observe employee behavior on a regular basis (daily if possible).

7   Interact with supervisees on a regular basis (daily if possible) and know or find out what they are doing and how they are doing it.

8   Observe the workplace or work setting of supervisees on a regular basis (sometimes supervisors do not work in the same physical location as the supervisee) as this will ensure that the supervisor has the opportunity to reinforce positive work behavior and to discourage negative work behavior. "Walking-around management" is frequently cited as an effective technique. Managers need to know at a minimum such things as how the job is being done by each supervisee, whether he or she needs more resources or training to do the job effectively, and how he or she interacts with coworkers and clients/the general public.

9   Make yourself available to those you supervise. The old "open door policy" is a good one. Supervisees should feel they can approach the supervisor with problems and issues related to job performance and job tasks.

10 Provide regular and informal feedback to employees. As most work by employees is done well, most of this feedback should be positive. But employees going down the wrong track need to be corrected, if possible, before, or in addition to, the formal evaluation.

In other words, employees need to be actively engaged in the process, and managers and supervisors need to be proactive in their supervision. If managers do not allow for participation in the process and neglect to engage in active observation and walking-around management, they may succumb to basing evaluations on exceptional and nonrepresentative incidents, gossip, or the production of poor performers who substitute obsequious behavior for real work. Nothing is more demoralizing for outstanding performers than to see poor performers rewarded because they have charmed a supervisor, rather than because of merit (Coutts and Schneider 2004).

Box 8.3 Judicial performance evaluations and judicial elections

In an effort to improve judicial performance, some states began instituting judicial performance evaluation programs in the 1970s. In a study of evaluation programs for judges in Washington State, Brody (2004) administered surveys to witnesses, jurors, and attorneys appearing before participating judges. The responses garnered from the witnesses and jurors did not match the perceptions of the same judges the attorneys had rated. Nevertheless, Brody (2004) noted that judges found the information collected from these surveys useful for improving their performance, and the cost of the study was relatively low. Brody argues that such evaluations can be a beneficial instrument for improving judicial performance and voter knowledge of it.

A final problem in appraisals

If these best practices are adopted, the criminal justice manager or supervisor is more likely to be able to fairly evaluate job performance and less likely to encounter the problems associated with appraisals. Similarly, if managers or supervisors allow for employee input into the process and make sure that the instrument itself fits the job it is being used to evaluate, there will be fewer problems. But a final problem with appraisals, which can be alleviated but not eliminated if these other issues are attended to, is the matter of over- or underevaluating performance. This is a problem that is associated with the manager.

Some managers tend to rate their employees too harshly, and others are too soft in their ratings (Wessel 2003). This is the Mama Bear, Papa Bear, and Baby Bear problem of performance appraisals. It is hard for managers to settle on the "just right" bed of evaluation. If "too hard" on employees, particularly those who are doing an excellent job, people tend to become discouraged. If "too soft," some employees may slack off, and the best employees may lose heart as even poor performers are rated highly. These disparities in ratings will seem particularly unfair if supervisors in the same unit or organization tend to vary a great deal in their evaluations. People will see and feel how unfair this situation is. Moreover, the problem of disciplining poor performers will be made harder because their evaluations will be lacking the feedback that would be necessary to support disciplinary action. Any manager or supervisor who has been on the job for more than a year is likely to have seen the deleterious effects of failing to evaluate accurately.

One means of alleviating the problem and moving supervisors closer to the "Baby Bear" perspective is to train supervisors on how to do the evaluation and how to use the performance appraisal instrument (Latham and Wexley 1981). Such training should allow some time to discuss appraisal scenarios and to play-act evaluation perspectives and techniques.

Retention strategies

Our final area of personnel policies and practices is keeping the best and the brightest working in criminal justice agencies. These strategies must be multifaceted, incorporating, at a minimum, adequate pay, career paths, and a fulfilling job design (e.g., McCampbell 2006).

Pay isn't everything, but it is something

Turnover can be acute when the economy is humming and the pay for criminal justice staff is not competitive with other public or private sector work. As is often said by those who espouse a human relations perspective on management, "pay isn't everything." But we would argue it is "something," and figures largely in the decision making of employees (DeFrances 2002;

Patenaude 2001; Petrecca 2011; Smith 1997; Stohr *et al.* 1992; Whisenand 2004; Yearwood 2003). As discussed earlier, working in some sectors of criminal justice (e.g., institutional corrections) is not the first career choice for some people (Conover 2000). Therefore, competitive pay for public sector work will keep employees on the job and motivated, even when other opportunities for employment are presented.

For instance, in a national survey of prosecutors, DeFrances (2002) found that low salaries were regarded as the primary reason why about a third of the offices were experiencing problems with recruitment and retention of deputy prosecutors. Yearwood (2003) found in an analysis of recruitment and retention issues in North Carolina detention centers that an annual pay increase was rated as the most effective retention technique an agency can employ. Similarly, in a study to explain a high turnover rate of correctional staff (35 percent from 1998 to 2001) working in Arkansas prisons, Patenaude (2001: 58) reported that "[p]ay and benefits were two primary concerns identified in the surveys and discussed by each focus group." About 18 percent of the respondents in Patenaude's study said they worked in the Arkansas Department of Corrections because they needed a job to support their families, and only about 10 percent saw that work as a long-term career choice. Meanwhile about 22 percent said they would leave if their pay and benefits did not increase and another 18 percent would leave if they could get better pay elsewhere. Patenaude (2001: 58) concluded that "[p]ay remains the major contributor to resentment and discontent within the correctional ranks and must be regarded as a major contributor to turnover."

Moreover, staff may be less likely to engage in corrupt activities and be more committed to their work if they are paid decently (Patenaude 2001). Recall, for instance, that on Maslow's hierarchy, the bottom two rungs include needs that are met primarily through financial compensation. For example, an employee of a criminal justice organization whose family qualifies for food stamps is a good indication that pay levels are far too low to motivate workers.

In 2007 the starting salary for NYPD new recruits was $25,100. The NYPD was only able to hire 1,100 of the 2,500 recruits they had hoped to sign up (*New York Times* editorial 2007). The most current starting salary for the NYPD is $34,970 (New York City Police Department 2013), which is an increase from the 2007 salaries, but is still comparatively low—especially considering the high cost of living in New York City. Combining a low salary, long hours, and stressful work conditions can make police work a daunting task.

According to the latest figures from the Bureau of Labor Statistics (2011), many work characteristics affect hourly wages: Whether the job is considered white-collar, blue-collar, or service-related; whether it is full or part-time, union or nonunion: the size of the organization; its location in a metropolitan location, or not, and the geographic area. As one might expect, white-collar positions, those in union shops, and those in metropolitan areas of New England or mid-Atlantic or Pacific regions of the country tended to pay the most. Unfortunately, prosecutors and defense attorneys are not separated out in these data, though mean hourly wages for lawyers ($62.74) and judges ($53.34), or roughly $113,310 and $110,940, are white-collar jobs. Of course, these figures grossly exaggerate what public sector defense attorneys and prosecutors make in most jurisdictions. Police officers and sheriff's patrol officers had a mean hourly wage of $27.05 and a mean annual salary of $56,260; probation officers (parole officers were not mentioned) and correctional treatment specialists had a mean hourly wage of $25.05 and an annual salary of $52,110; and correctional officers and jailers had a mean hourly wage of $20.82 and an annual salary of $43,300.

There is some variation in pay depending on the level of government. Federal judges and law enforcement and correctional staff make more than state or local actors in those professions. Also, public sector employees tend to make more than those in the private sector. Generally, and in terms of the whole pay and benefit package, those working at the federal level make more than those working in the states; those working in the adult system make more than those working with juveniles; those working in the state system make more than those working for counties or municipalities; those who work in a union shop make more than those who do not; and those working for a public sector organization make more than those working for the private sector. But, having said this, there is a wide range of pay across states and localities and job types that make these averages somewhat misleading. Of course, the cost of living in a given area of the country also accounts for some of these compensation differences; not surprisingly, however, in a survey on pay by Corrections Compendium, the researchers concluded (2003: 8) that "[t]he only common pattern or trend regarding correctional staff wages is the lack of any common pattern or trend."

Another generality, as the data from the Bureau of Labor Statistics indicates, is that correctional work tends to pay less than other public sector work, such as policing or work for the courts. But this does not always hold. One of the authors remembers being shocked when a lieutenant in a Nevada jail told her in 1990 that his compensation package was about $70,000 per year. When she indicated her surprise, he said that correctional officers who frequently worked overtime in his facility made even more. Not surprisingly, we found in research on that jail that the officers and other staff in his facility were some of the most satisfied with their work.

However, pay does not represent all the issues surrounding turnover for many criminal justice professionals. For example, Sexton (2006) found in a survey of police chiefs that rapid turnover was due, in part, to five main reasons: health, stress, personnel issues, politics, and job advancement. So pay isn't everything, but it is something.

Too much work

A common complaint raised by criminal justice workers is that they have too much on their work plate! Police officers in medium and large cities out of necessity ignore property crimes in order to focus their limited time on the more serious and violent offenses. Probation and parole officers at the state level are able to supervise only a fraction of their caseload each month. Correctional officers work in jails and prisons which are overflowing with inmates. Defense and prosecuting attorneys complain of staggering caseloads which prevent them from doing their legally mandated job. In a workload assessment of Virginia's attorneys and staff engaged in indigent defense carried out by Kleiman and Lee (2010: i), the authors found that Virginia's public defender offices statewide needed an additional 19.5 attorneys and 32.5 support staff in order to do their job effectively. Given the decreased monies allocated to the public sector at the local, state, and federal levels, it is unlikely that public defender's offices, or any other criminal justice agency for that matter, is going to see much relief in the "too much work" category any time soon.

However, there are long- and short-term consequences for criminal justice workers and their agencies when they are overburdened with work. Stress, health problems, and turnover are possible personal outcomes associated with too much work, and decreased or inferior work are organizational consequences. Although criminal justice managers can address some of this stress through scheduling and restructuring the work, at some point more resources will have to be allocated for staff in order to reduce negative workplace outcomes associated with too much work.

Career path

Once the basic compensation needs of staff are met, and if staff are not too overburdened with work, and if Maslow (1998) is correct, there are other elements of the job that serve as motivators. One such element is whether there is a clearly defined and attainable career path for staff. If staff are motivated by the higher level needs of respect, belonging (love), and self-actualization at work—as one might expect the best and brightest employees, in particular, to be—they will stay on the job if there is a future for them up the ranks. Specifically, they will be increasingly interested in shouldering greater responsibility and opportunities to make decisions about their work. To some extent, these needs can be met by structuring democratic participation into the work. Eventually, however, some of the best employees are going to want to become managers, or at least supervisors.

Current managers need to provide a clear and identifiable means for such people to advance by outlining for them work expectations (via performance appraisals and other means of feedback) and background requirements (training, work experience, and education levels), and by providing the training and work opportunities that allow people to develop the skills that will be needed for advancement. Likewise, some agencies even provide funding for employee continuing education or have coopera- tive agreements with local professional schools, colleges, and universities. For instance, Kiekbusch *et al.* (2003: 67) found in their examination of five jail settings in the United States that there was a positive influence on reten- tion when the sheriff in a jail communicated "realistic promotion support." Mentoring of the "water-walkers" by current managers will go far toward keeping those best and brightest employees motivated and on the job.

Job design: criminal justice work for the twenty-first century

The topic of job design tends to encompass all the other personnel prac- tices discussed in this and some of the other chapters. Job design just refers to how a job or task is structured. A job is said to be enriched if it pro- vides opportunities for meaningful work and input. Hackman and Oldham (1974) developed one of the most well-known and often used measures of job design in their Job Diagnostic Survey. To use this survey, respondents estimate on a seven-point scale the degree to which certain attributes pres- ently apply to their own job. Included in the instrument are questions geared toward deciphering the degree of task identification, autonomy, skill vari- ety, task significance, and feedback perceived to exist in one's work; these characteristics represent the attributes of an "enriched" job. According to Hackman and Oldham (1974), these five "core job dimensions" translate into three "critical psychological states," which result in personal and work outcomes of high internal work motivation, high quality of work perform- ance, high satisfaction with the work, and low absenteeism and turnover.

Skill variety, task identity, and task significance compose the critical psy- chological state of "experienced meaningfulness of the work"; autonomy measures the critical state of "experienced responsibility for outcomes of the work"; and feedback measures the critical psychological state of "knowl- edge of actual results of the work activities." Each of the job characteristic scores is weighted to reflect the relative importance of each dimension, and all the scores are combined to create a single "motivating potential" score. The motivating potential scores range from 0 to 360, with 0 reflecting a total absence of motivating potential and 360 indicating a total fulfillment of said potential.

Some colleagues and one of the authors used this instrument in a study of turnover and stress among correctional staff working in five jails around the country (Stohr *et al.* 1994). They found, among other things, that job enrichment, when combined with other model personnel and management practices, is associated with less stress and turnover. Furthermore, in a study including over seventy-three federal prisons, Wright *et al.* (1997: 525) found that "[j]ob autonomy and participation in decision making (by employees) are associated with enhanced occupational outcomes including higher job satisfaction, stronger commitment to the institution, greater effectiveness in working with inmates, and less job-related stress."

When we discuss job enrichment and job design in our criminal justice management classes we always ask students to consider what would be their "ideal" attributes of a job (see the exercise on job design at the end of this chapter). They often mention such issues as pay, work-hour flexibility, variety, and the ability to make a difference in the lives of others or in their community—not necessarily in this order. As our discussion of these personnel practices in this chapter would indicate, good people will be, and are, attracted to criminal justice work when the compensation is reasonable, but they will stay on the job, even in an economy where jobs are plentiful, if they have some control and say in their work and if it is designed to give them opportunities to make their mark in the world.

The research indicates that an enriched job tends to result in distinct and measurable outcomes (Bennett and Hess 2001; Sims 2001; Slate *et al.* 2001; Stohr *et al.* 1994; Zupan and Menke 1988). Lower turnover, greater job satisfaction, and less stress are some of the outcomes that are believed to accompany a more enriched job and longer tenure in criminal justice professions (e.g., Strickland 2006).

Conclusions

Managing the personnel processes in an organization is always difficult; it is doubly so in criminal justice agencies. The multilayered mission of these agencies makes personnel processes vitally important, as the very liberty and safety of other staff and community members/clients/inmates are at risk if serious mistakes occur. In this chapter we discussed all major aspects of personnel processes.

We discussed selection process, training, and performance appraisal in this chapter. These processes can certainly tax the resources of the organization, but if they are not done right, the cost can be very high. The *staff are* the organization when it comes to criminal justice agencies. They comprise 60–80 percent of costs, and the organization that fails to select, train, evaluate, and keep the best of their recruits is not achieving what would otherwise be possible. If the selection process is not valid, if the training is not useful or nonexistent, and if the appraisal process is inaccurate, the best staff will not be selected, nor will the better workers be persuaded to stay.

Organizations that do these things right (or as near to right as they can be done) must also make sure that the job itself pays a reasonable wage; has a clear career path that allows for, and even promotes, the advancement of the best and brightest; and provides as many enriched jobs as possible. Not all jobs in criminal justice can meet the ideal of "enrichment." Most, however, can provide avenues for advancement, training, or some variety to allow staff to appreciate their work and the meaningful contributions they are making.

Exercise: job design

Before we discuss job design in our management classes, we ask the students to fantasize about the attributes of their dream job. We think that this mental exercise, followed by some listing of these attributes on the board and discussion, helps people both to understand what job design is and to focus on what kind of work environment and tasks appeal to them. Finally, we ask the students to relate their desirable job characteristics to those described by Hackman and Oldham: Are the two sets similar in content?

Although we think these goals are best achieved if we do this exercise before the lecture on job design, the exercise might fruitfully be employed at the end of the lecture as well. As most of these students have some kind of work experience (few are "silver spooners" at the urban state school we currently teach at), our discussion usually includes references to jobs people have already held.

Discussion questions

1 Why is the cost consideration so important in personnel processes? Explain your answer.
2 How does the cost of each step in the selection process determine when those steps are taken? Explain your answer.
3 What does the term "job validity" mean, and how does it apply to selection and performance appraisal processes? Give an example of how it applies.
4 Why do correctional workers tend to receive less training than those who work for police departments? What does this difference in training mean for those respective roles?
5 What are the best methods for selecting and keeping the "water-walker" workers in criminal justice? Why don't all criminal justice organizations engage in more of these strategies?
6 Why does the selection process differ for criminal attorneys and for policing and corrections personnel?
7 How do management theories influence the way that selection, training, and performance appraisal are done in criminal justice agencies? Give an example.

> **Key terms**
>
> **job analysis:** allows the employer to determine what tasks are routinely required for the job and to ensure that those are evaluated on the performance appraisal instrument (Latham and Wexley 1981).
> **job design:** refers to how a job or task is structured.
> **job-valid qualification:** related to attributes or abilities that are needed to get the job done (age, weight, eyesight, etc.).
> **performance appraisals:** typically administered in most criminal, justice and other types of agencies, both formally and informally; they serve the same function of affirming good work, noting areas that may need improvement, and setting goals for the next appraisal period. Performance appraisals serve as formal departmental documents that can be used to establish a track record of work.

Note

1   Barbara Collins, executive director of the Juvenile Justice Trainers Association, kindly provided these figures after quickly surveying her contacts via e-mail. The Juvenile Justice Trainers Association in Ben Lomand, California, may be contacted by calling (831) 336–0611 or e-mailing www.jjta.org.

References

Austin, J. and Irwin J. (2001) *It's about time: America's imprisonment binge.* Belmont, CA: Wadsworth/Thomson Learning.
Bennett, W. W. and Hess, K. M. (2001) *Management and supervision in law enforcement,* 3rd edn. Belmont, CA: Wadsworth/Thomson Learning.
Bradford, D. and Pynes, J. E. (1999) Police academy training: Why hasn't it kept up with practice? *Police Quarterly,* 2: 283–301.
Brody, D. C. (2004) The relationship between judicial performance evaluations and judicial elections. *Judicature,* 87: 168–192.
Buerger, M. (1998) Police training as a Pentecost. *Police Quarterly,* 1: 27–64.
Bureau of Labor Statistics, US Department of Labor. (2004a) National compensation survey: Occupational wages in the United States, July 2003. Available at www. bls.gov/oco/ncs/ocs/sp/ncbl0658.pdf (last accessed January 31, 2013).
Bureau of Labor Statistics, US Department of Labor. (2004b) Occupational outlook handbook, 2004–05 edition, correctional officers. Available at www.bls.gov/oco/ocos156.htm (last accessed January 31, 2013).
Bureau of Justice Statistics, US Department of Justice. (2006) Law enforcement management and administrative statistics: Local police departments, 2003. May 2006, NCJ 210118. Washington DC: Office of Justice Programs.
Bureau of Justice Statistics, US Department of Justice. (2010) Law enforcement management and administrative statistics: Local police departments, 2007. Available at www.bjs.gov/content/pub/pdf/lpd07.pdf (last accessed January 31, 2013).

Bureau of Labor Statistics. (2011) Occupational employment statistics: May 2011 national occupational employment and wage estimates. Available at www.bls.gov/oes/current/oes_nat.htm#00-0000 (last accessed January 31, 2013).

Bureau of Labor Statistics (2013) Overview of BLS statistics by occupation. Available at http://www.bls.gov/bls/occupation.htm (last accessed January 31, 2013).

California Department of Corrections (2013). Sample test for correctional officers. Available at www.cdcr.ca.gov/Career_Opportunities/POR/docs/COYCOYCC%20Sample%2 Test.pdf (last accessed January 31, 2013).

Conover, T. (2000) *Newjack: Guarding Sing Sing*. New York, NY: Random House.

Cornett-DeVito, M. M. and McGlone, E. L. (2000) Multicultural communication training for law enforcement officers: A case study. *Criminal Justice Policy Review*, 11: 234–253.

Corrections Compendium. (2003a) Correctional officer education and training. *Corrections Compendium*, 28(2): 11–12.

Corrections Compendium. (2003b) Wages and benefits paid to correctional employees. *Corrections Compendium*, 28(1): 8–9.

Coutts, L. M., and Schneider, F. W. (2004) Police officer performance appraisal systems: How good are they? *Policing: An International Journal of Police Strategies and Management* 27: 67–81.

DeFrances, C. J. (2002) *Prosecutors in state courts. (2001)* Bureau of Justice Statistics Bulletin. US Department of Justice, Office of Justice Programs. Washington DC: GPO.

FBI Training Academy. (2013) New agents' training unit. Available at www.fbi.gov/about-us/training/sat (last accessed January 31, 2013).

Federal Bureau of Prisons (2013) About staff training centers. Available at www.bop.gov/about/train/index.jsp (last accessed January 31, 2013).

Ford, R. E. (2003) Saying one thing, meaning another: The role of parables in police training. *Police Quarterly*, 6: 84–110.

Fulton, B., Stichman, A., Travis, L. and Latessa, E. (1997) Moderating probation and parole officer attitudes to achieve desired outcomes. *The Prison Journal*, 77(3): 295–312.

Gaines, L. K., Worrall, J. L., Southerland, M. D. and Angell, J. E. (2003) *Police administration*, 2nd edn. Boston, MA: McGraw-Hill.

Haberfeld, M. R. (2002) *Critical issues in police training*. Upper Saddle River, NJ: Prentice Hall.

Hackman, J. R. and Oldham, G. R. (1974) *The job diagnostic survey: An instrument for the diagnosis of jobs and the evaluation of job redesign projects* (Tech. Rep. No. 4). New Haven, CT: Yale University, Department of Administrative Sciences.

Johnson, K. (2007) FBI relaxes policy on prior pot use by job applicants. *Idaho Statesman*, p. 15.

Jordan, L. (2003) Physical fitness standards in law enforcement. Paper presented at the Western and Pacific Association of Criminal Justice Educators Conference, Park City, UT.

Kiekbusch, R., Price, W. and Theis, J. (2003) Turnover predictors: Causes of employee turnover in sheriff-operated jails. *Criminal Justice Studies* 16(2): 67–76.

Kleiman, M. and Lee, C. G. (2010) *Virginia indigent defense commission attorney and support staff workload assessment: Final report*. Research Division, National Center for State Courts. Online. Available at www.ncsc.org (last accessed January 31, 2013).

Latham, G. P. and Wexley, K. N. (1981) *Increasing productivity through performance appraisal.* Menlo Park, CA: Addison-Wesley.

Lonsway, K. A. (2003) Tearing down the wall: Problems with consistency, validity, and adverse impact of physical agility testing in police selection. *Police Quarterly,* 6(3): 237–277.

Maslow, A. H. (1998) *Maslow on management.* New York, NY: Wiley.

Mays, G. L. and Winfree L. T. (2002) *Contemporary corrections.* Belmont, CA: Wadsworth/ Thomson Learning.

McCampbell, S. B. (2006) Recruiting and retaining jail employees: Money isn't the long-term solution. *American Jails,* 20(2): 9–15.

National Center for State Courts. (2013) Workload assessment. Available at www.ncsc.org/Services-and-Experts/Areas-of-expertise/Workload-assessment.aspx

New York Police Department. (2013) Frequently asked questions. Available at www.nyc.gov/html/nypd/html/faq/faq_police.shtml (last accessed January 31, 2013).

New York State Department of Corrections and Community Supervision. (2013) Correction officer exam. Available at www.doccs.ny.gov/jobs/CO_Exam.html (last accessed January 31, 2013).

New York State Division of Criminal Justice Services. (2013) Training. Available at www.criminaljustice.ny.gov/opca/training.htm (last accessed January 31, 2013).

New York State Police (2013) Basic school. Available at http://troopers.ny.gov/Academy/Basic_School (last accessed January 31, 2013).

New York Times. (2007) 'Enter police recruit, underpaid'. Available at www.nytimes.com/2007/02/03/opinion/03sat4.html (last accessed January 31, 2013).

North Carolina State Patrol. (2013) Job page. Available at http://agency.governmentjobs.com/northcarolina/default.cfm?action=viewjob&JobID (last accessed January 31, 2013).

Patenaude, A. L. (2001) Analysis of issues affecting correctional officer retention within the Arkansas Department of Correction. *Corrections Management Quarterly,* 5(2): 49–67.

Peak, K. J., Pitts, S. and Glensor, R. W. (2006) From FTO to PTO: A contemporary approach to post-academy recruit training. Paper presented at the Western and Pacific Association of Criminal Justice Educators Annual Conference, Reno, NV.

Petrecca, L. (2011) Tech companies top list of 'great workplaces': Survey finds trust, respect key to morale. *USA Today,* p. 7B.

Ruddell, R. and Main, R. (2006) Evaluating e-learning for staff training. *American Jails,* 20(3): 39–43.

Sexton, D. (2006) Tenure and turnover of small town police chiefs. *Police Forum,* 15(3): 13–20.

Sims, B. (2001) Surveying the correctional environment: A review of the literature. *Corrections Management Quarterly,* 5(2): 1–12.

Slate, R. N., Vogel, R. E. and Johnson, W. W. (2001) To quit or not to quit: Perceptions of participation in correctional decision making and the impact of organizational stress. *Corrections Management Quarterly,* 5(2): 68–78.

Smith, C. (1997) *Courts, politics, and the judicial process,* 2nd edn. Chicago, IL: Nelson-Hall.

Stohr, M. K., Lovrich, N. P. and Wood, M. J. (1996) Service v. security concerns in contemporary jails: Testing behavior differences in training topic assessments. *Journal of Criminal Justice,* 24(5): 437–448.

Stohr, M. K., Lovrich, N. P., Menke, B. A., and Zupan, L. L. (1994) Staff management in correctional institutions: Comparing DiIulio's 'control model' and 'employee investment model' outcomes in five jails. *Justice Quarterly*, 11(3): 471–497.

Stohr, M. K., Self, R. L., and Lovrich, N. P. (1992) Staff turnover in new generation jails: An investigation of its causes and prevention. *Journal of Criminal Justice*, 20(5): 455–478.

Strickland, M. J. (2006) Causations of stress among correctional officers. *American Jails*, 20(3): 69–77.

Thibault, E. A., Lynch, L. M. and McBride, R. B. (2004) *Proactive police management*, 6th edn. Upper Saddle River, NJ: Pearson–Prentice Hall.

US Equal Employment Opportunity Commission, US Department of Justice, Civil Rights Division. (2002) Americans with Disabilities Act: Questions and answers. Available at http://www.usdoj.gov/crt/ada/q%26aeng02.htm (last accessed January 31, 2013).

Utah Department of Public Safety. (2013) POST–the academy–basic training bureau. Available at http://publicsafety.utah.gov/post/academy/basic.html (last accessed January 31, 2013).

Vohryzek-Bolden, M. and Croisdale, T. (1999) *Overview of selected states' academy and in service training for adult and juvenile correctional employees*. Conducted for the California Commission on Correctional Peace Officer Standards and Training. Longmont, CO: National Institute of Corrections.

Weber County Sheriff's Office (2013) Corrections as a career. Available at www.co.weber.ut.us/sheriff/corrections/jobs.html (last accessed January 31, 2013).

Wessel, H. (2003) In search of the perfect performance appraisal. *The Idaho Statesman*, December 28, p. CB 1.

Whisenand, P. M. (2004) *Supervising police personnel: The fifteen responsibilities*, 5th edn. Upper Saddle River, NJ: Pearson–Prentice Hall.

White, M.D. (2008) Identifying good cops early: Predicting recruit performance in the Academy. *Police Quarterly*, 11(1): 27–49.

Wright, K. N., Saylor, W. G., Gilman, E. and Camp, S. (1997) Job control and occupational outcomes among prison workers. *Justice Quarterly*, 14(3): 525–546.

Yearwood, D. L. (2003) Recruitment and retention issues in North Carolina. *American Jails*, 17(4): 9–14.

Zupan, L. L. and Menke, B. A. (1988) Implementing organizational change: From traditional to new generation jail operations. *Policy Studies Review*, 7: 615–625.

9 Selection issues

Workforce 2000, diversity, and affirmative action

Today we hold that the Law School has a compelling interest in attaining a diverse student body. ... Major American businesses have made clear that the skills needed in today's increasingly global marketplace can only be developed through exposure to widely diverse people, cultures, ideas and viewpoints.

(Justice Sandra Day O'Connor,
writing for the majority
in *Grutter v. Bollinger et al.* June 2003)

Even though nearly two-thirds of respondents [in a 2003 Gallup Poll] say that race relations will always be a problem in America, when confronted with the prediction that in 2050, a majority of people in the U.S. will be non-white, the vast majority said it wouldn't matter or that it would be a good thing.

(Civil Rights Coalition for the 21st Century 2004: 1)

Introduction: the twenty-first-century workforce

The workforce of the twenty-first century will meld the talents, beliefs, and cultures of a diverse population. And that future is now.

In most criminal justice workplaces the number of women employed has increased significantly and the number of minority men sometimes mirrors their representation in the larger population (Langton 2010; Maguire and Pastore 2004). Criminal justice client populations have for some time now tended to include a much more ethnically and racially diverse group than those who were hired to handle them. Though there are not anywhere near the number of minority group members among employees as among typical client populations (Reaves 2010; Joseph *et al.* 2003; Lester 2003), there is a greater congruence in this regard than once was the case.

Criminal justice workplaces are much more diverse racially, ethnically, and gender-wise, and this can be laid squarely at the door of affirmative action. In practical terms, **affirmative action** simply means *that an organization takes* *positive steps to ensure that its hiring practices are fair and do not disparately impact a targeted underrepresented group.* The integration of the workplace generally, and specifically in criminal justice, did not occur until affirmative action plans had been mandated and implemented; this happened first on a limited scale affecting government contractors and universities. Because of the importance of this manifest change in criminal justice employment in the past thirty years, we spend some time in this chapter discussing diversity, its importance, and affirmative action as they pertain to personnel processes. But first it is worth discussing now, as we are squarely in the new millennium, Workforce 2000 and the job market generally.

Workforce 2000

In the 1990s there were a number of studies of "Workforce 2000" as the new century approached (Workforce Development Strategies 2004; see also Workforce 2000 reports on the web). Typically, such reports indicated that the workforce of the future would be more ethnically and racially diverse, and would include more females. Furthermore, such studies indicated that there would be a shortage of competent, educated, and qualified people to fill all the available jobs. Currently, as we shall see, there is a surplus of applicants for many positions advertised in criminal justice, though the vast majority of those applicants may not fit the qualifications for the jobs. But the authors of the Workforce 2000 reports thought this trend would reverse itself in the first decade of the new century as baby boomers retired and the next two generations, which are proportionately smaller, took their place in the workforce. Of course, the hope is that the new generations will have received the proper education necessary for these jobs.

Dealing with diversity

As the larger community becomes more diverse, so will that workforce. A key to dealing with or managing diversity in the workplace is raising awareness and understanding of diverse groups and cultures (Cox and Beale 1997). This need will become doubly important, literally, as the century proceeds. Indeed, the US Census Bureau (2012) projects that from 2012 to 2060 the proportion of minorities in the population will increase significantly. Specifically, the number of Hispanics and Asians as a percentage of the population will double, and the number of African Americans will increase, as will the percentage of other nonwhite racial and ethnic groups. By 2060 about 57 percent of the population (including white Hispanics) will belong to what we refer to now as a minority group, but which by then (2060) will likely not be (US Census Bureau 2012).

Cox and Beale (1997), in their book *Developing Competency to Manage Diversity*, argue that managing diversity is a business strategy that is central to increasing organizational effectiveness and performance. For instance, greater diversity in the workforce may contribute to the ability to problem-solve and innovate for public sector organizations faced with diverse clientele. They cite research that indicates that a failure to "manage" diversity, or to build awareness and understanding, leads to such negative organizational outcomes as absenteeism and turnover, harassment, discrimination suits, and stymied communications. They recommend that organizations interested in managing diversity develop individual and organizational-level competencies that dispel myths, misconceptions, and stereotypes about minority groups and at the same time build skills in handling situations in which diversity becomes an issue. Individuals for instance, would need to be trained to do the following:

- Understand group identities and how those affect self-concepts, perceptions of historical events, and cognitive styles.
- Recognize stereotyping and understand how stereotypes can act as a barrier to teamwork.
- Acknowledge cultural, age, and cross-gender differences and how these may affect perceptions of the quality of life.
- See the existence of prejudice and discrimination and their effects in organizations, including those revolving around race, ethnicity, and gender, but also disabilities and sexual orientation. (Cox and Beale 1997: 49–198)

Likewise, organizations and managers need be mindful of, and trained, regarding the following factors:

- Organizational culture, or the bicultural experience for minorities and religious diversity, as that affects organizations' culture.
- Formal and informal structure of the organizations, including affirmative action and mentoring programs.
- How to change the organization through education and a plan so that diversity is positively managed.
- How the organization and the individual can engage in continuous learning to ensure that diverse groups are well managed. (Cox and Beale 1997: 199–332)

In sum, employees and managers in the private and public sector will be more diverse in the near future. To tap into the talent and skills that diverse groups bring to the table, criminal justice managers will need to anticipate this trend and develop strategies and plans to accommodate the changing workforce. As indicated in Table 9.1 and 9.2, and by way of example, first-line supervisor/ managers of correctional officers are currently a diverse lot, with approximately 31 percent of workers from minority groups and 25 percent female (see also Box 9.1). As the population shifts in its proportion of minority group members, the corrections workforce for the twenty-first century will undoubtedly shift in the same direction.

Table 9.1 Number of people

Occupation	Total	W-NH	H	B-NH	AIAN-NH	A-NH
First-line supervisors/Managers of correctional officers	45,730	30,705	3,539	10,130	345	314

			Percentages			
Sex	Total	W-NH	H	B-NH	AIAN-NH	A-NH
	%	%	%	%	%	%
M	74.7	52.5	5.8	14.3	0.5	0.5
F	25.3	14.7	1.9	7.9	0.2	0.2
Total	100	67.1	7.7	22.2	0.8	0.7

Table key: W-NH—White Non-Hispanic (NH); H—Hispanic; B-NH—Black; AIAN-NH—American Indian/Alaskan Native; A-NH—Asian. Note: Some categories were left out due to lack of reported data. Also, percentages may not add to total due to rounding. For information on confidentiality protection, sampling error, nonsampling error, and accuracy of the data, see http://www.census.gov/prod/cen2000/doc/ (last accessed January 31, 2013).

Table adapted from: US interim projections by age, sex, race, and Hispanic origin, US Census Bureau. Available at www.census.gov

Table 9.2 State government employment data: 2011

	Occupation	Full-time employees	Part-time employees
United States	Judicial and Legal	167,030	9,790
United States	Police Protection – Officers	66,671	609
United States	Police – Other	36,601	1,999
United States	Correction	457,250	8,874

Table adapted from State government employment and payroll data: 2011, US Census Bureau. Available at http://www2.census.gov/govs/apes/11stus.txt (last accessed January 31, 2013).

Box 9.1 An organizational expert discusses the "business case" for diversity in justice organizations, by Jan Salisbury

For the past ten years, the most successful companies and businesses have willingly implemented diversity programs that vastly exceed affirmative action programs. Their efforts include ongoing training, active recruiting and mentoring, and measuring management on their ability to retain and manage. Their primary "business case" for this new strategic focus is that to sustain a competitive advantage, they need to recruit the best and the brightest and respond to an increasingly diverse customer and client base. Further, these organizations have realized that a functional diverse workforce enhances creativity and innovation in a diverse global economy. The "business case" for managing diversity in justice organizations is indisputable. Not only is there an escalating increase of people of color and women vying for jobs, but the population served in the justice system is overwhelmingly nonwhite, particularly in large urban areas.

The business of implementing justice is above all a people business, and effective justice professionals must have superior communications skills with which to rehabilitate and control diverse populations. For example, until women began entering corrections and policing in great numbers, there was a stereotype that the indirect, relationship-focused style of women would be disastrous for conflict situations. The result, however, has been the opposite. Women have been very effective in de-escalating conflict with inmates and creating relationships with the community that have led to more control, not less. Other dimensions of diversity are adding value as well. As in business, employing African Americans, Asians, different generations, and people with a variety of backgrounds creates a kaleidoscope of perspectives mirroring the diverse population served and encouraging culturally relevant solutions to workplace and institutional problems. For example, the often more direct style of African Americans is less threatening to someone whose own upbringing sees it as a style, and not as an invitation to a fight. As immigrants continue to enter the justice system, the need for multilingual employees also increases.

During the past decade, research has consistently shown that teams who are diverse in problem-solving styles, ethnicity, gender, etc. are more effective and successful than homogeneous groups in solving problems and accomplishing tasks. While homogeneous teams may be more emotionally comfortable for individuals, they do not encourage thinking "out of the box." However, this research also notes that diverse groups need the training and skills to recognize, appreciate, and utilize their diversity. Otherwise, teams may polarize and stereotype their differences! In addition, leaders need coaching and training to understand the value of their diverse teams and to lead them through conflict to cohesiveness. Creating an inclusive work environment also helps institutions retain great employees. When people know that they have an equal opportunity to contribute and where that input and backgrounds are appreciated, they are less likely to withdraw from work or to look for work elsewhere.

Finally, because that which gets rewarded tends to result in work completed, leaders in the justice community should consider articulating the skills and behaviors required for working with diverse populations (e.g., empathy, self-reflection, flexibility, and tolerance for ambiguity) in their performance evaluation systems. The commitment to implement diversity in justice organizations cannot be a strictly "training" effort, but must be part of a leader's strategic plan that implements inclusive policies and values in working effectively with diverse "others" as much as it does interrogation methods and other technical skills.

Jan Salisbury is president of Salisbury Consulting, which specializes in organizational development with a focus on developing leaders, team building, emotional intelligence, and implementing diversity. Salisbury's research is published in psychological journals, and she is the coauthor, with Bobbi Killian Dominick, of Investigating Harassment and Discrimination Complaints: A Practical Guide (2004).

Selection processes: who wants to work in criminal justice?

The answer to the question "Who wants to work in criminal justice?" is: Quite a few people. For every correctional officer position offered in the Ada County Jail, the local county jail in Boise, Idaho, there are usually at least twelve applicants.[1] According to Norm Brisson, Legal Administrator for the Denver Prosecutor's Office, when a prosecutor's job becomes available in Denver the office reviews the résumés on hand (usually 40–90) and interviews up to ten applicants. By extension, thousands of people apply for jobs in criminal justice agencies every year. What is worthy of note, however, is that many of these applicants may not be qualified for the job and some may not truly want to work in those positions permanently, but see them as stopgap employment until the factory reopens, or as steady employment in a state that has lost timber or manufacturing jobs (Bennett and Hess 2001; Conover 2000; Crouch and Marquart 1994; Lombardo 1989). Of course, in the latter case of downsized workers looking for steady employment, there can be successful work arrangements even though the job was not a new hire's first career choice.

In fact, data from the US Department of Labor (2004) indicate that government worker turnover is at least half that of the private sector (there are no specific figures for the different criminal justice positions in the public or private sectors). Interestingly, among all workers in the public and private sectors, however, workers are likely to hold an average of 9.6 jobs in a lifetime. These two facts, even though on their face contradictory, may mean that once drawn to work in a criminal justice position, people may be less inclined to leave it. But given the transient practices of the American worker, there are no guarantees that they will stay.

But people can and should be excluded from work in criminal justice when they lack obvious qualifications, such as the requisite education or age, or if they have a criminal background that disqualifies them. Moreover if the various jobs available in criminal justice are to be considered part of a desirable "profession" by the vast majority of Americans and by those who have prepared themselves for professional-level careers (e.g., those earning a college or university degree), then the standards for hiring need to reflect that aspiration.

Most of the students to whom the authors have spoken over the years (in the states of Washington, New Mexico, Missouri, and Idaho) are not interested in pursuing a career in institutional corrections, although some ended up working there because of the availability of positions (Mays and Winfree 2002). Many students *are* interested in working in policing, probation, and parole (adult or juvenile) and/or going to law school as preparation for employment as a prosecutor or defense attorney. The authors have been given the following reasons for this attraction to policing, courts, and community corrections work over correctional officer work in prisons, jails, and juvenile facilities:

1   Better pay;
2   Perception of a more professionalized workplace (qualifications require a college degree and more training comes with the job);
3   More perceived excitement and diversity of tasks in policing;
4   Less regular contact (of the total institution kind) with inmates/clients;
5   Dangerousness of prison and jail work (less true for juvenile facilities);
6   Better hours;
7   Unattractiveness of the idea of being "shut in or incarcerated along with" inmates;
8   Negative public image of institutional corrections.

Of course, the students are not factually correct about all these issues, and these perceptions are true or false depending on the locality, the level of government, and the type of job. In some states and localities, correctional officers and counselors are paid quite well. A certain amount of college credits or a college degree is required or encouraged and most work in the institution is not inherently dangerous. Also, correctional institution workers with any tenure in the job can have as good or better hours in comparison with attorneys in private practice, who when starting out can put in sixty-hour work weeks. But the necessity for regular contact with inmates, the sense that staff are enclosed like inmates, and the poor public image of institutional corrections are hard to dispute.

Moreover, the students are also partially correct about the other issues. Generally speaking, in any given state and locality, police, probation and parole officers, and attorneys do make more money, and they have more education and more freedom than workers in institutional corrections (see the Illinois and North Carolina examples provided in the sections that follow). The non-corrections jobs are also viewed as more "professional," in the sense that because of their education and training, jobholders are accorded more discretion in their work and more respect by the community. But regardless of whether the students' perceptions are always correct, the existence of such beliefs has implications for selection processes in criminal justice work. Some agencies may tend to get better or less qualified applicants because of these perceptions (see also the discussion of pay and training levels of criminal justice jobs we discussed in Chapter 8).

Entry-level corrections and police work in Illinois and North Carolina

To illustrate some of our points about jobs and hiring in criminal justice, let us examine some typical job offerings in Illinois and North Carolina. These two states were chosen at random from those listing jobs on the Internet. Job qualifications and salaries in the courts, for prosecuting attorneys, and for public defenders are not presented here in greater detail because they are not usually conveniently available on the Internet. Salary and qualifications for the police and corrections jobs in Illinois and North Carolina, relatively populous states in which the pool of applicants is theoretically more educated and more numerous, are likely to compare favorably with those elsewhere in the country.

Illinois

The position of correctional officer (CO) was advertised on the Illinois Department of Corrections website in April 2004. The basic qualifications for the job was that the applicant be an Illinois resident of 18 years of age or over; he or she should possess a valid driver's license, have a high school diploma or GED, be a US citizen or an authorized alien, and be able to speak, read, and write English.

The starting salary for a correctional officer trainee (as of April 2013) in Illinois was $42,432. During the first three months on the job, new hires are required to attend and pass a six-week corrections training academy, and then they are on probation for another four and one-half months. During the probationary period their salaries rise to $45,816 and the benefits are actually quite generous: 100 percent life insurance and a small co-pay on medical and dental.

Applicants fill out a data form and then begin a series of tests, much like those described in Chapter 8. Preference in scoring and ranking applicants is given to applicants with some post-high school education and to those with applicable work and military experience.

In contrast, in April 2013 the website of the Chicago Police Department indicated that an applicant to be a police officer in that city must be between the ages of 21 and 40, have a valid driver's license, be a resident of the City of Chicago (at least by the time of hiring), and have at least sixty semester hours of college from an accredited university or college, or forty-five hours and one year of military service.

New officers are on probation and make $43,104. They make $60,918 after one year and $64,374 after eighteen months. Probationary officers also are required to complete 480 state academy and 300 additional hours of training with the Chicago Police Department. The department offers very generous benefits of health, prescription drug, and vision and dental insurance and plans' 100 percent tuition reimbursement, even on advanced degrees; paid sick leave; twenty vacation days; and a retirement plan.

North Carolina

In April 2004 (and with some updated 2013 job postings), the North Carolina Department of Corrections website posted several corrections-related jobs, among which were correctional case manager (CCM), correctional officer (CO), probation/parole officer I, II (PPOI, PPOII), community services district coordinator (CSDC), and substance abuse counselor II (SACII).

These jobs called for applicants who were at least 20 years old, had passed a medical examination, possessed a high school diploma or GED, and were citizens of the United States. In addition to those basic qualifications, the website listed the following specifics:

- For the CCM position the applicant also had to have a two-year associate's degree in criminal justice or a related discipline or a high school degree and two years experience as a CO or in a human services position, or some similar combination of training and experience. The applicant also had to be certifiable by the North Carolina Training and Standards Council.
- No additional educational, training, or work experience requirements were listed for the CO position, though those with college degrees were encouraged to apply.
- The CSDC position required a college degree and one year of experience, a two-year degree and two years' experience, or some combination thereof, though the advertisement indicated that a trainee position required a four-year college degree.
- The PPOI/II position required a four-year degree in criminal justice or a related field and one year of experience as a PPO trainee, or another combination of experience and education.
- For the SACII position, a four-year degree and/or a master's degree were required with different levels of experience, primarily as a substance abuse counselor.

As might be expected, given the different levels of required education and experience, the beginning pay for these positions varied. The benefits package offered by North Carolina was also generous by current standards in that employees had full health insurance coverage for themselves, with dependent coverage available.

- CCM range in pay was $22,037–34,962
- CO range in pay was $22,894–34,962 ($28,826–$44,099, updated 2013)
- CSDC range in pay was $23,819–38,052
- PPOI range in pay was $25,781–41,569 (PPOII $37,125–$59,604, updated 2013)
- SACII range in pay was $25,781–41,569
- Note: the earlier numbers have likely increased similar to the CO range.

To apply for these positions in North Carolina, applicants fill out the state's application form and then proceed through a selection process that varies by position.

By way of contrast, in June 2013, the website of the City of Chapel Hill, North Carolina, listed the following requirements for a police officer: The ability to read, write, and perform mathematical calculations; a valid driver's license; a high school diploma or GED; and US citizenship. Persons so qualified must meet the standards set forth by the North Carolina Training and Standards Commission and pass all the required selection tests. A college degree and military experience were preferred. The starting salary was $37,048 annually. The city would also prefer to hire people after they have completed the academy. Benefits are generous, with health, disability, and life insurance for the recruit paid by Chapel Hill and optional dental insurance and tuition assistance. There is longevity pay that begins after five years.

Two-state comparison

This comparison of criminal justice jobs available in Illinois and North Carolina lends support to the belief that the jobs that require more education also tend to pay more. It also indicates that for some positions, the minimum requirements for employment are very basic and may make it difficult to regard those positions as "professional." This may mean that people may not be adequately prepared to engage in the decision making and the use of discretion necessary in professional-level positions. Also of note is that the policing positions tend to pay more and provide more benefits than those positions in corrections. Sometimes this is related to educational requirements (e.g., the Chicago police officer vs. the Illinois correctional officer), but sometimes it is not (e.g., the entry-level Chapel Hill police officer pay vs. the entry-level North Carolina probation officer pay). The explanation for the latter difference might rest with the professional regard and responsibilities that are vested in the police officer position over the corrections position, as well as environmental differences, such as urban vs. rural policing.

Qualifications

It used to be (and likely still is) possible to get a job in criminal justice in many areas of this country if you were/are "connected" through family or friends or politics. As we discussed in Chapter 4, criminal justice jobs, like all public sector work before the institution of civil service reforms, were handed out based on patronage and the spoils system. Recall that with the passage of the Pendleton Act or the Civil Service Reform Act of 1883 at the federal level, and the passage of similar civil service reforms in the states and localities, criminal justice jobs began to come under civil service requirements. The main purpose of civil service laws and protections is to ensure that people are hired, promoted, and fired based on their qualifications and how they behave rather than on whom they know or support in some way.

Nowadays, as discussed in the previous chapter, applicants for criminal justice positions are selected primarily based on merit. Agencies have a set application that queries for personal descriptors (e.g., gender, age), past employment, qualifications such as education and experience, and any criminal involvement or serious traffic offenses. Attorneys are required to have graduated from law school and to have passed, or be willing to take, the relevant state bar exam. In addition, military experience is often prized by criminal justice agencies and men and women who were honorably discharged may receive extra ranking points at the beginning or end of the process. This is not to say of course that "who you know" is completely irrelevant in the selection process. But it does mean that if you do not meet the basic requirements for the job, personal contacts will usually not be enough to get you a job in criminal justice agencies.

Equal opportunity and affirmative action

Any discussion of equal opportunity (EO) or affirmative action (AA) in the classroom or the workplace tends to stir debate, sometimes heated debate. This is understandable, as EO and AA initiatives in government and the private sector have had a real effect in the marketplace. Therefore some people are threatened and frightened by the existence of formal AA plans and their promotion.

As previously stated, in practical terms, **affirmative action** simply means that an organization takes positive steps to ensure that their hiring practices are fair and do not disparately impact a targeted underrepresented group. AA is a more proactive remedy for employment discrimination than EO (Camp *et al.* 1997). AA as law has been used to promote the hiring of minority group members and white women.

But let us just begin this discussion by recognizing that a form of affirmative action has always existed in criminal justice employment. In the past an informal qualification for police, court, or correctional work with adult males (where most of the jobs were) was that the applicant be white and male. For instance, between 1925 and 1965, some police departments actually had quotas to restrict the hiring of women to 1 percent or less of the workforce (Roberg and Kuykendall 1993). Moreover the roster of minority group men on any police force, correctional staff, or attorneys' list was minuscule before the civil rights movement. Thus there was a plan—albeit informal at times, but out in the open at others—that only white males would be hired to work in criminal justice.

For example, the state of California did not start hiring female correctional officers to work in male prisons until the early 1970s, or after the Civil Rights Act of 1964 had been amended in 1972 to apply to gender discrimination in hiring (*Pulido v. State of California et al. 1994*). The first woman police officer, with full police powers, was hired in 1968 in Indianapolis, Indiana (Roberg and Kuykendall 1993) Women were excluded from most law schools until the late 1800s, and from some until the mid-1900s. In 1970 only 3 percent of law students were female; today over 50 percent are (Merlo *et al.* 2000). Not so long ago, highly qualified women were discriminated against when they applied for positions as attorneys. For instance, after graduating near the top of her law school class, now retired Supreme Court Justice Sandra Day O'Connor was offered a "secretarial" position.

In all such cases, most women wishing to work in criminal justice were not hired before the gender provision of the Civil Rights Act was passed in 1972, and they had to sue to be hired and promoted (Martin 1989; Merlo *et al.* 2000). In many cases these organizations and law schools did not hire women until they were sued, and many other criminal justice agencies continued for years to refrain from hiring women.

Mary Stohr was only the second woman hired at the prison at which she began work in 1983. The first woman, a niece of a sergeant, had been hired only a month before Stohr; note this was more than ten years after the applicable statute passed and almost twenty years after the Civil Rights Act of 1964. The warden told Stohr in private that he had opposed hiring a woman and had fought the central office for five years before giving in. He also remarked that he had no intention of hiring African Americans and he proactively worked to prevent the promotion of the one Hispanic officer. The warden's behavior was nothing if not consistent: Upon informing Stohr that she was to serve on the affirmative action committee, he also instructed her to do nothing to recruit minorities. (Stohr told him she could not serve on the committee with that stipulation.)

Discrimination against minority men and women has been just as difficult to overcome as it has been for women in general. As late as 1991, the General Accounting Office found that there was a "glass ceiling" in federal employment that kept minority group men and women and white women situated at lower salaries and lower grades in federal employment (US Senate 1991). Though some real progress has been made in the hiring of minority group males into the criminal justice profession at the federal, state, and local levels, much remains to be done (Palacios 2003). McCluskey and McCluskey (2004) found, for instance, after a review of hiring data for the fifty largest American cities, that the employment of Latino officers has improved markedly for these police departments, but that the diversity of the department employees does vary by community served. Relatedly, Zhao *et al.* (2006) studied the influence of both internal institutional factors (e.g., affirmative action) and external environmental factors (e.g., city population, minority representation) on the hiring of female minority police officers. They found that the increased recruitment and hiring of African American and Hispanic female officers was due largely to an increase of minority representation within their respective cities. They also state that historically, affirmative action policies account for a portion of the initial increase in female officer employment, but those same policies have failed to sustain higher number of recruits due to the "differential retention patterns among male and female officers" (Zhao *et al.* 2006: 479).

Discrimination in hiring, both informal and sometimes formal, was common in American criminal justice until a few decades ago (Belknap 2001; Martin 1989; McCluskey and McCluskey 2004; Merlo *et al.* 2000; Palacios 2003; Walker *et al.* 2003). To establish this fact, one need only examine the employment rolls for criminal justice agencies before the 1970s. Very few women or minority men worked in American criminal justice agencies before agencies were forced to hire them (Merlo *et al.* 2000). Those few who did work in these agencies included women staff in women's prisons (in a few women's prisons only female staff were hired because of abuses that had occurred) and women's sections of jails, who were hired as "matrons" (institutional supervisors) and typically paid less than the men, or some women police officers or probation officers working with delinquent girls and women on probation. As mentioned earlier, formal discrimination was eliminated only with passage of the Civil Rights Act of 1964 and its amendment by Title VII in 1972, and numerous presidential executive orders (see Box 9.2) a few decades before that and since by presidents Franklin Roosevelt, Kennedy, Johnson, and Nixon.

Civil rights legislation

Civil rights legislation first appeared in 1866 and 1871 and was concerned with employment discrimination against former slaves. Despite a series of executive orders barring employment discrimination in federal employment and in organizations having federal contracts, starting with Franklin Roosevelt in 1941, criminal justice entities remained largely unaffected. In 1961 President Kennedy's executive order imposed the first requirement for affirmative action. He required that federal agencies and those with federal contracts institute a "plan" and implement a program to ensure that the methods used for employment practices were nondiscriminatory. Affirmative action plans were also to address the methods used to make up for past discriminatory practices in employment. In other words, affirmative action plans were premised on fair employment in the present and providing a remedy for past employment discrimination. Both Presidents Johnson and Nixon reaffirmed the importance of AA with their own executive orders.

The Civil Rights Act of 1964 (CRA) made it illegal to discriminate in voter registration requirements, public accommodations and facilities, and employment (for a brief social and political history of the CRA of 1964 and the movement that birthed it, see www.congresslink.org). The act also created the Equal Employment Opportunity Commission to review complaints, though the EEOC's ability to enforce change was weak. For our purposes the most important title of the CRA is Title VII, which came as an amendment to the act in 1972. Title VII essentially made it unlawful to discriminate in the hiring, maintaining, or discharging of people because of their race, color, religion, sex, or national origin.

The Civil Rights Act of 1964 originally only covered employers of more than twenty-five persons, but was eventually extended to cover both private and public employment agencies including those on the state and local level that employed fifteen or more people. With the passage of this act and its amendment in 1972, criminal justice agencies of any size were required to reform their hiring practices and to institute affirmative action plans. As Stohr's experience in 1983 in Washington State demonstrates, compliance with this law came only gradually and incrementally from facility to facility. Several years passed and countless lawsuits were initiated to compel compliance.

Box 9.2 Equal opportunity/affirmative action laws as cited by various government agencies

The following laws embody some of the major legislation covering equal opportunity, employment laws, anti-discrimination laws, and affirmative action laws. Sources and the descriptions of these laws have been directly quoted from several government agencies, such as the Equal Employment Opportunity Commission, the US Department of Justice, and US Department of Labor websites. Each entry represents several pages of condensed information. See the direct web links presented at the beginning of each entry to explore these laws further.

Employment law

Compensation discrimination in employment is prohibited by the Equal Pay Act of 1963, Title VII of the Civil Rights Act of 1964, the Age

Discrimination in Employment Act of 1967, and Title I of the Americans with Disabilities Act of 1990, all enforced by the US Equal Employment Opportunity Commission. Collectively, these statutes require employers to compensate employees without regard to race, color, religion, sex, national origin, age, or disability.

The law against compensation discrimination includes all payments made to or on behalf of employees as remuneration for employment. All forms of compensation are covered, including salary, overtime pay, bonuses, stock options, profit sharing and bonus plans, life insurance, vacation and holiday pay, cleaning or gasoline allowances, hotel accommodations, reimbursement for travel expenses, and [other] benefits.

Source: http://www.eeoc.gov/facts/fs-epa.html,
accessed April 30, 2013.

Equal Pay Act of 1963

The Equal Pay Act (EPA) requires that men and women be given equal pay for equal work in the same establishment. The jobs need not be identical [for this law to apply], but they must be substantially equal. It is job content, not job titles, that determines whether jobs are substantially equal. Specifically, the EPA provides: Employers may not pay unequal wages to men and women who perform jobs that require substantially equal skill, effort and responsibility, and that are performed under similar working conditions within the same establishment...

Source: http://www.eeoc.gov/facts/fs-epa.html,
accessed April 30, 2013.

Title VII of the Civil Rights Act of 1964

An Act:
To enforce the constitutional right to vote, to confer jurisdiction upon the district courts of the United States to provide injunctive relief against discrimination in public accommodations, to authorize the Attorney General to institute suits to protect constitutional rights in public facilities and public education, to extend the Commission on Civil Rights, to prevent discrimination in federally assisted programs, to establish a Commission on Equal Employment Opportunity, and for other purposes.

Source: http://www.eeoc.gov/policy/vii.html,
accessed April 30, 2013.

Age Discrimination in Employment Act of 1967

An Act:
To prohibit age discrimination in employment.

> Source: http://www.eeoc.gov/policy/vii.html,
> accessed April 30, 2013.

Title I of The Americans With Disabilities Act of 1990

An Act:
To establish a clear and comprehensive prohibition of discrimination on the basis of disability.

> Source: http://www.eeoc.gov/policy/vii.html,
> accessed April 30, 2013.

Discrimination—general

Executive Order 11246 and 11375 (1965 and 1967)

A four-part executive order, which enforces the following:
Part I, Nondiscrimination in Government Employment
Part II, Nondiscrimination in Employment by Government Contractors and Subcontractors
Subpart B—Contractors' Agreements
SEC. 202. Except in contracts exempted in accordance with Section 204 of this Order, all Government contracting agencies shall include in every Government contract hereafter entered into the following provisions:

During the performance of this contract, the contractor agrees as follows:

The contractor will not discriminate against any employee or applicant for employment because of race, color, religion, sex, or national origin. The contractor will take *affirmative action* [emphasis added] to ensure that applicants are employed, and that employees are treated during employment, without regard to their race, color, religion, sex or national origin. Such action shall include, but not be limited to the following: employment, upgrading, demotion, or transfer; recruitment or recruitment advertising; layoff or termination; rates of pay or other forms of compensation; and selection for training, including apprenticeship. The contractor agrees to post in conspicuous places, available to employees and applicants for employment, notices to be provided by the contracting officer setting forth the provisions of this nondiscrimination clause.

Part III, Nondiscrimination Provisions in Federally Assisted Construction Contracts

Part IV, Miscellaneous

Source: http://www.dol.gov/ofccp/regs/statutes/eo11246.htm, accessed April 30, 2013.

Title VI of The Civil Rights Act of 1964

Title VI, 42 U.S.C. §2000d et seq., was enacted as part of the landmark Civil Rights Act of 1964. It prohibits discrimination on the basis of race, color, and national origin in programs and activities receiving federal financial assistance. As President John F. Kennedy said in 1963:

> Simple justice requires that public funds, to which all taxpayers of all races [colors, and national origins] contribute, not be spent in any fashion which encourages, entrenches, subsidizes or results in racial [color or national origin] discrimination.

Source: http://www.justice.gov/crt/about/cor/coord/titlevi.php, accessed April 30, 2013.

Equal Employment Opportunity Act of 1972

An Act

To further promote equal employment opportunities for American workers.

Source: http://www.eeoc.gov/eeoc/history/35th/thelaw/ eeo_1972.html, accessed April 30, 2013.

Title IX, Education Amendment Action of 1972

Section 1681. Sex

(a) Prohibition against discrimination; … No person in the United States shall, on the basis of sex, be excluded from participation in, be denied the benefits of, or be subjected to discrimination under any education program or activity receiving Federal financial assistance.

Section 1682. Federal administrative enforcement; report to Congressional committees…

Section 1683. Judicial review …

Section 1684. Blindness or visual impairment; prohibition against discrimination…

Section 1685. Authority under other laws unaffected…

Section 1686. Interpretation with respect to living facilities...
Section 1687. Interpretation of "program or activity"...
Section 1688. Neutrality with respect to abortion...

> Source: http://www.dol.gov/oasam/regs/statutes/titleix.htm,
> accessed April 30, 2013.

Disability discrimination

Vocational Rehabilitation Act of 1973 and Rehabilitation Act of 1974

Section 503 of the Rehabilitation Act of 1973 prohibits federal contractors and subcontractors from discriminating against and requires affirmative action for qualified individuals with disabilities in all aspects of employment. Section 504 of the Rehabilitation Act of 1973 prohibits discrimination on the basis of disability in programs and activities that receive federal financial assistance and in federally conducted programs. Section 188 of the Workforce Investment Act of 1998 (WIA) prohibits discrimination against qualified individuals with disabilities in any WIA Title I-financially assisted program or activity.

> Source: http://www.dol.gov/dol/topic/discrimination/
> disabilitydisc.htm, accessed April 30, 2013.

Vietnam-Era Veterans Readjustment Act of 1974

Prohibits discrimination against and requires affirmative action for qualified special disabled veterans, as well as other categories of veterans. This law is enforced by the OFCCP (Office of Federal Contract Compliance Programs)

> Source: http://www.dol.gov/dol/topic/discrimination/
> disabilitydisc.html, accessed April 30, 2013.

Other

Pregnancy Discrimination Act (1978 Amendment of Title VII)

An Act
To amend Title VII of the Civil Rights Act of 1964 to prohibit sex discrimination on the basis of pregnancy.

> Source: http://www.eeoc.gov/laws/statutes/pregnancy.cfm,
> accessed April 30, 2013.

Immigration Reform and Control Act (1986, 1990, 1996)

In regards to immigration:
(h) Anti-Discrimination Provision.—(1)(A) For the purpose of applying the prohibitions against discrimination on the basis of age under the Age Discrimination Act of 1975 [42 U.S.C. 6101 et seq.], on the basis of handicap under Section 504 of the Rehabilitation Act of 1973 [29 U.S.C. 794], on the basis of sex under Title IX of the Education Amendments of 1972 [20 U.S.C. 1681 et seq.], or on the basis of race, color, or national origin under Title VI of the Civil Rights Act of 1964 [42 U.S.C. 2000d et seq.], ...

> Source: http://www.uscis.gov/ilink/docView/PUBLAW/HTML/
> PUBLAW/0-0-0-15.html, accessed April 30, 2013.

Americans with Disabilities Act of 1990

See Chapter 8, Box 8.1.

Civil Rights Act of 1991

An Act
To amend the Civil Rights Act of 1964 to strengthen and improve Federal civil rights laws, to provide for damages in cases of intentional employment discrimination, to clarify provisions regarding disparate impact actions, and for other purposes.

> Source: http://www.eeoc.gov/policy/cra91.html,
> accessed April 30, 2013.

Intentional discrimination

In an analysis of employment data provided in 1999 to the Equal Employment Opportunity Commission by employers of over fifty persons and supported by the Ford Foundation, two Rutgers University law professors, Blumrosen and Blumrosen (2002), found that there is a continuing pattern of widespread intentional discrimination in employment that impacts both minorities (African Americans, Hispanics, Asian-Pacific islanders, American Indians) and white women. What they found illustrates that discrimination in employment did not end with the institution of affirmative action plans, though they noted substantial improvement in the employment of minorities and women since 1979. For this study, Blumrosen and Blumrosen (2002) declared the existence of **intentional discrimination** when the employment of the minorities and women fell two standard deviations below the average for employment for those groups for that industry, job category, and metropolitan area.

As we might expect, they found that intentional discrimination differed by group and by state. For instance, in Georgia, there was a 33 percent chance that a minority group member or white woman would face intentional discrimination in employment. But the chance of discrimination was highest in this state for minority Hispanics (45 percent), Asian-Pacific Islanders (42 percent), blacks (36 percent), and white women (25 percent). In California, minorities faced this risk of intentional discrimination in employment about 25 percent of the time, and white women faced it about 20 percent of the time. Specifically, black people were most at risk in California (29 percent), followed by Asians (28 percent), Hispanics (24 percent), and white women (22 percent; Blumrosen and Blumrosen 2002; see the full text of their report at www.eeo1.com) Notably, when comparing just the two states of Georgia and California, one sees that the risk of being intentionally discriminated against in employment, though still high for some groups in our communities, can vary widely.

Reverse discrimination

The extent to which informal discrimination still occurs is not clear and presents some difficulties in terms of research, although the Blumrosen and Blumrosen (2002) report is more than suggestive. It is also not clear how often reverse discrimination, whether informal or formal, occurs. **Reverse discrimination** happens when a member of an overrepresented group is overlooked for jobs, promotions, college admission, or a related opportunity because of race, color, religion, sex, or national origin. Researching the extent to which reverse discrimination occurs is quite difficult, though there is some evidence that it exists in college admissions (see Box 9.3 on the *Bakke* [1978] and *Grutter* [2003] Supreme Court cases). Anecdotally this claim is not uncommon. Despite its blatant unfairness, in some instances the courts have allowed reverse discrimination to occur as a remedy for past discrimination. Courts also have used the reasoning that not everyone is equally privileged because of current or past discrimination in housing, education, and employment, which is sometimes determined along race and ethnicity lines.

For instance, in the *Grutter* (2003) case described in Box 9.3, a white female applicant to the University of Michigan's law school was denied admission based on a policy that considered the race or ethnicity of its applicants as part of its mission to increase the diversity of the student body. The Supreme Court agreed, ruling that because of the compelling interest of promoting diversity in the university and the community (a number of business organizations filed in support of the University of Michigan's position), colleges and universities can use race and/or ethnicity as one consideration in setting admissions policies.

Box 9.3 *University of California Regents v. Bakke* **(438 U.S. 265 [1978]) and** *Grutter v. Bollinger et al.* **(288 F. 3D, affirmed, U.S. 02–241 [2003])**

The two most well-known reverse discrimination cases—because they are from the Supreme Court—are *Bakke* of 1978 and *Grutter*, decided in 2003. Both are concerned with admissions to professional schools at prestigious universities. In *Bakke*, a white male claimed that he was the victim of reverse discrimination because applicants with lower academic qualifications were admitted to a University of California (UC) medical school while he was denied admission. He alleged that this occurred because he was white and the less qualified applicants were minority group members, some of whom were admitted to the school under a special admissions program that in practice was used to only admit minority group members. Justice Powell, writing for the majority, agreed in part with this assessment, and the Supreme Court ordered Bakke's admission to the medical school at UC Davis and invalidated the special admissions program. But the court did not say that race as a consideration in admissions was illegal. Indeed, Justice Stevens noted that more than academic credentials may be considered when developing criteria for admissions.

In the more recent *Grutter* case (2003), Grutter, a white female applicant to the University of Michigan's law school, maintained that she was denied admission because of her race, again while applicants with lesser academic credentials were admitted. As women, particularly white women, now make up about half of law school entrants, they are rarely now accorded protected status requiring affirmative action. Justice O'Connor, writing for the majority, wrote that the consideration of race as one factor in admissions policies was lawful. She noted that the law school's admission policy, which places a value on diversity, does not define that term only in relation to racial and ethnic origin. She argued that the majority opinion in this case was in keeping with the *Bakke* decision, which allowed some consideration of race and ethnicity in admissions policies.

Note: These cases are available in law libraries and can be accessed on the Internet by going to the Supreme Court Collection of the Legal Information Institute of Cornell Law School (www.law.cornell.edu/supremecourt/text/home) (last accessed October 3, 2013).

How the *Grutter* case will impact employment in criminal justice is not completely clear yet. It may mean that cases of reverse discrimination will continue to be given "strict scrutiny" by the courts, but that race and ethnicity of applicants can be considered in the making of employment decisions.

In fact, since the *Bakke* decision in 1978 there have been relatively few claims of reverse discrimination in employment before the federal courts, and very few of them have been found to have merit. In a study for the US Department of Labor's Office of Federal Contract Compliance Program, Blumrosen (1995) found that in federal district or appellate courts between 1990 and 1994 there were fewer than 100 cases (out of 3,000 discrimination opinions) involving reverse discrimination in employment, or about 1–3 percent of cases involving discrimination. Of these 100 opinions, only six ruled that discrimination had occurred and the rest were dismissed as without merit (Blumrosen 1995). Of course most folks do not report discrimination in employment, even if they are aware of it.

Some have argued, as more minority group members join the middle class and as white women have gained a more equal footing in the work world and in colleges and universities, where women typically make up at least half of the student body, that affirmative action should exist for those who are poor or for those who come from an impoverished background. In fact in the *Bakke* case it was noted that poverty was one of the qualifications for admittance via the special program. However, it was not noted *how* this factor was taken into consideration. Using poverty as a measure of disadvantage that merits remedy with affirmative action seems fair on its face; it cuts across racial and ethnic lines and gets at the disadvantage that poor people experience because of decrepit neighborhoods, underfunded schools, and reduced opportunities. Since minority group members are usually overrepresented among the poor in this country, there would be some consideration of minority status if poverty was used as a gauge for affirmative action. The difficulty lies, however, in establishing credentials as "poor" for anything but college admissions. College applicants could establish their "poverty" simply by supplying their parent's income tax returns. Even then there can be difficulties as people's income tends to fluctuate from year to year. Also, there is relative poverty across this country, insofar as someone who would be deemed middle class in a rural community could barely afford an apartment in a marginal neighborhood of a big city. How can relative poverty and these income fluctuations be accounted for in the process to make it "fair"?

Also, how would a person establish their "poverty" when applying for jobs? By describing current circumstances? The poverty experienced as a child? Many college students are relatively poor, as are those who do not yet have a steady income or a job, but does this mean they were disadvantaged by poverty when they were younger? Maybe, but maybe not. Clearly there are some difficulties inherent in using economic disadvantage as a consideration in school admissions, let alone employment decisions in criminal justice.

Finally, using AA only for those who would qualify as "poor" ignores the discrimination based on race or ethnicity that minority group members have experienced in employment based on their skin color. As indicated by the findings of Blumrosen and Blumrosen (2002), job discrimination based on race and ethnicity has not disappeared in this country. Given this fact,

AA may still be needed to ensure that all qualified persons are considered for employment in criminal justice.

Food for thought

Many people believe that affirmative action programs formally provide advantage for some groups over others. In our classrooms such opponents of AA tell us they are least likely to see the benefit for themselves of these programs. What opponents of AA may not consider however is that as our country becomes increasingly diverse, there will be a shift in advantage from group to group. California and New Mexico are already dominated numerically by "minority" groups, and other states, particularly in the Southwest, are moving in that direction. Remember those Workforce 2000 reports and the Census Bureau information presented earlier in this chapter indicating that the diversity of the American workforce and population will continue to grow. Consider these facts in tandem with the knowledge that women make up about half of most college majors and you have to conclude that formal plans in the future may tend to favor white males, who may increasingly become a "minority group" in terms of their representation in the workplace.

It is also possible that in their opposition to affirmative action some groups may be overestimating the opportunities it provides for minority group members. For instance, in two studies of affirmative action and personnel practices in the Federal Bureau of Prisons, Camp *et al.* (1997: 313) and Camp and Langan (2005) found that "white correctional officers tend to overestimate minority opportunities" provided by the existence of affirmative action policies. In the second study the researchers replicated the first finding and found that white men tended to overestimate job opportunities for women in the Bureau of Prisons as well (Camp and Langan 2005). In the period during which Camp *et al.* focused on African American officers and women (1991–1994), these populations were sometimes overrepresented among those promoted, but in other years were not. The authors conclude that "[i]t is probably more accurate to say that the playing field has been leveled [by affirmative action] for all races rather than to say [given the slight differences between racial groups] it favors any particular race" (Camp *et al.* 1997: 330).

Of course, in and of itself and beyond the self-interest of individuals, there is value for the community in having a diverse workforce. This is particularly relevant in the criminal justice environment where the clientele tend to be very diverse, both racially and in terms of ethnic background. Affirmative action and equal employment opportunity initiatives have served to increase the complementary diversity of staff and to bring a sense of balance and fairness in employment.

Conclusions

In this chapter we discussed one of the most divisive issues of our day—affirmative action—and the related issues of equal opportunity in employment and reverse discrimination. These are the issues that our students, and the rest of the country for that matter, are most sensitive to. Everyone can agree that we want the best qualified applicants to fill criminal justice jobs. But some argue that minority status should not be one of those qualifications. Our personal belief is that affirmative action is a necessary evil to ensure that the occupants of public and private sector jobs, but public sector jobs particularly, reflect as much as possible the communities they serve. It would be nice to believe that criminal justice organizations would hire minorities and women without the push that AA gives them, but our experience in this country is that they did not.

It is true that AA can lead to reverse discrimination in hiring and promotion. However, the incidence of these cases and their substantiation, as was illustrated by Blumrosen's (1995) findings, are likely to be much smaller than most people expect. If you look around this country you cannot fail to notice that most of the better paying jobs are occupied by whites. Most administrators and managers in criminal justice, forty years after passage of the Civil Rights Act, are still white men, though women and minority group men have made some progress here because of AA. Moreover, many people in the majority (usually white males, but in some cases white females) fail to realize that they may someday benefit from the protections that AA offers. Diversity levels by race and ethnicity are only increasing in our country, and those in the majority today may be in the minority in the years to come.

Exercise: tracking criminal justice employment

This exercise is useful in exposing students to the number and types of jobs available in criminal justice, locally and statewide as well as nationally. We suggest dividing a class into groups of five and assigning each group a locality in your state in which to do a job search (note: The counties and/or cities assigned must be large enough to be hiring criminal justice personnel on a regular basis). You might also consider assigning one group of students the state and one or two groups to the federal government. Alternately, each group could take a different state, to provide a spectrum across regions of the country or among neighboring states. Or you could assign them to garner information on jobs in policing, court, or corrections. The point is to expose students to the number and types of jobs available.

Have the students find descriptions of at least two criminal justice-related jobs for their locality/state. (If the locality is large enough, and/or sophisticated enough, this information should be available on the web.) Have each group write and present a brief summary report to the class. The class should note the similarities and differences between the advertised qualifications/pay and application procedures for these jobs.

Discussion questions

1   What do the Workforce 2000 reports predict for the future? How will you use this information in making your employment plans?
2   Should those predictions come true, how will employment in this country be affected? Explain your answer.
3   Why are Americans so "touchy" when they discuss affirmative action? How do you feel about it?
4   What is the difference between formal and informal affirmative action, and who tends to be hired under each? Explain your answer.
5   What benefits might we gain as a society if we were to base affirmative action on considerations of an impoverished background? Why is the basing of affirmative action on "poverty" (either current or during childhood) problematic? Explain your answer.
6   What is reverse discrimination, and why is it so harmful? Give an example and explain your answer.

Key terms

affirmative action: positive steps to ensure that an organization's hiring practices are fair and do not disproportionately impact a targeted underrepresented group.

intentional discrimination: according to Blumrosen and Blumrosen (2002), conditions under which the employment of the minorities and women falls two standard deviations below the average for employment for those groups for that industry, job category, and metropolitan area.

reverse discrimination: the result when an overrepresented group is overlooked for jobs, promotions, college admission, or a related opportunity because of race, color, religion, sex, or national origin.

Cases cited and laws/statutes

Pulido v. State of California et al. 1994
University of California Regents v. Bakke (438 U.S. 265 [1978])
Grutter v. Bollinger et al. (288 F. 3d, affirmed, U.S. 02–241 [2003])
Civil Rights Act of 1866, 14 Stat. 27 (1866)
Civil Rights Act of 1871, 17 Stat. 13 (1871)
Civil Rights Act of 1964, PL 88–352 (1964)

Equal Pay Act of 1963
Title VII of the Civil Rights Act of 1964
Age Discrimination in Employment Act of 1967
Title I of the Americans with Disabilities Act of 1990
Executive Order 11246 and 11375 (1965 and 1967)
Title VI of the Civil Rights Act of 1964
Equal Employment Opportunity Act of 1972
Title IX, Education Amendment Action of 1972
Vocational Rehabilitation Act of 1973 and Rehabilitation Act of 1974
Vietnam-Era Veterans Readjustment Act of 1974
Pregnancy Discrimination Act (1978 Amendment of Title VII)
Immigration Reform and Control Act (1986, 1990, 1996)
Americans with Disabilities Act of 1990
Civil Rights Act of 1991

Note

1   This number was provided by Gary Raney, Undersheriff at the Ada County Sheriff's Department, on April 27, 2004.

References

Belknap, J. (2001) *The invisible woman: Gender, crime and justice*, 2nd edn. Belmont, CA: Wadsworth/Thomson Learning.

Bennett, W. W. and Hess, K. M. (2001) *Management and supervision in law enforcement*, 3rd edn. Belmont, CA: Wadsworth/Thomson Learning.

Blumrosen, A. (1995) *Draft report on reverse discrimination commissioned by the Labor Department: How the courts are handling reverse discrimination claims*. Daily Labor Reports, March 23.

Blumrosen, A. and Blumrosen, R. (2002) *The reality of intentional job discrimination in metropolitan America—1999*. Available at www.EEO1.com (last accessed January 31, 2013).

Camp, S. D. and Langan, N. P. (2005) Perceptions about minority and female opportunities for job advancement: Are beliefs about equal opportunities fixed? *The Prison Journal*, 85(4): 399–419.

Camp, S. D., Steiger, T. L., Wright, K. N., Saylor, W. G. and Gilman. E. (1997) Affirmative action and the 'level playing field': Comparing perceptions of own and minority job advancement opportunities. *The Prison Journal*, 77(3): 313–334.

Civil Rights Coalition for the 21st Century (2004) *Civil rights and race relations*. Available at www.civilrights.org (last accessed January 31, 2013).

Conover, T. (2000) *Newjack: Guarding Sing Sing*. New York, NY: Random House.

Cox, T. and Beale, R. L. (1997) *Developing competency to manage diversity: Readings, cases & activities*. San Francisco, CA: Berrett-Koehler.

Crouch, B. and Marquart, J. W. (1994) On becoming a prison guard. In S. Stojokovic, J. Klofas and D. Kalinich (eds), *The administration and management of criminal justice organizations: A book of readings.* Prospect Heights, IL: Waveland Press, pp. 301–331.

Joseph, J., Henriques, Z. W. and Ekeh, K. R. (2003) Get tough policies and the incarceration of African Americans. In J. Joseph and D. Taylor (eds), *With justice for all: Minorities and women in criminal justice.* Upper Saddle River, NJ: Prentice Hall, pp. 105–120.

Langton, L. (2010) *Women in law enforcement, 1987–2008.* Bureau of Justice Statistics, Crime Data Brief. June 2010, NCJ 230521.

Lester, D. (2003) Native Americans and the criminal justice system. In J. Joseph and D. Taylor (eds), *With justice for all: Minorities and women in criminal justice.* Upper Saddle River, NJ: Prentice Hall, pp. 149–160.

Lombardo, L. X. (1989) *Guards imprisoned: Correctional officers at work,* 2nd edn. Cincinnati, OH: Anderson Publishing.

Maguire, K. and Pastore, A. L. (eds). (2004) *Sourcebook of criminal justice statistics.* Available at www.albany.edu/sourcebook/ (last accessed January 31, 2013).

Martin, S. (1989) Women on the move?: A report on the status of women in policing. *Women & Criminal Justice,* 1(1): 21–40.

Mays, G. L. and Winfree, L. T. (2002) *Contemporary corrections.* Belmont, CA: Wadsworth/ Thomson Learning.

McCluskey, C. P. and McCluskey, J. D. (2004) Diversity in policing: Latino representation in law enforcement. *Journal of Ethnicity in Criminal Justice,* 2(3): 67–82.

Merlo, A. V., Bagley, K. and Bafuma, M. C. (2000) In defense of affirmative action for women in the criminal justice profession. In R. Muraskin (ed.), *It's a crime: Women and justice.* Upper Saddle River, NJ: Prentice Hall, pp. 69–90.

Palacios, W. R. (2003) Where is Mayberry? Community-oriented policing and officers of color. In J. Joseph and D. Taylor (eds), *With justice for all: Minorities and women in criminal justice.* Upper Saddle River, NJ: Prentice Hall, pp. 65–78.

Reaves, B. A. (2010) *Local police departments, 2007.* Bureau of Justice Statistics, Crime Data Brief. December 2010, NCJ 231174.

Roberg, R. R. and Kuykendall, J. (1993) *Police & society.* Belmont, CA: Wadsworth.

Salisbury, J. and Dominick, B. K. (2004) *Investigating harassment and discrimination complaints: A practical guide.* New York, NY: Wiley.

US Census Bureau (2011) *State government employment and payroll data: 2011.* US Census Bureau Available at www2.census.gov/govs/apes/11stus.txt (last accessed January 31, 2013).

US Census Bureau (2012) *US Census Bureau projections show a slower growing, older, more diverse nation a half century from now.* Available at www.census.gov (last accessed January 31, 2013).

US Department of Labor (2004) *Labor statistics. Bureau of Labor Statistics.* Available at www.bls.gov (last accessed January 31, 2013).

US Senate, 102nd Congress (1991) *The glass ceiling in federal agencies: A GAO survey on women and minorities in federal agencies: Hearings before the committee on governmental affairs.*

Walker, S., Spohn, C. and DeLone, M. (2003) *The color of justice: Race, ethnicity and crime in America,* 3rd edn. Belmont, CA: Wadsworth/Thomson Learning.

Workforce Development Strategies. (2004) *State of the workforce report: Research reports, tables and charts.* Available at www.wdsi.org (last accessed January 31, 2013).

Zhao, J., He, N. and Lovrich, N. (2006) Pursuing gender diversity in police organizations in the 1990s: A longitudinal analysis of the factors associated with the hiring of female officers. *Police Quarterly,* 9(4): 463–485.

10 Reaching beyond the expected

Managing treatment, force, standards, and accreditation

The police are legitimate, bureaucratically articulated organizations that stand ready to use force to sustain political order. Anglo-American policing (AAP) is democratic policing: It eschews torture, terrorism, and counter-terrorism, is guided by law, and seeks minimal damage to civility...

(Manning 2005: 23)

Drug court treatment plans are different because they are court-mandated and reviewed periodically by the court. The judge makes ongoing determinations based on the input of both probation and treatment personnel. The client who is not progressing as required faces the immediate threat of incarceration for the original offense. This threat provides a powerful tool for treatment providers...

(Brown 2002: 19)

Brutalization begets brutalization. Violence begets violence. In Santa Fe we had a system of penology that was all punishment... When you take everything away from a human being, including his personal dignity, they become extremely dangerous... (John Salazar, former Secretary of Corrections in New Mexico, explaining what led up to the 1980 prison riot).

(ABC News Broadcast 1983)

The pains of life in contemporary prisons are real. There is no point in denying them. Nor does it make sense to see pain merely as an obstacle to correctional work, for it is an obstacle that can never be circumvented. Pain is an enduring feature of the correctional enterprise. We must accept this hard reality, and quite explicitly attempt to promote growth through adversity. This is a genuine correctional agenda. For men who cope maturely with prison, I will argue, are men who have grown as human beings and been rehabilitated in the process...

(Johnson 1996: 97)

Introduction: discipline and decency

A few years ago, when politicians' "lock 'em up and throw away the key" rhetoric was at its apex, there were calls to remove televisions and weight rooms from prisons, jails, detention centers, and long-term juvenile facilities. Many of these concerns emanated from the belief, fueled by the media and politicians, that inmates were being "coddled" in correctional institutions and that they were bulking up with weights as a means of increasing their ability to intimidate staff and other inmates (Merlo and Benekos 2000). To top it off, there was concern that taxpayer monies were being used to pay for such extravagances. So the solution was to take away the TVs, the satellite dishes, and the weight rooms.

Thankfully, sanity eventually prevailed. Once the public (and the politicians) were informed that the TVs, satellite dishes, and weights were paid for out of inmate funds (usually created from profits from the purchase of store items by inmates) and not from taxes, and that most correctional administrators considered the presence of TVs and weight rooms as essential to inmate management, the furor died down. Moreover, the argument can be made that inmates use the weight rooms to channel aggression, rather than to fuel it. But this tempest in a teapot did serve to illustrate how the ignorance of the public can be manipulated to drive criminal justice policy.

This kind of misrepresentation of facts is what we can expect when the public is ill-informed, in an atmosphere of little coverage or outside review of criminal justice activities beyond the infamous cases. Rumors and myths perpetrated by politicians and the media can take root and flourish in such an environment (Merlo and Benekos 2000). The most salient example of this is illustrated by the warm embrace given to DARE programs when they fit the political conception of how the drug war might be implemented in schools. It was not until years later and after empirical evidence had piled up that it became clear that DARE programs do not appear to "work" in reducing children's use of drugs (e.g., see Clayton *et al.* 1996). The point is: When people do not know any better, politics can drive policy.

Of course, given the nature of criminal justice programs and policy, it would be naïve and wrong to argue that program operations can or should be divorced completely from politics. The devil on the other side of this divide, however, is that too much political control—recall the discussion of democratic accountability vs. neutral competence—can render its own set of problems.

But like other jobholders, those who work in policing, courts, and corrections should attend at least equally to what is known from practice and research, for only thus will they be able to keep from falling each time for the latest passing political fad. Moreover, and relatedly, there is evidence that criminal justice entities that submit themselves to outside review by objective bodies are more able to ensure that there is decency, along with discipline, in their operations.

Therefore in this chapter we review some aspects of client management that are particularly salient these days, including treatment programming, drug courts, use of force in policing and corrections, standards, and accreditation. By way of setting the stage for a discussion of these elements of client management, however, we first discuss the false dichotomy that appears to prevail *vis-à-vis* security and treatment in court and correctional management. Our argument is that rather than either treatment or security, or one first and then the other, true security relies on the provision of treatment and other amenities.

Treatment

The false dichotomy: treatment or security?

In the book *Governing Prisons: A Comparative Study of Correctional Management* (1987), John DiIulio argues that before amenities and services can be provided in prisons, there must be order. There have been a number of critiques of the "control model" which he proposes for both staff and inmates in prisons, and its corollaries in policing (by James Q. Wilson, DiIulio's mentor, and Kelling 1982; e.g., see Crouch and Marquart 1990; Irwin 1985; Stohr *et al.* 1994; Walker 1984). Nevertheless, DiIulio makes a well-taken point about the importance of order. The problem is that his perspective, whether intentional or not, supports a logical fallacy that somehow security (order) and treatment are in opposition. In fact, it is often argued that treatment and the provision of amenities (such as those TVs and weight rooms) are *central* to maintaining order. To paraphrase an inmate of the New Mexico prison at the time of the riot in 1980, "you can't put a dog in a room with nothing to do for 24 hours a day and then let him loose and not expect him to bite you" (ABC News 1983).

Research on other social processes and institutions, such as parenting and teaching in schools, indicate that positive outcomes result when children are not just kept busy, but also engaged in productive activities of meaning to them (Wisconsin Education Association Council 2004). One of those outcomes is that there tends to be more "order" in the home and at school. The research shows that kids involved in sports, academic pursuits, or other prosocial interests are the most well adjusted and least likely to be involved in problems at school or home or with the law (Lindstrom-Johnson *et al.* 2012; Gottfredson 1997; Sherman *et al.* 1997). It also helps if the parents are involved in the school activities.

This research, of course, has relevance for all correctional facilities and programming and may apply generally to community members and work. If juvenile detainees are kept busy with prosocial and meaningful activities, they are more likely to positively reengage in the larger society. It makes sense that when human beings are busy and happy, they are less likely to be disruptive.

Though it would be nice to believe that inactivity and meaningless work or lack of programming are unique to the "prison experience" of the past and are no longer relevant, the evidence does not support that supposition. Our earliest conceptions of corrections include depictions of inmates "breaking rocks" as a means of both punishing them and keeping them busy. Today only a small fraction of any given correctional budget is devoted to treatment or educational programming. For instance, in 1995, the director of corrections for the State of Idaho indicated in a speech attended by one of the authors that only 1 percent of the adult corrections budget was devoted to treatment or other programming in prisons and in the community (this figure has since changed and was 1.76 percent for FY11; see http://www.idoc.idaho.gov for the IDOC FY11 annual report). As the economy has soured some states, such as Florida, have been forced to cut back on their treatment options at the same time that inmates are being added to the system (Royse 2003). Yet reports produced by and for some states (e.g., New Hampshire, Pennsylvania, and Connecticut) indicate that every dollar in treatment programming has the potential to save the state money in current and future correctional costs by reducing recidivism and the required level of supervision (Gioia 2004; Merrow and Minard 2003). Merrow and Minard (2003: 1) found that the New Hampshire Department of Corrections' community-based programs "saved the state and county governments as much as two dollars for every dollar they have invested in the programs, saving approximately $10 million over six years" and "helped hundreds of nonviolent offenders stay in their jobs and with their families as they worked successfully through treatment and counseling programs."

So both in institutions and on the streets, there is a need for people to have something to do that allows them to either better themselves or contribute in a meaningful way to their communities. In short, the most effective regimen in correctional client management is not order first and then the provision of services and amenities, but order and services and amenities together.

Box 10.1 Whistling while they work

Author Mary Stohr, who worked in a prison in the 1980s, noted ironically that there was not enough work to keep about a third of the inmates busy. In this prison, half the men worked in the surrounding forests for the state's Department of Natural Resources. These jobs were generally prized, as it was meaningful work (planting trees, clearing trails, maintaining roads, fighting fires in the summer and fall). Such jobs also presented the chance for the men to get away from the prison and be out in the fresh air. Other than the GED program during the day, chapel on Sunday, and 12-step meetings (which were staffed by the inmates themselves and a few volunteers from the community) in the evenings, no treatment programs were provided. Once the kitchen, cleaning, and facility maintenance staffs were full, no other jobs or activities were available.

But because there were not enough jobs and because this was a "work camp" where everyone, save a few trustees, were required to be off their bed and out of the TV and weight rooms during the day, many tasks were trivial and repetitive "make work," devised to keep people busy. For instance, one inmate was assigned to polish the brass door handles every day. Because the prison itself housed only about 110 inmates at that time, the inmate would often polish the same knob twice a day. Other inmates were continuously engaged in raking and re-raking the facility perimeter, in part for security, but also for something to do. Other inmates were assigned to dig dirt for a garden that was never planted or to clear a trail around the prison perimeter for a fence that was never constructed.

At the time it seemed surprising that so many inmates complained bitterly about being assigned such pointless tasks. Before working in this prison, the author had half bought into the popular perception that all inmates were lazy. This was certainly true of some who, by their actions did appear to prefer inactivity; but the vast majority wanted to work and wanted to do something, anything, that mattered. Such inmates always claimed that working made "their time" go faster.

Mature coping and finding a niche

Robert Johnson devotes one chapter of his book *Hard time: Understanding and reforming the prison* (1996) to a discussion of the importance of inmates coping maturely and finding a niche during their incarceration. This idea is of course related to our discussion of the need for correctional clients not only to engage in activities, but also to find those that have meaning for them.

By "**mature coping**," Johnson (1996: 98) means "[d]ealing with life's problems like a responsive and responsible human being, one who seeks autonomy without violating the rights of others, security without resort to deception or violence, and relatedness to others as the finest and fullest expression of human identity." Johnson argues that inmates, like all human beings, have a natural inclination to desire autonomy, security, and relatedness to others and that prison can build on or accentuate those proclivities.

Much like correctional staff members, inmates and correctional clients in general would do better if they had some sort of say about the circumstances of their lives (Toch *et al.* 1989). Those who have such autonomy are less likely to be disruptive in the prison and, once they leave it, are also less likely to experience emotional and physical distress and illness because of their incarceration (Listwan *et al.* 2013; Goodstein and Wright 1989; Johnson 1996).

Another point made by Johnson is that inmates, like most humans (remember Maslow's hierarchy), place a premium on security. Johnson (1996) notes that "mature coping" requires that inmates achieve this security without resort to deception or violence. Unfortunately, in the prison, as on some mean streets, deception and violence may be accepted—even *valued*—practices. "Indeed, not to take advantage of others is to show a kind of moral weakness, to advertise a potentially fateful failure of nerve in a social jungle. Correspondingly, not to be ready for violence at any time is a fateful— and often deadly—departure from prison norms" (Johnson 1996: 106). The problem is that if this primitive resort to violence and this trust-destroying deception are to flourish in the prison, people will not be prepared to live prosocially or to maturely cope in the prison or in the free world.

Thus Johnson (1996) advocates that inmates, and by extension all correctional clients, learn how to "self-actualize" by caring for themselves and others. Caring for others comes from the recognition that inmates in prisons, jails, and juvenile facilities are part of a community that is interdependent. Johnson does not believe this will be a selfless caring, but rather a means of deserving this care from others. He believes that inmates should act as "altruistic egoists" who are generous to those in need around them, but are not saints. By acting in this way they can form security niches composed of other inmates interested in helping each other in return for assistance when needed. Predatory inmates, even in prisons plagued by violence, are less likely to go after other inmates who are seen as part of a group. Unfortunately, though, this banding together for security purposes has been one of the reasons for the spread of gangs in prisons.

Johnson (1996) is not advocating the formation of gangs, however, when he recommends that inmates look for niches. Rather, he defines a **niche** as a private world that inmates try to carve out to serve as a sanctuary that offers "[s]heltered settings and benign activities that insulate [inmates] from the mainline prison" (Johnson 1996: 120).

Barbara Owen (1998), in her book *In the Mix*, relates the findings from her study of the prison life of inmates in California's largest women's prison. She found that the inmates who adjusted best in prison were those who related to others in a caring way and avoided those areas (e.g., the yard) where the most deviance was likely to occur. Such niches might be found in living units for trustees or other work settings, or in the art, school, or drug and alcohol programs. Though Johnson and Owen were describing inmates in prisons, finding a welcoming and productive niche can happen for inmates of an institution or for clients on probation or parole. The point is to have a common and worthwhile purpose that binds people and allows them to care for and protect each other while also becoming more than they were.

Treatment programming

Treatment programming in its broadest sense has always existed in prisons and jails, but particularly in juvenile facilities and for probation and parole clientele. Beyond the juvenile court and a century-long focus on rehabilitation programming for juveniles, a newer twist has been the development of courts devoted to promoting treatment as an alternative to a correctional institution and often in conjunction with a form of probation.

But whether treatment is provided on the streets or in jails or prisons, there are many forms it can take. This is because treatment programming often encompasses work programs, education programs, counseling programs, and all manner of rehabilitation/habilitation programs. It is easy to see why this broad conception aligns treatment with work and school; for, as we discussed with niches, these productive activities can also be therapeutic. In this sense, the earliest jails where inmates worked had therapeutic purposes attached to their requirements for work and a quiet life of penance that was believed to lead to reform. The juvenile court was formed with the "best interests of the child" in mind, and even the most primitive of juvenile ranches and reformatories included some form of school program. Probation and parole programs too were developed to assist the client to transition back into the community. Historically this usually included assistance in finding a job, and these days it might call for participation in a salient rehabilitation program.

In other words, treatment, broadly defined, has always been an integral part of courts, but particularly correctional operation. It has also been one aspect of client and inmate management that has spurred much debate and research. As criminal justice reforms have waxed and waned in popularity, so too has the belief in the integrity and validity of some such programs.

Death to all programs! and the nothing works mantra

From 1966 to 1970, a research team headed by Robert Martinson undertook to study rehabilitation for the state of New York (Lipton *et al.* 1975; Martinson 1974). They were asking "what works" in correctional reform (Martinson 1974). To answer this question, they reviewed all evaluations of rehabilitation programs that had been published in the English language from 1945 to 1967. They then eliminated studies that did not evaluate a treatment method and did not adhere to conventional standards of social science research. Dropped from the study at this point were programs without a control or comparison group, those lacking an independent measure of improvement, and those that were divorced from the treatment method. The team was most interested in whether the treatment programming resulted in a reduction in recidivism of those engaged in the program versus similar individuals who were not. In the end, they included 231 studies in their analysis. These studies spanned the breadth of court-sanctioned or correctional rehabilitation programming, including education and vocational training, training programs for adult inmates, individual and group counseling programs, milieu therapy in institutions, medical treatment, the effects of sentencing and decarcerating inmates, psychotherapy in community settings, probation and parole supervision, intensive supervision for juveniles and adults, and various community treatment programs.

What Martinson and his colleagues (1974: 25) found was that "[w]ith few and isolated exceptions, the rehabilitative efforts that have been reported so far have had no appreciable effect on recidivism." They never said "nothing works" in correctional programming, but they came pretty close, and their study outcomes were interpreted that way in the popular press. In rehabilitation's stead, Martinson (1974) suggested that the value of deterrence and punishment merited greater attention and study by scholars.

This research was widely cited by politicians who were interested in shifting away from treatment programming to a greater focus on punishment and deterrence in corrections (Cullen and Gilbert 1982). In fact, this shift directly tracked the larger societal shift to a conservative approach to crime in general. Given these findings and the effect they had on policy, it is indeed ironic that the Governor's Special Committee on Criminal Offenders that originally commissioned the Martinson study was organized on the premise that "[p]risons could rehabilitate, that the prisons of New York were not in fact making a serious effort at rehabilitation, and that New York's prisons should be converted from their existing custodial basis to a new rehabilitative one" (Martinson 1974: 23).

Despite the original intent of the Martinson study, the stage was perfectly set to misinterpret the findings as stating that "nothing works" in correctional programming. The country was primed politically to disavow treatment as a legitimate approach to correctional reform and the Martinson report was embraced widely and used to eliminate funding for, or justify the death of, a number of correctional programs that served clients on the streets and in the institutions (Andrews *et al.* 1990; Cullen and Gilbert 1982). This is why when one of the authors worked in a prison in the 1980s, there were very few programs available in the institution and not many more available in the community for the men for whom she wrote parole plans (see Box 10.1).

But despite this abandonment by politicians, Cullen and Gilbert (1982) were able to demonstrate that the public never lost complete faith in "rehabilitation" as a justification for the existence of correctional institutions or programs. They noted over twenty years ago, and after the Martinson report had had a chance to sink in, that in a national survey administered in 1981, the percentage of respondents (37 percent) who thought that rehabilitation should be the primary purpose of putting people in prison was higher than the percentage of those (31 percent) who thought punishment should be its primary purpose.

Of course the Martinson report had its critics, especially in the years and decades following its publication (e.g., see Palmer 1975; 1983; 1995). These critiques, called meta-analyses, were structured reviews of the major published reports in the area. Among their criticisms was an assertion that Martinson had misconstrued the findings from the recidivism studies he had written about. Palmer (1983) noted that although no single program had worked for all targeted offenders, some programs had reduced the recidivism of some offenders. In fact Martinson himself later recognized that individual programs might work for targeted groups even when whole groups of programs do not (Palmer 1983). Other meta-analyses of correctional programming (e.g., Antonowicz and Ross 1997; Leukefeld and Tims 1992; Logan and Gaes 1993; Wright 1995) have also raised serious questions concerning the veracity of claims of success for correctional program components.

Moreover, of the forty-four programs that had adequate research designs, only twenty were found to be "effective" (Antonowicz and Ross 1997: 313). The programs that achieved some success in this and other meta-analyses (e.g., see Andrews *et al.* 1990; McMurran 1995) were stronger in the areas of conceptualization (programs with cognitive/behavioral models, structuring, and role-playing). The better programs included a greater variety of programming options and techniques; they also targeted factors that were actually related to criminal involvement and matched offender learning styles to complementary services.

Programs also falter because of external factors, some of which they have little or no control over. Leukefeld and Tims (1992) caution that programs must be given time to succeed or fail on their merits. That is, to succeed, programs must have sustained, adequate funding over a period of time and must be designed with evaluation in mind. Such a design should be realistic in scope and timeline with respect to outcomes and subject participation. Lipton and his colleagues (1992) note that the history of the demise of therapeutic community programs over the past two decades was oftentimes tied to factors eternal to the programs, such as administrative changes and funding reductions, and not to the efficacy of the programs themselves.

Drug courts

The nexus between drugs and crime is well established. At least 60 percent of jail inmates admit they were under the influence of drugs or alcohol at the time of their offense, or were regular substance abuse users (James 2004; Wilson 2000). Drug courts, first developed in the 1980s at the local level, represent another strategy in the drug war—one that eschews locking people up without addressing underlying addiction issues. Drug courts were developed as a means of diverting people from jail or prison time by engaging them in the treatment process in the community under the close supervision of the court (Brown 2002). At the same time, it was expected that drug courts would reduce the dependence on both courts and corrections for processing relatively-low level drug and alcohol offenders and/or people who commit crimes to sustain their drug use (Bell 2005). General Accounting Office reports (2005; 2011) note that as of 2011 there were about 2,500 (up from 1,200 in 2005) drug courts established in the United States.

Drug courts will either defer prosecution or order drug court involvement as a means of "encouraging" participants. Substance abuse treatment, mandatory drug testing, and involvement of court actors, particularly judges, are central to the operation of drug courts. Attendance at regularly scheduled status hearings before a judge is considered a key element of drug courts. Typically, one year of successful participation in drug court is required for participants to clear their sentence.

The participants in these programs, and the programs themselves, vary widely. According to the GAO (2005; 2011) reports, participants have usually committed a nonviolent drug or property offense, although some had extensive criminal justice histories. Most substance abuse treatment is conducted on an outpatient basis. Some courts include participants with prior convictions, while others do not. Most programs, recognizing that addiction is a disease, will accommodate relapse with either increased sanctions or treatment, rather than immediate termination.

What works, or using science to separate the wheat from the chaff in programming

The truth is that many of the well-intentioned and even well-funded programs out there do not deliver much in the way of reform of clients or inmates. On the other hand, there are many programs that are outright successes and/or show much promise in these areas. The difficulty is dividing the wheat from the chaff in programming, an enterprise that necessarily requires a scientific approach to research on programs (e.g., see Box 10.2).

Box 10.2 The scientific approach in social sciences

The scientific approach in the social sciences is based on logic, rationality, and the collection or analysis of data (Babbie 1992). If researchers want to know why a phenomenon occurs—for instance, why inmates join gangs—they first need to review any research that might exist on this topic. If research does exist, they might test a hypothesis that emanates from that research or replicate a test by other researchers (deductive approach). If there is no research, then the researchers will want to find some means (methods) to investigate the topic (inductive approach). In either case, whether replicating or testing hypotheses from the extant research or engaging in a new area of research where little has been done, researchers need to collect data or analyze existing data. Such data, in the case of gang studies, could come in the form of surveys/police records/observations and so on. There are many methods to employ when doing science! But whatever method is chosen, it needs to allow the researcher to test, support or refute, or develop hypotheses. The researcher also reviews the data to determine whether any patterns or trends, noted or not noted, in other research, become apparent. After a period of study and taking the body of research into consideration, the researchers might propose a theory about why inmates join gangs. That theory should include hypotheses that are testable, and the process then begins again.

It is of the utmost importance that criminal justice managers have some basic understanding of research methodology. Managers are top consumers of research findings, and need the ability to sort out valid and reliable findings and to correctly implement policy changes that are directed by empirical evidence. Furthermore, as many managers can attest, outsourcing research jobs is a critical process for those who do not have the time or the in-house resources to evaluate, explore, describe, or explain the many questions that arise in day-to-day operations. The manager then becomes a contract monitor, and they must possess the necessary research skills to effectively supervise the job and, in the end, justify the research expenses.

In their meta-analysis, Andrews *et al.* (1990) noted that although it is true that no program "works" for all offenders in all circumstances, plenty of rehabilitation programs in fact help reduce recidivism. In other words, in rehabilitation and treatment programming, as in life, there are no easy answers or silver bullets that will "cure" everyone from engaging in criminality. But there are some programs that do appear to "work."

According to Andrews *et al.* (1990), such programs can be distinguished from less successful programs by three principles: Risk, need, and responsivity. By "risk" the authors are referring to the risk level represented by the offender. Those programs that target higher-risk offenders are more likely to have an effect in reducing recidivism. Those programs that focus on "criminogenic needs" or factors that are associated with criminal involvement—such as substance abuse, antisocial attitudes, poor role models, and parenting—and are replaced with more prosocial attitudes and behavior are more likely to be successful. Programs that have styles and modes of program service delivery, or "responsivity," such as modeling, cognitive self-change, role-playing, and behavioral and social learning, coupled with the following factors, are also likely to be more successful in reducing criminal involvement (Andrews *et al.* 1990: 295):

- The use of authority (a "firm but fair" approach and definitely not interpersonal domination or abuse).
- Anti-criminal modeling and reinforcement (explicit reinforcement and modeling of alternatives to pro-criminal styles of thinking, feeling, and acting).
- Concrete problem solving and systematic skill training for purposes of increasing reward levels in anti-criminal settings.
- High levels of advocacy and brokerage are also indicated as long as the receiving agency actually offers appropriate service.
- Service deliverers relate to offenders in interpersonally warm, flexible, and enthusiastic ways, while also being clearly supportive of anti-criminal attitudinal and behavioral patterns.

Some programs that are showing particular promise in rehabilitation programming include substance abuse treatment in adult prisons (Bahr *et al.* 2012; Peters and Steinberg 2001), cognitive self-change coupled with hormonal treatment for sex offenders (Nagayama Hall 2001), and academic and vocational correctional education programs (Gerber and Fritsch 2001). In fact, the literature on substance abuse and related programming is replete with research evaluations indicating that successful treatment programming can be designed and implemented in the correctional environment (Bahr *et al.* 2012; Andrews *et al.* 1990; Applegate *et al.* 1997; Knight *et al.* 1997; Lipton *et al.* 1992; Lipton 1998; Wexler *et al.* 1999).[1] The most successful programs are those that deliver substantive knowledge in an environment that is suited to therapeutic change (Bahr *et al.* 2012; Inciardi 1995; Lipton 1998; Lipton *et al.* 1992). Research also indicates that cognitive attributes, positive modeling, behavioral redirection, emotional therapy, a treatment environment engendering trust and empathy, and clients' intensive involvement in problem solving in their own treatment are also key to attaining actual behavioral change upon release (Bahr *et al.* 2012; Andrews *et al.* 1990; Antonowicz and Ross, 1997; Gendreau and Ross 1987, 1995; Henning and Frueh 1996; Inciardi 1995; McMurran 1995; Smith and Faubert 1990). Treatment programs directed at drug offenders also appear to achieve greater success in reducing recidivism when services were continued post-release (Bahr *et al.* 2012; Lipton 1998; McMurran 1995; Tims and Leukefeld 1992).

In fact, research conducted by Bahr *et al.* (2012) indicates that there are positive outcomes associated with cognitive-based programs in changing criminal activity. There is also now a substantial body of literature that documents the success of prison-based therapeutic community (TC) programs in reducing substance abuse and recidivism, especially when combined with an aftercare component (Bahr *et al.* 2012; Gendreau 1996; Knight *et al.* 1997; Knight *et al.* 1999; Linhorst *et al.* 2001; Martin *et al.* 1995; Martin *et al.* 1999; Pearson and Lipton 1999; Peters and Steinberg 2001; Wexler *et al.* 1999).

Many correctional agencies have come to believe in, and are attempting to implement, cognitive behavioral and social learning approaches because they suspect these treatment components answer the question "What works?" (Bahr *et al.* 2012; Andrews *et al.* 1990; Peters and Steinberg 2001). However, these jurisdictions may be frustrated in their ability to combine these "best practices" in a complementary continuum of services.

The preliminary research on drug courts is also quite promising. In its review of twenty-seven evaluations of adult drug courts, the General Accounting Office (2005: 1) found that "[l]ower percentages of drug court program participants than comparison group members were rearrested or reconvicted" and that "[p]rogram participants had fewer recidivism events than comparison group members." Moreover, the lower recidivism effect remained even for offenders with different offenses. The GAO study authors did not find, however, that one particular mode of operation in the drug court, such as the behavior of the judge, affected the participants' recidivism.

The challenges of managing treatment programming

Research by a number of scholars indicates that the many criminal justice managers in courts or corrections (among other sub-fields) who are interested in providing and maintaining effective treatment programming face several challenges (Ahn-shik *et al.* 2003; Caeti *et al.* 2003). The greatest obstacle by far is that of garnering resources. In fact, most management difficulties associated with treatment programming are associated with the funding issue.

Almost every prison, jail, juvenile facility, and community of any size in this country has volunteers who provide 12-step programs or church-related activities. Undoubtedly, the attraction of such programming is that it can be provided at either no or a very low cost (institutions may need to provide space and supervisory staff), and it can be effective in turning around some offenders. But other kinds of programming, which meet the principles outlined by Andrews *et al.* (1990), are going to cost.

As governmental entities are rarely so flush with funds that all such treatment needs can be met, dollars for treatment or rehabilitation programming are usually narrowly targeted primarily at education programs at the GED or high school diploma level, and at some limited work skills training programming. Substance abuse treatment of late, however, has received a boost in terms of federal funding targeted at detainees in juvenile and adult facilities (e.g., see the National Institute of Justice website for summaries of programs and research funded by NIJ: www.ojp.usdoj.gov). Moreover, other federal agencies, such as the National Institute on Alcohol Abuse and Alcoholism, have provided resources for community-wide drug and alcohol prevention programs targeted at youth. The surge in drug court development has been spurred by the authorization of federal monies, beginning in 1994 with grants under Title V of the Violent Crime Control and Law Enforcement Act (GAO 2005; 2011).

So there are some limited and targeted resources available from the federal government and states that have opened up programming options for administrators, particularly within the past ten years. But it is a rare agency that can match programming to all or even most of the criminogenic needs of offenders.

Related to cost considerations are other management challenges, such as staffing and space. Staff, as per the criteria of Andrews *et al.* (1990), need be qualified and trained to provide the programming effectively. In a fifteen-month process evaluation of a local therapeutic community substance abuse program, we found that too often programming was provided either by other inmates or by staff who had not received adequate training (Stohr *et al.* 2003). Of course, a collateral problem is the low pay for people assigned to staff such programming in some institutions. In treatment programming, as with any service, you get what you pay for—which often results in inadequately trained and paid staff or, worse yet, programming provided by inmates or offenders themselves, which violates the principles described by Andrews *et al.* (1990).

Space is usually in short supply in correctional facilities and in some communities, which is another big problem requiring management attention. If the programming is provided in the community, a local school or church might be used after hours; but correctional institutions with security concerns do not have such options. In some cases the space predicament can be solved by co-opting the chapel or recreational facilities (when such exist) in the off-hours. Or it can be solved by the more costly and thus less likely option of building an expansion to the facility to provide more programming space.

As with the cost and staffing challenges, there are no easy answers to the shortage of space for programming. It will take more than broad recognition of the value of treatment by politicians, other policymakers, and citizens before these hurdles of cost, staffing, and space can be fully addressed. Research by Applegate *et al.* (2001), however, indicates that the public supports treatment for offenders. Therefore it will take the political will and sacrifices necessary to fund treatment before these matters can be addressed. In the interim, managers will need to be creative in their resolution of these issues.

Although we may not have time to address all of the creative ways in which we can resolve treatment and programming issues, one way to start is for managers to tap into their local college(s) or university/ies for help. Often outside state agencies will tap a university for (relatively inexpensive) resources such as graduate research assistance. Many of our students have been hired as interns, with or without pay. Networking within this resource is one way in which criminal justice managers can be creative in getting good and economical help, and it benefits students as well by giving them valuable work experience.

Use of force

Managing the use of force in policing and corrections is at least as problematic as managing treatment and rehabilitation programming. After all, at the very heart of criminal justice is force; its existence, use, and constraint. The threat of force, and the willingness to use it, lie behind the willingness of community members, suspects, and offenders to comply with directives about what they can do, where they are housed, where they work, what they eat, what programs they attend, and who they associate with (Pratt *et al.* 1999).

Certainly there are social controls exerted by family, friends, and community moral beliefs that induce people to act lawfully. But the coercive power of the state in influencing behavior cannot be underestimated. Kids hanging around on the corner will move when asked to by an officer because they know he or she has the ability to bring more attention to their activities than they might like. People comply with court orders because they know that if they do not, they may be fined or compelled into custody. People allow themselves to be supervised by probation and parole officers because they know that if they do not, they will be forced to submit themselves (or be physically taken) to incarceration in a correctional facility. They allow themselves to be housed in a juvenile detention or prison facility or an adult jail, where offenders always outnumber correctional staff by anywhere from 10 to 100 or more to 1, because they know that they have no choice; if they resist, they will be restrained in some way. They also know that there are few avenues of escape from such facilities, and if they try they are likely to be caught and probably will be punished more with a longer sentence.

Recall that power is the ability to get people to do what they otherwise would not. The ability to use coercive power or force is a big reason why people comply, despite what the correctional officers in Hepburn's study thought (see Chapter 6 for a review of the discussion of Hepburn's 1990 study and types of power). In other words, in the everyday operation of police, courts, and corrections, force is either implied or explicitly displayed, and it is useful.

The use of force has been problematic throughout criminal justice history and its abuse is usually highlighted only in infamous cases (Hickman and Atherley 2012; Thomas *et al.* 2010; Alpert and Smith 1999; Pratt *et al.* 1999), particularly for the police and corrections. The worst abuses of force have ranged across the gamut of human hell, including beatings, shootings, isolation, overwork, starvation, torture, rape, and murder. But other than isolation for disruptive behavior, most of these uses and abuses of force have been constrained or eliminated by statute from most police or correctional agencies. Of course, certain organizations and programs have staff who abuse force, but this is by no means the norm.

Documenting the abuse of force in policing and corrections is difficult, if at times impossible. As Thibault *et al.* (2004: 255) indicate, police violence takes place in an environment typified by "secrecy, solidarity and social isolation"—descriptors that certainly apply to correctional work as well. There are indications, however, that the use of excessive force is not as rare as one might think. For instance, in 2005 alone, the American Civil Liberties Union complained about police practices entailing the use and abuse of force in Boston, Santa Fe, and Denver (ACLU 2005a; 2005b; 2005c). In all three cities, the police engaged in the questionable use of lethal and "non-lethal" force (specifically use of Tasers) that resulted in the death of citizens. Relatedly, the Department of Justice signed an agreement with the City of Cincinnati, Ohio, in 2002 that limits the use of force by police officers in that city (CNN 2002). The city signed this agreement when the DOJ was threatening to sue over departmental practices related to the police shootings of young black men in Cincinnati. The death immediately preceding the agreement was that of an unarmed black man shot by a Cincinnati police officer, an incident that spurred four days of rioting in the city. Similar cases have arisen in cities since 2002, as exemplified by the recent consent decree that was signed by the city of Seattle in conjunction with the threat of a lawsuit from the DOJ (see Hickman and Atherley 2012).

The US Attorney General's Office typically handles over a hundred cases of civil rights violations of institutionalized persons every year. The attorney general can investigate such violations in accordance with the Civil Rights of Institutionalized Persons Act (CRIPA).[2] "Since May 1980, when CRIPA was enacted, through September 2001, the Department investigated conditions in 355 jails, prisons, juvenile correctional facilities, and nursing homes" (US DOJ 2001: 1). In 2001 alone, 187 facilities were involved in CRIPA cases, and 11 facilities were investigated, 53 investigations were continued, and monitoring continued over 105 facilities. These cases in 2001 existed in thirty-three states, the District of Columbia, and US territories. In a number of these cases one issue was the abuse of force, or at least protection from harm (US DOJ 2001). For instance, the complaint in a case involving five jails in Maricopa County (Phoenix), Arizona, which was filed in 1997 and settled in 2001, alleged:

> [T]hat the defendants used excessive physical force and restraints in violation of the constitutional rights of individuals detained in the jails. The settlement agreement provided for adequate staffing; staff

training, particularly in use of force issues; prohibition of "hogtying" procedures; revised policies on pepper spray and stun guns that prohibits their use where hands-on control can be used; proactive measures to prevent excessive use of force and restraints; and procedures to receive and investigate inmate grievances.

(US Department of Justice 1998: 2)

As this example illustrates, the appropriate use of force in criminal justice settings is shaped by the circumstances. Typically policies allow the use of force only when there is real or potential danger, and even then there is a preference for a graduated use of force or progressive behavior control. For instance, item 804 of the Arizona Department of Corrections Policy (#804) regarding the use of force in prisons states in part that:

[f]orce shall only be used after every other reasonable attempt to neutralize the real or potential danger has been considered and determined ineffectual. The use of force is reserved for situations where no other reasonable alternative is available to prevent escape, imminent death, serious bodily harm, or the taking of hostages. Verbal abuse by inmates does not constitute cause for the use of force. The use of force shall never be used as punishment or retaliation … Physical force shall be used only when persuasion, direct orders, counseling and warnings are found to be insufficient to obtain cooperation from the inmate: Only the amount of force necessary to gain control of the inmate and minimize injury to staff and the inmate shall be used; once an inmate becomes cooperative, the physical force control techniques shall be consistent with the inmate's amended behavior. However, staff safety shall continue to be the governing consideration; No unorthodox, radical or extreme control techniques that might cause positional asphyxia or bodily injury to staff or inmates is to be used.

(www.azcorrections.gov)

The policy even delineates the maximum use of force in given circumstances. Furthermore, according to the department's policy, staff who violate the use-of-force policy or fail to report a violation or a suspected violation are subject to disciplinary action.

The Minnesota Department of Corrections Field Services Policy for community services staff also details the precise steps that staff should take and matters they should consider when a use-of-force incident occurs (Division Directive no. 201). Unlike the Arizona Department of Corrections use-of-force policy for institutions, however, the Minnesota policy for parole officers focuses more on identifying danger and putting some distance between themselves and the offender who may be endangering them or others. If, however, the officers cannot leave they are authorized to use force to defend themselves and others:

Staff must avoid or leave any situation in which they do not feel safe or in which they are threatened. In the event that staff find themselves in a situation in which the offender or others appear to present a potential or immediate threat to the staff's safety or the safety of others, and the staff are not able to leave or have those presenting the threat leave, staff are authorized to respond in their own defense and the defense of others according to the Use of Force Continuum as defined in this directive and to the extent that they have been trained. The best protection against potential harm comes from:

a   Recognition and awareness
b   Preventive practices
c   Self-protection plans and skills
   (www.doc.state.mn.us/DocPolicy2, last accessed January 31, 2013)

In the Minnesota policy, the *use of force continuum* explicitly links the type of behavior with the appropriate response (e.g., see Figure 10.1). For instance, noncompliance with a request that an offender leave should be paired with a request by staff for an offender to leave, then a directive for the person to leave, then a command. If none of these actions by the staff induce the offender to leave, the officer should leave and get assistance and allow the offender to leave as well. But if the offender should threaten the officer, "either verbally or physically," the officer is justified in using chemical spray and/or physical self-defense tactics.

Alpert and Smith (1999), in their review, note that some police use-of-force continuum policies are adjusted based on the suspect's resistance and the officer's response level. Therefore the officer would merely use verbal commands if the suspect resistance level was characterized by just verbal resistance. However, the officer's response or "level of control (force)" would necessarily adjust to take in the use of physical tactics and/or weapons should the suspect resist physically (Alpert and Smith 1999: 61).

As you can see from these examples, the abuse of force is formally prohibited by criminal justice entities and actors. The use of force is carefully prescribed and delimited by policy and statute. But those who work in and manage police and corrections departments have to be most concerned with ensuring that the informal abuses are not occurring. As much of this abuse is hidden, the best way to stop abuse of force is to engage in preventive measures:

1   Ensure that your policies and procedures are appropriate and sufficient to cover regular and reoccurring interactions between staff and community members/suspects/clients/inmates.
2   Engage in progressive personnel practices that include hiring and maintaining the best people and training them well initially, and throughout their careers, about what constitutes the acceptable use of force.

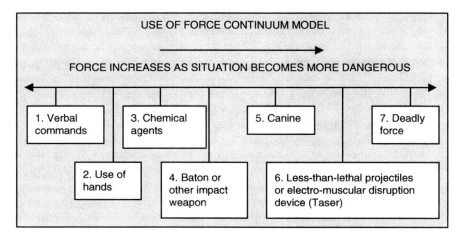

Figure 10.1 Use of force continuum model.

3 Monitor the use of force carefully and consistently to ensure that staff are complying with policies and statutes.
4 Provide a reporting or whistleblowing mechanism and process so that staff and community members/suspects/clients/inmates can report the abuse of force by staff without repercussions (see Box 10.3 for a discussion of whistleblowing).
5 Develop an "early warning" system to identify officers who have received excessive use-of-force complaints or incidents (Thibault *et al.* 2004).
6 Investigate all reports thoroughly and according to established procedures.
7 Discipline violators of the policy.

In sum, there is nothing wrong with using force in criminal justice operations; it comes with the territory. The problems arise when that force is abused. A number of the CRIPA settlements by the US Attorney General's Office included requirements regarding the need for agencies to adequately staff facilities and to train personnel on the appropriate use of force (US DOJ 1998; 2001). The general sentiment seems to be that agencies that take proactive steps in this regard are much less likely to experience abuses of the use of force.

Box 10.3 "The answer, my friend, is blowing in the wind"

The answer to some management prevention issues is indeed blowing in the wind of the organization, and if employees feel they can report on problems without getting punished they will do just that. The idea of whistleblowing probably originated from sporting analogies—that the official blows the whistle on wrongdoing in a game (Miceli and Near 1992). An employee who has observed wrongdoing in an organization can "blow the whistle" on the person or persons responsible by reporting the improper action.

A definition of the term **whistleblowing** offered by Miceli and Near (1992: 15) is: "[t]he disclosure by organization members (former or current) of illegal, immoral, or illegitimate practices under the control of their employers, to persons or organizations that may be able to effect action." As these authors note in their book *Blowing the Whistle: The Organizational and Legal Implications for Companies and Employees*, whistleblowing is a courageous and necessary act if any organization is to remain as free of corruption as possible. But since whistleblowing can be hazardous to the career of that employee, the authors advocate the creation of organizational mechanisms for anonymous reporting, the protection of whistleblowers, and the rewarding of whistleblowing that saves the public money or preserves its safety or health.

Standards and accreditation

Criminal justice standards have evolved over the centuries as a means of improving the professionalism of staff and the operation of agencies, including in relation to the abuse of force. Standards typically cover all aspects of operation, from prescribing the amount of training different classes of staff should have, to drafting procedures for relating to community members, to determining the amount of space an inmate needs in a jail, to setting the ratio of staff to clients on probation. **Accreditation** is the process of determining whether an agency operates according to set standards. The best standards for criminal justice organizations are set by outside professional organizations. In turn, the best accreditation is done by these agencies. Such professional entities are best positioned to be aware of the level of standards necessary to operate the agency professionally; ideally they are also, hopefully, disinterested enough to provide an unbiased assessment or accreditation.

Courts

State and federal courts, as loosely construed organizations, are not typically subjected to accreditation processes. The American Bar Association (ABA), however, rigorously accredits law schools and continuing legal education (CLE) credits, required by many states for practicing attorneys, are usually subjected to accreditation processes. The ABA also has a certification process for lawyers. Some states (e.g., Indiana) require certification of courses in specialty areas like consumer bankruptcy (American Board of Certification), elder abuse (National Elder Law Foundation), and others (Indiana Commission for Continuing Legal Education 2005). Generally speaking court actors, particularly attorneys, are subjected to professional norms and standards through the American Bar Association, their law schools, and state requirements for CLEs; however, these organizations are not always subjected to standards development and accreditation processes in the same way that police and corrections are.

However, in 1995, following an eight-year initiative (beginning in 1987), the Commission on Trial Court Performance Standards—composed of sitting judges, court clerks, and political scientists—along with person-nel from the Bureau of Justice Assistance, the National Center for State Courts (NCSC), and the Trial Court Performance Standards Project Staff, developed standards for self-assessment of state trial courts (NCSC 2001). The NCSC, with funding assistance from the Bureau of Justice Assistance, created the commission to develop a set of standards. The standards were pre-tested in twelve courts in the four states of Ohio, New Jersey, Virginia, and Washington State by over a hundred personnel. The impact of the stand-ards was intended to be narrow, and the self-assessment would not include the review of outside professional entities that might be more prone to objectivity: "The resulting measurement system is intended to be a versatile tool for self-assessment and improvement, and not a means for evaluating the performance of individuals or for drawing comparisons across courts" (NCSC 2001: 2). Having said this, the development of some standards is a step in the right direction. The twenty-two standards, with sixty-eight meas-ures, cover the following areas (NCSC 2001: 6; 2013):

- access to justice;
- expedition and timeliness;
- equality, fairness, and integrity;
- independence and accountability;
- public trust and confidence;

Many of the measures under these five performance areas include a mix of data collection techniques, including surveys of staff and clients, obser-vation, interviews, and the review of court documents. The point is to get a clear picture of how the court operates so that administrators can improve performance in problematic areas. It appeared that the commis-sion intended that the standards be used in administrative decision making involving budgetary determinations and strategic planning.

In the more specialized area of courts and child abuse and neglect cases, the American Bar Association, the National Center for State Courts, and the National Council of Juvenile and Family Court Judges took four years to develop a "guide and toolkit" to measure court performance in this area (American Bar Association 2005). The goal of these organizations was to provide tools for the assessment of performance and judicial workload, and to tailor the assessment to the capabilities for data collection of individual courts. The performance measures for courts dealing with child abuse and neglect cases incorporated national goals developed by the Adoption and Safe Families Act of 1997, including safety, permanency, and well-being for children. They added other performance measures for courts to these three, such as due process and timeliness (American Bar Association 2005). The methods or measures used to assess these performance areas are varied and include surveys, focus groups, case file review, and observation. Again, the process and performance areas were developed as a means for courts or court systems in the states to engage in self-assessment and to improve their performance without outside review.

It is not yet clear how many courts engage in these self-assessments developed by the National Center for State Courts and the ABA. Though time-consuming, such assessments are likely to be beneficial for courts that engage in them because they have the potential to systematize the available information and consequently to improve decision making.

Police

Police organizations have established voluntary accreditation through the Commission on Accreditation for Law Enforcement Agencies, or CALEA[3] (CALEA 2013). The International Association of Chiefs of Police, the National Organization of Black Law Enforcement Executives, the National Sheriffs' Association, and the Police Executive Research Forum established CALEA as an independent accrediting agency in 1979. CALEA is governed by a board composed of eleven law enforcement practitioners and ten members from the public and private sector. CALEA was established to improve and standardize service delivery by the police. There is a small staff and an executive director who produce a newsletter and workshops to explain the standards and the accreditation process. Accreditations are conducted by specially trained CALEA members.

CALEA claims that adherence to its standards, and thus accreditation, will reap benefits for police organizations including improvement of administrative and supervisory service and accountability, reduction in liability costs and lawsuit success (and insurance), and greater support from the community and political actors. The standards themselves address nine areas of law enforcement, running the gamut from operations to personnel structure to traffic operations. To earn accreditation, an agency must demonstrate compliance with 188 standards at Tier 1 (regular accreditation program) and 481 at Tier 2 (advanced accreditation program), although standard applicability varies by agency size and function. The accreditation process starts with an agency self-assessment that can take as long as two years and is followed by a visit by an assessment team. The accreditation lasts for three years.

It is not clear from the CALEA website whether all or most law enforcement agencies engage in voluntary accreditation through the commission. But a perusal of various agency websites indicates that several agencies around the country are proud of their accreditation status through CALEA or are interested in achieving it. For instance, the City of Mesa, Arizona, claims to have been the 186th agency accredited by CALEA, in 1993; it was reaccredited in 2001 (Mesa Police Department 2005). Similarly, the police department of the City of Plantation, Florida, earned accreditation in 1998. In Florida it is possible to also be state-accredited, and Plantation achieved that the following year (Plantation Police Department 2005). The Metro Police Department in Harris County, Texas, the Winston-Salem Police Department in North Carolina, and the County Police Department in Arlington, Virginia all had accreditation requests soliciting community support/comment and postings on their websites at some point in the past five years (Arlington County Police Department, 2005; Metro Police and Traffic Management 2005; Winston-Salem Police Department 2005). Additionally, the CALEA website has a search engine that lists all agencies that are either accredited or attempting to gain accreditation. At the time of the authors' search (May 2013), the website stated that 614 agencies had been awarded law enforcement accreditation (CALEA 2013).

Corrections

As of 2004, most correctional agencies in this country were not accredited (see the American Correctional Association website, www.aca.org). The reasons cited for failure to seek accreditation typically include cost, time, and concern that the agency might not meet the defined standards of professional operation.

A number of corrections and related organizations provide information on the standards of care and operation of correctional entities. The American Probation and Parole Association, which was founded in 1975 by a group of probation practitioners and later joined by those in parole, has served as the professional entity for community corrections professionals. The organization's website (www.appa-net.org) indicates a history of trying to professionalize and standardize the delivery of services and the operation of agencies. For instance, in 1982 the APPA released position papers regarding organizational issues such as budgeting, workload, professionalization in general, and how best to use community resources. As a means of promulgating their message of professionalization, the association also publishes a newsletter which includes research articles as well as anecdotes and commentary on probation and parole practice, and management. Currently the APPA claims a membership of over 26,000 practitioners worldwide.

Like the APPA, the American Jail Association (AJA), founded in 1981, is heavily involved in training jail professionals at its annual training conferences and via its research/practice-based magazine, *American Jails.* According to its website (www.aja.org), the AJA instituted a certification program for jail managers that focuses on inculcating acceptable professional practice and standards for those who work and lead in the field. The managing editor of *American Jails*, Dr. Ken Kerle, has done extensive research on jail standards and has visited hundreds of jails nationally and internationally in an effort to push for professional practice. In *Exploring Jail Operations* (2003: 74), Kerle includes this comment regarding self-audits by jails:

> A self-audit would make it extremely difficult for a person to be objective about his own jail operation. Bias in an individual cannot be totally eradicated in such an exercise. This is somewhat analogous to a teacher giving the students an essay examination and then asking them to score their own papers; bias inevitably creeps in. A jail audit could be greatly improved and possess more credibility if the jail auditors came from outside the state with no prior knowledge of the jail's operation.

But the American Correctional Association (ACA), founded in 1870 with future US president Rutherford B. Hayes as its first president, is the largest and most engaged organization in the standardization and certification of correctional personnel and organizations. With a worldwide membership in the tens of thousands, the ACA sponsors a number of training and knowledge-enhancing opportunities at its annual meeting and in other venues. The ACA publishes the well-known *Corrections Today* and the more research-based *Corrections Compendium* to promulgate professional standards of practice and emerging research in corrections. The ACA is an emerging force in the academic publishing market, with a repertoire of scholarly books. The ACA is also heavily engaged in the accreditation of adult and juvenile prisons, jails, and community corrections agencies.

In fact, staff and facilities in the area of juvenile and adult corrections are audited for accreditation by the ACA. Although the ACA accreditation program is primarily focused on training and staff development programs for personnel, it also considers such characteristics of the agency as its physical plant, its mission, and the number of clients/inmates it is responsible for. Specifically, as part of accreditation, an ACA audit assesses matters that cover "[a]dministration and management, the physical plant, institutional operations and services, and inmate programs" (www.aca.org/standards/benefits.asp). The ACA believes that accreditation will allow a correctional organization to assess its strengths and weaknesses, better defend itself against lawsuits, establish criteria for improvement, and increase the professionalism of staff.

Because it is time-consuming and costly to get accredited by the ACA, many correctional agencies have not sought accreditation or have tried to improve standards by other means. For instance, as of April 2004, the ACA listed only 1,274 correctional agencies as accredited, which means that thousands of other facilities remain unaccredited (www.aca.org/ searchfacilities). For instance, according to the ACA website, only one local jail (the Cumberland County Jail in Maine) and one federal prison (the FCI-Sheridan in Oregon) had completed accreditation (yet each state has numerous county jails and detention centers, probation and parole departments, prisons, and work release programs that are not accredited). In contrast, sixteen Illinois, thirty-four South Carolina, and seventy-seven Texas juvenile detention centers, adult jails, adult transition centers, proba-tion/parole departments, work release programs, and prisons, both public and private and at the local, state, and federal levels, had been accredited by the ACA as of 2004 (www.aca.org/searchfacilities). Of course, these larger states have many more correctional entities than the small states, so these raw figures may be misleading. For example, there might be pro-portionally more correctional entities accredited by the ACA in Idaho (the ACA currently lists only one prison in Idaho) than in Texas. Unfortunately, there is no easy way to determine this as there is no source listing all the correctional entities. But these ACA numbers, randomly selected from six states, appear to indicate that more accreditation is taking place in larger states; this is perhaps because the funding is there, but a tradition of valuing outside review by professional organizations may be more pronounced in larger states as well.

As a side note, we mention that accreditation by any agency, even an outside agency such as the ACA, is not perfect. An institution that wants to fudge the numbers or misrepresent facts can probably get away with it. For instance, in the early 1990s, while visiting a medium security prison in a southwestern state, one of the authors learned from a lieutenant that the officer's institution was able to get ACA accreditation despite being grossly overcrowded, by moving inmates around in buses from facility to facility to avoid having them counted by ACA auditors.

Conclusions

In this chapter we discussed a number of issues related to the management of key issues in criminal justice organizations: Treatment, use of force, and standards and accreditation. Each of these issues presents a special set of problems and concerns for those who work in and manage criminal justice agencies.

Treatment, broadly defined, has always existed in corrections and has been a focus of the courts for some time. It was integral to the genesis of correctional institutions as prisons for adults and of detention centers and juvenile facilities for children, as well as to the mission of probation and parole. Treatment has recently emerged as a central facet of courts as the popularity of drug courts has spread. Treatment still enjoys support from the general population and from correctional administrators, though that support has waxed and waned over the years. The good news is that empirically based research indicates that soundly structured treatment programs can and do have a real and measurable impact on recidivism, as well as other outcome measures.

The use and abuse of force have concerned policing and correctional entities since their inception. By definition these agencies are in the business of forcing people to do what they might not want to do and compelling them to be confined and/or supervised. Force is integral to the mission and operation of criminal justice organizations. The problems arise when employees of organizations abuse force, something that history tells us is not uncommon. Criminal justice managers and workers interested in insulating their organization from the abuse of force should focus on standards, training, and reinforcement of positive and professional behaviors by staff.

Clearly the development of standards is key to the professional management of criminal justice organizations generally, whether in the area of treatment delivery, the use of force, or some other sphere of operation. Because of the political nature of the operation of criminal justice entities, and hence the need for objective assessment, the best method for managers to obtain a level of adherence to standards is to subject their agencies to regular accreditation audits by an outside professional agency. Such an audit is much more likely to be respected by the public, the courts, and policymakers than self-assessment or reviews by like agencies in a state. Outside accreditation is also much more likely to breed an environment of professionalism among those who labor in, and for, criminal justice agencies.

Exercise: Take an informal poll

Since one of the authors began teaching criminal justice classes over eighteen years ago, students' attitudes toward rehabilitation programming have changed drastically. Both authors know this because we routinely engage in nonscientific polls. Faculty, students, and criminal justice practitioners might consider doing the same thing by polling their colleagues or students. Of course, as was mentioned in this chapter, to some extent those attitudes are based on how you define "treatment" and what kind of organization and population you are talking about. Here is how a version of our poll works. Before starting the discussion of treatment programs and rehabilitation generally, we ask students to respond, by raising their hands, to the following questions:

1   Do you support the existence of treatment programs for clients/ offenders/inmates?
2   Do you support the existence of education programs (GED, High School diploma) for incarcerated persons?
3   Do you support the existence of drug and alcohol treatment programming for offenders in the community? How about via drug courts? How about in jails or prisons?
4   Do you support the existence of these programs for adults?
5   Do you support the existence of these programs for children?

Without giving the game away, you can imagine, and we believe you will find, that the level of support for treatment voiced by your students or colleagues depends on a number of factors. But we have also found that the amount of support for treatment in general, and certain programs in particular, has increased markedly in the last few years. This change is perhaps a reflection of the growing support in communities as people become disillusioned with the "lock 'em up and throw away the key" philosophy of the 1980s and 1990s, and as research emerges tallying the successes of some treatment programming. To test this last premise—that communities are supportive of treatment—students might consider doing a nonscientific poll of their friends and family to determine how much support there is for treatment and how that support varies by characteristics of the population and type of programming. They might also notice generational, gender, and other differences in the people they poll that appear to be related (remember that this is a nonscientific poll) to levels of support for treatment.

Discussion questions

1   Why is the dichotomy between treatment and security false? What would be a better way of viewing the relationship between treatment and security?
2   What does Johnson mean by "mature coping" in corrections? How might this concept apply to other areas of criminal justice? Explain your answer.
3   What is a niche, and how are niches related to mature coping? Give an example.
4   What attributes of a treatment/rehabilitation program are likely to "work"? Explain why.

5 How do drug courts operate? Briefly describe each step in the process.

6 Does the extant research indicate that drug courts "work"? Cite some examples in your answer.

7 What sorts of policies exist to determine when the use of force is appropriate in policing? How about in corrections? Explain your answers.

8 What are the best methods that can be employed in policing and corrections to control the abuse of force? Why? Give an example.

9 What are standards and accreditation? How are professional organizations involved in promoting standards? If you were a manager, would you want to go through the accreditation process? Why or why not?

10 What are the advantages that derive from the use of outside agencies to accredit criminal justice agencies? Given these advantages, why don't most criminal justice organizations get involved in the accreditation process? Explain your answer.

Key terms

accreditation: the process of determining whether an agency operates according to set standards.

niche: a private world that inmates try to carve out that serves as a sanctuary that offers "[s]heltered settings and benign activities that insulate them [inmates] from the mainline prison" (Johnson 1996: 120).

mature coping: "[d]ealing with life's problems like a responsive and responsible human being, one who seeks autonomy without violating the rights of others, security without resort to deception or violence, and relatedness to others as the finest and fullest expression of human identity" (Johnson 1996: 98).

standards: typically cover all aspects of operation, from prescribing the amount of training different classes of staff should have, to drafting procedures for handling community members, to determining the amount of space an inmate needs in a jail, to setting the ratio of staff to clients on probation.

whistleblowing: "[t]he disclosure by organization members [former or current] of illegal, immoral, or illegitimate practices under the control of their employers, to persons or organizations that may be able to effect action" (Miceli and Near 1992: 15).

Notes

1   See also Bowman *et al.* 1997; Brewster 2003; Calco-Gray 1993; Field 1985, 1989, 1992; Gendreau and Ross 1995; Hartmann *et al.* 1997; Henning and Frueh 1996; Inciardi 1995; Kelley 2003; Lockwood *et al.* 1998; McMurran 1995; Office of Justice Programs 1998; Palmer 1995; Rice and Remy 1998; Siegal *et al.* 1999.
2   See also http://www.justice.gov/crt/about/spl/documents/split_cripa11.pdf (last accessed January 31, 2013).
3   More info can be accessed at http://www.calea.org/content/standards-titles (last accessed January 31, 2013).

References

ABC News. (1983) *Death in a Southwest prison.* ABC News Special. Narrated by Tom Jarret.

ACLU (2005a) ACLU calls on Denver officials to deliver on promised police reform. Available at www.aclu.org/PolicePractices (last accessed January 31, 2013).

ACLU (2005b) In testimony before commission, ACLU of Massachusetts calls for change in Boston police department's lethal force policies. Available at www.aclu.org/PolicePractices (last accessed January 31, 2013).

ACLU (2005c) ACLU sues New Mexico sheriff's deputies for beating two young men. Available at www.aclu.org/PolicePractices (last accessed January 31, 2013).

Alpert, G. P. and Smith, M. R. (1999) Police use-of-force data: Where we are and where we should be going. *Police Quarterly*, 2: 57–78.

American Bar Association (2005) *Building a better court: Measuring and improving court performance and judicial workload in child abuse and neglect cases.* Chicago, IL: National Council of Juvenile and Family Court Judges. Available at www.abanet.org (last accessed January 31, 2013).

Ahn-shik, K., Devalve, M., Devalve, E. Q. and Johnson, W. W. (2003) Female wardens. *The Prison Journal*, 83(4): 406–425.

Andrews, D. A., Zinger, I., Hoge, R. D., Bonta, J., Gendreau, P. and Cullen, F. T. (1990). Does correctional treatment work? A clinically relevant and psychologically informed meta-analysis. *Criminology*, 28(3): 369–404.

Antonowicz, D. H. and Ross, R. R. (1997) Essential components of successful rehabilitation programs for offenders. In J. W. Marquart and J. R. Sorensen (eds), *Correctional contexts: Contemporary and classical readings.* Los Angeles, CA: Roxbury, pp. 312–317.

Applegate, B., Cullen, F. T. and Fisher, B. S. (2001) Public support for correctional treatment: The continuing appeal of the rehabilitative ideal. In E. J. Latessa, A. Holsinger, J. W. Marquart and J. R. Sorensen (eds), *Correctional contexts: Contemporary and classical readings.* Los Angeles, CA: Roxbury, pp. 268–290.

Applegate, B. K., Langworthy, R. H. and Latessa, E. J. (1997) Factors associated with success in treating chronic drunk drivers: The turning points program. *Journal of Offender Rehabilitation*, 24(3/4): 19–34.

Arlington County Police Department (2005) *At a glance.* Available at www.arlingtonva.us/Departments/Police/PoliceMain.aspx (last accessed January 31, 2013).

Babbie, E. (1992) *The practice of social research*, 6th edn. Belmont, CA: Wadsworth.

Bahr, S. J., Masters, A. L. and Taylor, B. M. (2012) What works in substance abuse treatment programs for offenders? *The Prison Journal*, 93(2): 155–174.

Bell, V. (2005) A content analysis of adult drug courts in the Pacific Northwest. Paper presented at the Western and Pacific Association of Criminal Justice Educators, Vancouver, BC, Canada.

Bowman, V. E., Lowrey, L. and Purser, J. (1997) Two-tiered humanistic pre-release interventions for prison inmates. *Journal of Offender Rehabilitation*, 25(1/2): 115–128.

Brewster, D. R. (2003) Does rehabilitative justice decrease recidivism for women prisoners in Oklahoma? In S. Sharp (ed.), *The incarcerated woman: Rehabilitative programming in women's prisons*. Upper Saddle River, NJ: Prentice Hall, pp. 29–48.

Brown, J. R. (2002) Drug diversion courts: Are they needed and will they succeed in breaking the cycle of drug-related crime? In L. Stolzenberg and S. J. D'Alessio (eds), *Criminal courts for the 21st century*. Upper Saddle River, NJ: Prentice-Hall, pp. 5–37.

Caeti, T., Hemmens, C., Cullen, F. T. and Burton, V. S. (2003) Management of juvenile correctional facilities. *The Prison Journal*, 83(4): 383–405.

Calco-Gray, E. (1993) The dos pasos: Alternatives to incarceration for substance abusing women of childbearing age. *American Jails*, 7(4): 44–53.

CALEA (2013) *CALEA online*. Available at http://www.calea.org/ (last accessed January 31, 2013).

Clayton, R. R., Catterello, A. M. and Johnstone, B. M. (1996) The effectiveness of drug abuse resistance education (Project D.A.R.E.): 5-year follow-up results. *Preventive Medicine*, 25: 307–318.

CNN (2002) Cincinnati signs pact with U.S. over police. Available at www.cnn.com/lawcenter (last accessed January 31, 2013).

Crouch, B. and Marquart, J. (1990) Resolving the paradox of reform litigation, prisoner violence and perceptions of risk. *Justice Quarterly*, 7: 103–123.

Cullen, F. T. and Gilbert, K. E. (1982) *Reaffirming rehabilitation*. Cincinnati, OH: Anderson Publishing.

DiIulio, J. J. (1987) *Governing prisons: A comparative study of correctional management*. New York, NY: Free Press.

Field, G. (1985) The Cornerstone Program: A client outcome study. *Federal Probation*, 49(2): 50–55.

Field, G. (1989) The effects of intensive treatment on reducing the criminal recidivism of addicted offenders. *Federal Probation*, 53(4): 51–56.

Field, G. (1992) Oregon prison drug treatment programs. In C. G. Leukefeld and F. M. Tims (eds), *National Institute on Drug Abuse research monograph series: Drug abuse treatment in prisons and jails*. Rockville, MD: National Institute on Drug Abuse.

Gendreau, P. and Ross, R. R. (1995) Correctional treatment: Some recommendations for effective intervention. In K. C. Haas and G. P. Alpert (eds), *The dilemmas of corrections: Contemporary readings*. Prospect Heights, IL: Waveland Press, pp. 367–380.

Gendreau, P. and Ross, R. R. (1987) Revivification of rehabilitation: Evidence for the 1980s. *Justice Quarterly*, 4, 349–407.

Gendreau, P. (1996) The principles of effective intervention with offenders. In A. Harland (ed.), *Choosing correctional options that work*. Newbury Park, CA: Sage, pp. 117–130.

General Accounting Office (2005) *Adult drug courts: Studies show courts reduce recidivism, but DOJ could enhance future performance measure revision efforts.* Washington DC: GAO-12-53.

General Accounting Office (2011) *Adult drug courts: Evidence indicates recidivism reductions and mixed results for other outcomes.* Washington, DC: GAO.

Gerber, J. and Fritsch, E. J. (2001) Adult academic and vocational correctional education programs: A review of recent research. In E. J. Latessa, A. Holsinger, J. W. Marquart and J. R. Sorensen (eds), *Correctional contexts: Contemporary and classical readings.* Los Angeles, CA: Roxbury, pp. 268–290.

Gioia, P. (2004) *State corrections needs comprehensive re-examination: Connecticut business and industry association report.* Norwich Bulletin. Available at www.norwichbulletin.com

Goodstein, L. and Wright, K. N. (1989) Inmate adjustment to prison. In L. Goodstein and D. L. MacKenzie (eds), *The American prison: Issues in research and policy.* New York, NY: Plenum Press, pp. 229–251.

Gottfredson, D. (1997) School-based crime prevention. In L. W. Sherman, D. Gottfredson, D. MacKenzie, J. Eck, P. Reuter and S. Bushway (eds), *Preventing crime: What works, what doesn't, what's promising. A report to the United States Congress.* Rockville, MD: Department of Criminology and Criminal Justice, University of Maryland.

Hartmann, D. J., Wolk, J. L., Johnston, J. S. and Colyer, C. J. (1997) Recidivism and substance abuse outcomes in a prison-based therapeutic community. *Federal Probation,* 51(4): 18–25.

Henning, K. R. and Frueh, B. C. (1996) Cognitive-behavioral treatment of incarcerated offenders: An evaluation of the Vermont Department of Corrections' cognitive self-change program. *Criminal Justice and Behavior,* 23(4): 523–541.

Hepburn, J. R. (1990) The exercise of power in coercive organizations. In S. Stojkovic, J. Klofas and D. Kalinich (eds), *The administration and management of criminal justice organizations.* Prospect Heights, IL: Waveland Press, pp.249–265

Hickman, M. J. and Atherley, L. T. (2012) Police use of force in Seattle, January 2009 – March 2012. Available at http://www.nwjs.org/docs/SeattleUOF.pdf (last accessed January 31, 2013).

Inciardi, J. A. (1995) The therapeutic community: An effective model for corrections-based drug abuse treatment. In K. C. Haas and G. P. Alpert (eds), *The dilemmas of corrections: Contemporary readings.* Prospect Heights, IL: Waveland Press, pp. 406–417.

Indiana Commission for Continuing Legal Education. (2005) Independent certifying organizations for Indiana. Available at www.in.gov/judiciary/cle/ico.html (last accessed January 31, 2013).

Irwin, J. (1985) *The jail: Managing the underclass in American society.* Berkeley, CA: University of California Press.

James, D. J. (2004) *Profile of jail inmates, 2002. Bureau of Justice Statistics, Special Report.* Office of Justice Programs. Washington DC: US Department of Justice.

Johnson, R. (1996) *Hard time: Understanding and reforming the prison.* Belmont, CA: Wadsworth.

Kelley, M. S. (2003) The state-of-the-art in substance abuse programs for women in prison. In S. Sharp (ed.), *The incarcerated woman: Rehabilitative programming in women's prisons.* Upper Saddle River, NJ: Prentice Hall, pp. 119–148.

Kerle, K. (2003) *Exploring jail operations.* Hagerstown, MD: American Jail Association.

Knight, K., Simpson, D. D., Chatham, L. R. and Camacho, L. M. (1997) An assessment of prison-based drug treatment: Texas' in-prison therapeutic community program. *Journal of Offender Rehabilitation*, 24(3/4): 75–100.

Knight, K., Simpson, D. D. and Hiller, M. L. (1999) Three year reincarceration outcomes for in-prison therapeutic community treatment in Texas. *The Prison Journal*, 79(3): 337–351.

Leukefield, C. G. and Tims, F. M. (eds) (1992) *National Institute on Drug Abuse research monograph series: Drug abuse treatment in prisons and jails*. Rockville, MD: National Institute on Drug Abuse.

Linhorst, D. M., Knight, K., Johnston, J. S. and Trickey, M. (2001) Situational influences on the implementation of a prison-based therapeutic community. *The Prison Journal*, 81(4): 436–453.

Lindstrom-Johnson, S. R., Finigan, N., Bradshaw, C., Haynie, D. and Cheng, T. L. (2012) Urban African American parents' message about violence. *Journal of Adolescent Research*, 28: 511–553.

Lipton, D. S. (1998) Treatment for drug abusing offenders during correctional supervision: A nationwide overview. *Journal of Offender Rehabilitation*, 26(3/4): 1–45.

Lipton, D., Falkin, G. P. and Wexler, H. K. (1992) Correctional drug abuse treatment in the United States: An overview. In C. G. Leukefeld and F. M. Tims (eds), *National Institute on Drug Abuse research monograph series: Drug abuse treatment in prisons and jails*. Rockville, MD: National Institute on Drug Abuse, pp. 8–30.

Lipton, D., Martinson, R. and Wilks, J. (1975) *The effectiveness of correctional treatment: A survey of treatment evaluation studies*. Springfield, MA: Praeger.

Listwan, S. J., Sullivan, C. J., Agnew, R., Cullen, F. T. and Colvin, M. (2013) The pains of imprisonment revisited: The impact of strain on inmate recidivism. *Justice Quarterly*, 30(1): 144–168.

Lockwood, D., McCorkel, J. and Inciardi, J. A. (1998) Developing comprehensive prison-based therapeutic community treatment for women. *Drugs and Society*, 13(1/2): 193–212.

Logan, C. H. and Gaes, G. G. (1993) Meta-analysis and the rehabilitation of punishment. *Justice Quarterly*, 10: 245–263.

Manning, P. K. (2005) The study of policing. *Police Quarterly*, 8: 23–43.

Martin, S. S., Butzin, C. A. and Inciardi, J. A. (1995) Assessment of a multi-stage therapeutic community for drug-involved offenders. *Journal of Psychoactive Drugs*, 27: 109–116.

Martin, S. S., Butzin, C. A., Saum, C. A. and Inciardi, J. A. (1999) Three-year outcomes of therapeutic community treatment for drug-involved offenders in Delaware: From prison to work release to aftercare. *The Prison Journal*, 79(3): 294–320.

Martinson, R. (1974) What works? Questions and answers about prison reform. *Public Interest*, 35(Spring): 22–54.

Martinson, R. (1974, reprinted in 2001) What works?—Questions and answers about prison reform. In E. J. Latessa, A. Holsinger, J. W. Marquart and J. R. Sorensen (eds), *Correctional contexts: Contemporary and classical readings*. Los Angeles, CA: Roxbury, pp. 268–290.

McMurran, M. (1995) Alcohol interventions in prisons: Towards guiding principles for effective intervention. *Psychology, Crime & Law*, 1: 215–226.

Merlo, A. V. and Benekos, P. J. (2000) *What's wrong with the criminal justice system: Ideology, politics and the media*. Cincinnati, OH: Anderson Publishing.

Merrow, K. and Minard, R. A. (2003) *Under the influence. Part 2: Treating addictions, reducing corrections costs.* Concord, NH: New Hampshire Center for Public Policy Studies. Available at www.nhpolicy.org

Mesa Police Department. (2005) Mesa Police Department accreditation. Available at www. ci.mesa.az.us/police/admin/accred.asp (last accessed January 31, 2013).

Metro Police and Traffic Management. (2005) Accreditation & professional standards. Available at www.hou-metro.harris.tx.us/PDWebsite/standards.html (last accessed January 31, 2013).

Miceli, M. P. and Near, J. P. (1992) *Blowing the whistle: The organizational and legal implications for companies and employees.* New York, NY: Lexington Books.

Nagayama Hall, G. C. (2001) Sexual offender recidivism revisited: A meta-analysis of recent treatment studies. In E. J. Latessa, A. Holsinger, J. W. Marquart and J.R. Sorensen (eds), *Correctional contexts: Contemporary and classical readings.* Los Angeles, CA: Roxbury, pp. 268–290.

National Center for State Courts (NCSC) (2001) Trial court performance standards & measurement system. Available at www.ncsconline.org (last accessed January 31, 2013).

National Center for State Courts (NCSC) (2013) Trial court performance standards & measurement system. Available at www.ncsconline.org

Office of Justice Programs. (1998) *Residential substance abuse treatment for state prisoners.* Washington DC: Department of Justice.

Owen, B. (1998) *In the mix.* New York, NY: State University of New York Press.

Palmer, T. (1975) Martinson revisited. *Journal of Research in Crime and Delinquency,* 12: 133–152.

Palmer, T. (1983) The effectiveness issue today: An overview. *Federal Probation,* 46: 3–10.

Palmer, T. (1995) The 'effectiveness' issue today: An overview. In K. C. Haas and G. P. Alpert (eds), *The dilemmas of corrections: Contemporary readings.* Prospect Heights, IL: Waveland Press, pp. 351–366.

Pearson, F. S. and Lipton, D. S. (1999) A meta-analytic review of the effectiveness of corrections-based treatments for drug abuse. *Prison Journal,* 79(4): 384–410.

Peters, R. H. and Steinberg, M. L. (2001) Substance abuse treatment in U.S. prisons. In E. J. Latessa, A. Holsinger, J. W. Marquart and J. R. Sorensen (eds), *Correctional contexts: Contemporary and classical readings.* Los Angeles, CA: Roxbury, pp. 268–290.

Plantation (Florida) Police Department. (2005) Accreditation. Available at www. psd.plantation.org/accreditation-section.html (last accessed January 31, 2013).

Pratt, T., Maahs, J. and Hemmens, C. (1999) The history of the use of force in corrections. In C. Hemmens and E. Atherton (eds), *Use of force: Current practice and policy.* Lanham, MD: American Correctional Association, pp. 13–22.

Rice, J. S. and Remy, L. L. (1998) Impact of horticultural therapy on psychosocial functioning among urban jail inmates. *Journal of Offender Rehabilitation,* 26(3/4): 169–191.

Royse, D. (2003) State prisons lock up 3,000 new inmates. *The Miami Herald,* August 19. Available at www.MiamiHerald.com (last accessed January 31, 2013).

Sherman, L. W., Gottfredson, D., MacKenzie, D., Eck, J., Reuter, P. and Bushway, S. (1997) (eds), *Preventing crime: What works, what doesn't, what's promising. A report to the United States Congress.* Rockville, MD: Department of Criminology and Criminal Justice, University of Maryland.

Siegal, H. A., Wang, J., Carlson, R. G., Falck, R. S., Rahman, A. M. and Fine, R. L. (1999) Ohio's prison-based therapeutic community treatment programs for substance abusers: Preliminary analysis of re-arrest data. *Journal of Offender Rehabilitation*, 28(3/4): 33–48.

Smith, J. and Faubert, M. (1990) Programming and process in prisoner rehabilitation: A prison mental health center. *Journal of Offender Counseling, Services and Rehabilitation*, 15(2): 131–153.

Stohr, M. K., Hemmens, C., Baune, D., Dayley, J., Gornik, M., Kjaer, K. and Noon, C. (2003) *Residential substance abuse treatment for state prisoners: Breaking the drug-crime cycle among parole violators*. NIJ Research for Practice-Web Only Document. US Department of Justice, Office of Justice Programs, National Institute of Justice. Available at www.ncjrs.org. (last accessed January 31, 2013).

Stohr, M. K., Lovrich, N. P., Menke, B. A. and Zupan, L. L. (1994) Staff management in correctional institutions: Comparing DiIulio's 'control model' and 'employee investment model' outcomes in five jails. *Justice Quarterly*, 11(3): 471–497.

Thibault, E. A., Lynch, L. M. and McBride, R. B. (2004) *Proactive police management*, 6th ed. Upper Saddle River, NJ: Pearson–Prentice Hall.

Thomas, K. J., Collins, P. A. and Lovrich, N. P. (2010) Conducted energy device use in municipal policing: Results of a national survey on policy and effectiveness assessments. *Police Quarterly*, 13(3): 290–315.

Tims, F. M. and Leukefeld, C. G. (1992) The challenge of drug abuse treatment in prisons and jails. In C. G. Leukefeld and F. M. Tims (eds), *National Institute on Drug Abuse research monograph series: Drug abuse treatment in prisons and jails*. Rockville, MD: National Institute on Drug Abuse.

Toch, H., Adams, K. and Grant, J. D. (1989) *Coping: Maladaptation in prisons*. New Brunswick, NJ: Transaction Publishers.

US Department of Justice (1998) *Introduction and overview of CRIPA activities. 1998 CRIPA Report*. Available at www.usdoj.gov (last accessed January 31, 2013).

US Department of Justice (2001) *Introduction and overview. CRIPA Activities in FY 2001*. Available at www.usdoj.gov (last accessed January 31, 2013).

Walker, S. (1984) 'Broken windows' and fractured history: The use and misuse of history in recent police patrol analysis. *Justice Quarterly*, 1: 57–90.

Wexler, H. K., DeLeon, G., Thomas, G., Kressel, D. and Peters, J. (1999) The Amity Prison TC evaluation. *Criminal Justice and Behavior*, 26(2): 147–167.

Wexler, H. K., Melnick, G., Lowe, L. and Peters, J. (1999) Three-year reincarceration outcomes for Amity in-prison therapeutic community and aftercare in California. *The Prison Journal*, 79(3): 321–336.

Wilson, D. J. (2000) *Drug use, testing, and treatment in jails. Bureau of Justice Statistics. Office of Justice Programs*. Washington, DC: Department of Justice.

Wilson, J. Q. and Kelling, G. L. (1982) Broken windows: The police and neighborhood safety. *Atlantic Monthly*, March: 29–38.

Winston-Salem Police Department (2005) Police department undergoing re-accreditation, public comment invited. Available at www.ci.winston-salem.nc.us (last accessed January 31, 2013).

Wisconsin Education Association Council (2004) Great schools issue paper: Parent and family involvement. Available at www.weac.org/greatschools (last accessed January 31, 2013).

Wright, R. A. (1995) Rehabilitation affirmed, rejected, and reaffirmed: Assessments of the effectiveness of offender treatment programs in criminology textbooks, 1956 to 1965 and 1983 to 1992. *Journal of Criminal Justice Education*, 6(1): 21–41.

11 Strategic planning and budgeting

There is a connection between planning and doing...

(Hrebiniak 2005: 65)

Zero-based budgeting sounds great in theory. But theory is not reality.

(Roger Simmons, County Commissioner of Ada County, Idaho 2001)

Public budgeting involves making and carrying out decisions regarding acquisition, allocation, and the use of resources, particularly money, by government. Although public and private budgeting are similar in many respects, public budgeting is often more controversial, more open to multiple influences, and more heavily regulated than private budgeting.

(Nice 2002)

Introduction: strategic planning and budgeting are at the very center of all things organizational

People tend to think of strategic planning, but particularly budgeting, as very dry topics. Many students hem, they haw, they yawn, when these topics come up. As hard as we try, it is difficult to raise the enthusiasm for budgeting or strategic planning to the level elicited by, say, selection! People who have not worked in criminal justice agencies before, or have not paid attention to organizational management and politics, often just do not see the relevance to themselves of strategic planning or of a budgeting discussion. That many should find planning and budgeting boring is not necessarily surprising; these can be much neglected areas of study and comment that have not been presented creatively. A scholarly lament on the "arid landscape" of the literature on budgeting (Key 1940) remains applicable over a half-century later.

Of course, attitudes of boredom and nonchalance about strategic planning and budgeting are completely out of step with what these disciplines represent for public (and private) sector criminal justice organizations. For such organizations, and the people who work in and supervise in them, strategic planning and budgeting are at the *very center of the organizational universe.* This is true, regardless of whether it is recognized, because strategic plans spur and justify budgets. The budget, in turn, controls just about everything done by the organization as a whole, and by individual actors. Budgets determine pay, wage raises (or not), whether programs are funded, buildings built, computers and furniture purchased; budgets determine staffing levels, availability of promotions, training amounts, research, and on and on. Concomitantly, budgets and strategic plans affect stress levels, satisfaction with the job, and turnover of employees. In low-budget years or when budgets do not fit the strategic plan, even criminal justice agencies, with burgeoning numbers of clients, can be cut or—almost as bad—not funded at a level that allows them to continue operating as previously (Bryson 1995; Campbell 2003; Gaines *et al.* 2003; Hrebiniak 2005; Hudzik and Cordner 1983; Royce 2003; Smith 1997; Swanson *et al.* 1998; Wallace *et al.* 1995).

In short, for those who work in public and private criminal justice organizations, for those who have pursued such careers or want to, and for those who study such organizations, understanding strategic planning and budgeting is of paramount importance. Every topic that has been touched upon in this book is affected by how, or whether, an organization plans and budgets. In a very real sense, then, plans and budgets will influence who we are in any criminal justice organization and what we can become.

In this chapter, and keeping the proper recognition of the importance of planning and budgeting in mind, we explore some recent history on the following topics: Methods of planning, effects of planning, types of budgeting, and innovations in budgeting. We will first define strategic planning and budgeting and then, with politics ever on our minds, we will begin our discussion of budgeting with "some things to remember about public sector budgets" that are derived from the literature on this topic.

Strategic planning: definition, benefits, and the difficulties of implementation

According to Bryson (1995: 4–5) strategic planning is "[a] disciplined effort to produce fundamental decisions and actions that shape and guide what an organization is, what it does, and why it does it." To plan well, managers of an organization must have valid and reliable information, be aware of viable alternatives, and consider the future implications of all planning decisions. Should the organization be in a position to engage in strategic planning, Bryson (1995: 7) identifies the following benefits:

- the promotion of strategic thought and action;
- improved decision making;
- enhanced organizational responsiveness and improved performance;

- benefit the organization's people [as policymakers and key decision makers can better fulfill their roles and meet their responsibilities, and teamwork and expertise are likely to be strengthened among organizational members].

In sum, the organization that engages in strategic planning consciously develops a map for organizational operation. (Figure 11.1 is a simplified flowchart for the strategic plan of a criminal justice system in Anytown, USA.) As pointed out in Chapter 4, in our discussion of the systems perspective, most strategic plans will reflect the organization's overall goals and mission, which are influenced by environmental, external, and internal processes, inputs, outputs, and feedback. So again, the strategic plan as Bryson defined it explicates what the organization is and does, and the reasons for its actions.

In most locations, for instance, the public defender's office can rationally choose to allocate its resources to certain types of cases while de-emphasizing others based on a plan. Bryson (1995) cautions, however, that there is no guarantee that a strategic plan will yield the benefits he lists, since for that to happen there must be leadership, the will to carry out the plan among organizational members, and the budget to implement the plan (Hrebiniak 2005). Hrebiniak argues, in fact, that the planning, as arduous as it can be in some organizations, is actually the easy part. Execution or implementation is really the most difficult part of strategic planning, and it is where most managers fail (Pressman and Wildavsky 1973; Rothman 1980). Therefore, that public defender's office may suffer politically (and potentially budgetarily) when it shifts resources to one type of case over others if the managers of the organization do not first persuade interested stakeholders (e.g., the police, courts, prosecutor's office, and community members) to buy into the plan.

Implementing the plan

The execution of a strategic plan follows the layout of Figure 11.1 (also keep in mind how this planning process relates to the systems theory presented in Chapter 4). Notice that the "Crucial Stage" label is applied to the implementation section. It is here that all the plans are put into action. However, some very important steps must precede implementation if organizational goals are to be met. First, during the initial planning stage, representatives from the organization, key stakeholders, and all other individuals involved should come together and pose questions that feed into objectives, which (in theory) reflect the general goals of the organization (Welsh and Harris 1999). This is done for several reasons; one is to flush out possible problems with planning design, and another is to explain why one particular design may be better than another. For example, if a state Department of Correction's ultimate goal is to increase funding for all treatment services

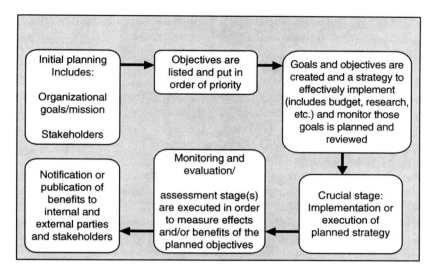

Figure 11.1 Example of a strategic planning flow chart

available, the agency must gather information from several sources, both to help in the acquisition of more state or federal funding and to provide empirical evidence to guide and support decision making and policy planning. During the initial stage, then, the state agency might bring together professionals in the field for advice in the form of technical assistance (TA), for research support, and to field and answer the all-important questions that will direct the plan's objectives.

During that initial meeting or thereafter, the managers and stakeholders responsible for overseeing all stages of the strategic plan will position objectives in order of importance or priority (Welsh and Harris 1999). For example, in building a case for increased use of community policing, a planning group may prioritize a list of research objectives, and the most important will address or reflect the substantive question(s) posed in the planning stage (e.g., Does community policing increase positive interactions between the police and the public?).

Once the list of objectives, priorities and goals has been completed, a strategy to effectively implement and monitor those goals is planned and reviewed. The proper planning of this stage (which includes budget, research, etc.) is critical to the actual implementation stage for several reasons. Organizations often are faced with limited resources, and their proper management may make or break the whole planning process. Therefore, budgeting the right amount of resources is paramount to success. The budget must cover all stages of a program's existence, and it must be understood that these resources will provide a continuum of support throughout the process. We shall return to this topic shortly.

We can also see that it is at this juncture that we map out how to effectively monitor and evaluate our plan. The evaluation may cover several key points in the plan at a variety of times (e.g., pre and post; multiple points during the progression of the plan), and it may include a strategy to effectively monitor and assess the proposed time line for implementation, contracts and contracted employee oversight, communication, budgeting, information gathering/data analysis/packaging and presentation, post assessment, and criteria for success (Welsh and Harris 1999).

It is during the final decisive stage, implementing the plan, that all previous measures are put into action and must be effectively managed. Here monitoring and evaluation/assessment stage(s) are executed to measure effects and/or benefits of the planned objectives and notification or publication of benefits to internal and external parties and stakeholders. It is here, too, that the organization planning committee, stakeholders, and all relevant parties assess whether the objectives are being met.

Failure of execution

The reasons for failure of execution are multifaceted (Hrebiniak 2005). For one thing, managers are often trained on how to plan, but not on how to implement. Therefore, they may neglect to build support for programs and initiatives and to restructure the culture to support the plan; they may not understand how power will shape and influence implementation; and they may continue to emphasize the importance of plan execution without having constructed control and feedback mechanisms to monitor implementation (Hrebiniak 2005).

The very best of intentions by policymakers will not guarantee that a plan will be faithfully funded and implemented (Rothman 1980). In fact, at times, as with the implementation of juvenile courts in the first half of the twentieth century, just the opposite of the "best interests of the child" can play out when there is little oversight of powerful actors such as judges (Rothman 1980).

But even assuming that the money is there and there is widespread support for the strategic plan, "the best laid plans of mice and men," as John Steinbeck said, "often go awry." Pressman and Wildavsky (1973), in a classic study of the failure to implement a well-funded and agreed-upon anti-poverty program—economic development to increase minority employment in Oakland, California—found that it was the little things, the devil in the details, that stymied program implementation. Specifically, it was the lack of follow-through that kept this program from being adequately implemented. Agreements made for work should have been maintained, approvals and clearances from all interested parties were needed. These are the small and ordinary, but important, matters that should have been attended to but were not. And these are the types of things, according to Pressman and Wildavsky (1973), that are often neglected in implementation. "Failure to recognize that these perfectly ordinary circumstances present serious obstacles to implementation inhibits learning. If one is always looking for unusual circumstances and dramatic events, he cannot appreciate how difficult it is to make the ordinary happen" (Pressman and Wildavsky 1973: xviii). Thirty-plus years later, Hrebiniak (2005) makes a similar point: That achieving effective execution and change in organizations requires not just a plan and a budget, but sustained effort on the part of organizational members.

What is a budget?

The implementation of a strategic plan is dependent on the development and execution of a budget; that is, a summary of expenses for a given program or organization. If as a student you were to devise a budget for your college education, you would likely list tuition and fees, books, rent, and food (or room and board), clothing, recreation, and miscellaneous items. Similarly, a transitional program for juvenile boys would budget for staff, housing, food, utilities, clothing, programming, school costs, recreation, maintenance, and miscellaneous. As with a personal budget, under each of these major headings for the transitional program would be subsidiary cost breakdowns, as in different salaries for the full-time and part-time staff positions, pay that varies by role (e.g., the director vs. the counselors), and health care and retirement benefits.

Table 11.1 gives a sample governmental budget. The proper planning (budgeting), implementation, and evaluation of an organization's goals and objectives takes fundamental, and in some cases advanced, mathematical and analytical skills, along with foresight and other managerial know-how. In the formation of fiscal policy and yearly budgets, most criminal justice organizations employ computer spreadsheets and other statistical software. A strong working knowledge of various computer programs (e.g., Microsoft Excel, Microsoft Access, and SPSS [the Statistical Package for the Social Sciences]) is a must at the managerial level and, in some instances, for the day-to-day operations of the whole organization. Technological tools such as these provide the manager and the organization with the ability to both plan and implement objectives, goals, services, and research within the organization and then interpret and benefit from the use of that information.

The four stages of the budget process

There are at least four stages in the budget process for organizations (Graham and Hays 1986; see Figure 11.2 for a chart of the budget process and Box 11.1 for an example). Before embarking on the development of a budget, however, a criminal justice agency must first consider the fiscal environment that affects their funding entity (Padovani and Young 2012). If tax revenues are up and the political actors (members of the legislative and executive branches at their level of government) are supportive, the agency will be able to develop a more generous budget than if the opposite is true. With this fiscal environment in view, the first stage of the budgeting process, which involves the preparation of

Table 11.1 Highlights of recent budget for the US Department of Justice (millions of dollars)

Spending	2010 actual	2011 estimate	2012 estimate
Discretionary Budget Authority			
Federal Bureau of Investigation	7,749		8,076
Drug Enforcement Administration	2,050		2,012
Federal prison system	6,185		6,791
US Marshals Service	1,151		1,253
Bureau of Alcohol, Tobacco, Firearms and Explosives	1,121		1,147
Detention trustee	1,439		1,595
United States attorneys	1,935		1,995
General Legal Activities	877		955
National Security Division	88		88
Office of Justice Programs, COPS, Office of Violence Against Women	3,552		2,964
Organized Crime and Drug Enforcement Task Force	527		
All Other	925	541	
Subtotal: Discretionary budget authority	27,599	30,351	754
Less Crime Victims' Fund discretionary offset	—	–5,820	28,171
Less Assets Forfeiture Fund cancellation	—	–387	–6,641
			–620
Total: Discretionary budget authority	27,599	24,144	20,910
Memorandum:			
Budget authority from supplements	206	—	—
FBI Overseas Contingency Operation	101	—	—
Total Discretionary outlays	27,736	26,731	24,074
Mandatory Outlays	1,828	6,770	
Existing Laws	—	—	8,977
Legislative proposal	1,828	6,770	100
Total Mandatory outlays		33,501	9,077
Total Outlays		29,564	33,151

Source: Adapted from Department of Justice Budget, April 8, 2013. Available at http://www.whitehouse.gov/sites/default/files/omb/budget/fy2012/assets/justice.pdf (last accessed January 31, 2013).

the budget, may be begun. Often budgets are prepared with several objectives in mind, and they are not created out of whole cloth every year. Typically, the starting point for staff preparing the budget is previous years' budgets. Staff will examine these budgets and allocate a similar amount of money to each item, while accounting for inflation. Briefly, the US Department of Labor defines

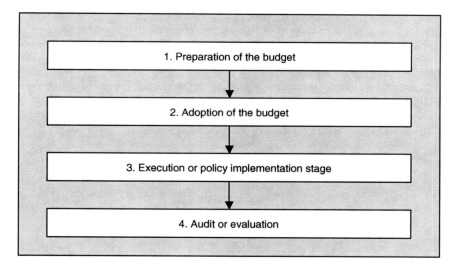

Figure 11.2 The four stages of the budget process.

inflation as "the overall general upward price movement of goods and services in an economy." If new monies are likely to be available, they will be budgeted to account for the likely increase in expenses and/or used to fund new initiatives. The more discretionary parts of the budgets are then often examined to determine whether they fit, and further, the plan for the program or organization. In other words, for our juvenile transition program, housing, food, the cost of running the building, and even staffing remain somewhat fixed, if not requiring moderate increases from year to year. On the other hand, programming, recreation, and other special project costs vary from year to year—that is, are discretionary—depending on the budget priorities set in a given year, the availability of funding, the approval of the transitional program's board or funding agency, or the next step in the process.

Box 11.1 Reduced budgets for juvenile corrections in Florida

The budgetary crises that many states have confronted in the past several years have led some states to reduce their budgets for corrections and other services (Florida Department of Juvenile Justice 2013; Lauth 2003). A case in point is the budgets for the Florida juvenile justice system for fiscal year 2005 through 2013 (www.djj.state.fl.us). According to the Florida Department of Juvenile Justice (legislative update) in 2005, a total of $7 million was cut from juvenile facilities and community corrections. These cuts included detention, probation and community corrections, residential and correctional facilities, and more. Across these areas, the cuts affected jobs for staff and administrators, programs, placements, and secure and nonsecure beds for juveniles. Fast forward to the present and we find that the department is still being cut. In a press release from the Florida Department of Juvenile Justice dated January 2013, the department touts the fact that its proposed budget of $513.6 million for 2013–2014 will be $9.7 million less than its current budget. Moreover, the department claims they have shifted their focus from residential beds to "investing in health and front-end services," or prevention over incarceration.

The next stage in the budgeting process, after preparation, is adoption of the budget. This is usually a process that is dominated by politics, economics, and the perceived and real performance of the program. If the current political actors, such as state legislators and the governor in the case of our transitional program, support such programs for youth, think there is enough money in the state budget to continue funding it at the requested level, and believe it fills an important need in juvenile corrections, the budget proposed by our transitional program director will be approved. But if these important people think such programs are unnecessary, or disagree with them philosophically, then the funding request will be slashed or denied. If there is a recession, or if tax collections have decreased or are projected to decrease in the upcoming year, our transitional program's budget request is also likely to suffer. Or if there is little evidence to indicate that our transitional program is successful in reducing the criminal engagement of troubled youth, or if it is perceived to have failed in some capacity, the budget request will not be approved, as submitted, by either the governor or by the state legislators.

Should our transitional program's budget remain somewhat intact for the next year, it will enter the third stage of the budgeting process, which is the execution or policy implementation stage. Note that this stage takes the whole year, as the budget is intended to fund a year's worth of operation. Many states, cities, and counties count their fiscal year from July 1 through June 30. The federal government's fiscal year runs from October 1 through September 30. The vast majority of operations in criminal justice continue from year to year, and so the implementation of the budget for these organizations holds few surprises. New staff might be hired or computers purchased in our transitional house for juvenile boys, but normal operations are not disrupted much by the implementation of the budget. It is when new programs are funded or initiatives pursued that the agency feels the jolt and then the urgency that an infusion of, or reduction in, money brings. If, for instance, our transition program was funded to add more treatment space and programming, staff would need to undertake a number of tasks to ensure that expansion is accomplished. For instance, implementation of the budget will possibly require the construction of the space, and hiring and scheduling of new staff (for examples, see also Winkler and Smith 2006). The development of a curriculum or curriculums may also be necessary. Usually all this activity will happen within the span of that budget year, if so specified in the budget plan.

The final stage in the budget process is the audit or evaluation. Typically, organizations of any size will employ internal or external financial auditors to go over their books to ensure that money budgeted for certain programs and activities was spent as intended. Even small organizations, if they are wise, will subject themselves to this kind of review. Some criminal justice organizations will also employ program auditors who, after examining the operation of a program, will make an assessment of its relative success. Both financial and program auditing are very important for at least the following reasons: They can help catch, reduce, or prevent corruption; they can improve financial and program records; they give successful programs some leverage in making their budgeting case to their funding agency; and they provide the organization with the information it needs to make valid budgeting decisions.

Some things to remember about public sector budgeting

According to several authors of articles and books on budgeting, there are at least four central facts to remember about all budgets in the public sector that have remained true for some time (Blomquist *et al.* 2004; Ebdon and Franklin 2004; Graham and Hays 1986; Key 1940; Lauth 2003; Nice 2002; Padovani and Young 2012; Poulson 2001; Pyhrr 1977; Schick 1966; Whisenand and Ferguson 1996, 2002):

1   As budgets are created in a political and economic environment, they are products of that environment.
2   Budgets are a mix of science and art.
3   Budgets, as political documents, reflect to some extent public priorities.
4   There is always more demand for public resources than there are resources.

Item 1 means that decisions about the funding of criminal justice agencies are always taken by political actors (Nice 2002). For instance, budgets for sheriff's departments are typically determined and appropriated by elected county commissioners (usually based in large part on agency head proposals). Likewise, budgets at the county and city level for police, city and county courts, jails, detention centers, and juvenile probation and parole organizations (often through the county courts) are mulled over and funded by county commissions and city councils/city managers who are either elected or politically appointed.

For much of the twentieth century, funding criminal justice agencies was not always seen as politically popular, and some agencies were underfunded. As a result, inmates languished in overcrowded facilities, people received little meaningful supervision by community corrections officers, police were unable to investigate all serious crimes, court dockets were overflowing, there were few programs or staff in juvenile or adult institutions, pay was poor, and facilities were nonexistent or falling down. Not surprisingly, these factors led to infamous abuses in any number of agencies and allowed serious offenders to remain on the streets to wreak additional havoc and pain. In the 1980s, as political priorities shifted and lawsuits forced funding, a building and hiring boom in many agencies began, and continues today (Austin and Irwin 2001; Campbell 2003; Wallace *et al.* 1995).

Relatedly, as mentioned in item 2, budgets are a mix of science and art (Nice 2002). The science these days lies in basing the budget on some definable, and even measurable, public good. If a jail is double- or triple-bunked with serious and repeat offenders, then some public good, such as continued public safety, would be achieved by floating a bond to fund construction of a new jail or expansion of the current one. The science comes in when the jail and those who oversee and set its budget (often county commissioners) study its practices, and those of related entities such as the courts and the police, to determine whether that need for space (population forecasting) and funding is real or whether some changes could be made to avert putting more money into the jail (for examples, see also Surette *et al.* 2006). Similarly, if that jail is interested in adding a drug and alcohol program for its long-term residents, it might seek funding at the local level or a grant from the state or the federal government, which in turn may allocate such money based on reigning political priorities (balancing treatment and security concerns, for instance). The "art" in all this is related to negotiating in the political realm to get the funding that is needed for current programs and priorities, while not neglecting to garner funds for any initiatives on the horizon.

Which means, as was noted in item 3, that budgets reflect public priorities (Blomquist *et al.* 2004; Ebdon and Franklin 2004; Nice 2002). Politicians, though often beholden to powerful political interests that are not aligned with everyday citizens, still have to be elected. When jockeying for votes, political actors will tend to shape their message to fit what they believe the public views as important. If the public is concerned about crime, as many polls indicated in the 1980s and 1990s (Merlo and Benekos 2000), the politicians will respond by funding criminal justice agencies more. It is not a coincidence that a building boom in corrections and increased hiring in police and prosecutor's offices in the 1980s and 1990s (and continuing in some jurisdictions) tracked public support and concern about crime control (Austin and Irwin 2001; Wallace *et al.* 1995).

Lipsky (1980) made a point similar to our item 4: There is always more demand for resources in the public sector than there are resources. This is a point that particularly applies to public sector criminal justice agencies, as the clients of these agencies tend to be poor, to have less education than is the norm, and to be "nonvoluntary": That is, they usually did not ask for contact with a criminal justice actor, though the actions of offenders have dictated their entrance into the system. In other words, putting aside what the clients of criminal justice agencies did, this population is relatively powerless and sometimes cannot vote, even when released from incarceration. The clients' relatives and friends may be able to vote, but often they do not. So with a public good like safety prominently on voters' and politicians' minds, coupled with more recent concerns about the costs, criminal justice funding and practice can be affected.

For example, according to data provided by the Judicial Council of California, the number of court filings in Superior or trial courts in California involving criminal and civil cases increased by 14 percent and 6 percent, respectively, from 2002 to 2011 (Judicial Council of California 2012: 73, 76). During this same time period the number of filings per judicial position increased by about 6 percent, which means that not enough judges were hired to keep up with the increased caseloads (Judicial Council of California 2012: 72). Though a distinctive state in many ways, what is happening in California courts is representative of what is occurring in courts across the nation. The use of courts, particularly when involving criminal matters, continues to rise, but not enough judges or other court personnel are being hired to handle those increases.

Large caseloads appear to be a theme not just for the courts, but also for other sectors of the system. According to a study done by the American Probation and Parole Association (2007: 44), 68 percent of the respondents thought their caseload was too large for community corrections officers. In fact, the average caseload they reported for officers was 106 offenders, whereas the optimal caseload they identified was seventy-seven offenders (APPA 2007: 44). The authors of the study and the respondents acknowledged that in reality what this means is that most offenders on these caseloads are not being supervised with any regularity. As some of these offenders will never commit another crime, or may do something that is a less serious threat to public safety, their lack of supervision is not of much consequence. It is these officers' need to focus on the more serious and violent offenders which concerned the respondents to the APPA survey, as high caseloads make it more difficult to respond to such offenders. In other words, public safety is compromised by the politically, and economically, determined decision to increase the number of crimes that require a prison sentence (drug crimes come to mind), but also by decisions to release people from overcrowded prisons, not to build more prisons, and then to release offenders out onto the streets with virtually no supervision. Based on all these complicated reasons, the status of clients, the politics of crime, the tightness of budgets, the input of a public both concerned for public safety and balking at higher taxes, there is always more demand for resources than there are resources.

Recent history of budgeting and planning

Given the foregoing budgeting maxims, let us consider some recent history on the topic. Recall that before the reform of public agencies, contracts, and hiring ushered in by the civil service reforms, public sector agencies were openly ruled by the politics of the day (see the discussion of this matter in Chapter 2). Political ideology and connections, before the twentieth century, had a much greater impact on the operation of public sector agencies than is true today, though—as mentioned earlier—that political influence is still quite apparent in budget determinations. Corruption and misspending of public funds made the need to control budgets and prevent their abuse a major concern for those in the policymaking and management spheres (Schick 1966). An adherence to Taylorism in management, with its emphasis on control, also influenced the reformation of budgeting determinations. Budgeting was to be done by rote, in a dry and objective fashion. This approach is known as **line item budgeting**, which we will discuss shortly. Tradition has some influence in determining what was funded: If it was funded last year, then it should be funded this year, with perhaps a bit more thrown in to cover inflation. In other words, formally, budgeting was very controlled and was regarded as a very staid and predictable process; the political and economic influences that inevitably intruded were little recognized in the literature on budgeting.

Key (1940), writing over sixty years ago, lamented what he regarded as "a lack of budgetary theory" in his article by the same name. He noted that the prevailing thought about budgeting at the time was consumed with a concern over technique (i.e., forms and their structure), with little attention or recognition of the influence of politics and economics. In contrast, he defined the budgetary process and document as "[a] judgement upon how scarce means should be allocated to bring the maximum return in social utility" (Key 1940: 117). He argued that determining the "social utility" of a given public program was not that difficult, but that budget analysts and managers needed more standardized ways to evaluate and guide choices. He urged such folks to consider the merits or return in social utility of a program and to not be afraid to decrease or end programs that do not yield such benefits.

Schick built on the work of Key when he wrote more than twenty years later that budgeting should be a systematic process that is related to planned objectives: "In this important sense there is a bit of PPB (planning, programming, budgeting) in every budget system" (Schick 1966: 300). He thought that budgeting should involve strategic planning, which considers the objectives and resources of the organization in tandem, as well as the policies that govern the resources. He also believed in management and operational control to ensure task efficiency in operation, to monitor resource acquisition, and to avoid the misuse or abuse of resources. He thought the "watchdog" approach taken by managers married to line item budgeting was an understandable reaction to the graft and corruption that prevailed in the public sector in the nineteenth century. Because the potential for abuse still exists, Schick did not advocate that public sector agencies abandon the controls and oversight of budgets, hence his emphasis on operational and management control; he did, however, think the agencies should lighten up a bit. He thought the line item analysis and work-cost assessments were appropriate tasks for the mid managers, but that top-level managers in the organizations should take a "big-picture" approach to planning and budgeting. Keep in mind that the big-picture approach is analogous of the systems perspective we discussed in Chapter 4, in that top-level managers must be able to understand and react to environmental, external, and internal demands or processes, output, and feedback, and then make adjustments according to such information.

Schick (1966) notes that as we became more sophisticated in economic analysis and informational acquisition in the 1960s, long-range planning for organizations became more doable. His central message was that managers needed to plan and analyze more, or pay attention to the forest as well as the trees.

In the 1970s an innovation in budgeting, perhaps reflective of the fiscal crisis looming at the national level, became popular and was premised on the ability to effectively analyze budgetary and program data. That innovation, which was wildly popular at first, was **zero-based budgeting**. Two questions are addressed under zero-based budgeting (Pyhrr 1977: 496):

1 Are the current activities efficient and effective?
2 Should current activities be eliminated or reduced to fund higher priority new programs or to reduce the current budget?

The appeal of this approach to budgeting was its fiscal conservatism and its related emphasis on limiting governmental growth. Every program would be examined for its social utility (as Key would have defined it) and for its performance as that related to cost. Programs that did not pass muster or produce results would be eliminated or have their funding reduced. Zero-based budgeting requires that program managers defend their entire budgetary appropriation for each year.

Zero-based budgeting became a true budgeting fad, in that it was first adopted by Texas Instruments in 1969 and then by Governor Jimmy Carter for the state of Georgia (Pyhrr 1977). After Carter was elected president in 1976, the use of zero-based budgeting spread to the federal government, and several other states and localities eventually adopted its principles (see Box 11.2).

Then reality set in. Despite its appeal, zero-based budgeting has a number of problems, the most damning of which is the lack of an easy way to know whether a program is "working." There are problems in defining performance (what is good, what is bad, what is mediocre) and appropriate costs for public sector or public sanctioned programs, such as the courts. Moreover, though part of the appeal of zero-based budgeting was its promised limits on government, carrying out thorough evaluations of program performance is ironically very costly. Moreover, an outcome evaluation requires good solid data on every program, and such information does not always exist in the real world. Finally, some pieces of programs are not measurable. How does one define and measure "justice" in the courtroom, for instance? How about rehabilitation? Is the true measure of rehabilitation only absence of recidivism? What about new programs? Are they likely to produce outcomes in the span of months or a year that would justify their continued existence?

Imagine a court administrator or a judge who could avoid budget cuts only by defending all her programs, every year, for funding (see Box 11.2). Imagine the funding bodies having to review every little program to determine its value. Imagine the redundancy and tedium in this whole process. Simply put, zero-based budgeting was great in theory, but in practice it was unintentionally costly and time-consuming. Not surprisingly, it was quickly abandoned by most organizations once these realities set in, although it is still used, at least to some extent, in some communities.

In the 1980s and 1990s budgeting continued to emphasize controls, as represented by line item budgets and audits, but with planning. Thus around this time **planning, programming, budgeting systems (PPBS) budgeting** came into vogue (Graham and Hays 1986; Whisenand and Ferguson 2002). **Budgeting by objective** (BBO) **budgeting** also became popular as the sister of the managing-by-objective (MBO) movement (as described in Chapter 4) during this time period. As with MBO, BBO involves greater input from organizational members into a central part of organizational operation: developing, implementing, and evaluating the budget.

Box 11.2 Zero-based budgeting is enjoying a resurgence in popularity

Due to the work involved in justifying each program, zero-based budgeting for the most part fell into disfavor and disuse for a large part of two decades. Increasingly, however, there is a movement by some lawmakers in states and counties to use zero-based budgeting as a means of cutting government programs. The city of Phoenix, the state of Georgia, and Montgomery County, Pennsylvania have all incorporated zero-based budgeting in the review of at least some of their programs in the last few years (Bonner 2012; Bui 2011; DeHuff 2012; Jones 2011). Usually the adoption of such budgeting, if utilized widely, can be quite controversial, because the decision about whether to fund or not fund certain programs is a political decision as much as a cost-cutting one (Jones 2011).

One County Commissioner in Ada County, Idaho argued that zero-based budgeting did not yield the predicted savings when his county tried it. The county commissioners of Ada County, Idaho used both zero-based and expenditure control (aka mission-driven) budgeting systems in the 1980s and early 1990s. According to a former county commissioner, Roger Simmons, it didn't work very well (Simmons 2001: 8):

> Zero-based budgeting sounds great in theory. But theory is not reality. There are several reasons why zero-base hasn't worked in government budgeting. Zero-based requires department supervisors to start at zero each year and justify every expenditure to the county commissioners. The reality is that any qualified supervisor knows their department's needs far better than the commissioners. Meanwhile, each supervisor, in hopes of funding what they consider to be legitimate needs, argues furiously for every expenditure. That, unfortunately, puts them in an untenable position when it comes to saving. As they approach the end of the fiscal year, they start looking for ways to spend their entire budget. They do that, not because they are bad people, but they are stuck in a system that encourages it.

This is because, as Commissioner Simmons argues, if they don't spend that money then they won't be believed when they ask for the money again next year. Moreover, should they save money, it is pooled and may be given to departments that are less frugal. Commissioner Simmons (2001: 8) concludes by saying, "In all the years Ada County used zero-base, we saved nothing—nothing."

In contrast, he notes that after the county moved to an expenditure control budgeting system, it did save money. "Under expenditure-control budgeting, each department is allowed to roll over 75 percent of its savings into the next budget year, thus eliminating the 'spend it or lose it' philosophy that prevails in zero-base. In Ada County, under expenditure control, we have been rolling over on average of about $3 million in savings each year" (Simmons 2001: 8).

Both initiatives, PPBS and BBO, represent an attempt to rationalize budgets and to tie them to the strategic plan and identifiable and measurable objectives (BBO). As such, both represent an attempt to insert more science and less art into the budgeting process.

Another initiative, **mission-driven budgeting** (aka expenditure control budgeting), is touted as a way of combining some of the science of the PPBS and MBO approaches with the input of workers, while rewarding frugality and keeping the realities of taxpayer revolts and worker calculations in mind (Whisenand and Ferguson 1996). Under a mission-driven budget, each unit and its actors engage in developing a budget that is submitted to a department head. The budget for the organization will be allowed to grow only by the amount of inflation and the amount of community growth. Units that save money from year to year are allowed to keep all or a portion of those savings to reinvest in program activities. As funding is allocated in a lump sum, not line item, determination of how the money is to be spent rests with each unit, or those closest to the program delivery.

The beauty of this approach is that it averts the well-known problem of federal or state managers and workers trying to spend all of their allocation by the end of the budget year to ensure that their budget request for next year can be at the same or a higher level. One cannot blame these workers. They know that they might well need the extra funds next year, even if they did not spend their whole allocation this year. But they will not be able to justify a budget request in the same amount if they had money left over this year. Mission-driven budgeting allows these workers to hoard their funds for next year, thus rewarding frugality, and allowing them to use the funds where they were most needed.

Whisenand and Ferguson (2002), in their book on police management, nicely summarize six budgeting approaches used by both public and private agencies.

1   Line item budgets: These are budgets that are largely based on previous budgets. Each unit of an organization may have input about a given line item. This budget approach is focused on keeping costs down, or at least stable. There is not much attention paid to performance or to public need, and ongoing program costs are allowed to continue.
2   Performance budgets: This approach is focused on measuring the performance of a program. Unfortunately, the output of some organizations is not easily quantifiable, though output for some programs may be.
3   Planning, programming, budgeting systems: This approach ties all parts of the organization, its present and future plans, together with its budget proposal, funding, and implementation. The difficulty with this system, as with performance budgets, is that it requires the generation and review of so much data on programs that it can become overwhelming to use a full-scale PPBS approach for an organization. Also, good data may not be available. This process tends to put budgeting in

the hands of technically oriented people who collect and analyze data (i.e., those who can generate and examine statistics).

4   Program or outcome budgets and/or budgeting by objectives: This approach allows for much more input by each unit in the development of the budget or that pesky human element again (recall this discussion as part of the management theories reviewed in Chapter 4). Activities are related to outcomes, but decision making is also allowed at the unit level.

5   Zero-based budgeting: This approach requires that you start with a clean budgetary slate every year. Much data must be collected every year to justify the continued funding of each program. The approach is time-consuming and costly, hence very difficult to implement.

6   Mission-driven budgeting or expenditure control budgeting: This approach, suggested by Whisenand and Ferguson (1996), focuses on limiting expenditure growth to inflation and community growth, retaining year-end savings in organizations to encourage frugality, and basing funding on lump sums, not line items, to allow program employees some decision-making autonomy. These authors like it because they believe it "[p]romotes sound management, simplifies the budget process, focuses on the big picture, restores trust in the budget process and promotes savings" (Whisenand and Ferguson 1996: 314–315). The problem with mission-driven budgeting is that there appears to be no formal approach to performance or outcome evaluation. Despite the difficulty of these activities, the truth is that in an environment of tight budgeting, program performance cannot be ignored, even as one acknowledges that it can't always be assessed effectively, either. But the problems in evaluation of effectiveness do not justify the skirting of the issue altogether.

In reality, most budgeting processes include a mix of these approaches. Because of accounting principles, it is difficult to believe that the basis for most budgets should be anything but line item. Indeed, line item budgets can be the rampart for other budgets that are more focused on performance, planning, and outcomes and that allow for more employee input (Blomquist *et al.* 2004: Ebdon and Franklin 2004). Many governmental agencies use a form of zero-based budgeting for some limited types of programming, however, despite the problems (Simmons 2001).

Budget strategies

At the beginning of his book *Public Budgeting*, Nice (2002: 10–13) outlines ten different strategies that organizations and interested stakeholders adopt to increase their success in influencing budgetary decisions. These strategies, which may come in handy for managers and/or for those who study criminal justice organizations, are briefly discussed next.

Cultivating client support

The first strategy mentioned by Nice (2002) is cultivating client support. As a democratically operated organization presupposes some client input, some organizational scholars believe that both support and input by clients are just a given in the development of a healthy budget (Blomquist *et al.* 2004; Ebdon and Franklin 2004). The clients of criminal justice enterprises in this case, and as defined by Nice, might be conceived broadly. They could include community members, suspects, clients, inmates, and supervisees; in budgetary matters, however, they are more likely to include employees and administrators, the pertinent elected representatives in both the legislative and executive branches of government, and the general public. For instance, if the Department of Corrections in a given state were interested in building a work release facility in a community, it would behoove the administrators to solicit the support, and input, of those most affected by it. At a minimum the DOC would need to garner support from the larger community, but particularly prospective neighbors, local leaders such as the mayor and/or county commissioners, state legislators in that district, and the governor's office—not necessarily in this order.

Gaining the trust of others and documenting a need

It should be a given in public service that one acts with honesty and integrity in all interactions (see the discussion of ethics in Chapter 3). Unfortunately, experience teaches us that this expectation of the "honest broker" is not always realized in either public or private sector work. Ideally and over the long term, however, being honest and upfront about factual matters usually pays off in a number of ways. In our work release example, the DOC should bring together all the affected persons and discuss with them the need for, costs of, and likely consequences of building and maintaining the work release. After all the facts are on the table, and the DOC has brought all the arguments and evidence to bear, the department may well fail to convince the appropriate parties that a work release is necessary at this time. But in subsequent discussions on the need for a work release, and other topics, the DOC is more likely to be believed and supported because its representatives are thought to operate with integrity.

Looking for sympathetic decision makers

That said there is nothing wrong with approaching the decision makers who are most inclined to be receptive and who are willing to advocate for your organization's budgetary initiative. As Nice indicates, if one branch of government is not likely to be supportive, the other branches and/or public support can be solicited. Nice (2002: 11) points out that "[w]ith many decision-making arenas and many decision makers, people may shop around for the decision they want."

Coping with painful actions and minimizing the risk of future cuts

In tight budgetary times, when all levels of government are forced to consider and reconsider funding options, Nice (2002) argues that agencies tend to develop strategies to avoid or reduce cuts. When painful cuts are threatened, he notes that agencies may tend to blame others for the budget crisis. They may also cut less visible positions or programs, and/or do the opposite and cut those that are popular to raise the ire of the program supporters. Another strategy which organizations sometimes employ to minimize the risk or threat of cuts at such times is to quickly spend the monies they have, to avoid having to return them to the state. Another tactic is to pad the original budget proposal with the understanding that less essential items may have to be cut later.

The camel's nose

A different budgetary strategy might be employed when an organization is starting or enhancing a program. Nice (2002) observes that in such instances, some organizations may tend to de-emphasize the eventual cost of a program by asking for a small amount in the first couple of years and escalating the amount of their requests later as the program becomes more popular. This tactic is premised on the belief that a small allotment is less likely to alarm decision makers and that incremental increases in funding will be the norm.

Making the program appear to be self-supporting

Funding for a program/policy or agency may be justified if it is partly self-funded. For instance, adding state patrol officers might appear more palatable to decision makers budgetwise if the director can argue that the new hires' salaries will be partly supported by increased tickets paid by traffic violators.

Capitalizing on temporary circumstances

Some programs and organizations can effectively argue for more money in their budgets in the immediate aftermath of a crisis (Nice 2002). This phenomenon has occurred in corrections on many occasions in reaction to such events as riots and court orders to remedy conditions of confinement and practices. Correctional managers are quite cognizant of the advantages that such events can produce. For instance, one of the authors attended a conference organized by the National Institute of Corrections for progressive jail managers in 1992. Some of the participating managers wondered aloud how they could get the staff, training, capital inflow for buildings, and programs for inmates from their county budgets if the ability of inmates to sue the jail was decreased. This is not to say that they liked being sued per se, but the prospect of lawsuits gave them leverage to argue for the funds they needed to properly run their jails.

Deception and confusion

Though he does not recommend such strategies for garnering more resources, Nice (2002) recognizes that some organizations will engage in deception and confusion to increase or maintain their budget. To that end, agency representatives may hide information in their budget, provide misinformation, or engage in doublespeak by telling decision makers that the money will be used for something other than what they intend it for. In this sense, the ignorance about the agency or organization of those in the public and among the decision makers can be used to advantage to conceal budget priorities unlikely to meet with general approval.

An additional strategy: Agency consolidation

It is an accepted truism about criminal justice practice that most things are local. We have city/county/state policing, corrections, and courts (as well as federal, but that is not local!) that vary widely from jurisdiction to jurisdiction and so reflect, to some extent, the local character and culture of each area. The problem is that there is a great deal of duplication of costs when we have each a separate administrative staff for every little city and county criminal justice agency (not to mention state). We also have overlapping services, and thus duplicated costs, when jurisdictions overlap geographically, as they commonly do when cities grow big enough to occupy most of counties. In Box 11.4 Scott Sotebeer discusses why consolidation of some of these agencies and services makes real fiscal sense for some of these localities.

Conclusions

Those unfamiliar with organizational operations often regard strategic planning and budgeting as dry and irrelevant exercises. If you have ever gotten a raise, or not gotten one, because of the political or economic environment, or if your program funding was cut or increased for the same reason, you quickly begin to appreciate the relevancy of these organizational functions. How does one, as a political leader or a policymaker, make a bureaucracy more responsive? The answer is cut, or threaten to cut, the agency's budget, forcing a change in plans. Bureaucrats, or wannabe bureaucrats, are also positively influenced (read: Motivated!) by budget increases. Planning and budgeting really are at the center of all things organizational.

The types of budgeting discussed in this chapter reflect the various approaches and techniques that have been attempted over time. The attempts to both control and evaluate budgeting decisions in the twentieth century were a laudable improvement over public sector operation of the 1800s. Criminal justice organizations interested in twenty-first-century practice and with improved access to information will likely be increasingly called upon to evaluate and assess their programs' success, and to tie each budget to a strategic plan that outlines the organization's future.

Part of that plan, if even at the informal level, involves strategies to maintain or increase the organization's budget and/or to make that budget stretch through the consolidation of agencies and services at the local level. Some of these strategies, as outlined by Nice (2002) and Sotebeer (in Box 11.3), reflect real-world efforts to secure funding for criminal justice agencies.

Box 11.3 Government Consolidation 101

Changing the business model of local government

M. Scott Sotebeer, PhD, CEO

USA Strategics, www.usastrategics.com

The extended recession is accelerating a serious problem with local governments: Budget cuts, layoffs, wage and benefit freezes or reductions, and outright city (town, borough, or village) bankruptcies are happening everywhere. The costs associated with operating local government are outstripping the amounts coming in—and taxpayers have made it clear that they will not continue to pay more and more for government. As a result, some states and a growing number of local governments have begun to aggressively merge operations and create regional partnerships as a way to save money and sustain basic services. The practice is often referred to as shared services or consolidation.

Actions by the federal government indicate that resources flowing to states are most likely to be severely reduced this year and in the foreseeable future. That impacts the flow of money to local governments. In other words, it is likely to get worse at the state and local level as nationally, most states get as much as 30 percent of their general budget from the federal government in a variety of forms (from Medicaid reimbursement to highway, parks, and other types of grant money). The problem is not going away and will not fix itself on its own.

The immediate problem with our local government setup is primarily driven by redundant administrative infrastructures. It is easy to understand by doing simple math: In my county, we have thirty-nine individual cities with separate police, fire, EMS, parks, library, roads, and other departments—all duplicated to some degree by the county and, in many cases, federal agencies as well. We most likely do not need fewer police officers or parks maintenance workers for the same geographic region because most governments have already significantly cut these types of department workers in the past several years. But in the twenty-first century, there is neither an arguable need nor financial justification for duplicated administrative structures. Our current small government structure is a post-WWII growth and expansion model that has been in place for over sixty years.

The other problem is that in many states, there are too many independent taxing districts that function as separate units of government. Fire, cemetery, PSAP (911 and emergency call centers), library, sewer, school, and many others all get funding from individual households through various taxing structures. Most have some sort of governing board or commission, and the ability to extract increasing amounts of revenue from the public. The various layers are evident when looking at a cable TV, cell phone, public utility, energy, or property tax assessment.

As one example, we have over 6,000 emergency 911 call centers in the US. They all have independent taxing authority. Most have separate governance boards and complete managerial infrastructures and the real estate and operational/administrative overhead to go with it. Communications experts will argue that there should be no more than one to five 911 call centers per individual state. We need the call receivers to take the calls—but not the redundant infrastructures.

Law enforcement and the criminal justice system are generally the single biggest drain on local budgets. Contracting police services between a county and a city, or between cities, as one of several models, has shown to save from 20 to 34 percent annually. Other strategies in use nationally in a variety of service areas also work.

Consolidation has been around for a long time—but it is the "renewed" strategy that might be the answer for some communities to cut costs, protect services, and stabilize community budgets for the long haul. Consolidation has several forms:

1   Merger: Two or more departments combine under a single banner to form a single department serving a larger area and population.

2   Shared services: Two or more departments in a region collaborate on any number of operations.
3   Contracting: One department contracts to provide services for another unit of government. Usually from a county to a city—but not always. Types of government units (townships, villages, towns, cities, boroughs, etc.) vary from state to state.
4   Regionalization or metropolitan arrangements: Several agencies reconstruct themselves legally into one new, regional organization (Las Vegas, Louisville, Indianapolis, Salt Lake City, and Northern York County, PA have done this in policing. Other examples exist in fire, courts, watershed, sewer, library districts, and others).

The most common areas of opportunity for consolidation

* Criminal justice, including police, courts, EMS, and related services
* 911 call centers*
* Roads*
* Parks and recreation*
* Solid waste
* Public works
* Libraries*
* Health/human services*
* Non-criminal prosecutorial/legal services
* Finance
* Human resources
* IT management/records
* School districts*
* Assessor
* Fire departments & fire districts*
* Cemetery and other specialty purpose districts
* Cooperative purchasing.

*may include taxing authority that could be reprogrammed, redistributed, or eliminated

Common concerns—the things that most often surface as objections to consolidation

* Loss of local control (someone else is running my show and making my decisions).
* Loss of identity (this is no longer OUR city's police department).

- Personality and quality of citizen contact (Officer Friendly has left the building).
- Unions/complex contracts (how are all workers affected by change?).
- Lack of political cooperation- (no one [politicians] wants to "give up the kingdom").
- Potential for complex legislative hurdles (does state law and county/city code allow for this?).
- Loss of services (what are we giving up to save money?).
- Cost of change and threat of "buyer's remorse"— there may be no turning back.

Universal advantages—where consolidation works well, there are some common themes and outcomes

- Economies of scale—if all the math works, the idea is that the same number of resources (people/things) can provide a given level of service over a larger geographic area at a lower per-unit cost.
- Lower cost per capita—total per household cost is possible across a broader population base when the right model is used. It should be a measure and goal of a consolidation.
- Risk is spread—this is a major issue for small cities/communities. Insurance and other liability expenses (employee lawsuits, for example) can be spread out in most service partnership deals.
- Improved uniformity, consistency, and coordination of services— the research supports that a region of partners can have a better level of service through uniform policies and management.
- Improvement in personnel (more job competition).
- Improved management and supervision (more job competition).
- Improved training and expanded personnel opportunities (specific to police, fire, and most high-cost, skilled service workers).

Consolidation, when it works, provides for important options to local communities:

1 It can act as a stop-gap to serious financial decline or (local government) bankruptcy;
2 It can simply stop the decline of critical services (parks closed, police officers cut, libraries closed, school programs cut, roads maintenance deferred, etc.);
3 It can provide for better services, depending on the model;

4   It can provide communities the opportunity to "repurpose" financial resources found through savings.

Consolidation is not a magic fix. It is not a guarantee. It is a decision-
making and analytical process designed to help communities survive.

Exercise: develop a criminal justice budget

The goal of this group exercise is to acquaint participants with the
likely costs of doing business in criminal justice. Here is one thing
to remember: It almost always costs more than you think—unless, of
course, you happen to be familiar with police, courts, or corrections
budgets! The following steps will allow folks to reconcile their projections with reality.

1   Divide the participants into manageable groups of four or five.
These always seem to work best if people in each group choose
specific tasks (there can be more than one person assigned to each
task) and are held responsible for them. In this exercise, specific
tasks might include doing the web research, writing the report,
and presenting the report. Ask the groups to do the following.
2   Choose a type of criminal justice agency, institution, or program in
a city or state, and devise a budget for it. (The group may need to
choose more than one city or state, as not all have their budgets
available on the web). Hint: States and large cities and counties are
more likely to post their budgets on the web.
3   Make an extensive and detailed list of likely expenses for the chosen agency, institution, or program (there should be 20–40 items
listed).
4   Assign yearly costs to each of these budget items. To do this for
some items on their list, it may be necessary to figure out the daily
costs and then project the amount for the year. For instance, a
group could calculate the costs of supervising one client on probation, multiply that by 365, and then multiply the product by the
number of clients supervised in that community. Costs of buildings, and so on, can more easily be estimated by year. It is okay to
make a reasonable guess. That is part of the fun!
5   Search the website chosen for the state or locality, and locate the
posted budget. Again, not all states and localities post this material, so the group may have to use more than one resource. Also
remember that some agencies and facilities are managed only by

a certain level of government. Usually cities do not manage prisons and, with a few exceptions, states do not manage jails. Cities, counties, states, and the federal government all have some form of law enforcement. Adult probation and parole usually are handled at the state or federal level, and juvenile probation/ parole and detention at the county or city level. Courts are funded at the local, state, or federal level, depending on type.

6 Examine the most recent posted budget and compare the items to the preliminary budget. Make changes in item categories of the preliminary budget so that they are comparable with the "real" budget, but do not change the figures.

7 Write a brief report (3–5 pages) on the "budget development process" that your group engaged in and include an analysis of the preliminary and real budgets. Be sure to note the differences and similarities between the budgets and try to explain them. Also report on whether there were any surprises for the group upon examining the two budgets in tandem.

8 Present the report to the larger group and discuss.

Discussion questions

1 What are the four stages of the budgeting process, and how might politics intrude in each? Give an example for each one.

2 Why is budgeting regarded as both a science and an art? Explain your answer.

3 Where is planning likely to falter and why? Explain your answer and offer some examples.

4 What are the four things to remember about budgeting, and how are they related to the four stages of budgeting and the budgeting approaches discussed in this chapter?

5 What do you think are the most important matters to consider in the development of a plan and a budget for a criminal justice organization? Why?

6 What groups do you think are most represented in the development of criminal justice plans and budgets? Why? Explain your answer.

7 What groups do you think are least represented in the development of criminal justice plans and budgets? Why? Explain your answer.

8   Which budgeting approach appeals to you? Why?
9   Why are auditing and/or evaluation important in the opera-
     tion of public and private sector criminal justice? Explain your
     answer.

Key terms

budget: a summary of expenses for a given program or organization.
inflation: "the overall general upward price movement of goods
     and services in an economy" (US Department of Labor (2007:
     www.dol.gov/dol/topic/statistics/inflation.htm).
line item budgets: budgets largely based on previous budgets. Each unit
     of an organization may have input about a given line item. This
     budget approach is focused on keeping costs down, or at least sta-
     ble. There is not much attention paid to performance or to public
     need, and ongoing program costs are allowed to continue.
mission-driven budgeting or expenditure control budgeting: an
     approach suggested by Whisenand and Ferguson (1996) that
     focuses on limiting expenditure growth to inflation and community
     growth, retaining year-end savings in organizations to encourage
     frugality, and funding on the basis of lump sums, not line item, to
     allow program employees some decision-making autonomy.
performance budgets: budgetary approach focused on measur-
     ing the performance of a program. Unfortunately, the output
     of some organizations is not easily quantifiable, though that of
     some programs might be.
planning, programming, budgeting systems: an approach that ties all
     parts of the organization, its present, and its future plans together
     with its budget proposal, funding, and implementation.
program or outcome budgets and/or budgeting by objectives: this
     approach allows for much more input by each unit in the devel-
     opment of the budget or that pesky human element again.
     Activities are related to outcomes, but decision making is also
     allowed at the unit level.
strategic planning: "[a] disciplined effort to produce fundamental
     decisions and actions that shape and guide what an organization
     is, what it does, and why it does it" (Bryson 1995: 4–5).
zero-based budgeting: the approach that requires starting with a clean
     slate every year. Much data must be collected every year to justify
     the continued funding of each program. This time-consuming
     and costly approach is very difficult to implement.

References

American Probation and Parole Association (APPA) (2007) Probation and parole's growing caseloads and workload allocation: Strategies for managerial decision making. Available at www.appa-net.org/eweb/docs/appa/pubs/SMDM.pdf (last accessed January 31, 2013).

Austin, J. and Irwin, J. (2001) *It's about time: America's imprisonment binge*, 3rd edn. Belmont, CA: Wadsworth/Thomson Learning.

Blomquist, G. C., Newsome, M. A. and Stone, D. B. (2004) Public preferences for program tradeoffs: Community values for budget priorities. *Public Budgeting and Finance*, 24(1): 50–71.

Bonner, J. (2012) Zero-based budgeting resurfaces. Georgia Public Broadcasting. Available at www.gpb.org/news/2012/01/17/zero-based-budgeting resurfaces (last accessed January 31, 2013).

Bryson, J. M. (1995) *Strategic planning for public and nonprofit organizations*. San Francisco, CA: Jossey-Bass.

Bui, L. (2011) Phoenix lays plans for zero-based budgeting: Spending controversies mark transparency push. *The Arizona Republic*. Available at www.azcentral.com/news/articles/2011/06/25/20110625phoenix-budget-plan zero-based-budgeting.html (last accessed January 31, 2013).

Campbell, R. (2003) Dollars and sentences: Legislators' views on prisons, punishment, and the budget crisis. The Vera Institute of Justice. Available at www.vera.org/publications (last accessed January 31, 2013).

DeHuff, J. (2012) Montco commissioners unveil 2013 "zero-based budget." *Montgomery News*. Available at www.montgomerynews.com/articles/2012/11/18/montgomery_life/news/doc50a 38d9a0baf999028939.txt?viewmode=2 (last accessed January 31, 2013).

Ebdon, C. and Franklin, A. (2004) Searching for a role for citizens in the budget process. *Public Budgeting and Finance*, 24(1): 32–49.

Florida Department of Juvenile Justice. (2013) Governor Scott's 2013–14 juvenile justice budget promotes reform, public safety. Available at www.djj.state.fl.us/news/press-releases/press-release-detail/2013/01/31/governor-scott-s-2013-14-juvenile-justice-budget-promotes-reform-public-safety (last accessed January 31, 2013).

Gaines, L. K., Worrall, J. L., Southerland, M. D. and Angell, J. E. (2003) *Police administration*, 2nd edn. New York, NY: McGraw-Hill.

Graham, C. B. and Hays, S. W. (1986) *Managing the public organization*. Washington, DC: Congressional Quarterly Press.

Hrebiniak, L. G. (2005) *Making strategy work: Leading effective execution and change*. Upper Saddle River, NJ: Wharton School Publishing.

Hudzik, J. K. and Cordner, G. W. (1983) *Planning in criminal justice organizations and systems*. New York, NY: Macmillan.

Jones, W. C. (2011) State's zero-based budgeting program to focus on education. *Athens Banner-Herald*. Available at http://onlineathens.com/local-news/2012-06-11/states-zero based-budgeting-program-focus-education (last accessed January 31, 2013).

Judicial Council of California. (2012) 2012 Court statistics report: Statewide caseload trends 2001–2002 through 2010–2011. Available at http://www.courts.ca.gov/documents/2012-Court-Statistics-Report.pdf (last accessed January 31, 2013).

Key, V. O. (1940) The lack of budgetary theory. In J. M. Shafritz and A. C. Hyde (eds), *Classics of public administration*. Chicago, IL: Dorsey Press, pp. 116–122.

Lauth, T. P. (2003) Budgeting during a recession phase of the business cycle: The Georgia experience. *Public Budgeting and Finance*, 23(2): 26–38.

Lipsky, M. (1980) *Street-level bureaucracy: Dilemmas of the individual in public services.* New York, NY: Russell Sage Foundation.

Merlo, A. V. and Benekos, P. J. (2000) *What's wrong with the criminal justice system: Ideology, politics and the media.* Cincinnati, OH: Anderson Publishing.

Nice, D. (2002) *Public budgeting.* Belmont, CA: Wadsworth/Thomson Learning.

Padovani, E. and Young, D.W. (2012) *Managing local governments: Designing management control systems that deliver value.* London: Routledge.

Poulson, B. W. (2001) Surplus expenditures: A case study of Colorado. *Public Budgeting and Finance*, 21(4): 18–43.

Pressman, J. L. and Wildavsky, A. (1973) *Implementation*, 2nd edn. Berkeley, CA: University of California Press.

Pyhrr, P. A. (1977) The zero-base approach to government budgeting. In J. M. Shafritz and A.C. Hyde (eds), *Classics of public administration*. Chicago, IL: Dorsey Press, 495–505.

Rothman, D. J. (1980) *Conscience and convenience: The asylum and its alternatives in progressive America.* Glenview, IL: Scott, Foresman.

Royce, D. (2003) State prisons lock up 3,000 new inmates. *The Miami Herald*, August 19. Available at www.MiamiHerald.com (last accessed January 31, 2013).

Schick, A. (1966) The road to PPB: The stages of budget reform. In J. M. Shafritz and A. C. Hyde (eds), *Classics of public administration*. Chicago, IL: Dorsey Press, pp. 299–318.

Simmons, R. (2001) Zero-based budgeting hasn't worked well for Ada County. *The Idaho Statesman*, June 8. Local: p. 8.

Smith, C. E. (1997) *Courts, politics, and the judicial process*, 2nd edn. Chicago, IL: Nelson-Hall.

Surette, R., Applegate, B., McCarthy, B. and Jablonski, P. (2006) Self-destructing prophecies: Long-term forecasting of municipal correctional bed need. *Journal of Criminal Justice*, 34: 57–72.

Swanson, C. R., Territo, L. and Taylor, R. W. (1998) *Police administration: Structures, processes and behavior*, 4th edn. Upper Saddle River, NJ: Prentice Hall.

United States Department of Justice. (2013) No title. Available at http://www.whitehouse.gov/sites/default/files/omb/budget/fy2012/assets/justice.pdf (last accessed January 31, 2013).

Wallace, H., Roberson, C. and Steckler, C. (1995) *Fundamentals of police administration.* Englewood Cliffs, NJ: Prentice Hall.

Welsh, W. N. and Harris, P. W. (1999) *Criminal justice policy and planning.* Cincinnati, OH: Anderson Publishing.

Whisenand, P. M. and Ferguson, R. F. (1996) *The managing of police organizations*, 4th edn. Upper Saddle River, NJ: Prentice Hall.

Whisenand, P. M. and Ferguson, R. F. (2002) *The managing of police organizations*, 5th edn. Upper Saddle River, NJ: Prentice Hall.

Winkler, G. and Smith, J. (2006) Long-term budgeting for operations in construction and design planning for jails. *American Jails*, 20(4): 53–55.

12 Decision making and prediction

To be, or not to be, that is the question: Whether 'tis nobler in the mind to suffer the slings and arrows of outrageous fortune, or to take arms against a sea of troubles, and by opposing end them?

Hamlet, Act III, Scene I

Ours is a time of uneasiness and indifference—not yet formulated in such ways as to permit the work of reason and the play of sensibility. Instead of troubles—defined in terms of values and threats—there is often the misery of vague uneasiness; instead of explicit issues there is often merely the beat feeling that all is somehow not right. Neither the values threatened nor whatever threatens them has been stated; in short, they have not been carried to the point of decision. Much less have they been formulated as problems of social science. ... The great sociologist C. Wright Mills comment[s] on the failure of social scientists to focus on core issues of "our times." Mills laments the jettisoning of reason and the failure to connect larger movements to individual existence.

(Mills 1959: 11)

Introduction

One of the most representative titles of a criminal justice textbook, in terms of its content, is *Screwing the System and Making It Work* (Jacobs 1990). In essence, this not so well-known book is about a juvenile probation officer faced daily with no-win decisions regarding resources and his clients. Jacobs routinely had to decide how to reconcile his desire to help his clients with the fact that he had limited time, too many probationers to supervise, and too few programmatic options to refer them to. What to do? What to do? Or: Not whether to be or not to be a probation officer (as Hamlet might ponder), but how to be an effective one.

Ultimately, the probation officer's decision was to "screw the system to make it work," or to truly focus his time and talents on only the few clients he deemed most in need of his services, reluctantly ignoring the rest. By making this Solomonic choice, he believed that he might be "screwing" the system and perhaps his more neglected clients, but "making it work" for the youths he could focus attention on. He was not necessarily "happy" or "satisfied" with this decision, but he believed it was the best he could do with limited resources.

Such a scenario—scarce resources and too many clients—is emblematic of social service work for SLBs, as discussed earlier with reference to the work of Lipsky (1980). This reality fits the work of criminal justice practitioners today as much as it did more than twenty-five years ago, when Lipsky published his classic work. As Mills wrote almost fifty years ago, there is a tendency in human history to fail to make the logical connection between what happens globally and the individual experience; yet the phenomena are inextricably intertwined: "Neither the life of an individual nor the history of a society can be understood without understanding both" (Mills 1959: 3). One global truth that fits public sector work with few exceptions is that resources are always short and demand is always great; the SLB must make a determination, a decision, about how to reconcile these conditions.

So, given these constraints, how do criminal justice practitioners and managers make decisions? What sorts of influences are likely to affect how they make those decisions? Do they always act as our erstwhile juvenile probation officer did, focusing their resources on the most deserving and hard cases? What sorts of factors are likely to hamper effective decision making, and to improve it?

In this chapter we review the act of decision making: What it is, obstacles to effective decision making, and how that act might be improved. In addition, and relatedly, we will discuss decisions of one type, namely predictions, exploring how they are made and the typical errors associated with them. On this note we will touch on how brain cognition, and thus decision making, may be influenced by biology and environment and the implications of these connections for criminal justice actors and their work.

Decisions, decisions, decisions: what they are and who makes them (the decision makers)

A **decision** is simply a choice made by a person who is given the *discretionary power* to do so. There can be alternate options available to the decision maker, or it may be that no other choices are apparent. In our example, the juvenile probation officer made a decision to concentrate his time and resources on certain probationers, rather than spreading himself too thin. But what if he had not done this? What if he had tried to serve all his clients by rationing out limited time and resources to offer a little bit to everyone? In other words, what if he had maintained the status quo? Would this have been a decision? The answer is yes, it would. People in the criminal justice system, and in all other aspects of their lives, are forever making decisions to maintain the current operations even when they might be flawed.

Effective decision making

With little reservation, we can assume that the majority of criminal justice agency managers and actors are interested in making what we will define here as "effective" or "good" decisions, or those most likely to further the ends of justice. It is useful here to repeat the definition of *justice* given in the American Heritage Dictionary (1992: 456), as stated in Chapter 2: "[t]he quality of being fair; fairness. 2. The principle of moral rightness; equity. 3. The upholding of what is just, especially fair treatment and due reward in accordance with honor, standards, or law." Distinctions between formal and natural justice (law and morality) and how justice is precisely and fully defined are matters best left to philosophers. However, in this text, "justice" means that those who are guilty are caught, processed, and sanctioned, as befits community, professional, and moral standards, by system actors. We think that justice for our purposes also means that those who are innocent are given ample opportunity and the due process necessary to ensure that if they are caught up in the system, they do not remain there long and are not sanctioned. In terms of internal organizational operations, justice might also mean that employees are treated fairly and honestly by management and given the opportunity to develop and "give back" to their community. Effective or good decision making in criminal justice agencies, then, in our view, has to do with furthering the ends of justice for those processed by the system, and for the criminal justice actors who work in it.

To act or not to act: that is but one of the questions!

The decision not to act is perhaps the most common decision of all. The police choose not to ticket or arrest, the prosecutor chooses not to prosecute, the community corrections officer or correctional officer in the jail or prison chooses not to pursue violations of rules. The truth is that we who study the behavior of criminal justice actors really have no idea how often such decisions *not to act* are made, since they usually do not come to official notice. Given the number of cases that flood the system each year and are sifted out, plus the official review that often accompanies decisions to act, it is likely there are more decisions not to act than otherwise (Bohm and Haley 2005). Judicial decisions made inside courtrooms or in front of legal actors, even concerning the least important of matters, are usually recorded for posterity. But so many other decisions by criminal justice actors, especially when they involve the decision not to act, are never reviewed or reviewable, simply because they are not known. For instance, police officers often do not file reports detailing why they did not write certain tickets for speeding. So the police organization, the public, and sometimes the alleged speeders, do not know why the decisions were made, or even that there were decisions; only the officers know.

Yet when a police officer does write a ticket, any number of people will know of that decision and some will review it, not the least of whom will be the alleged speeder! Such a decision to act then presents the greatest risk for the officer organizationally and therefore must be supported with ample evidence that a real violation occurred (through observation, but better yet because of unbiased evidence as provided, e.g., by a radar reading). Notice however that if the officer thinks, based on comparable evidence, that a speeding violation occurred but chooses not to act, there is usually no need to justify that decision, even though the dispatcher and perhaps a video recorder in the police car may document that the officer made the stop. But whatever way you look at it, it is just easier for an officer who witnesses a minor offense, absent organizational pressure to do otherwise, to decide not to act. This is the reason why criminal justice organizations, particularly police organizations that may stand to receive revenue from each traffic ticket, will pay careful attention to how many tickets are written by individual officers. In fact, they will often include that information in the officer's performance appraisal as a measure of how much work she is accomplishing on her shift, for example.

Such organizational surveillance or pressure regarding decision making may be both beneficial and detrimental to the ultimate goal of "good" decision making. Obviously, we want criminal justice actors to decide *to act* when there has been a violation of the law. But we also want them to have the discretion, as professionals, to determine when that is likely to have happened and to weigh the value of acting. So of course it is necessary for the criminal justice organization managers to watch and monitor how and why decisions are made, although an organization that applies too much pressure to make a decision one way or the other may thereby impose an obstacle to "good decision making."

Obstacles to good decision making: let us count the ways

Obstacles to "good" or effective decision making can come in many forms and from several sources. As we have seen, *the realities of the work of street-level bureaucrats* can force criminal justice actors to make less than optimal decisions. In essence, our juvenile probation officer was not "screwing" the system, but most of the clients, in order to "make it work" for those deemed most deserving or needy.

As was discussed in Chapter 7, *groupthink* has derailed many a decision-making process, and thus it constitutes a second and serious hindrance to effective decision making (Janis 1972). A prosecutor surrounded by only "yes people" who fail to challenge the status quo (or at least to question it) and who provide no alternative routes for action will often make decisions that do not achieve the best interests of justice for the community.

A third obstacle, as illustrated by police officers faced with ticket-writing decisions, indicates that *organizations can be both obstacles to, and facilitators of, effective decision making.* To repeat, because inertia or inaction is easier for officers in many cases of minor offenses—they do not have to do the paperwork and have it reviewed by others—organizational pressure to act may be inappropriate in some situations. Discretion with respect to minor offenses gives the officer the leeway she would not have with major offenses, where she would be compelled to act by law, practice, or conscience—or some combination of these. If the organization pressures her to act, to write the ticket when she otherwise would not, this can be an obstacle to good decision making only if the ticket was not warranted. As mentioned in Chapter 3 on ethics, organizational pressure can also lead to decisions, which involves *organizational deviance* that violate the laws or professional practices one would expect from criminal justice actors and thus constitute poor decision making (Lee and Visano 1994; Walker 1993).

A fourth obstacle to good decision making is the *politics of organizational operation.* As we have discussed in several chapters, starting with Appleby's conception of the nature of public organizations early in the text (Chapter 2) through the later treatment of budgeting and planning (Chapter 11), we have established that criminal justice agencies are centered in a political context. Laws and budgets that are formulated through give and take by political actors wrangling among themselves guide the actions of criminal justice organizations. What this means is that courtroom actors facing known time and resource constraints will tend to process cases more expeditiously than they might if there were more courtrooms, more judges, more prosecutors, more defense attorneys (Blumberg 1984). The numbers of those actors and those courtrooms are determined by political actors, presumably acting in the public interest, and they will allocate funding at the level that would allow more cases to be given more time, or not.

Of course, central to this discussion of politics is *money,* a fifth potential obstacle to good decision making, particularly when it is lacking. The example given of the courts and their processing of cases is really about both money and politics, or politics determining how much money will be allocated for criminal justice operation. An organization that is strapped for funds may decide, like our intrepid juvenile probation officer, to "screw the system" and focus on "making" only a part of it "work." Thus, courts might focus most resources on only the most serious cases, or systemwide policy may be to plead down even the most serious cases, to diminish prosecutorial or courtroom time expended on them.

Relatedly, space constraints in jails and prisons and *extremely heavy defense and prosecutorial caseloads and court dockets* represent a sixth obstacle to effective decision making for criminal justice actors. In Idaho, the lack of berths in treatment programs in the community has meant that judges sentence some offenders to prison, where they can in fact get treatment. Some might ask why this is a "poor" decision. The answer here is simple: Because it does not serve the ends of justice as we defined it. Judges in such cases will admit that some of the offenders did not *need* to go to prison for punishment, but they *desperately needed* substance abuse treatment. Why wasn't there substance abuse treatment available for indigent offenders in the community, one might ask? Because establishing and funding such programs is a political decision. So the state, courtesy of the taxpayers, ends up spending much more to incarcerate low-level offenders (about $20,000 annually for adult males) so that they can receive treatment. In turn, many offenders are more severely punished than their crimes warranted, according to the judges, and they are separated from their families and jobs, thus leading to a harder transition into the community once they parole.

This gets us to the point, and the seventh obstacle, that a *lack of available alternatives* or knowledge of such alternatives can also hinder good decision making. If judges have alternative sanctions or means of handling addicts—and in Idaho and other states, drug courts are providing such an alternative in large urban centers—then they might be able to improve their decision making and in turn better serve the ends of justice. Unfortunately, information about such alternatives, regardless of whether they "work," is sometimes sorely lacking in the criminal justice system. There are problems with getting up-to-date and applicable research on criminal justice practices, programming, and processes, and undoubtedly such a gap in knowledge impairs the criminal justice decision maker's ability to make good decisions (we will discuss the value of research a bit more in the following).

The eighth and final obstacle also relates to information as it affects decision making. The problem here is that there is *too much information* for the decision maker to sift through and use effectively. For example, there is now a plethora of information about the relative effectiveness of treatment programming. So the criminal justice planner reviewing that information for the first, or even the sixth time, could be overwhelmed by its complexity and depth. Yet somehow, people who make decisions about the content and duration of treatment programming will need to determine what information to pay the most attention to. A rule of thumb in terms of reviewing scientific research, as in this instance, is to look for studies that are well designed (Babbie 1992). That is, do they fit their subject, use multiple sources of both qualitative and quantitative data (also known as triangulation), and include enough subjects, and are they replicated?

However, when science cannot come to the rescue, so to speak, the decision maker will tend to evaluate the usefulness of information based on both logical and illogical factors. Illogical factors might include media presentations of infamous or non-representative cases, the order in which conflicting statements are received (what is seen or heard first or last will be given most credence), the mode of delivery (people will better remember information put to a tune or dramatically presented vs. spoken in a lecture), or who delivers it (famous or infamous persons, or those who have a dramatic flair, are more likely to be "heard" than others; Chiricos 2002;

Dye and Zeigler 1989; Merlo and Benekos 2000). Other influential factors include who delivers the information (a trusted person or personality or someone with accepted expertise on a topic) and the mode of delivery (in a peer-reviewed academic journal vs. the popular press). It also makes a difference whether information fits the conventional wisdom or common-sensical notions about what is true and/or whether it is congruent with what has happened before.

People will also review information from the perspective of each individual's role as an organizational actor and make determinations about its truth and usefulness from that vantage point. Both the formal (training, official positions) and informal (subcultural and actual) practices of the organization will help people decipher the value of information. In other words, when faced with too much information, and absent any assurances about its validity from a scientific standpoint, the criminal justice manager and actor will try and sort through it using all sorts of filters; the danger arises when people are influenced by their own biases and predispositions, which may have been shaped by logical fallacies.

Logical fallacies

One of the authors became acquainted with common logical fallacies in an undergraduate logic class. The professor was interested in preparing his students to "watch out for" and "beware" of failures in logic that frequently appear in public and private discourse and inevitably hamper the ability to make reasoned decisions. Classes on logic often include some discussion of logical fallacies or common errors in rhetorical arguments. Such fallacies are the refuge of the desperate and the deceitful, which is why we often see such tactics used in political discourse and over the airwaves. However, since criminal justice agencies and practices are guided mightily by the prevailing political winds, we often see such tactics used by those in or those critiquing criminal justice agencies or actors. The point of identifying common logical fallacies here is to prevent people from "falling" for them and thus making decisions that are influenced by the wrong conclusions they promote. Therefore, no discussion of decision making would be complete without touching on at least a few of the most common of these fallacies, including *ad hominem attacks, straw men, red herrings, begging the question* or *circular reasoning, the exception makes the rule,* and *appeals to patriotism/religion/ emotion.* (Type "logical fallacies" into Google and you will be astounded at how many deceptive rhetorical tactics we humans have devised.)

Ad hominem attacks occur in arguments or discussions when the speaker or writer is attacked or slurred, without reference to the merits of what that person argued or stood for (Bassham *et al.* 2008). So for instance, if a police chief were to argue against the establishment of a certain crime control program, a person launching an ad hominem attack would make disparaging comments either directly or indirectly about the chief, perhaps accusing the person and his or staff of being "soft" on crime, rather than addressing the merits of the argument. Whether the research or current practice supports the development of such a program is irrelevant for people who launch an ad hominem attack in this instance, because their goal is to influence the decision making of stakeholders (not just the public, but also the mayor, the city council, and others), and they do not want the facts to get in the way.

The **straw man** logical fallacy is used by those who want to divert attention from the merits of the real argument or situation (Bassham *et al.* 2008). To do this they will construct an argument that is as easy to "push over" as a "straw man" would be. A person using this tactic will set up a false or weak (straw man) argument and, once it is shown to be false, will act as if the opponent's argument is false in its entirety. To cite Watters (2013: 5), a straw man argument can take this or many other forms, including the following:

1   Present the opponent's argument in weakened form, refute it, and pretend that the original has been refuted.
2   Present a misrepresentation of the opponent's position, refute it, and pretend that the opponent's actual position has been refuted.
3   Present someone who defends a position poorly as the defender, refute that person's arguments, and pretend that *every* upholder of that position, and thus the position itself, has been defeated.
4   Invent a fictitious persona with actions or beliefs that are criticized, and pretend that the person represents a group that the speaker is critical of.

Let's make our crime control program example more specific. Suppose a city council member who favored the establishment of a COMPSTAT program by the police department was to use a "straw man" argument (Chapter 13 discusses "the COMPSTAT phenomenon" in some detail). The council member might start by noting that failure to implement such a program will lead to greater crime in the streets. So an exchange between the police chief and the user of the straw man tactic might go something like this:

> **Police chief:** We should not develop a COMPSTAT program in the city until the research indicates that it "works" to improve our ability to control crime.

> **City council member:** Drug dealing on our streets should be stopped. COMPSTAT is a proactive solution that can solve our drug and larger crime problem.

Now of course by opposing the adoption of COMPSTAT now, the chief is not arguing that drug dealing on the streets should be allowed to go on. This is the straw man portion of the argument, because nobody wants drug dealing to continue. Thus, when the council member implies that to oppose COMPSTAT is to argue against a proactive crime control measure that will solve drug crimes, he deflates the chief's point about prudently waiting for research results and makes the chief appear to be reactive and perhaps "weak."

A **red herring** logical fallacy—the straw man fallacy could be a subgroup of the red herring—is also a diversionary tactic. As with all these tactics, it is used to divert attention from or mask the truth (Bassham *et al.* 2008). The difference is that the *red herring* tactic often entails an emotional twist, which is used to impair the listener's ability to make good decisions. Our police chief arguing against implementation of COMPSTAT now might have been educated at an elite Ivy League school, and his opponent might use this fact to argue that "the chief doesn't understand how things are done in this town." Now the police chief may in fact be well acquainted with how the department operates, having served in it for several years, but the person wielding this tactic is not interested in the truth. Rather, they are interested in making an argument in a fashion designed to convince members of a community in which reverse snobbism about education is widespread. The city councilman is also playing to the emotions of his audience, intimating that the chief is an outsider and not "one of us." Therefore group solidarity against those Ivy League outsiders requires that the community oppose what the chief wants to do in this matter. Where the police chief went to school of course has nothing to do with the merits of the COMPSTAT program.

Begging the question or circular reasoning involves restating in the conclusion the point on which the argument was based (Bassham *et al.* 2008). Thus the city council member might argue that "we know COMPSTAT is effective in reducing crime, because it is successful in reducing crime." The latter part of this statement "begs the question" about the program's effectiveness by stating that the program should be used precisely because it is (said to be) effective.

Another common logical fallacy used in public discourse about crime is **the exception makes the rule**, or "If it happens once or was true once, it must happen all the time or be true in every case" (Bassham *et al.* 2008). We often see this argument used by practitioners who will tell an anecdote and then apply the lessons from that story to all like circumstances and clients/suspects/offenders. Such an anecdote might begin: "You can't trust a such and such type of offender, because this one time I did and the person violated that trust," or "This treatment program should be adopted everywhere because we have seen fewer offenders return after they graduated from it." The point is that both statements may well describe what happened in the instances related, and they might even apply to all like instances, as these practitioners imply. But we do not know for sure that the statements apply to like circumstances or offenders, because each anecdote is only a single instance (the exception); there may be other explanations for what happened then, or comparable circumstances in which the same outcome would not occur (make the rule).

Thus a proponent of COMPSTAT might use this logical fallacy by arguing that "COMPSTAT 'worked' to reduce crime in New York City in a given decade and so it should be adopted in all cities." Again, it may be true that COMPSTAT "worked" to reduce crime in New York City in the given decade. Alternatively crime may have dropped in New York for the same reasons (e.g., changing demographics, decline in violent drug trade, increased social supports for some offenders, increased income of the poor in the latter part of the 1990s, displacement of the poor from urban corridors, etc.) that led to its decline nationally over the same period, none of which had anything to do with COMPSTAT (Bureau of Justice Statistics 2007). But the point is that one exception—the success of COMPSTAT in New York City even if true—would not be a valid basis for making the rule for all cities. Of course if scientific studies had empirically tested the relative worth of COMPSTAT programs and the evidence indicated that the programs were instrumental in helping reduce crime, then the success of the program in New York City would no longer constitute an exception.

Finally, a very popular set of logical fallacies comprises those that have to do with **appeals to emotions/patriotism and religion.** These tactics can take many forms, but essentially they use emotional events or scenes (e.g., this child was made homeless because of drug crimes, so we must implement COMPSTAT) and appeals to God and country (e.g., people who don't support COMPSTAT are godless commie-lovers—this might also be considered an ad hominem attack) to make their point. Again, and obviously, decision making is improved when it is based on valid information, not name calling of opponents, diversionary tactics, appeals to emotions, and/or nasty insinuations about opponents.

Biology and cognition (social intelligence): a possible undue influence

There is much emerging science that indicates our biology and environment are constantly interacting to shape our behavior (Walsh and Beaver 2009; Walsh and Ellis 2007; Walsh 2002). The reason a discussion of biology, as it affects cognition, fits in this chapter on decision making is obvious: Cognition, or thinking and understanding is central to decision making. An important popular press book, *Social Intelligence: The New Science of Human Relationships*, describes how our reactions to each other and to our environment literally affect and are affected by our brain chemistry. As the author, Daniel Goleman (2006: 4), puts it:

> Neuroscience has discovered that our brain's very design makes it sociable, inexorably drawn into an intimate brain-to-brain linkup whenever we engage with another person. That neural bridge lets us affect the brain—and so the body—of everyone we interact with, just as they do us.

Clearly there is much we do not know about the brain and how it interacts with its environment, but the current science tells us that *spindle cells*, which guide social decisions, are much more prevalent in the human brain than in the brains of other animals (Goleman 2006). We also know that *mirror neurons* allow humans to anticipate the activity and emotions of others and to empathize with them, which probably explains why fallacious appeals to emotions are so persuasive for humans. According to Goleman (2006), we "catch" the emotions of others and they have an effect on our own chemistry and subsequently our behavior. When those around us display anger or are upset at us or others we tend to feel it in a bodily sense, and our own wellbeing and attitude are affected. Luckily the opposite is also true: those who exhibit a happy, contented, or hopeful outlook are more likely to inspire such feelings in others.

The knowledge that our brains can be affected in such a manner, needless to say, has major implications for all criminal justice agencies and their management. Our conception of how best to lead, communicate, motivate—you name it—are all likely to be affected by a greater understanding of how the brain operates in this social context.

Understanding that decisions are often affected by the emotional impact of others is important because it means that decision makers need to be aware of this impact and account for it in their decisions. A judge must think about whether his sentencing decision in a case is influenced by the actual crime committed or is being unduly affected by the community's and the victim's emotions. If the case involves a heinous crime where victim statements are taken into account in sentencing, are we not agreeing that the sentencing decision should reflect some emotional affect? What about police handling of a suspected "cop killer"? How might the emotions of all involved affect the decisions made in that context? What about parole boards or correctional officials who are overly swayed by emotional appeals of an unrepentant inmate, who has every intent of committing the same types of crimes once released? In each case the criminal justice actor must be aware that his own emotions and those of others are likely to have an effect on cognition, and that he may need to compensate for that effect.

Prediction

It is probably not an exaggeration to state that millions of decisions are made every day in the criminal justice system. One key type of decision making is "prediction," or making a decision about what will happen in the future. As defined by Vogt (2005: 244), **prediction** in a scientific context is "(a) using data to make a statement about the future ... (b) the more common use of the term ... refers to using data to "predict" outcomes that have already occurred." An example might be using data gathered on a cohort of offenders who were all released from prison during the same time period to investigate what variables or measures have an impact on recidivism. Later, these findings can influence the decision making of correctional program managers as they work to control or impact those measures that turned out to be key "predictive" factors.

As indicated by this definition and example, criminal justice decisions might be aided by the valid (true) and reliable (consistent) information that can be obtained through scientific investigation. Such investigations might be done qualitatively (e.g., using interviews or observations) or quantitatively (e.g., using surveys or agency data; Babbie 1992; Dillman 2000). Ideally such methods should fit the subject under study and be designed to best determine what is true about theory or well supported about the practice. Criminal justice managers and actors who fail to use scientifically obtained information to inform their decisions risk making predictions that do not fit reality and do not further the ends of justice.

Having said this, there are two types of errors common to prediction: false positives (or overpredicting the occurrence of phenomena; Type I error) and false negatives (or underpredicting the occurrence of phenomena; Type II error). It is likely because of real-world concerns about safety and security, not to mention political and media influence, that criminal justice actors, with the possible exception of defense attorneys, are more inclined to make false positive mistakes than false negative ones. Police officers, prosecutors, judges, and community and institutional correctional officers are more likely to predict future offending by persons who have been accused and convicted than the opposite. Because the vast majority of people who enter the criminal justice system do not in fact commit another crime, if indeed they are guilty of the one they were apprehended for, the overprediction of this outcome by criminal justice actors is likely.

Naturally, overprediction of reoffending or dangerousness leads to greater use of the whole criminal justice system, greatly enhances the monetary expenses of that system, and mars the ability to maintain a "just" system for those who are processed in it. On the other hand, if criminal justice actors were to commit the opposite error—that of false negatives or underpredicting reoffending or dangerousness—as sometimes also happens, the outcome would be a threat to the safety and security of the community, and impairment of justice likewise. The "solution" to this tendency to commit either type of error in prediction is to focus on developing a system and a series of processes and practices that improve decision making generally, which will have the collateral effect of improving predictions specifically.

Ways to improve decision making

Based on what we have presented in this text and this chapter, we have come to believe that decision making in criminal justice agencies can be greatly improved by managers and other criminal justice actors. Generally speaking, the first step towards improvement is to *be aware of all the obstacles, errors, and rhetorical traps* (e.g., logical fallacies) that can impair effective decision making. Second, one must work to develop an atmosphere that *values organizational integrity* or one whose actors as a whole are honest, ethical, and can be trusted by the agency's members and by the community. An organization that has this reputation probably gained it by making effective decisions regarding its staff and the people they work with and for. Third, as much as is possible, one should work to *provide enough resources* so that staff can make the decision to devote the requisite time and effort to doing their jobs well. In addition to these more global ways to improve organizational decision making, the savvy criminal justice manager might also do the following:

- As much as is possible, insulate most criminal justice decision making, and decision makers, from political influence.
- Hire educated people, or support employees in educational endeavors that will prepare them for the complexity of their work (e.g., criminal justice or related classes that will give them the theoretical, historical, and research-based information they need to contextualize their decision making).
- Emphasize professional practices as a guide to effective decision making.
- Focus on the validity and reliability of information that informs decisions. In tandem, make efforts to encourage and enhance research done in and for the agency.
- Be aware of, and account for, the biological processes that are at play in decision making.
- Foster creative and open decision making processes, which encourage discussion and even dissent, and the consideration of alternative courses of action.

Conclusions

Criminal justice actors are constantly called upon to make decisions; yet often the information they have is incomplete or flawed in some way. Since at times that information is purposefully misleading, the criminal justice actor needs to be a wary consumer and a thoughtful reviewer of the source and validity of information. It is always best if solid research on a topic has been done, and then done again and again, so that the decision maker has a good basis for making a decision. But most of the time, considering criminal justice decisions on any number of topics, such research does not exist or is not developed enough to give real guidance to criminal justice practitioners and managers.

In such cases, which are most cases, decision makers need to fall back on professional practices, training, education, and known and legitimate actions or decisions that "worked" in the past for themselves or their colleagues. Awareness of the logical fallacies used to bend the truth by those trying to illegitimately persuade and distract decision makers is also critical. As one of our undergraduate professors, who shall remain unnamed here, cautioned: "When you hear such crap [in the popular press], your shit detectors should be going off." Thankfully, and as noted in this chapter, there are ways to improve the organizational environment so that decision makers are not floundering alone or, in some cases, relying on a personal "shit detector" to determine whether a given piece of information is true or worth listening to.

Exercise: the false argument

The point of this exercise is to better acquaint students with the failures of logic (logical fallacies) commonly used in arguments over criminal justice practices and policies.

1   Allow each student, or group of students, the opportunity to select an initiative from a list of criminal justice programs or practices (e.g., drug courts, therapeutic communities, community policing, the balanced approach in juvenile courts, unit management in corrections, problem-solving policing, parole, indeterminate/ determinate sentencing, mandatory sentencing, human relations theory of management, traditional theory of management).

2   As a single-student exercise, assign a one- to two-page paper (to be written in or out of class) using each of the logical fallacies to argue for or against one of these initiatives. As a group exercise, have the group select a speaker and a scribe (writer of the group's notes), and have the whole group use each of the logical fallacies to argue either for, or against, one of the initiatives.

3   Have a few students, or all the groups, present their arguments (without naming the logical fallacy used) to the class, and have the class critique the arguments and identify each logical fallacy used.

Discussion questions

1   What is a decision? What do you think are everyday decisions made by criminal justice actors?

2   Why is the decision not to act often easier for criminal justice actors? When is it appropriate?

3   Provide some current examples of logical fallacies used by policymakers. Can you think of any that are specifically directed at criminal justice agencies or actors?
4   What are some common obstacles to effective decision making? How might these obstacles be overcome?
5   Why should scientifically derived information be weighted more heavily by the decision maker than information from other sources?
6   What are the types of common errors associated with prediction? Which error is most common for criminal justice decision makers, and why is that error more ubiquitous?
7   How might the decision making environment in criminal justice organizations be improved? Is the ability to make such improvements solely in the hands of criminal justice managers? If not, why not?

Key terms

ad hominem attacks: occur in arguments or discussions when the speaker or writer is attacked or slurred, passing over the merits of what that person argued or stood for.

appeals to emotions, patriotism, and religion: these tactics can take many forms, but essentially they use emotional events or scenes and appeals to God and country to make a point that is not supported in logic.

begging the question or circular reasoning: restating as the conclusion a point in the argument.

decision: a choice made by a thinking being.

exception makes the rule: a logical fallacy that states that if it (i.e., the focus of the discourse) happens once or was true once, it must happen all the time or be true in every case.

prediction: in a scientific context, "(a) using data to make a statement about the future ... (b) the more common use of the term ... refers to using data to "predict" outcomes that have already occurred" (Vogt 2005: 244).

red herring: a logical fallacy—the straw man fallacy could be a subgroup of the red herring—and also a diversionary tactic since, like all these tactics, it is used to divert attention from the truth or mask it. The difference is that the red herring tactic often entails an emotional twist, which is used to impair listeners' or readers' ability to make good decisions.

straw man: a logical fallacy used by those who want to divert attention from the merits of the argument or the facts of the situation.

References

American Heritage Dictionary (1992) *American heritage dictionary*, 3rd edn. New York, NY: Delta/Houghton Mifflin.

Babbie, E. (1992) *The practice of social research*, 6th edn. Belmont, CA: Wadsworth.

Bassham, G., Irwin, W., Nardone, H. and Wallace, J. M. (2008) *Critical thinking: A student's introduction*, 3rd edn. Boston, MA: McGraw-Hill.

Blumberg, A. S. (1984) The practice of law as a confidence game: Organization cooptation of a profession. In G. F. Cole (ed.), *Criminal justice: Law and politics*. Monterey, CA: Brooks/Cole, pp. 191–209.

Bohm, R. and Haley, K. N. (2005) *Introduction to criminal justice*, 4th edn. New York: McGraw-Hill.

Bureau of Justice Statistics (2007) Crime characteristics. Office of Justice Programs, U.S.Department of Justice. Available at www.ojp.usdoj.gov/bjs/cvict (last accessed January 31, 2013).

Chiricos, T. (2002) The media, moral panics and the politics of crime control. In G. F. Cole, M. G. Gertz and A. Bunger (eds), *The criminal justice system: Politics and policies*. Belmont, CA: Wadsworth/Thomson Learning, pp. 59–79.

Dillman, D. (2000) *Mail and internet surveys: The tailored design method*, 2nd edn. New York, NY: John Wiley & Sons, Inc.

Dye, T. R. and Zeigler, H. (1989) *American politics in the media age*. Belmont, CA: Wadsworth.

Goleman, D. (2006) *Social intelligence: The new science of human relationships*. New York, NY: Bantam Books.

Jacobs, M. D. (1990) *Screwing the system and making it work: Juvenile justice in the no-fault society*. Chicago, IL: University of Chicago Press.

Janis, I. L. (1972) *Victims of groupthink: A psychological study of foreign-policy decisions and fiascoes*. Boston, MA: Houghton Mifflin.

Lee, J. A. and Visano, L. A. (1994) Official deviance in the legal system. In S. Stojokovic, J. Klofas and D. Kalinich (eds), *The administration and management of criminal justice organizations: A book of readings*. Prospect Heights, IL: Waveland Press, pp. 202–231.

Lipsky, M. (1980) *Street-level bureaucracy: Dilemmas of the individual in public services*. New York, NY: Russell Sage Foundation.

Merlo, A. V. and Benekos, P. J. (2000) *What's wrong with the criminal justice system*. Cincinnati, OH: Anderson Publishing.

Mills, C. W. (1959) *The sociological imagination*. London: Oxford University Press.

Vogt, W. P. (2005) *Dictionary of statistics and methodology: A nontechnical guide for the social sciences*, 3rd edn. Thousand Oaks, CA: Sage.

Walker, S. (1993) *Taming the system: The control of discretion in criminal justice, 1950–1990*. New York, NY: Oxford University Press.

Walsh, A. (2002) *Biosocial criminology: Introduction and integration*. Cincinnati, OH: Anderson Publishing.

Walsh, A. and Beaver, K. M. (eds). (2009) *Biosocial criminology: New directions in theory and research*. New York, NY: Routledge.

Walsh, A. and Ellis, L. (2007). *Criminology: An interdisciplinary approach*. Thousand Oaks, CA: Sage.

Watters, J. G. (2013) A very little guide to logical argument and fallacies. Available at: http://angellier.biblio.univ-lille3.fr/etudes_recherches/alittleguidetofallacies.pdf (last accessed January 31, 2013).

13 Model management practices

You will see at once why I believe that the Enlightenment thinkers of the seventeenth and eighteenth centuries got it mostly right the first time. The assumptions they made of a lawful material world, the intrinsic unity of knowledge, and the potential of indefinite human progress are the ones we still take most readily into our hearts, suffer without, and find maximally rewarding through intellectual advance. The greatest enterprise of the mind has always been and always will be the attempted linkage of the sciences and humanities. The ongoing fragmentation of knowledge and resulting chaos in philosophy are not reflections of the real world, but artifacts of scholarship.

(Wilson 1998: 8)

Today arbitrary treatment of citizens by powerful institutions has assumed a new form, no less insidious than that which prevailed in an earlier time. The "organization" has emerged and spread its invisible chains. Within the structure of the organization there has taken place an erosion of both human values and the broader value of human beings as the possibility of dissent within the hierarchy has become so restricted that common candor requires uncommon courage.

(Nader 1972: 3)

Select a person, set expectations, motivate the person, and develop the person: these are the four core activities of the "catalyst" role. If a company's managers are unable to play this role well, then no matter how sophisticated its systems or how inspirational its leaders, the company will slowly start to disintegrate.

(Buckingham and Coffman 1999: 61)

Those elements of COMPSTAT that correspond with existing bureaucratic structures are more likely to change organizational practice, while those that do not, have a much more limited effect. Furthermore, rather than streamlining the organization, COMPSTAT's operation

appears to be hindered by the same bureaucratic features that it purportedly transforms.

(Willis *et al.* 2004: 490)

Parallel findings from two differently constituted Compstat programs
on two different continents provides evidence that the primary component of the Compstat model is focusing, not broken windows enforcement, and the primary impact is on property crime.

(Jang *et al.* 2010: 387)

Introduction: criminal justice agencies in a continuing crisis, in need of a solution

Ever since we started working in and studying criminal justice—some
thirty-five-plus combined years now—justice system agencies have been
in crisis. Of course, these problems did not start when we began to pay
attention to them! The history of criminal justice agencies and institutions indicates that there has always been a crisis of varying proportions in
evidence. Common themes of crises occurring for at least the last two centuries include understaffing, burgeoning numbers of clientele, dilapidated
facilities, brutality and other abuses, a lack of professionalism, inadequate
training and pay, funding shortfalls, a lack of adequate or effective programming, and so on and so on.

Unfortunately, these problems have only been exacerbated as the
number of people coming into contact with the criminal justice system has
boomed. The latest figures from the Bureau of Justice Statistics (BJS) and
the Federal Bureau of Investigation (FBI 2011) indicate that in recent years
there have been fewer people arrested, adjudicated, sentenced, supervised,
or incarcerated, in one form or another, by the criminal justice system, but
the people involved as suspects and offenders remains at a very high level
as compared to thirty years ago (Bureau of Justice Statistics 2007; Glaze
and Parks 2012; Maruschak and Parks 2012; Snyder 2012) This sustained
demand for services has only served to strain agency resources and personnel already grappling with a changing and dynamic environment.

Surprisingly, however, a number of criminal justice agencies are weather-
ing these crises rather well. Yes, there are manifestations of problematic
behavior in many forms. Stories of brutality and abuse by the police or in
the courts leak out and then explode on the national news. Harassment of
inmates and staff, by employees and by other inmates, is hidden behind
the screen of officialdom and becomes evident only as lawsuits reach the
courts. Serious disturbances may fester for years on the streets and in institutions and then reach the tipping point as demands for service are not
met. The accused and the guilty sometimes leave the system no better off,
and at times much worse, than when they entered. Moreover, turnover,
stress, and dissatisfaction with the work plague some criminal justice staff,
and ultimately their agencies.

What is amazing about this whole cycle of crises that afflicts the adult and juvenile criminal justice system, however, is that somehow, and despite the challenges presented from the external and internal environments, many agencies, institutions, and programs are managing to sustain operations. Some are flourishing and innovating and have created enjoyable places to work, if not to live in. Clearly, there is a vast difference between a well-run agency and a poorly run agency. As the capstone chapter in this book, we are going to focus on the former, or the elements that contribute to success in a criminal justice operation: The "solutions" rather than the all-too-evident factors that can lead to failure.

All things being equal, and assuming some level of reasonable support for criminal justice operations in a state or locality, or at the national level, the following factors are likely related to its success: Human relations management practices, a professional staff, proactive and shared leadership, an embedded subcultural belief in ethical practice, the availability of "best practices" programming that itself is evidence-based, and an engaged and informed community. In this chapter we revisit and explore these factors, which are part and parcel of model management practices, but first let us note that such practices derive from several sources.

Salvation through consilience

The discipline of criminal justice is perhaps the most consilient of all. Harvard professor and author of two Pulitzer Prize-winning books, Edward O. Wilson (1998), describes consilience as a unity of knowledge among seemingly disparate disciplines. Criminal justice was birthed in part from several other disciplines (sociology, psychology, social work, political science, public administration, business, chemistry, history, English, the arts, and, more recently, biology) and continues to be influenced by them; ideas from these disciplines, in combination with our own, forge a cogent understanding of crime, justice, and the associated practices (Guarino-Ghezzi and Trevino 2005) We mention this here because a true understanding of criminal justice operations, or any management for that matter, requires the melding of many disciplines and a creative utilization of the knowledge they provide. This book presents but a sampling of the vast knowledge that one might employ in criminal justice management.

So as we begin the discussion of a "model criminal justice manager and model management practices," we would note that the best managers are well educated, either formally or informally—and really both—and are tempered by experience. This statement is true because knowledge is a prerequisite to the understanding and practice of management. Experience is often valued in criminal justice practice, so it needs no defense here, but education is not always similarly valued.

Effective and just criminal justice management is impossible if managers have no, or little, exposure to the literature on the origin and nature of crime (sources include the disciplines of criminal justice, but also sociology, psychology, biology, and world literature) How will managers know what is likely to "work" if they do not study the history of institutions/agencies and solutions tried in the past (as discernible from sources on criminal justice, but also history, sociology, public administration, and business)? How will managers know how to evaluate practice if they do not understand principles and evidence in this area or know why programs are successful (from sources including not only criminal justice, but also psychology, sociology, social work, business, the arts, public administration, and chemistry)? How will managers know how to work well with other human beings, either their staff or clients, if they do not understand what motivates people (using as sources criminal justice, but also business, psychology, public administration, biology, and the humanities)? Finally, and perhaps most importantly, how will managers appreciate, and distinguish between, procedural and substantive justice in their organizations without the knowledge one can garner only from a number of disciplines (e.g., criminal justice, but also political science, law, public administration, philosophy, social work, literature, and history)? Only with such knowledge and understanding can the criminal justice manager avoid the dangers inherent in all organizations (as briefly identified by Ralph Nader in the quote at the beginning of this chapter), and troubles that are particularly problematic for criminal justice agencies (as was discussed in Chapter 3).

In sum, effective criminal justice management requires vast knowledge of many topics. The best managers are of a Renaissance frame of mind, in that they either have the knowledge themselves or make it their business to acquire it, and use the brain-power of their colleagues in collaborative processes.

Communication, leadership, and culture change

The intersection of communications, leadership, and culture change is clear; their relationship is clearly dialectic. Leaders interested in changing their organization's culture, beyond approaching the work with a well-rounded education, use communication channels to convey that message. Yet the culture shapes the leader and the mode and style of the communication. In this way there is interplay between the three, and all must be considered, and calibrated, when cultural change is attempted.

Cultural acceptance of the change will depend on any number of factors, such as the substance of the change, the extent of the change, the perceived and real effects of the change, leadership, and norms in the workplace. When the proposed change involves a movement from a sole focus on incapacitation for corrections to the inclusion of rehabilitation programming based on "best and evidence-based practices" (as discussed in Box 13.1), enormous effort is needed to effectuate such change. On many levels this need for change must be "sold" to the organizational members by leaders, but then, if it is to be successful, other members must be persuaded to "buy in."

Currently, police agencies are faced with the latest effort at organizational change, the COMPSTAT phenomenon. COMPSTAT, which stands for either "computer-statistics meetings" or "compare stats," was first implemented by New York City Police Commissioner William Bratton (Jang *et al.* 2010; Raney 2005; Willis *et al.* 2004: 464) It is heralded for sparking the huge decrease in crime in New York City in the 1990s, and because of its perceived success in a city where crime was regarded as particularly intransigent, COMPSTAT has attained a number of acolytes in police departments around the country.

Integral to the COMPSTAT philosophy are the following six elements: "mission clarification, internal accountability, geographic organization of operational command, organizational flexibility, data-driven analysis of problems and assessment of department's problem-solving efforts, and innovative problem-solving tactics" (Willis *et al.* 2004: 465–466) Some of these elements would appear to contradict each other. For instance, how does internal accountability, highly prized in bureaucratic organizations, coexist with an emphasis on organizational flexibility? How does one engage in innovation, where risks and chances are taken, when practices must also be both accountable and data-driven? Such questions were also raised by Willis and his colleagues (2004) when they tried to reconcile the elements of COMPSTAT with its practice in a small, bureaucratically organized police department. Simply put, they found that at times the bureaucracy got in the way of true COMPSTAT implementation (see the quote from the authors at the beginning of this chapter and the quote from the Jang *et al.* [2010] article about what makes COMPSTAT successful [focus rather than Broken Windows] and what crimes it tends to affect [property and not violent]).

But then, COMPSTAT implementation presents the real challenge of change in organizations that are bureaucratically arranged and are shaped by paramilitary practices. How to reshape the culture so that it prizes progress, innovation, excellence, and ethics is not always clear. It would appear that most organizations, public or private, that are interested in organizational change are struggling with just these issues. Willis and his colleagues (2004: 493) conclude their article on a pessimistic note *vis-à-vis* COMPSTAT implementation: "Most significant, COMPSTAT'S reinforcement of the bureaucratic hierarchy of policing stifles creative problem-solving approaches." However, this pessimism regarding COMPSTAT does not mean that leadership cannot effectuate positive cultural change via communication; rather, it just means that these authors are not optimistic about this program in these types of agencies, in particular. Change might well be more possible if an agency has a less paramilitary structure (e.g., is fatter and flatter) and is more amenable to engagement of the workers, who construct the culture, in the change. For example, Box 13.1 presents a manager's account of an attempt at culture change of a corrections department.

Box 13.1 Making a culture change as we move toward evidence-based "best practices", by Gary Barrier

Prison culture change can be slow, and seeing change, when you are immersed in the organization, can be even harder. The IDOC Idaho Department of Corrections embarked on a remarkable era of change—matching what national researchers were saying was a needed diversion from "Nothing Works" to a "What Works" perspective in corrections. The latter concept is based on evidenced-based "Best Practices" and the shift to this began in the early to mid-90s for the IDOC.

The Idaho Department of Corrections has always been viewed as an agency which assures public safety by locking up dangerous criminals. Reducing offender risk and providing opportunities for the offender to change is part of our mission. Because the vast majority of those who are incarcerated in Idaho prisons will someday be in our communities, this is reason enough to ensure inmates leave the institutions better than when they entered them. The following facts are quite sobering in this regard:

- 3,237 incarcerated offenders were released from Idaho prisons in 2003
- 6,235 offenders were incarcerated
- 97% of all offenders will leave prison and return to our communities

I have personally worked in the corrections field for approximately twenty-eight years. I began my career in corrections as a juvenile probation officer and counselor in the late 1970s and graduated to adult supervision of probation and parole in the early 1980s. I have served in programs and treatment, been a deputy warden, a warden and ended my career in an administrative capacity with Programs/Education. My experience with prisons began in the early 1990s. It was then I realized the problems and conflict day-to-day prison management was having with prison programs. We conducted and completed some research on prison ethics in partnership with then BSU professors Dr. [Mary] Stohr and Dr. [Robert] Marsh. This was the starting point for IDOC to take a look at the problems we had with a number of areas (e.g., communication and culture) and provided an impetus to gear our efforts toward cultural change. Part of this shift in focus would be used to standardize programs into research-based Best Practices for the IDOC. (e.g., communication and culture) and provided an impetus to gear our efforts toward cultural change. Part of this shift in focus would be used to standardize programs into research-based Best Practices for the IDOC.

In relation to these efforts, and national recognition and support for correctional change, in 2001 the governor, Dirk Kempthorne, initialed and signed into law the Substance Abuse Initiative Act. As a result of this act, [authorization for] 47.5 FTEs [full-time employees], along with $2,500,000 for substance abuse assessments, treatment, and program evaluations, was signed into law. Unfortunately, subsequent budget cuts in 2002 and 2003 negated these funds and positions. This initiative, however, served as another catalyst for a philosophical shift in the IDOC, which resulted in the implementation of new research-based programs and the enhancement of our existing programs. Being consistent with legislative intent, IDOC formulated partnerships with Health and Welfare and community treatment providers. These collaborations and partnerships have continued to grow with judicial and other state agencies, such as Idaho Housing, Vocational Rehabilitation, faith-based community services, and many others.

IDOC has been committed to providing research-based programs. In 1998 the IDOC opened up its first of four therapeutic communities. We built on that success to develop a core program continuum of treatment which begins with a battery of assessments, and a personalized offender treatment/release plan. As a result of a comprehensive update of our data system and better documentation, IDOC is now able to process outcome research reports.

The foundation has been successfully built. Before I retired, the average rate of Idaho offenders revoking parole and returning to prison from 1996–2003 was 39 percent. Meanwhile our population continued to surge, with court commitments rising for violent and nonviolent offenders. In the 2000s Idaho had one of the fastest growing populations in the US, with an average rate of yearly growth exceeding 10 percent for new inmates.

Clearly, we are at a crossroads. A bulging prison and community supervision population threatens our ability to deliver effective programs and to fulfill our mission and vision for making our communities safe, while providing offenders opportunities to change.

A continuing challenge is the need for the IDOC to work together with our state and community partnerships to proceed with our efforts to ensure that we do not lose sight of the need to support these changes.

Gary Barrier is a retired warden and administrator of programs for the Idaho Department of Corrections.

As we discussed in Chapter 4, there has been a movement in both the private and public sectors toward the adoption of a more human relations management-style practice. Much like the other management theories discussed in Chapter 4, human relations management derived from the work of scholars and practitioners in a number of disciplines. In that sense, it is consilient, and thus it renders interrelated practices, as should become evident in the following.

The latest manifestations of the human relations movement come in the form of the push for "learning organizations" and "teaming" in businesses and governmental agencies. These initiatives of themselves represent a unity of knowledge from the disciplines of education, public administration, business, psychology, and, of course, criminal justice. But beyond these current thrusts in management, styles of leadership, personnel practices, and processes and types of budgeting are all fitted, to some extent, to either a more traditional or a more human relations perspective of management.

The reality is that a human relations perspective on management could never be fully adopted in criminal justice organizations. Given their multi-layered mission, their bureaucratic shape, and the need for accountability and some privacy protection, the implementation of this perspective, much like that of COMPSTAT, must always be relative to the mission of the organization. So the extent to which a human relations management perspective could be implemented in criminal justice agencies depends on the primary mission for that organization and the situation it finds itself in. For instance, traditional management is better fitted to correctional institutions that must be more secure. But a juvenile halfway house and an adult maximum security prison can and should be managed differently. The maximum security prison is more likely to need hierarchy, bureaucracy, rule of law, and paramilitary apparatus in its organization than is the halfway house. The halfway house, on the other hand, might benefit from less structure, more open communication lines, greater flexibility, and empathy— characteristics that are aligned with a human relations perspective.

Moreover, all criminal justice agencies, whether police departments, courtrooms, or halfway houses for juveniles, must be concerned with accountability. Recall the discussion of Appleby's (1945) thesis that "government is different" from private sector work in part because of the need for accountability. Since it is the agencies' business to legally deny liberty to citizens in a democracy, managers and workers need always be accountable for their actions to ensure proper use of this awesome power.

Having said this, there is room for a human relations perspective of management in every criminal justice facility, though it should be adjusted for circumstances. We say this because one thing remains constant whether we are discussing a maximum security prison or a halfway house, a police department or a courtroom, and that is the need to manage human beings, as both clients and staff. As we found from our discussion of management theories in Chapter 4, human beings have motivating needs, some of which are fulfilled, or not, at work. If these needs are not fulfilled, there is a real chance that workers will not be motivated; that production will decrease; and that problems with negative stress, turnover, and job dissatisfaction will increase.

Recall the six basic tenets for those adopting a modern version of human relations theory, as noted in Chapter 4:

1 A fatter and flatter organizational structure, or a less pyramidal shape to the organization than is typical of traditional agencies.
2 Shared decision making by all sectors of the organization.
3 A mechanism or mechanisms for sharing in decisions.
4 Empowered employees who are willing and able to participate fully in decision making that affects their workplace.
5 Enhancement of top-down communication with bottom-up, horizontal, and diagonal communication avenues.
6 Acceptance and expectation that the organization and its members must adapt, grow, and even take risks, if they hope to achieve objectives.

The theory is that the organization and manager who can employ these tenets are more likely to avoid a number of the maladies common to unsuccessful management practice (Stohr *et al.* 1994; Wright *et al.* 1997) It is also thought that an organization that can successfully employ all these tenets, taking into account the twin concerns of security and accountability that criminal justice agencies face, is likely to experience positive outcomes, such as a highly motivated and engaged staff, a willingness to innovate by staff, and excellence in service delivery to clients.

It is the people and their goals that matter

Appleby's powerful argument that "government is different" from the private sector notwithstanding, we can learn a great deal from studying business management practices (Raney 2005) For example, Buckingham and Coffman (1999) interviewed over 80,000 managers, primarily in the private sector. The study continued for almost twenty-five years, beginning in 1975. The managers hailed from large and small companies and agencies of all stripes. Each manager was interviewed for an hour and a half about his or her work, employees, reaction to situations, and recommendations. Their answers were audio recorded. The responses of the "best" managers were separated from those who had been identified by others as "average" managers, and the two sets were compared.

The researchers found that the "best" managers were diverse demographically and stylistically. In most senses of the word they differed wildly from each other. However, Buckingham and Coffman were able to isolate and present some gems of wisdom that they distilled from the thousands of hours of tapes. These gems regarding workers in organizations included the following (Buckingham and Coffman 1999: 57):

- People don't change that much.
- Don't waste time trying to put in what was left out.
- Try to draw out what was left in.
- That is hard enough.

In other words, choose carefully who will work in your agency. Train and develop those persons to their fullest potential. If you have employees who are not going to work out, and you are sure of that, do not waste your time and the company's resources trying to make them something they are not, or cannot be.

Such wisdom fits the perspective that criminal justice agencies should focus considerable resources at the selection and development end of personnel processes so that talented people will be identified, selected, and promoted. In their quote appearing at the beginning of this chapter, Buckingham and Coffman indicate that if a manager does not select well, set expectations, motivate, and develop the personnel, then the organization will not survive for long with any degree of effectiveness intact.

Once good people have been hired, they must be motivated. Sirota, Mischkind, and Meltzer (2005) analyzed four million survey responses, as well as a mix of focus groups, interviews, and observations of mostly business, but some public sector organizations, in over eighty countries over a period of thirty years. They concluded that employee enthusiasm for work is tied directly to management practices. One startling finding from their research was that morale declines significantly for most employees in most companies after six months on the job. The authors claim that this decline is not just attributable to the novelty of the job wearing off, but it is tied to management practices. They find that in 90 percent of companies management kills enthusiasm, but this does not happen in the other 10 percent (Sirota *et al.* 2005: xxix). Their question is: What distinguishes the 10 percent from the 90 percent? Their answer, as one would expect, is multifaceted and has to do with what people want from work.

What they found was that most employees in most cultures have three basic goals for their work: "equity, achievement and camaraderie" (Sirota *et al.* 2005: 9). The researchers think that organizations which provide the opportunities for workers to achieve these goals will benefit in the form of heightened morale and better performance. To set the stage for this achievement, management must establish policies and practices that promote these goals. Of course, these three goals closely mirror what Maslow (1961) identified as needs that motivate people in the workplace, Sirota and his colleagues (2005) merely provide some empirical evidence to support Maslow's theory.

A consilience of topics too: the unity of knowledge in criminal justice management practice

Did you notice? All of the management topics discussed in this book are interrelated, not just because they derive from several disciplines, but because excellence in one area, or lack of it, inevitably influences the other areas. Of course if a human relations approach allows staff and clients to be more engaged in decision making and in shaping the agency in a positive way, the agency will inevitably succeed. Organizational success, in turn, affects many areas, as we have seen:

- The management of trouble, or unethical practice, becomes less problematic when the organization is more open internally and externally (Chapter 3).
- There are improvements in ability and willingness to communicate (Chapter 5).
- There are changes in how people are socialized into the roles they adopt and in their use of power (Chapter 6).
- The leadership styles people choose and respect manifest personal growth (Chapter 7).
- The understanding of the importance of selection, performance appraisal, and training in building and shaping the workforce and culture is increased (Chapter 8).
- The organization's openness to, and appreciation of, the need for diversity are enhanced (Chapter 9).
- Standards in treatment and the use of force, and general practice, are seen as necessary conditions to creating a professional workforce (Chapter 10).
- Efforts are made to conduct strategic planning and budgeting in the most effective way (Chapter 11).
- People learn how to make positive and effective decisions in light of all the obstacles that are present (Chapter 12).

In several chapters we used extant research and knowledge on management from a number of sources, from several disciplines, to formulate suggestions for improving criminal justice management. All these topics are interrelated, not because of some grand scheme orchestrated by the authors, but because management practices in one area necessarily affect practices in another. The management theory adopted by an organization, whether it is closer to human relations or to a more traditional focus, and the ways in which focus become translated into practice by all organizational members via the leadership and the culture, in turn affect everything.

Based on the literature in this area (as cited throughout the book), and using our six basic tenets noted earlier, here are some suggestions for incorporating a human relations-flavored version of model management practices into the criminal justice workplace:

1 Maintain and respect civil service rules and protections.
2 Uphold and respect the due process rights of staff and clients.
3 Increase training hours on all aspects of the organization (what it is and how it operates) and the role (what it involves and how to practice it) so that the role at least matches that of a profession.
4 Ensure that the substantive portion of training includes such topics as leadership and supervisory techniques, problem solving, interpersonal and communication skills, participatory management, ethics, diversity and cultural issues, the importance of best and evidence-based practices, and innovation/creative thinking, as well as the typical and necessary topics related to security, accountability, report writing, and the legal aspects of practice.
5 Make it a priority to hire people with a college degree (from an accredited college or university) and to support employees working to earn college credits.
6 Pay to all employees a livable wage that is commensurate with their professional status.
7 Select, evaluate, and promote based on formal and informal adherence to ethical practice.
8 Establish a whistleblowing program so that staff have a safe and anonymous means to report wrongdoing.
9 As much as possible, open the agency to scrutiny by outsiders, including researchers, the media, citizen groups, and other interested stakeholders.
10 Maintain the appropriate professional standards for operation, and submit the organization to an accreditation regimen.
11 Encourage and support innovation and the implementation of new ideas in the workplace.
12 Increase the avenues for communication, input, and involvement of staff in the workplace:

- develop a newsletter with regular contributors from all ranks
- organize work teams that include a mix of ranks and perspectives (e.g., security and treatment personnel), and do not neglect support staff
- solicit input regarding management decisions, optimally before decisions are made

- have some joint training sessions that include management and line workers
- as needed, organize formal problem-solving sessions that involve a mix of ranks
- involve all ranks in personnel processes (e.g., let entry-level workers sit in on some selection interviews or be involved in the development of a new performance appraisal instrument)
- engage in regular discussion of the value of policies, the ethics code, and the budgetary process

13 Improve the management of clients:

- provide meaningful opportunities for clients to work, participate in treatment programs, and grow
- develop a newsletter for clients/the community with contributions from them
- periodically survey or interview clients/the community about their needs and the services with which they are being provided
- ensure that grievance procedures are fair
- use evidence-based programming and practices

These suggestions for model management practices are not, of course, comprehensive, and their implementation is likely to vary from agency to agency (see also Box 13.2). But if employed with care and to the degree necessary and possible, the organization, the workers, and the clients should benefit in an enriched and more productive work environment for staff, and safer, better and just treatment and service for the community and clients (Buckingham and Coffman 1999; Drucker 1954; 1964; Gaines *et al.* 2003; Heil *et al.* 2000; Kiekbusch *et al.* 2003; Maslow 1961, 1998; McGregor 1957; Ouchi 1981; Parker Follett 1926; Patenaude 2001; Peters 1987, 1995; Schein 1992; Slate *et al.* 2001; Sirota *et al.* 2005; Stohr *et al.* 1994; Whisenand and Ferguson 2002; Wright *et al.* 1997).

Box 13.2 The IACP and the role of police executives

In 1999 the International Association of Chiefs of Police held a conference entitled Police Leadership in the 21st Century: Achieving and Sustaining Executive Success. The roles of police executives were discussed and analyzed by conference participants, who later developed several recommendations. Notably, many of the recommendations from the IACP conference fit our own recommendations regarding model management in criminal justice agencies generally.

To summarize how to foster key leadership attributes and activities for police executives and within police organizations, the attendees listed the following (IACP 1999: i–ii):

- The profession is obligated to ensure the continuing presence of an abundant pool of candidates who possess the personal attributes, academic preparation, and formal training to meet the demands of the 21st century leadership.
- Competition for chief executive positions will increase among younger and better educated generation of professionals.
- Executive development education and training capacity must multiply to produce this pool.
- Police executives must become more intensely involved in framing executive development curricula, especially with the premier national training institutions.
- Forming and constantly reinforcing ethical values and behavior are paramount in leadership preparation and performance.
- Communities, governments, and especially the workforce look increasingly to a chief for clarity and precision in setting forth a vision and mission for the department, and constructing a framework of shared values.
- Chiefs are increasingly expected to conceptualize systematically— to define the role and place of policing and the police officer in society and the community.
- Transition to participatory management seems irreversible. In the empowerment milieu of contemporary organizations, chiefs must work collaboratively with members of many hierarchical levels and stakeholder centers, especially to constructively effect change.
- Mutual expectation guidelines, fashioned jointly by mayors, city managers, and chiefs, are paramount for building and sustaining executive success and tenure.
- In striving to prioritize customer service and satisfaction, traditional and unalterable obligations to victims and crime prevention and control must be diligently pursued and guarded.
- Numerous and complex issues and the changing environment demand that 21st century police leaders bring special passion for the workplace—that they regard their obligations as a calling that requires total commitment— not just a job.

Conclusions

It has been our contention from the outset that there are very powerful reasons why criminal justice organizations should move further in the direction of a human relations perspective on management in the workplace. Our hope is that these pages have cogently conveyed this argument, along with the concomitant case for greater professionalism and funding. The gist of this book is that criminal justice agencies, and their actors, need not fall into the "big" and "bad" of management. There is much that is "beautiful" about the best-managed criminal justice entity, and management practices can be fashioned to showcase and promote that beauty.

Discussion questions

1 How are all the management topics covered in this book related? Give an example.
2 Why are all the management topics covered in this book related?
3 How do criminal justice organizations benefit from traditional management practices? Give an example and explain your answer.
4 Are any traditional management practices included in the model management practices listed in this chapter? If so, which ones are they?
5 How do criminal justice organizations benefit from human relations management practices? Give an example, and explain your answer.
6 Identify the human relations management practices included in the model management practices listed in this chapter. List them and give examples to show why each one is important.

Key terms

Consilience: a unity of knowledge among several seemingly disparate disciplines (Wilson 1998).

References

Appleby, P. (1945, reprinted in 1987) Government is different. In J. M. Shafritz and A. C. Hyde, (eds), *Classics of Public Administration*. Chicago, IL: Dorsey Press, pp. 158–163.

Buckingham, M. and Coffman C. (1999) *First, break all the rules: What the world's greatest managers do differently*. New York, NY: Simon and Schuster.

Bureau of Justice Statistics (2007) *State Court caseload statistics.* Bureau of Justice Statistics, Office of Justice Programs, US Department of Justice. Available at www.bjs.gov/index.cfm?ty=tp&tid=30 (last accessed January 31, 2013).

Drucker, P. F. (1954) *The practice of management.* New York, NY: Harper and Row.

Drucker, P. F. (1964) *Managing for results.* New York, NY: Harper and Row.

Federal Bureau of Investigation (2011) *Persons arrested.* FBI, US Department of Justice. Available at www.fbi.gov/about-us/cjis/ucr/crime-in-the-u.s/2011/crime-in-the-u.s. 2011/tables/table-29 (last accessed January 31, 2013).

Gaines, L. K., Worrall, J. L., Southerland, M. D. and Angell, J. E. (2003) *Police administration.* Boston: McGraw-Hill.

Glaze, L. E. and Parks, E. (2012) *Correctional populations in the United States, 2011.* Bureau of Justice Statistics, Office of Justice Programs, US Department of Justice. Available at www.bjs.gov/content/pub/pdf/cpus11.pdf (last accessed January 31, 2013).

Guarino-Ghezzi, S. and Trevino, A. J. (2005) *Understanding crime: A multidisciplinary approach.* Florence, KY: Anderson Publishing.

Heil, G., Bennis, W. and Stephens, D. C. (2000) *Douglas McGregor revisited: Managing the human side of the enterprise.* New York: Wiley.

IACP. (1999) *Police leadership in the 21st century: Achieving and sustaining executive success. International Association of Chiefs of Police: Recommendations from the president's first leadership conference, May 1999.* Alexandria, VA: IACP.

Jang, H., Hoover, L. T. and Joo, H-J. (2010) An evaluation of Compstat's effect on crime: The Fort Worth experience. *Police Quarterly,* 13(4): 387–412.

Kiekbusch, R., Price, W. and Theis, J. (2003) Turnover predictors: Causes of employee turnover in sheriff-operated jails. *Criminal Justice Studies,* 16(2): 67–76.

Maslow, A. H. (1961, reprinted in 1998) *Maslow on management.* New York, NY: Wiley.

Maslow, A. H. (1998, first published in 1961) *Maslow on management.* New York, NY: Wiley.

Maruschak, L. M. and Parks, E. (2012) *Probation and parole in the United States, 2011.* Bureau of Justice Statistics, Office of Justice Programs, US Department of Justice. Available at http://www.bjs.gov/index.cfm?ty=pbdetail&iid=4538 (last accessed January 31, 2013).

McGregor, D. (1957, reprinted in 2001) The human side of enterprise. In J. M. Shafritz and J.S. Ott (eds), *Classics of Organization Theory,* 5th edn. Fort Worth, TX: Harcourt College Publishers, pp. 152–157.

Nader, R. (1972) An anatomy of whistle blowing. In R. Nader, P. J. Petkas and K. Blackwell (eds), Whistle blowing: The report of the conference on professional responsibility. New York, NY: Grossman, pp. 3–11.

Ouchi, W. (1981) *Theory Z: How American business can meet the Japanese challenge.* Reading, MA: Addison-Wesley.

Parker Follett, M. (1926, reprinted in 2001) The giving of orders. In J. M. Shafritz and J. S. Ott (eds), *Classics of Organization Theory.* Fort Worth, TX: Harcourt College Publishers, pp. 152–157.

Patenaude, A. L. (2001) Analysis of issues affecting correctional officer retention within the Arkansas Department of Correction. *Corrections Management Quarterly,* 5(2): 49–67.

Peters, T. (1995) *Two complete books: Thriving on chaos and a passion for excellence (with Nancy Austin).* New York, NY: Random House.

Peters, T. (1987) *Thriving on chaos: Handbook for a management revolution.* New York, NY: Harper and Row.

Raney, G. (2005) *Shining the star: Identifying priorities, processes and outcome goals of a strategic plan for the Ada County Sheriff's office.* Boise, ID: Unpublished master's project, Boise State University.

Schein, E. H. (1992) *Organizational culture and leadership,* 2nd edn. San Francisco, CA: Jossey-Bass.

Sirota, D., Mischkind, L. A. and Meltzer, M. I. (2005) *The enthusiastic employee: How companies profit by giving workers what they want.* Upper Saddle River, NJ: Wharton School Publishing–Pearson Education.

Slate, R. N., Vogel, R. E. and Johnson, W. W. (2001) To quit or not to quit: Perceptions of participation in correctional decision making and the impact of organizational stress. *Corrections Management Quarterly,* 5(2): 68–78.

Snyder, H.N. (2012) Patterns and trends: Arrest in the United States, 1990–2010. Bureau of Justice Statistics, Office of Justice Programs, US Department of Justice. Online. Available at http//www.bjs.gov/content/pub/pdf/aus9010.pdf (last accessed January 31, 2013).

Stohr, M. K., Lovrich, N. P., Menke, B. A. and Zupan, L. L. (1994) Staff management in a correctional institution: Comparing DiIulio's 'control model' and 'employee investment model' outcomes in five jails. *Justice Quarterly,* 11(3): 471–497.

Whisenand, P. M. and Ferguson R. F. (2002) *The managing of police organizations,* 5th edn. Upper Saddle River, NJ: Prentice Hall.

Willis, J. J., Mastrofski, S. D. and Weisburd, D. (2004) COMPSTAT and bureaucracy: A case study of challenges and opportunities for change. *Justice Quarterly,* 21(3): 463–496.

Wilson, E. O. (1998) *Consilience: The unity of knowledge.* New York, NY: Knopf.

Wright, K. N., Saylor, W. G., Gilman, E. and Camp, S. (1997) Job control and occupational outcomes among prison workers. *Justice Quarterly,* 14(3): 525–548.

Index

Note: Tables are indicated in bold; graphs in italics.